"O BIBLIOS"

THE BOOK

"O BIBLIOS"

THE BOOK

by

Alan O'Reilly

Published by The Covenant Publishing Ltd
for The National Bible College
121 Low Etherley,
Bishop Auckland,
Co. Durham
DL14 0HA
UK

Designed and typeset by J. W. Arrowsmith Ltd, Bristol
Printed by Antony Rowe Ltd, Eastbourne

Contents

Author's Preface

The most important event in my life took place on July 19th, 1967, when I received the Lord Jesus Christ as Lord and Saviour.

The most important event for me since then as a child of God has been to come to know the Holy Bible, known as the Authorised King James Version, AV1611, as the perfect word of God and the FINAL AUTHORITY in ALL matters of faith and practice.

To believe that the AV1611 as the FINAL AUTHORITY is also to believe that it is superior not only to the modern "bibles" but also to ALL Greek and Hebrew texts and manuscripts and to the so-called, non existent "verbal, plenary, inspired, original autographs".

These do not correct the Holy Bible. The Holy Bible corrects both THEM and all of the scholars who use them to alter the pure words of Holy Scripture **"given by inspiration of God"** 2 Timothy 3:16.

After I was saved, I spent 17 years as a member of the Bible denying group that Dr. Peter S. Ruckman of Pensacola Bible Institute rightly calls "the Alexandrian Cult". I am particularly indebted to Dr. Ruckman's ministry via his books and tapes for my deliverance from this cult and for belief in the AV1611 as the perfect Bible. This belief has of course been greatly encouraged by the works of Dean Burgon, Dr. Hills, Dr. Otis Fuller, J.J. Ray, Dr. Gipp, Dr. Mrs. Gail Riplinger, Dr. Grady and others whose books are listed in the Bibliography and References of this work. See Volumes 1 and 5.

Some years ago, I was engaged in correspondence with the Protestant Truth Society over the issue of the Bible. In a letter to that organisation, dated 5th August 1986, I stated the following:

"The view that I express is that of a BIBLE BELIEVER who takes the AV BIBLE in ANY edition as inerrant with respect to its words, punctuation, order of Books and chapter and verse divisions. It is Holy Scripture given by inspiration of GOD, 2 Timothy 3:16 and is THE FINAL AUTHORITY in ALL matters of FAITH and PRACTICE and is SUPERIOR to ANY set of 'originals', ANY set of manuscripts in either Hebrew or Greek, ANY English Bible published before or since 1611 and ANY Hebrew or Greek Testament, including the "Textus Receptus"."

My stance for the AV1611 is now as it was then, except that today I would add inerrancy with respect to paragraph divisions. I hope that by reading this book, others will be encouraged to maintain the same stance.

"Stand therefore, having your loins girt about with truth, and having on the breastplate of righteousness; And your feet shod with the preparation of the gospel of peace; Above all, taking the shield of faith, wherewith ye shall be able to quench all the fiery darts of the wicked, And take the helmet of salvation, and the sword of the Spirit, which is the word of God" Ephesians 6:14-17.

Notes for Readers

1. Quotations from the Holy Bible, frequently referred to in the text as the AV1611, are given **bold**, and enclosed in double quotes.
2. Quotations of Greek and Hebrew words, or their literal English equivalents and quotations from both ms. sources and modern bibles are given in normal text, enclosed in double quotes.
3. Quotations from various authors or other reference material are given in *Italics*, enclosed in double quotes, except for tabulated reference material, which is given in normal text. Reference sources within the quotations are given in normal text.
4. Quotations of detailed criticisms of the Holy Bible, which are discussed in this work, are given in ***bold Italics***, enclosed in double quotes. This includes some chapter headings. If such a quotation is repeated, it has not (usually) been emboldened.
5. Loose quotations, which may not be referenced in the text of this work, are given in normal text, in single enclosed quotes.
6. Titles of books, papers and other source material stated in the text of this work, are given in *Italics*, with no quotes, or in normal text within Italicised quotations.

The author wishes to apologise in advance to readers for any deviations from the above format, all of which are unintentional and is happy to have them drawn to his attention via the publishers, together with any other typographical errors, which may have escaped notice prior to publication.

General Introduction

"This ain't lucky! You've gone and cut this out of a Bible. What fool's cut a Bible?"
"Long John" Silver *Treasure Island* by R.L. Stevenson

"I can getcha a load o' Bibles, Sir! Good discount – all King James, no rubbish!"
Private Joey Walker"Walmington-on-Sea Platoon", Home Guard Dad's Army

"In all these instances the Bible means the translation authorised by King James the First...to this day the common human Britisher or citizen of the United States of North America accepts and worships it as a single book by a single author, the book being the Book of Books and the author being God."
George Bernard Shaw cited in *The Men Behind the KJV* by Gustavus S. Paine

"But God hath chosen the foolish things of the world to confound the wise; and God hath chosen the weak things of the world to confound the things which are mighty;"
1 Corinthians 1:27

Perhaps nothing could be more foolish than an endorsement of a 400-year-old work of Bible translation by two notorious characters of fiction and an atheistic playwright, especially when contemporary scholars would assure us that the equivalent works available today are far superior. The main reason advanced by these scholars for this modern superiority is that today's translators have older and more reliable sources at their disposal upon which to base their work. We are also assured that today's scholars have greatly benefited Bible students by cutting out or altering many of the familiar readings in the older work that are now deemed spurious.

One would therefore expect to find a much greater enthusiasm for the words of Holy Scripture on the part of the general populace of these isles than has ever been witnessed in the past. However, here one observes a strange anomaly, described as follows by Rev. M.J. Roberts of Greyfriars Free Church, Inverness, quoted in the TBS *Quarterly Record*, No. 529, October to December 1994.

> *"The Bible is a lost book in Britain today. It has little influence on national life any more . . . We have to admit that we are not seeing souls converted in great numbers. It does not matter where you go. Go to Wales, to Scotland, or to England here. Few are being converted in these days. Where are the days when the Bible was being blessed to the conversion of thousands and ten thousands? . . . The problem is here. This book is not being read so as to bring light to bear upon men's lives. Therefore the tragedy is that men are not being converted to Christ. Could any curse in this life be greater? Could any judgment be more awful than this?"*

What is equally alarming is that many national leaders, whether in the church, or in politics or part of royalty seem indifferent to the nation's lamentable spiritual condition as outlined by Rev. Roberts. (The Prince of Wales recently won a prize at the Chelsea Flower Show for his "*Muslim Garden*"! Although the Archbishops of Canterbury and York have advised voters to give consideration to the beliefs of candidates in the forthcoming general election, they have maintained a deafening silence over the raft of ungodly enactments that successive governments have imposed in the last 50 years.)

Moreover, there are aggressive forces abroad in the land and adjacent to our shores whose apparent aim is to forbid Bible preaching altogether. American author Robert Morey wrote almost 10 years ago in the introduction to his book *The Islamic Invasion*, Harvest House Publishers 1992, that some Muslims had laid claim to England as the first European Muslim country. They have not publicly given up on this aspiration and it is common knowledge that Islam tolerates no serious rivals ideologically when it seizes power.

Across the channel, the Baptist Press, Paris, drew attention to a report published on July 3rd, 2000, entitled *EVANGELISM TO BE OUTLAWED - PROPOSED FRENCH LAW.* The report states

> *"Missionaries and lay persons who share their faith in Jesus could be imprisoned for up to two years under a proposed French law that accuses religious proselytisers of "mental manipulation" of the public. French Justice Minister Elisabeth Guigou last week called the bill "a significant advance giving a democratic state the legal tool to efficiently fight groups abusing its core values."*

Can this report be taken at face value? If so, is it the start of a renewed persecution of Christian believers such as the Dragonnades of the 17th century and might it even be a resurgence of the kind of Holy Inquisition that herded millions of hapless Jews into the extermination camps of World War 2? What is certain is that the European Union, in which France is a leading player, has nothing but contempt for Britain's laws, customs and Protestant Biblical foundations and is blatantly intent on consigning them to the dust heap of history. The evidence in support of this statement, from the books by Lindsay Jenkins, *Britain Held Hostage*, Adrian Hilton, *The Principality and Power of Europe* and Ashley Mote, *Vigilance – a defence of British liberty*, is overwhelming.

How could all this have happened to the people who were once, according to the historian Green *"the people of the Book - and that Book the Bible"* if the word of God is much more readily available today than ever before and purportedly "in the language of the people"?

One has to ask, are the scholars telling the truth?

Are the modern bible translations, based on supposedly more ancient and reliable sources, really authentic bibles? If they are really so superior, why have none of them succeeded in even arresting the nation's spiritual decline, let alone blessed it with revival, in the way that the Old Book authorised by King James has done time and again? Why is it that none of them are memorable, in the way that the Old Translation is? What words and phrases from any modern bible translation have actually passed into common household usage like those from the Old "King James" Version?

Could it be that the scholars aren't telling the truth? Could it be that they have been deceived by the Devil into passing off *"rubbish"* as the genuine article so that whole generations now definitely *"ain't lucky"*? In other words, have we all been 'shafted' by Christian, *fundamental*, APOSTATE 'scholarship'?

This author believes unequivocally that the answer to each of the last three questions is a resounding *YES* and the work that follows is the proof. He exhorts each and every reader of this work unreservedly to get back to believing the Old Book from cover to cover and by it to get right with its Author, while there is still time.

"Give glory to the Lord your God, before he cause darkness, and before your feet stumble upon the dark mountains and, while ye look for light, he turn it into the shadow of death, and make it gross darkness" Jeremiah13:16.

"I must work the works of him that sent me, while it is day; the night cometh, when no man can work" John 9:4.

The night is fast approaching, the darkness is gathering, the cold wind from the desert wilderness is already buffeting our faces with the bitter chill of the Great Tribulation. The hour is late, the need is so great and it is time for you to shine, Christian.

"Do all things without murmurings and disputings: That ye may be blameless and harmless, the sons of God, without rebuke, in the midst of a crooked and perverse nation, among whom ye shine as lights in the world" Philippians 2:14, 15.

The author wishes to thank Pastor Dave Myers, Dr. Dennis Lloyd, Mr. Matthew J. Browning, Mr. Michael A. Clark and all those of the National Bible College who have helped with the compilation of this work.

Alan O'Reilly
Guisborough, N. Yorks
May 2001

1

What is the Bible?

"*O Biblios*" – The Book, John Chrysostom, AD 345–407 (1) p48

1.1 INTRODUCTION

That question demands a right answer. The need for the right answer has never been more pressing than it is today. A famous preacher once said to his congregation

> "*The Bible is God's word, and when I see it, I seem to hear a voice saying, "I am the Book of God, man, read me; I am God's writing: open my leaves, for I was penned by God' . . . I plead with you, I beg of you, respect your Bibles, and search them out. Go home and read your Bibles . . . O Book of books! And wast thou written by my God? Then I will bow before thee, thou Book of vast authority! For He has written this Book Himself . . . let us love it, let us count it more precious than fine gold!*" Charles Haddon Spurgeon (1), p 23.

In spite of this exhortation, many Christians now believe that the popular, modern bible translations are superior to the Authorised Holy Bible, known simply as the Authorised Version or "King James" Version, because they are based on a superior Greek text. This belief no doubt stems in large part from the views expressed in the Prefaces of the modern translations, where sweeping allusions to "*the best Greek text*" or "*the best available Greek text*" or "*the earliest and best manuscripts*" may be found. In fact, the Greek text upon which most of the modern New Testaments are based is actually a corrupt text devised by the Gnostic philosophers of Alexandria, Egypt, chief of whom was Origen (184–254 AD). Less than 10 percent of extant Greek manuscripts of the New Testament conforms to this corrupt text. Historically, the true text

emanates from Antioch of Syria (Acts 11:26, 13:1, 2) and has been preserved not only in the vast majority of Greek manuscripts but also in various faithful early translations, such as the Old Latin, Old Syriac and
Gothic. These translations, together with the Syrian manuscripts, constitute the Bibles of the true believers during the Dark Ages and on into the
Reformation. Other valuable witnesses to the Syrian text as the true text
type are early Christian writers, known as church 'fathers.' Even the
Alexandrian mss. contain much of the Antiochan text.

This text eventually emerges in the 16th century as an edited Greek
New Testament, later called the *"Received Text"* or *"Textus Receptus"*.
Following numerous editions involving only minor modifications, the
Textus Receptus re-appears in pure form in the 17th century as the
Authorised Version of 1611, AV1611; in English, the language of the
end times. Subsequent Editions of the AV1611 differ from the 1611
Edition only in matters of spelling, punctuation and Italics, where obvi-
ously variation is possible without discrepancy. Allowing for correction
of typographical errors by later Editions, the actual TEXT of any
AV1611 available today is the same as that of 1611.

Throughout history, the Syrian text type, especially in its pure form
as the AV1611, is invariably associated with great movements of the
Spirit of God in revival, missionary outreach, social and material
progress and with the lives and ministries of great men and women of
God. The Alexandrian text type, by contrast, forms the basis for the
'bibles' of the Roman Catholic 'Church' via the Latin Vulgate of
Jerome. It is thus always associated with spiritual deadness, social and
moral degeneration, abominable idolatries and savage persecutions
against true Bible believers, even to this day, as in Ulster, the Republic
of Ireland, Latin America, Spain and the Philippines.

Sadly, it is this Alexandrian text type which the Body of Christ in this
last century has been deceived into accepting as *"the oldest and best."*
This deception stems from the conniving of Westcott and Hort, two
Cambridge theologians who masterminded the 1881 Revision
Committee which produced the Revised Version, RV, progenitor of
most of the modern translations. The success of the deception may be
attributed mainly to the attitudes of born-again, fundamental, conservative, evangelical Christians who have shown more regard for naturalistic scholarship than for the living words of the living God.

Nevertheless, there remains a formidable body of witnesses for the
AV1611, provided by the works of Burgon, Burton, Fuller, Gipp, Grady,
Hills, Ray, Riplinger, Ruckman, Ward, the Trinitarian Bible Society and

others. John Burgon was a true Christian scholar and contemporary of Westcott and Hort (2) p 139. Dr. David Otis Fuller was a pastor and Bible teacher for over fifty years and Chairman of the *Which Bible?* Society. Drs. Samuel Gipp and William Grady are seasoned Bible believing Baptist pastors. Dr Edward F. Hills was a graduate of Yale and Harvard Universities and another true Christian scholar, (3) p 6. Jasper J. Ray is a business manager, missionary and Bible teacher (3) p 2. Norman Ward and Barry Burton are informed laymen whose books are invaluable primers. Dr. Mrs Gail Riplinger devoted several years of full time research in order to produce the definitive book *New Age Bible Versions* showing the occult roots of the modern bibles. Dr. Peter S. Ruckman is President of the Pensacola Bible Institute and probably the most forthright advocate of the AV1611 in the world today. The TBS is the only Bible society loyal to the AV1611 in this country.

This work has been undertaken to show that the AV1611 King James Bible is the pure word of God, given by inspiration of God, infallible and finally authoritative. A second reason for this work is to expose the modern translations for what they are - satanic counterfeits which either omit or distort genuine Scriptures or impugn them by means of equivocal marginal notes. It may come as a surprise to some readers to discover how the text of a popular, supposedly 'evangelical' translation such as the NIV repeatedly matches that of the Roman Catholic Douay Rheims and Jerusalem bibles and the New World Translation of the Jehovah's Witnesses. However, this is to be expected, given that the basic Greek text of these four 'bibles' is largely that of the Alexandrian mss., particularly B or Vaticanus and Aleph or Sinaiticus, which are in turn the basis for Jerome's Roman Catholic Latin Vulgate.

It is common for fundamental, evangelical Christians to defend discrepancies between the AV1611 and the modern versions. They insist that "*not one fundamental of the faith is affected.*" Inspection of the evidence will reveal that such statements are at best half truths. It is true that ANY translation (including the NWT!) contains "the fundamentals of the faith" such as the Trinity, Virgin birth, blood atonement, resurrection, ascension, second advent. However, it is also true that the modern versions often weaken the testimony of Scripture to these fundamentals by omission or distortion of words preserved in the AV1611. However, the main issue is not 'the fundamentals.' The main issue is that of FINAL AUTHORITY in ALL MATTERS of faith and practice - not merely those which are deemed 'fundamental' by saved, conservative, evangelical apostates.

It is hoped therefore, that as he reads the following pages, the sincere Bible believer will see that FINAL AUTHORITY rests with the BOOK and not with the 'preferences' of born again, Bible rejecting fundamentalists.

1.2 THE SOURCES OF THE HOLY BIBLE, AV1611

(2) pp 26–27, (4) pp 69–91, (5) pp 115–121

Vindication of the AV1611 as the pure word of God rightly begins with a study of its roots. Examination of the sources of the AV1611 shows how the Lord preserved his pure word down through the centuries in order to bring it forth during the English Protestant Reformation in pure form.

Much more detailed manuscript evidence on the sources of the AV1611 and comparison of its readings with those of the modern bibles will be found in the works of Rev. J.A. Moorman, published by *The Bible for Today*, 900 Park Avenue, Collingswood, N.J. 08108, USA. These works are highly recommended.

1.2.1 Sources of the AV1611 New Testament
In brief, these are as follows.

1. The Greek manuscripts, uncial or upper case, cursive or lower case, lectionary and papyrus. Collators have designated uncial mss. by capitals, e.g. Aleph ℵ, A, B, C, D, Delta Δ, Theta Θ, Psi Ψ, etc. Cursives, lectionaries and papyri have mainly been catalogued numerically, e.g. Cursive 28, Lectionary 547, Papyrus or P66 etc.
2. The ancient versions, e.g. Old Latin, Old Syriac, of which there are several variants, Coptic, Gothic etc., whose texts date from the 2nd to the 6th centuries. The Old Latin mss. are catalogued alphabetically, e.g. a, aur, d, f etc. or alphanumerically, e.g. ff2, r1 etc.
3. Quotations from early 'church fathers'.

This triad overwhelmingly vindicates the AV1611 Text according to Scriptural principle: Deuteronomy 19:15, Matthew 18:16, 2 Corinthians 13:1. See Abbott, *Bible League Quarterly*, p 123–128, No. 353, 1988 and p 147–153, No. 354, 1988 and Watts *The Lord Gave the Word* TBS, 1998.

A more detailed listing of the AV1611 New Testament sources follows.

1.2.2 New Testament Greek Manuscripts, mss.
Most of these mss. contain only parts of the New Testament. Burton gives the total as 5309 (6) p 58. Watts gives the following totals for 1989.

Type of ms.	Century When Written	Number of Copies
Uncials, upper case,	4th–9th	299
Cursives, lower case,	9th–16th	2812
Lectionaries, responsive		
readings,	9th–16th	2281
Papyri, fragments,	3rd	96
Total:		5488

The majority of the Greek mss. conform to the 'syrian' or 'Byzantine' Text type, also known as the "Traditional Text". This is essentially the text of the AV1611. The remainder of the mss. are of the so-called 'Alexandrian' Text type. Codex B, Vaticanus and Codex Aleph, Sinaiticus are the most famous - or infamous - of the Alexandrian mss. (6) p 57ff.

1.2.3 New Testament Ancient Versions

Version	Century When Written	Approximate Number of Copies
Old Latin	2nd-4th	50
Old Syriac	2nd-4th	350
Gothic of Ulfilas,		
"*the Little Wolf*"	4th	6 (5) p 120.
Armenian	5th	1244
Other, e.g Coptic,		
Georgian etc., (5) p 120.		

A complete Latin Bible, the Italic version, was circulating in northern Italy by 157 AD and contained the Johannine Comma (2) p 213, (4) p 77, (7) p 98. The Johannine Comma is 1 John 5:7, 8 as it reads in an Authorised Version:

"**For there are three that bear record *in heaven, the Father, the Word, and the Holy Ghost: and these three are one.* And there are three that bear witness *in earth*, the spirit, and the water, and the blood: and these three agree *as one*.**"

The same passage in an NIV reads as follows:

"For there are three that testify: the Spirit, the water and the blood; and the three are in agreement."

The 19 words that have been italicised in the reading from the Authorised Version are either omitted from modern bibles, or disputed in the margin. The omission is a direct attack on vital Christian doctrines, including the Trinity, or Godhead and the strength of witness to the First Coming in the flesh of the Lord Jesus Christ. There was a trio of witnesses *in heaven*, a trio *on earth* and both sets agreed amongst themselves and with each other *as one*. See also the discussion on this passage in Sections 7.3 and 14.1.

Overall, the texts of the ancient versions agree with the Syrian type text of the majority of the Greek mss. except where known corruptions have been introduced by Alexandrian scribes (4) p 81.

1.2.4 *Quotations of Early Church "Fathers"*
1. Western

Irenaeus	130–202 AD
Tertullian	150–220 AD
Cyprian	200–258 AD
Augustine	354–430 AD

With the exception of Tertullian, these men were the 'founding fathers' of the Roman Catholic church (4) p 76.

2. Alexandrian

Clement	150–215 AD
Origen	182–254 AD

Both Clement and Origen were Gnostics. Origen rejected the Deity and High Priesthood of Christ, the physical resurrection and the Second Advent. He believed in infant baptism, universal salvation and forgiveness of sin through communion (6) p 64–65, (8) p 8. He repeatedly corrupted Bible mss. to conform to his beliefs (4) p 55–56, (6) p 64–65. Origen is also most closely associated with the LXX or 'septuagint" (4) p 40–54.

3. Antiochan

Polycarp	69–155 AD
Tatian	120–200 AD
John Chrysostom	345–407 AD

Tatian's 'Diatessaron' or 'Harmony' of the Gospels bears witness to AV1611 readings in Luke 2:33, John 5:3b-4, 9:35 and elsewhere (1) p 69, 192, (4) p 80, 209. John Chrysostom was known as the *"golden mouthed"* preacher.

These men and others quote the New Testament more than 35,000 times (1) p 322. Most of the New Testament can be reconstructed from their writings (11) p 30. Despite the heretical beliefs of the Western and Alexandrian Fathers, the Fathers' quotations support the Syrian text in ratio 3:2 against the Alexandrian text and in ratio 3:1 in 30 important doctrinal passages (3) p 237–238.

1.2.5 Old Testament Sources
(2) p 181

The following should be noted:

1. The Old Testament was in a *"settled condition"* by the time of Christ.
2. Hebrew Scriptures were preserved intact by Masoretic Scribes until the advent of printing, 1450 AD (5) p 92.
3. Many scholars insist that an allegedly BC Greek translation of the Old Testament, the LXX or Septuagint, was used by the Lord and His Apostles. The facts (4) p 41–54 are:
4. The only evidence for a BC LXX is the spurious writing *"Letter of Aristeas"*.
5. All LXX mss. are extant from 200 AD or later.
6. The original LXX is the 5th column of Origen's 6 column parallel Old Testament 'Hexapala' and contains the Apocrypha.
7. Brenton's LXX Edition, Zondervan, uses texts of Codex B Vaticanus, 4th century AD and Codex A Alexandrinus, 5th century and declares the Apocrypha to be *"a portion of the Bible of Christendom"*.

The LXX is highly regarded by Greek scholars. If they can convince the Body of Christ that the LXX was the Lord's 'bible', they could easily and significantly extend their influence over that Body (9) p 48. The book *The Mythological Septuagint* by Dr. Peter S. Ruckman, 1996, available from the Bible Baptist Bookstore, provides a detailed study of the dubious nature of the LXX.

1.3. TWO SETS OF GREEK MSS.

Figure 1, *The Mss. Pyramid* (10) p 2, shows relative proportions of the two main groups of Greek New Testament manuscripts. The two main centres of mss. compilation were Antioch, Syria and Alexandria, Egypt.

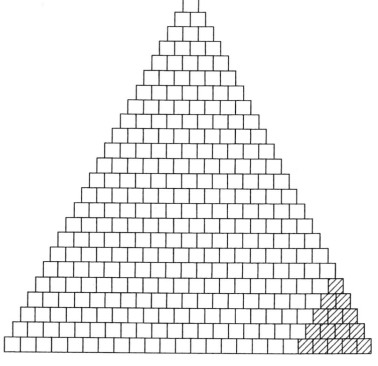

Figure 1 The Mss. Pyramid
(courtesy J. C. Coad)

The pyramid of exactly 300 blocks represents the sum total of New Testament Greek manuscripts. The most recent list gives 96 papyrus mss., 299 uncials or upper case mss. and 2812 cursives or lower case mss.. Many of these are fragments and most do not contain the entire New Testament. Each one, however, is a valuable testimony.

Each block represents approximately 10 mss.. The shaded portion represents Codex Sinaiticus, Codex Vaticanus and a few supporting mss.. The textual critics, enemies of the AV1611, set aside the whole weight of the text of the 95% mss. which have been the Church's Inheritance and guiding testimony for 1800 years in favour of the 5% depraved, corrupted and "corrected" text. The NIV coming 100 years after the failure of the RV of Westcott and Hort shows identical OMISSIONS!

The essential features of these mss. groupings may be summarised as follows.

1.3.1 The Antiochan Mss.:
1. 95 % of all Greek mss. belong to this group.
2. They were faithfully preserved by the Bible believers of Antioch of Syria (2) p 187, (6) p 57, (11) p 31.
3. They agree closely with each other (2) p 187.
4. At least 90 % support the AV1611 Text (2) p 26.
5. They are the basis for the Received Text or Textus Receptus, the Greek Text underlying the AV1611 and other Protestant Bibles.
6. At least 80–90 % of ALL mss. support the AV1611 Text (2) p 26, (12) p 476.

1.3.2 The Alexandrian Mss.:
1. Only 5 % of all Greek mss. belong to this group.
2. They are either originally Antiochan mss., corrupted by Gnostics of Alexandria, especially Origen (2), p 188–193, (6) p 57–64, (11) 44–46, or corrupt copies of Antiochan mss..
3. They disagree significantly from Antiochan mss. and even with each other, (2) p 136, 272, (5) p 222, (6) p 60.
4. 80 heretical sects existed in the 4th century (2) p 182, 2 Corinthians 2:17, aggravating the problem of mss. corruption.
5. They form the basis for all 'bibles' of the Roman Catholic church (2) p 193, (11) p 46–47.
6. They form the basis for most modern versions. Most of the differences from the AV1611 arise from these mss., for all modern versions including the NKJV (1) p 127ff, (4) p 92ff, (6) p 57, 65, (7) p 17–72, (11) p 49–51.

1.3.3 Mss. offshoots.
They stem from both sets of mss.
1. Some Antiochan type mss. are called 'Caesarean'. They were probably corrupted by Origen (1) p 285.
2. Some Alexandrian type mss. are called 'Western'. They exhibit additions - and subtractions - probably introduced in Rome (5) p 121–125.

1.3.4 'Older' but not 'Better'
Although Alexandrian mss. are OLDER than Antiochan, it will be

shown later that they are not BETTER (11) p 32–34, (13) p 271–288. There are several reasons why extant Alexandrian mss. have survived longer than their Antiochan counterparts.

1. The Egyptian climate was more conducive to mss. preservation than the Syrian.
2. Persecution of Antiochan Christians was more protracted and intense.
3. The Antiochan mss. material was papyri or parchment. These mss. were therefore more fragile than the Alexandrian, which consisted of best quality vellum or antelope skin.
4. The Antiochan mss. were more used than Alexandrian.
5. The Antiochan mss. were often destroyed after recopying.
6. Some scholars allege that the Antiochan mss. stem from the so called *"Lucian Recension"*, an alleged 4th century standardisation of the Antiochan text type. It is then further alleged that this standard text then supplanted the older Alexandrian type, supposedly closer to the original mss.. There is no historical evidence to support these allegations, which were utterly refuted by Dean Burgon (13).

1.4 ANTIOCH VS. ALEXANDRIA IN THE BIBLE

(1) p 310–311, (14) p 54–56

The Scriptures themselves testify to the location of the centre for mss. compilation and distribution which the Lord ordained.

1.4.1 Antioch, Syria
1. The church in Antioch sent out the first Bible teachers, Acts 13:1.
2. The first missionary trip went from Antioch, Acts 13:1–6.
3. The word **"Christian"** originated in Antioch, Acts 11:26.

1.4.2 Alexandria, Egypt
1. God called His Son out of Egypt, Matthew 2.
2. God called Jacob out of Egypt, Genesis 49.
3. God called Israel out of Egypt, Exodus 15.
4. God called Joseph's bones out of Egypt, Exodus 13.
5. God never wanted His people to return to Egypt, Deuteronomy 17:16.

Which city would GOD choose to compile a New Testament? 1 Corinthians 14:33.

Which city would YOU choose? Do you suppose that GOD has as much sense as YOU? Isaiah 55:8, 9

1.5 TWO LINES OF BIBLES

(2) p 187, (4) p 71, (7) p 15–18, 71, 87, (8) p 7

Figure 2, *The Mss. Dichotomy* (14), shows how two main streams of Bibles have been derived from the two major mss. groupings.

1.5.1 The Antiochan Stream

1. This stream stems from the Antiochan mss..
2. This stream appears with very little change in many Protestant Bibles and culminates in the AV1611.
3. The Waldenses, or Vaudois, were Bible believing Christians of Northern Italy. Their Italic Bible dates from the 2nd century AD and essentially matches the Text of the AV1611.
4. Wycliffe appears to have used both the Old Latin and the Vulgate for his Bible, 1382. Wycliffe's Bible did NOT contain the Apocrypha (16) p 309–311.

1.5.2 The Alexandrian Stream

1. This stream stems from the Alexandrian mss.
2. Constantine, 331 AD, ordered the historian Eusebius to produce 50 bibles from Origen's mutilated mss. (2) p 3.
3. Codex B Vaticanus and Codex Aleph Sinaiticus are probably of this group. Codex Alexandrinus is from the 5th century.
4. The Latin Vulgate of Jerome became the official 'bible' of the RC church for 1000 years (7) p 20, (11) p 46.
5. The NKJV, 'Jerry Falwell Version' JFV, is based on the Textus Receptus but contains many Alexandrian readings and is therefore a hybrid. Jerry Falwell, leader of 'The Moral Majority' in the USA in the 1980's, was the leading promoter of this version.
6. Westcott and Hort were the two Cambridge academics who masterminded the Revision Committee which produced the Revised Version in 1881.
7. Rome tried to flood England with the Jesuit Rheims bible of 1582 but the English people rejected it. She then resorted to the Armada of 1588 in order to catholicise the people of England against their will.

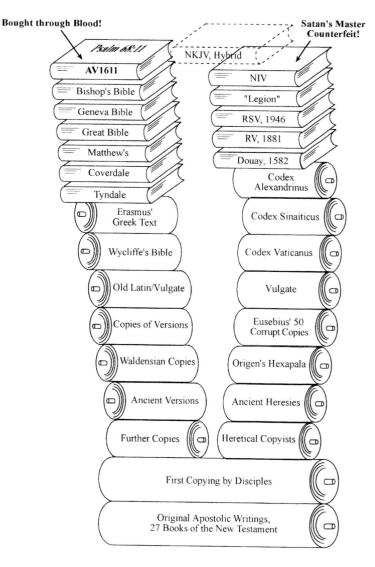

Bought through Blood!

Satan's Master Counterfeit!

NKJV, Hybrid

Psalm 68:11

AV1611	NIV
Bishop's Bible	"Legion"
Geneva Bible	RSV, 1946
Great Bible	RV, 1881
Matthew's	Douay, 1582
Coverdale	Codex Alexandrinus
Tyndale	
Erasmus' Greek Text	Codex Sinaiticus
Wycliffe's Bible	Codex Vaticanus
Old Latin/Vulgate	Vulgate
Copies of Versions	Eusebius' 50 Corrupt Copies
Waldensian Copies	Origen's Hexapala
Ancient Versions	Ancient Heresies
Further Copies	Heretical Copyists

First Copying by Disciples

Original Apostolic Writings, 27 Books of the New Testament

Figure 2 Manuscript Dichotomy
(courtesy J. C. Coad)

1.6 CODEX B AND CODEX ALEPH, THE "SIN-VAT"

(6) p 60–61, (17) p 408

The two most prominent Alexandrian mss. are Codex B Vaticanus and Codex א, Aleph, Sinaiticus. A summary of their history and contents reveals their corrupt nature.

1.6.1 Codex B Vaticanus

1. It was found in excellent condition in the Vatican library in 1481 and never influenced the Protestant Reformation.
2. It omits Genesis 1:1–46:28, parts of 1 Samuel, 1 Kings, Nehemiah, Psalm 105:26–137:6, Matthew 16:2–3, John 7:53–8:12, the Pauline Pastoral Epistles, Hebrews 9:14–13:25, Revelation.
3. It leaves blank columns for Mark 16:9–20, (18) p 67, thus providing additional testimony for the existence of this passage.
4. It includes the Apocrypha as part of Old Testament Text. Protestant Bibles do NOT (5) p 98.

1.6.2 Codex א, Aleph, Sinaiticus

1. It was found in a trash pile in St. Catherine's Monastery near Mt. Sinai in 1844 by Tischendorf.
2. It omits Genesis 23:19–24:46, Numbers 5:27–7:20, 1 Chronicles 9:27–19:17, Exodus, Joshua, 1 and 2 Samuel, 1 and 2 Kings, Judges, Hosea, Amos, Micah, Ezekiel, Daniel, Mark 16:9–20, John 7:53–8:12.
3. It adds *Shepherd of Hermes* and *Epistle of Barnabas* to the New Testament Text.

Codices Aleph and B disagree with each other over 3,000 times in the Gospels alone (6) p 60. Nevertheless, they have been designated as "*The most reliable early manuscripts*" and "*The earliest and most reliable manuscripts*" by the NIV New Testament, p 70, 127.

> "*The impurity of the Texts exhibited by Codices B and Aleph is not a matter of opinion but a matter of fact. These are two of the least trustworthy documents in existence. So far from allowing Dr. Hort's position that 'A Text formed by taking Codex B as the sole authority would be incomparably nearer the truth than a Text similarly taken from any other Greek or single document' we venture to assert that it would be on the contrary, by far the foulest Text that had ever seen the light: worse, that is to say, even than the Text of Drs.*

Westcott and Hort. And that is saying a great deal." Dean Burgon
(13) p 315–316.

1.7 TWO LINES OF CHURCH HISTORY

(2) p 176–318, (16), (20) p 6

Figure 3 shows two lines of church history, according to the two lines
of Bibles descending from the two major mss. divisions.

1.7.1 The Bible Believing Line
1. The Bible of Antioch goes to the ends of the earth via the Waldenses
   and other Protestant or Bible believing groups, including English
   Methodists and Anabaptists.
2. This Bible was translated into Indian and Chinese dialects long before
   1890.
3. Every major language had access to the AV1611 Text in their own
   language before 1901.
4. All revivals, reformation, soul-winning and interest in Bible study
   follow this Text.
5. The acknowledged great men of God, Bunyan, Wesley, Carey,
   Moody, Finney, Spurgeon and others follow this Text, for all or most
   of their public ministries.
6. Material prosperity, political stability, humanitarian effort, progress
   in art, literature, music, science and technology and the emergence
   of a stable, productive, law abiding, morally upright, educated
   'middle class' follow the dissemination of this Text.

1.7.2 The Bible Rejecting Line
1. The 'bible' of Alexandria was used by Jerome to translate the so-
   called *"Vulgate"*.
2. This text predominated in Europe throughout the Dark Ages.
3. This was or is the text of the Popes, the Jesuits, the Inquisition, and
   by association catholic dictators such as Charlemagne, Bloody Mary,
   Philip II, the Hapsburgs, Mussolini, Hitler and catholic terrorist
   groups such as the IRA and those like them such as the ANC.
4. This is the text that produced Italy, Latin and South America, Spain,
   Portugal, South Ireland, the Philippines and - indirectly - Russia, both
   Czarist and Marxist. The history of these nations is one of widespread
   poverty, political instability, corruption and repression, terrorist
   movements, lack of true missionary zeal, lack of true Christian

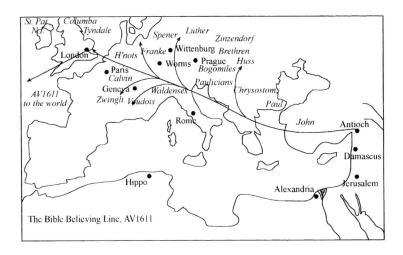

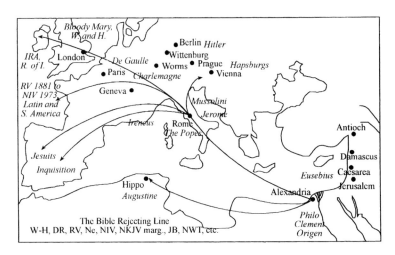

Figure 3   Two Lines of Church History

conduct and - until recently - absence of religious freedom (1) p 119.

5. No Scriptural work for God ever stems from this text but every major war since 400 AD DOES (16) p 378–381.

6. This text was resurrected in 1881 by Westcott and Hort in place of the Reformation Textus Receptus as the *"Revised Version"*. The latter part of the 19th century marks the beginning of Britain's decline as a world power.

1.8 THE WORK OF THE MISSIONARIES

"In the silent watches of the night, along the lonely paths of Asia Minor where robbers and wild beasts lurked, might have been seen the noble missionaries carrying manuscripts, and verifying documents from the churches of Judea to encourage their struggling brethren under the iron heel of the Papacy" (2) p 214.

The Vaudois, or Waldenses of Northern Italy took a solemn oath to maintain the purity of the Scriptures, 1561 (21) p 88–91, for the sake of future generations.

> *"We promise to maintain the Bible, whole and without admixture, according to the usage of the true Apostolic Church, persevering in this holy religion, though it be at the peril of our life, in order that we may transmit it to our children, intact and pure, as we received it from our fathers".*

These early and devoted believers maintained a faithful witness to the Gospel of Christ throughout Medieval times and laid a sure foundation for the Reformation which came about in the 16th century through the ministry of Martin Luther.

> *"There was no kingdom of Southern and Central Europe to which these missionaries did not find their way, and where they did not leave traces of their visit in the disciples whom they made . . . their track being marked with the edifices for worship and the stakes of martyrdom that arose around their steps"* (21) p 16.

> *"The fog was rolling away from the plains and hills of Europe. The pure Bible which long had sustained the faith of the Vaudois, was soon to be adopted by others so mighty that they would shake Europe from the Alps to the North Sea. The light had begun spreading unobserved, and the Reformation was on the point of being*

anticipated. The demon Innocent III was the first to decry the streaks of day on the crest of the Alps. Horror-stricken, he started up, and began to thunder for his pandemonium against a faith which . . . was threatening to dissolve the power of Rome" (2) p224.

The retaliation of Rome was characteristically savage. John Milton gave testimony to her brutality in his poem *On The Late Massacre at Piedmont, 1655* (21) p 150.

> "*Avenge, O Lord, Thy slaughtered saints, whose bones*
> *Lie scattered on the Alpine mountains cold;*
> *Even them who kept Thy truth so pure of old,*
> *When all our fathers worship stocks and stones . . .* "

An eyewitness account of the massacre had this to say.

"*My hand trembles so that I scarce can hold the pen, and my tears mingle in torrents with my ink, while I write the deeds of these children of darkness - blacker even than the Prince of Darkness himself*" Jean Leger, Waldensian pastor 1655, (21) p 144.

"*Alexandria*" replacing "*Antioch*"…

For more details, see *Fox*'s *Book of Martyrs*, edited by Forbush.

2

The Restoration of the Received Text

(2) p 216–217, 225–246, (5) p 193–208

With the dawning of the Reformation, God used a number of distinguished scholars to produce editions of the New Testament in Greek, from the faithfully preserved mss. of Antioch. These Greek editions were to culminate in the publication of the AV1611 a century later.

2.1 ERASMUS OF ROTTERDAM

1. Refugees from the fall of Constantinople, 1453 AD, brought thousands of Greek mss. to Europe.
2. Desiderius Erasmus was the intellectual giant of Europe, an outstanding scholar who travelled widely in pursuit of his researches. Although a catholic, he publicly denounced the RC church in many books. He classified Greek mss. and studied the church fathers extensively.
3. Between 1516 and 1535, Erasmus published 5 editions of the Greek New Testament Received Text. The 3rd, 1522, includes the Johannine Comma, 1 John 5:7. He mainly used 5 Antiochan mss. to compile his New Testaments but had access to many more. He rejected the Vulgate of Jerome and knew of almost all the important variant readings in the Greek New Testament mss..

"The pedigree (of the Received Text) stretches back to remote antiquity. The first ancestor of the Received Text was, as Dr. Hort is careful to remind us, at least contemporary with the oldest of our extant mss., if not older than any of them" (2) p 227.

"I would have the weakest woman read the Gospels and the Epistles

*of St. Paul . . . I would have those words translated into all languages,
so that not only Scots and Irishmen, but Turks and Saracens might read
them. I long for the plowboy to sing them to himself as he follows the
plow, the weaver to hum them to the tune of his shuttle, the traveller to
beguile with them the dullness of his journey . . . Other studies we may
regret having undertaken, but happy is the man upon whom death comes
when he is engaged in these. These sacred words give you the very
image of Christ speaking, healing, dying, rising again, and make Him so
present that were He before your very eyes you would not more truly see
Him"* Erasmus (11) p 37–38.

2.2 ROBERT STEPHANUS

1. Stephanus was a French printer and scholar.
2. He produced two editions of the Hebrew Old Testament. The first
   nominally Christian publication in Europe of the Hebrew Old
   Testament appeared in 1522 and was mainly the work of Cardinal
   Ximenes (22) p 12.
3. He produced 4 editions of the Greek New Testament Reccived Text.
   The Interlinear Greek English New Testament first published by
   George Ricker Berry in 1897 is the 3rd Edition of Stephanus, 1550.
4. Stephanus was forced by Roman Catholics to leave Paris in 1550
   because of his work on the New Testament. He settled in Geneva and
   became a Protestant.
5. With Beza, he was largely responsible for the verse divisions of the
   AV1611 and ALL subsequent versions, TBS *Quarterly Record* No.
   462, Jan-Mar. 1978.

2.3 THEODORE BEZA

1. Beza was Calvin's disciple and successor at Geneva.
2. He produced 10 editions of the Greek New Testament Received Text.
3. The AV1611 Text is based largely on his 4th Edition, 1588–1589.
4. His editions upheld AV1611 readings for Matthew 6:13, Mark
   16:9–20, Luke 2:14, John 7:53–8:11, 1 Timothy 3:16 and 1 John 5:7,
   which are omitted, altered or disputed by all modern versions.
5. Beza *"astonished the world . . . with the mss. he unearthed"* (2) p
   210.

2.4 THE ELZEVIR BROTHERS

1. They were Dutch printers of Leiden, in the Netherlands.
2. They produced 2 editions of Greek New Testament Received Text, in 1624 and 1633. A further 5 editions were published between 1633 and 1678 (23) p 138.
3. The phrase *"Textus Receptus"* first appears in the preface to the 1633 edition. *"You have therefore the text now received by all (textum ab omnibus receptum) in which we give nothing changed or corrupt."*

Note that the Received Text had therefore made its appearance over 20 years BEFORE the Piedmont massacre of 1655. The damage was done but Rome is *"semper Eadem."* SHE DOES NOT FORGIVE OR FORGET.

3

The Men Behind The English Bible

"Go now ye that are men and serve the Lord; for that ye did desire" Exodus 10:11.

As the Greek New Testaments were being published on the Continent, God was at work preparing the English Bible, before and during the Reformation. These were the Englishmen whom He used for this purpose.

3.1 JOHN WYCLIFFE, 1324–1384

1. John Wycliffe has been called *"The Morning Star of the Reformation"*, Revelation 2:28, *"the father of the English Reformation"* and the founder of English Non-conformity, (24) p 13.
2. He was also called *"The flower of Oxford"*. He was converted about the time of the Black Death, 1348, (24) p 9–10, to become the *"Evangelical Doctor"*.
3. Of the Pope, he said *"Anti-Christ, the proud, worldly priest of Rome and the most cursed of clippers and purse-kervers (bag snatchers)"* (24) p 26.
4. He compiled the first complete Bible in English, 1382. See Figure 2. Wycliffe's Bible was later revised by Nicholas of Hereford and John Purvey, in order to match the Vulgate of Jerome more closely (16), p 310–311.

Of the Bible Wycliffe said:

"As the doctrines of our faith are in the Scriptures, believers should

*have the Scriptures in a language familiar to the people . . . It is
impossible for any part of the Holy Scriptures to be wrong. In Holy
Scripture is all the truth; one part of Scripture explains another*" (24)
p 47–48.

5. In 1415, his body was exhumed and burnt and the ashes cast into the
    River Swift:

    "*The little river conveyed Wycliffe's remains into the Avon, Avon
    into the Severn, Severn into the narrow seas, they into the main
    ocean. And thus the ashes of Wycliffe are the emblem of his doc-
    trine, which is now dispensed all the world over*" (24) p 75.

3.2 WILLIAM TYNDALE, 1495 (1484?)-1536

1. He was a student of Erasmus, at Cambridge. He was probably
    converted there under the ministry of Latimer, Bilney and Cranmer.
2. He was "*so skilled in seven languages, Hebrew, Greek, Latin, Italian,
    Spanish, English, French, that whatever he spoke you would suppose
    it his native tongue*" (2) p 228–229, citing Herman Buschius.
3. He is said to have "*stamped his genius upon English thought and
    English language*" (2) p 228.
4. He produced two editions of the New Testament, in 1526 and 1534.
    This was the first English New Testament translated from the Greek
    Received Text (2) p 228–229. He was actively engaged in translating
    the Old Testament certainly up until the time of his arrest in 1534.

To the Abbots of Winchcombe and Tewkesbury he had said:

"*I defy the pope and all his laws. If God spare my life, ere many years
I will cause a boy that driveth the plough to know more of the
Scriptures than thou doest*" (25) p 10.

5. He was betrayed, strangled and burnt at the stake at Vilvorde on
    October 6th 1536. His last words were: "*Lord, open the King of
    England's eyes.*"

    In 1538 King Henry VIII decreed that the Great Bible be set up in
    every Parish church, in answer to Tyndale's prayer.
6. The AV1611 New Testament is 90% that of Tyndale.

    "*I perceived by experience how that it was impossible to establish
    the lay people in any truth, except the Scripture were plainly laid*

before their eyes in their mother-tongue, that they might see the process, order, and meaning of the text" Tyndale's Preface to the Pentateuch (26) p 4.

3.3 JOHN ROGERS, 1500–1555

1. He was educated at Cambridge and converted by the Scriptures and the witness of Tyndale, 1534 (27) p 94.
2. He was responsible for the printing of the Matthew's Bible, in which Tyndale's work is reproduced as far as possible, supplemented where necessary by that of Miles Coverdale, taken largely from Luther's German (27) p 99–101, (28) p ix.
3. Matthew's Bible is the English foundation of the Great Bible 1539, the Geneva Bible 1560, the Bishop's Bible 1568 and the Authorised King James Bible of 1611, the AV1611.
4. John Rogers was burnt at the stake, February 4th, 1555, the first to suffer thus during the short and tyrannical reign of Mary Tudor.

3.4 GOD'S ENGLISHMEN...

The men who produced the early English Bibles had these things in common:
1. They were genuine scholars who approached the Scriptures believing them to be the true words of God.
2. They had a God-given desire to impart the pure words of God to the ordinary people, NOT keep it locked up in the original languages.
3. They rejected the RC church and suffered as a result. It follows that Bible believers are anti-Catholic and Bible reading countries are NOT catholic countries.

4

The Company Of 1611

"The Lord gave the word: great was the company of those that published it" Psalm 68:11.

To complete the work of Tyndale and the other pioneers of the 16th century, the Lord raised up **"a band of men, whose hearts God had touched"** 1 Samuel 10:26, **"valiant for the truth upon the earth"** Jeremiah 9:3.

4.1 KING JAMES 1, THE BRITISH SOLOMON

The following statements are extracts from *Battle Cry* September/October 1985:

1. James was the first man to unite the feuding tribes of Scotland into one nation.
2. James united Scotland and England, laying the groundwork for the British Empire, birthplace of the greatest missionary movement of the modern age.
3. James founded of the Province of Ulster, by far the most Bible believing, prosperous and Christian sector of Ireland.
4. James was the first earthly monarch on record to encourage the propagation of God's word in the language of the people (1) p 164.
5. James believed in salvation by grace and in the word of God, never wavering from his personal adherence to Protestant belief.
6. James broke the back of witchcraft in Scotland.
7. James was an accomplished scholar. He knew Latin, Greek and French perfectly, Italian and Spanish adequately and wrote poetry, theology and a tract against the use of tobacco!
8. He has been called *"The most hated character in English history for Greek and Hebrew scholars in the Protestant church, especially the*

modern fundamentalist branch" (16) p 412. This distinction appears
to have been bestowed by fundamental scholars for the reason given
in point 4 above.

9.   James gave Royal Assent to the Puritan proposal for a new Bible
     translation, 1604.

*"To fulfil Acts 1:8 . . . All the Lord needed was a Bible in line with
what He had already written and preserved; since He had already
decreed (in 1000 BC) that there had to be present "the word of a
King" Ecclesiastes 8:4 before there could be any spiritual "power"
in that word (Romans 13:1–4), and since His king was a JEW (John
18:34) . . . God needed a king with a Jewish name; He got one . . .
this time it was JAMES. James is the English word for JACOB"*
(16) p 374.

4.2 SCHOLARS OF 1611

(2) p 13–24, (14) p 183–195
   These were some of the 47 men chosen to produce the 1611 Bible.

1. Dr. John Reynolds
He was the Regius Professor of Divinity at Oxford, 1585. Reynolds was
the leading Puritan who petitioned the king for a new translation of the
Bible. Noted as a distinguished Greek and Hebrew scholar, "*his memory
and reading were near to a miracle*".

2. Dr. Miles Smith
He was Bishop of Gloucester, 1612 and writer of the preface to the
AV1611, *The Translators to the Reader*. "*He had Hebrew at his fingers'
ends; and he was so conversant with Chaldee, Syriac, and Arabic, that
he made them as familiar to him as his native tongue*".

3. Dr. Laurence Chaderton
He was Fellow of Christ's College and a noted Puritan. Distinguished as
a Latin, Greek and Hebrew Scholar, he was still actively preaching at
age 85. His sermons had won about 40 of the clergy to Christ.

4. Dr. John Boys
Fellow of St. John's, Cambridge, to which he was admitted at age 14, he
was able to read Hebrew at the age of 5. As a distinguished Greek scholar, he sometimes devoted himself to his studies of Greek in the university library from 4 a.m. to 8 p.m.

5. Dr. Lancelot Andrewes

He was Bishop of Wincester and Chaplain to Queen Elizabeth 1. *"His knowledge in Latin, Greek, Hebrew, Chaldee, Syriac and Arabic . . . was so advanced that he may be ranked as one of the rarest linguists in Christendom . . . in his last illness he spent all his time in prayer-and when both voice and hands failed in their office, his countenance showed that he still prayed and praised God in his heart, until it pleased God to receive his blessed soul to Himself'*.

6. Dr. Richard Kilbye

Regius Professor of Hebrew at Oxford, 1610 and an excellent Hebrew scholar, he was also expert in Greek. He once heard a young preacher give three reasons why a particular word in the AV1611 should have been translated differently. He explained to the young preacher how he and others had considered all three reasons *"and found thirteen more considerable reasons why it was translated as now printed"*.

Many have followed, however, in that young preacher's train . . .

Not only were the translators of 1611 exceptional scholars *"but also Bible believers to whom the Scriptures were "God's sacred truth". With the bloody Reformation still afresh in their mind's eye, the translators of the Authorised Version were fully cognizant of the inestimable value of the word of God"* (11) p 41.

4.3 MATERIALS USED FOR THE AV1611
(11) p 42

The following list shows that the translators of 1611 had more than sufficient material for their vital task.

1. All preceding printed English and foreign language Bibles. These included the JesuitRheims Version.
2. The printed Greek texts of Erasmus, Stephanus and Beza.
3. The Complutensian Polyglot with the Masoretic Text of the Hebrew Old Testament. The translators also had the Antwerp Polyglot of 1569–1572, (22) p 12.
4. Several important uncial mss. and a great mass of cursive mss.
5. The Old Latin.
6. The Italic, Gallic and Celtic versions.
7. Jerome's Vulgate.
8. Variant readings from Codices A and B (2) p 250–254.

"The translators of 1611 had substantially the same selection of readings from which to choose as did the revisers of 1881, 1952, 1973 and 1979".

4.4 THE ORIGINAL TITLE PAGE FOR THE AV1611

An exact reprint of the 1611 Authorized Version is available from the Oxford University Press. Inspection of the title page tends to dispel some of the myths about the AV1611, which have often been propagated by apostate fundamentalists.

1. The title is THE HOLY BIBLE.
2. The title is NOT 'The Authorised Version'. Its "authorisation" came from its AUTHOR (29) p 21–23.
3. The title is NOT 'The King James Version', although this term is commonly used even by Bible believers. The term was first applied long after the publication of the AV1611, originally to avoid the word 'authority' (29) p 21–23.
4. The title does NOT include the Apocrypha as part of the Scriptures.

5

The AV1611 – The Pure Word of God

"No book ever published has had a greater influence on civilization than has the AV1611. It is the pure, perfect, inerrant and infallible word of God" (11) p 40.

"We Anglo-Saxons have a better Bible than the French or the Germans or the Italians or the Spanish. Our English translation is even better than the original Hebrew and Greek. There is only one way to explain this: I have no theory to account for the so-called inspiration of the Bible, but I am confident that the Authorized Version was inspired" William Lyons Phelps, Lampson Professor of English Literature at Yale University, 1923.

"If accuracy, fidelity, and the strictest attention to the letter of the text, be supposed to constitute the qualities of an excellent version, this, of all versions, must, in general, be accounted the most excellent" Alexander Geddes, Roman Catholic priest, circa 1792 (22) p 30.

"We are poor instruments to make God's holy Truth to be yet more and more known unto the people" The Epistle Dedicatory, AV1611.

Why is the AV1611 the perfect word of God? The reasons are given below. The titles for the sections which follow have been taken from the references listed, in particular those of Dr. Ruckman, (29) and (30). I cannot improve on them.

5.1 THE ABSENCE OF COPYRIGHT

(6) p 80, (29) p 22–24, (30) p 3,4.

The AV1611 in all its editions carries no copyright. All modern versions are copyrighted by their respective publishing companies. *"By taking out a copyright on a so-called "Bible", the copyright owner ADMITS that this is not God's word but THEIR OWN WORDS"* (6) p 80.

"Copyright: Exclusive right given by law for term of years to author, designer, etc., or his assignee to print, publish, or sell, copies of his original work". The Concise Oxford Dictionary, 5th Edition, 1964.

5.2 THE TIME OF ITS PUBLICATION

It was published before the advent of French atheism, German rationalism and English deism. God could work through men whose minds had not been infected by modern philosophy and **"the oppositions of science falsely so called"** Colossians 2:8, 1 Timothy 6:20. Questionable texts and words in the Bible do not become questionable until AFTER 1611. The first 'textual critic' of the AV1611 in the modern sense is Richard Simon, a ROMAN CATHOLIC priest (1) p 91.

The translators lived at a time when the reign of Bloody Mary was still in living memory. They made no attempt to honour the man-made traditions of Rome. Compare Matthew 1:25, 23:14, Acts 8:37, Colossians 1:14, James 5:16, 2 Peter 1:20 in the AV1611 with the equivalent readings in the New International Version, NIV or Jerusalem Bible, JB.

The English language in the 16th and 17th centuries was perfectly suited to expressing the thoughts and concepts of Hebrew and Greek. English words were *"simple, broad and generic"* (8) p 22. Examples are **conversation, bowel, frame, instant, discover, savour, meat, corn** and **church**. However, the language of the AV1611 is not 16th or 17th century English style, which was very different. It is not a type of English that was ever spoken anywhere. It is Biblical English, which was not everyday speech in the 17th century, as even the AV1611 Preface shows. Even the singular *"thee"*, *"thou"* etc. had been replaced by the plural *"you"* in ordinary conversation (5) p 218.

5.3 THE HONESTY OF ITS PRESERVATION

No translation from one language into another can be verbatim, or word-for-word. The AV1611 translators inserted words in Italics which had no direct equivalents in the Hebrew or Greek texts but which were necessary for clarity, good English style and grammatical sense. The translators also rendered the second part of 1 John 2:23 in Italics because it was absent from the Received Text, although attested by other ancient witnesses. See the TBS *Quarterly Record*, No. 453, Oct.-Dec. 1975 and also Gipp, (9) p 52.

The practice of inserting Italics shows that the AV1611 is an honest translation, Romans 12:17. Most modern translations do not exhibit this degree of honesty. The exception is the NKJV, which was obviously forced to emulate the AV1611 in this respect. Note the importance of the word "**is**" in Italics in 2 Timothy 3:16. Although the NKJV follows the AV1611 here, the NIV does NOT.

As work on the AV1611 progressed, the translators kept the rest of the clergy informed and invited help from them (7) p 103. This is another testimony to the honesty of the translators.

5.4 THE INSTRUMENTS OF ITS PRESERVATION

See Chapter 4.

5.5 THE FRUITS OF ITS PRESERVATION

See Section 1.7 and note that God has accomplished FAR MORE with the AV1611 than He ever did with the originals. This is only ONE reason why the AV1611 is SUPERIOR to the original mss.. For the 'fruits' of the modern translations, Dr. Gipp, (9) p 113, has this analysis:

"Today's modern translations haven't been able to spark a revival in a Christian school, let alone be expected to close a bar. In fact, since the arrival of our modern English translations, beginning with the ASV of 1901, America has seen:

1. God and prayer kicked out of our public school.
2. Abortion on demand legalised.
3. Homosexuality accepted nationally as an "alternate life style".
4. In home pornography via TV and VCR.
5. Child kidnapping and pornography running rampant.
6. Dope has become an epidemic.
7. Satanism is on the rise.

If this is considered a "revival" then let's turn back to the King James to STOP it".

For a British evaluation of the results of rejecting the AV1611 and the corrupt fruit of the modern versions, Luke 6:43–45, see *Britain in Sin*, 1998, available from *Christian Voice*, Wemlwyd, Pen-y-bont, Carmarthen, SA33 6QN.

5.6 THE PRE-EMINENT PLACE IT GIVES TO THE LORD JESUS CHRIST

The AV1611 is unique in this respect.

ALL modern translations detract from the Person and Deity of the Lord Jesus Christ. The NIV and NKJV omit the definite articles from Isaiah 9:6. The NIV omits "**Lord**", "**Jesus**", "**Christ**", "**God**" or similar terms 162 times in the New Testament (31) and slanders the Lord further in Daniel 3:25, Micah 5:2, Matthew 20:20, Luke 2:33, 23:42, John 1:3, 3:13, 16, 9:35, Acts 3:13, 4:27, 30, Romans 14:10, 1 Timothy 3:16, Hebrews 4:8 and 1 John 5:7. The NKJV (JFV) margin upholds many of the corruptions in the NIV text for these verses and retains in its text the NIV readings in Matthew 20:20, John 1:3, Acts 3:13, 4:27, 30, 7:45, Hebrews 4:8.

A definitive analysis of attacks on the Deity of Christ in the modern versions will be found in the work by Riplinger, (12) and the work by C. Salliby, *If The Foundations Be Destroyed*, 1994. These books can be obtained through Penfold Book and Bible House, P.O. Box 26, Bicester, Oxfordshire, OX6 8PB or B. McCall Barbour, 28 George IV Bridge, Edinburgh, EH1 1ES.

5.7 THE PRIDE AND INCONSISTENCY OF ITS CRITICS

"Most of the fervency against the Authorised Version is not so much due to a conscious hatred against the Book, as much as it is a show of one's education. This fact, which is a conscious malice, is then coupled with the "flesh" or "natural man" . . . to form a constant antagonism toward the true Word of God. This "old nature" exists in every person, even Christians. It will not change until the rapture. This nature manifests itself in an innate desire not to submit to the authority of God" (14) p 169.

Critics accuse the AV1611 as follows:

5.7.1 The AV1611 contains many archaic words which need to be updated.

Such words could easily be explained in the margin or in a glossary without altering the Text. Comprehensive but inexpensive glossaries are available (32). Many supposedly archaic words are little changed from their modern equivalents and may be found in a Concise Oxford Dictionary. Moreover, alteration of a word in the AV1611 Text may destroy its full range of meaning. See Section 5.2.

Critics also overlook the fact that the AV1611 contains many 'modernisms'. Examples are **addict** (!), **artillery, God save the king, powers that be, head in the clouds, housekeeping** (!), **communication, learn by experience, labour of love, shambles, advertise, publish, beer** (!), **the course of nature** and many others. Much of the *"archaic words"* criticism is directed against the personal pronouns **"thee"** and **"thou"** etc. However, these supposedly archaic forms enable the reader to distinguish between the second person singular ('thee') and the second person plural ('you'), a distinction lost in modern English. The retention of 'thee', 'thou' etc. therefore makes the AV1611 Text CLEARER. Compare Luke 22:31,32 in an AV1611 with an NIV or NKJV. The NIV has to insert a marginal note to enlighten the reader. (Why not change the TEXT??!)

Finally, one should be guided by the Bible itself in the treatment of 'archaic' words. See 1 Samuel 9:9, 11. The 'archaic' word **"seer"** is explained, v.9 but retained in the Text, v.11.

A definitive work on supposedly archaic words in the AV1611 is *Archaic Words and the Authorized Version*, by Dr. Laurence M. Vance, 1996, available from the Bible Baptist Bookstore, Pensacola, Florida.

5.7.2 The AV1611 is hard to understand and therefore we need modern versions.

If the AV1611 is *"hard to understand"* why did its Text cause the English people to become a Bible loving people, *"the people of the Book"* in the words of the historian Green? This commendation cannot be bestowed on ANY modern version. For example, the RAV, Revised Authorised Version, which was supposed to replace the AV1611, went bankrupt within a few years and now can only be obtained as its American counterpart, the NKJV.

Gail Riplinger (12) p 195–214, cites the results of a survey carried out by the Flesch-Kincaid Research Company on the ease of reading of various Bible versions, including the NIV and NKJV. The AV1611 was found to be the easiest Bible to read in 23 of 26 comparisons. The AV1611 is also acknowledged to be the easiest to memorise. The NIV is particularly defective in this respect because it uses, on average, twice as many syllables as the AV1611 in any given passage.

Further, the belief that modern renderings are necessary for understanding denies the principles of interpretation stated by Joseph, Genesis 40:8, Solomon, Proverbs 2:1–5, Daniel, Daniel 2:18–27 and the Lord Himself, John 14:26, 16:13.

Finally, the AV1611 was not hard to understand for those converted under its preaching, when it was, allegedly, 120 years out of date:

> *"Two hundred miners standing in the field near the colliery at Bedworth, Warwickshire, listened with astonishment while a young Oxford graduate explained how they might have their sins forgiven. In the town of Bedworth colliers were rated heathen, animals, brutes who had no use in life other than to wrest coal from the earth. To be treated with respect and interest was a new experience. The unlicensed preacher could see "white gutters made by their tears, which plentifully fell down their black cheeks."*
>
> *It was a new experience for George Whitefield as well . . . "* (33)
> p 291.

5.7.3 The AV1611 is a translation and translations are made by imperfect men. Therefore the AV1611 must be imperfect.

This criticism overlooks the fact that the originals were written by imperfect men. Moses murdered a man, Exodus 2:12, David committed adultery and murder, 2 Samuel 11:2,15,21, Solomon apostatised, 1 Kings 11:1–8, Daniel committed sacrilege, Daniel 2:46, Peter cursed, swore and denied the Lord, Matthew 26:74, Paul disobeyed the Lord and spent two years in prison, Acts 21:4,11–13, 24:27, John tried to worship an angel, not once but twice, Revelation 19:10, 22:8,9. Moreover, if a translation is held to be imperfect for that reason, what of the ORIGINALS for Genesis 42:23, Moses' conversations with Pharaoh, Exodus 4–14, Peter's speech from Joel, Acts 2:17–20, the reading from Isaiah 53 in Acts 8:32 and Paul's speech in Acts 22:2–21? The written originals of these passages were translations. Were THEY imperfect?

Critics should note that God has promised to PRESERVE the word which He gave by inspiration: **"The words of the Lord are pure words: as silver tried in a furnace of earth, purified seven times.**

Thou shalt keep them, O Lord, thou shalt preserve them from this generation forever" Psalm 12:6,7.

A variation on this criticism is that 'good, godly men corrected the AV1611 on occasion, so it must need correcting'. The simple answer is that when any man "**holds the truth in unrighteousness**" Romans 1:18, by exalting HIS own authority over that of the BIBLE, he CEASES to be 'good' and he ceases to be 'godly'.

"**My glory will I not give to another**" Isaiah 42:8, not Torrey, not Spurgeon, not Ryle, not Calvin, not Wesley, not Moody, not Scofield, not ANY other.

5.7.4 The original edition of the AV1611 contained the Apocrypha and the AV1611 still has pro-catholic readings.

The Apocrypha in the AV1611 was contained BETWEEN the Testaments. It was NOT part of the Old Testament and was not stated to be Scripture in the title page of the AV1611. See Section 4.4. The Apocrypha was removed from the 1613 edition and several subsequent, major editions published before the 19th century, when it became usual for publishers of the AV1611 to omit the Apocrypha. As for pro-catholic readings, these are a feature of the modern versions. See Section 5.2. The alleged "*pro-catholic*" readings in the AV1611 are insufficient for it to be sold by the Catholic Truth Society, although the CTS do sell the NIV!

5.7.5 The AV1611 is obscure in some passages and inaccurate in others and therefore it should be improved.

One should consider whether "Nephilim" Genesis 6:3, "curds" Isaiah 7:15, "carved stones" Numbers 33:52, "demons" Matthew 4:24, 7:22, 8:16 etc. and "Hades" Revelation 1:18, 6:8, 20:13 in the NIV are 'clearer' than the AV1611 renderings, "**giants**", "**butter**", "**pictures**", "**devils**" and "**hell**", even if the NIV terms were more 'accurate', which they are not. Note that "demons" and "Hades" are transliterations, not translations and are perpetuated throughout the NIV, NKJV, although neither the NIV nor the NKJV transliterated "ouranos" for "**heaven**"!

One should also consider whether the pro-catholic readings in the NIV and NKJV listed above, see Section 5.2, are more 'accurate' than the AV1611 even if 'clearer', which they are not.

Critics will change a 'clear' verse in the AV1611 to make it more 'accurate' and alter an 'accurate' verse to make it 'clearer'. Obviously the overriding aim is to alter the AV1611 Text at any cost. Note that

where the AV1611 correctly translates "**Jesus**" in Acts 7:45 and
Hebrews 4:8, the critics insert "Joshua" because they cannot understand
that Joshua is an Old Testament type of the Second Coming of Jesus
Christ, associated with the destruction of an accursed city, Joshua 7:26
and Revelation 18, 19:2, (17) p 337–338. Moreover, Joshua 5:13–15
shows that the Lord Jesus Christ did command the people of Israel during their invasion of the Promised Land as "**captain of the host of the
Lord**", Who received worship from Joshua, just as He did from the disciples centuries later, Matthew 14:33. This Old Testament appearance of
the Lord "**whose goings forth have been from of old, from everlasting**" Micah 5:2, was promised in Exodus 23:20–23, which refers to
"**Mine Angel**" of Whom God says "**for my name is in him**". The modern translations all overlook this essential feature of the conquest of
Canaan and in so doing fail to give glory due to the Lord Jesus Christ.

5.7.6 The AV1611 of today is not the same as the original AV1611 but has been changed in 20,000 places. Therefore we can legitimately introduce MORE changes.

The changes in the AV1611 are mainly changes in spelling, punctuation,
Italics, marginal references, capitalisations and rectification of printing
errors. According to the American Bible Society, 1852, "*The English
Bible as left by the translators has come down to us unaltered in respect
to its text*" (11) P 43.

It is true that the original AV1611 has "**he**" in Ruth 3:15, while
today's Editions have "**she**". Each Edition is correct because BOTH
Ruth and Boaz "**went into the city**". See Ruth 3:16, 4:1. Moreover, this
alteration 'does not affect one fundamental of the faith'. What is good
for the goose is good for the gander.

Changes in the modern versions include elimination of words, phrases, verses and whole passages of Scripture, resulting in the denial of the
virgin birth, the blood atonement, salvation by faith alone and the deity
of Christ. These changes are therefore of an entirely different NATURE
from those in the AV1611 Editions. The same comments apply to the
notion that because the Alexandrian text is said to be 90% similar to the
Antiochan Text (4) p 89, 90, 211, there is therefore little difference
between bibles from either text.

It should be noted that Vaticanus B, the most highly regarded ms. of
the Alexandrian text, is only 50% similar to the Received Text (12) p
551.

The AV1611 of today is Dr. Blaney's edition, published 1769 (34) p 3. The AV1611 Text therefore has definitely not changed for over 200 years, which is more than can be said yet for the NIV and NKJV.

5.7.7 *The AV1611 can be tolerated but surely any translation is satisfactory so long as it contains the fundamentals of the faith and we win souls.*

The 'fundamentals of the faith' can be written on the back of an envelope and found even in a JB or NWT, New World Translation of the Jehovah's Witnesses. This does not mean that they are Bibles. The AV1611 will always give greater emphasis on the 'fundamentals' than the modern versions. As Gail Riplinger shows (12), progressive modern versions for the 'New Age' will continue to undermine fundamental doctrine until it is no longer 'fundamental'. See also comments by Dr. Gipp, (14) p 181–82.

A young preacher once said that he could preach from ANY Bible on "*justification by faith*", even if we could only be sure of "*98%*" of God's words. Not only are there no Scriptures to support this view but a 2% uncertainty in the Scriptures yields approximately 600 doubtful verses. Any concordance will show that the word "**justify**" or its equivalent with respect to faith, occurs in no more than about 30 verses in the New Testament. Are THESE verses among the doubtful 600? Who decides and by what authority?

Concerning 'soul winning', see Sections 1.7, 5.5 and George Whitfield's experience at Bedworth.

Finally, if a bible is to be selected on the basis of preference, which is what the above criticism implies, perhaps one should ask what Bible does GOD prefer?

5.7.8 *The AV1611 may be tolerated but it is still inferior to "the Greek".*

To this criticism, it may reasonably be asked WHICH Greek, because there are about two dozen different Greek texts (1) p 150, (4) p 176, (11) p 3–4. They can roughly be divided into three groups:

1. The 'Received Text', such as the editions of Erasmus, Stephanus etc..
2. The 'Alexandrian text', such as those of Tregelles, Tischendorf, Griesbach, Hort and Nestle, who is probably the best known editor.
3. The 'Majority text' of which there are two rival editions, by Farstad and Hodges, 1982 and Robinson and Pierpont, 1991 (22) p 73–74.

The 26th edition of Nestle (1979) restored 467 Receptus readings which had been deleted in previous editions for the past 100 years (1) p vi, (29) p 7–8. Nestle's editors supposedly did this on the basis of evidence from the papyri, indicating that Receptus readings actually predate Alexandrian readings (1) p 329. Moreover, while Nestle will use Codex B repeatedly to alter Receptus readings, he may abruptly switch to another ms. if B agrees with the Receptus. "**Him**" is omitted from John 14:7 by Nestle's 21st edition using B, but all of Luke 24:12 is omitted using Codex D, although B agrees with the Receptus (4) Chapter 7, (29) p 71–85. Note that these omissions bear on the Deity of Christ and the resurrection of Christ. Ricker Berry's text retains the Receptus readings. See also (1) p 328–331. Similar inconsistencies exist in the selection of the texts for the NIV and other modern versions (12) p 499–503.

This criticism really amounts to a denial of the promise of God to preserve His word, Psalm 12:6,7. Similar comments apply where the critic insists that the AV1611 is inferior to 'the originals', with the added observation that the originals no longer exist and that the verses usually used to justify this criticism, 2 Timothy 3:15,16, are NOT a reference to the originals! They refer to "**the holy scriptures**", copies of Old Testament Books that Timothy had known "**from a child**".

There are at least 8 reasons why the AV1611 is in fact superior to 'the Greek' – and to 'the Hebrew' (1) p 332–343:

1. The AV1611 uses "**synagogues**" in Psalm 74:8, instead of the Hebrew "meeting places", showing that the reference is yet future, to the great tribulation.
2. The Pre-millennial order of the books from 2 Chronicles to Psalms in the AV1611 preserves the order of events in the history of Israel from the destruction of Jerusalem, 70 AD, to the Second Advent. This order is superior to that of the Hebrew Bible.
3. In an age ruled by the television, "**pictures**" in Numbers 33:52 is far superior to the original Hebrew of "carved stones".
4. The AV1611 alone uses "**forces**" in Daniel 11:38 instead of the literal Hebrew "fortresses". The AV1611 reading is superior because it is a reference to the use of electricity, Luke 10:18, the highest form of energy, especially in the tribulation. See Revelation 13:13.
5. The AV1611 has "**churches**" in Acts 19:37, showing where pagans devoted to the "**Queen of heaven**", Jeremiah 44:19, actually WORSHIP. This is far superior to the 'original Greek', which gives "temples".

6. The AV1611 has "**easter**" in Acts 12:4 instead of the literal Greek equivalent "passover". Herod was an Edomite and would therefore observe Easter, not the Passover. See also Dr. Gipp's comments, (9) p 3–8.

7. The tense of the Greek in Galatians 2:19 is "I have been crucified" but Luke 9:23 shows that a man is to take up the cross DAILY. The AV1611 reading, "**I am crucified**" is therefore both correct and superior to "the Greek".

8. The AV1611 alone has "**corrupt**" in 2 Corinthians 2:17, where the 'original Greek' is "peddle", according to the modern revisers. There is no danger in selling the AV1611, because it isn't corrupt. However, there could be a great danger in the selling of CORRUPT 'bibles'. It would be rather like selling contaminated milk, 1 Peter 2:2!

For detailed discussions of the superiority of the AV1611 to 'the Hebrew' and 'the Greek', with over 60 examples, see (1) Appendix 7 and *Bible Believers' Bulletin*, February, March 1989, November 1991. See also Dr. Gipp's discussion of the distinction that should allegedly be drawn between the Greek words "phileo" and "agape", which are both translated as "**love**" in the AV1611 (9) p 124–131. The English Bible's comment on this alleged distinction is found in John 21:17 and comparison of 'the Greek' with the English in Luke 11:43, John 5:20, 42, 16:27, 1 Corinthians 16:22, Titus 3:4, 15, Revelation 3:19 will yield valuable further insight.

Many critics of the AV1611 may still insist with Ricker Berry that *"Without some knowledge of Greek and Hebrew, you cannot be an independent student, or reliable interpreter of the word of God"*. The Lord's comment on this type of condescension is in Luke 10:21. Ricker Berry's statement can also be "interpreted" as follows:

1. All translations are made by men who are imperfect and therefore their translations are imperfect (see above).

2. Any translation is therefore inferior to the original which was perfect.

3. The original was in Greek (and so is the LXX which Christ and the Apostles (allegedly) used).

4. I KNOW GREEK AND YOU DON'T. THEREFORE YOU WILL HAVE TO COME TO ME (OR BUY MY BOOKS) TO FIND OUT WHAT GOD ACTUALLY SAID.

5.7.9 *The AV is out of date and modern man needs a modern version.*

"The sluggard is wiser in his own conceit than seven men that can render a reason" Proverbs 26:16.

Critics of the AV1611 should note that:

1. NO Bible version has received anything like the criticisms which have been levelled at the AV1611, as this list shows.
2. Modern versions come and go, with 100 appearing in the last 100 years (22). None last for more than a few decades.
3. God Himself has intervened at times to deprive some of the more prominent revisors of the power of speech (12) p 446–452. Those affected include Tregelles, early editor of a Hort-Nestle type text, Westcott, Philip Schaff, editor of the NASV, which is similar to the NIV, Kenneth Taylor of the 'Living' bible and J.B. Phillips, whose New Testament bears his name.

Psalm 12:3 should be a warning to all: **"The Lord shall cut off all flattering lips, and the tongue that speaketh proud things"**.

6

The Defection of the Church of England

6.1 WESTCOTT AND HORT

(2) p 262–318, (7) p 23–34, (14) Ch. 7, 8

The Devil was not slow to oppose the great blessings of revival, soul-winning and enterprise brought about by the God honoured AV1611 Holy Bible. Through the agency of his own papal church, Satan concentrated his attack on the nation which had produced the Book. His attack culminated in the efforts of Westcott and Hort, two Cambridge academics, to displace the AV1611 as the English Bible by means of their own Revised Version, RV, based mainly on the text of the Alexandrian mss., which in turn formed the basis of Roman Catholic bibles such as the Latin Vulgate and the Jesuit Douay Rheims. The attack developed as follows:

1. The Jesuit Counter-Reformation had begun even before the publication of the AV1611 (2) p 231–243.
2. Jesuits dominated the Council of Trent, 1546, convened to defeat the Reformation.
3. This council declared that belief in justification by faith alone was accursed, Canon IX, thus cursing the Lord Jesus Christ, John 3:16 and that the Apocrypha and church tradition were of equal authority with the Bible (2) p 4.
4. Jesuits tried unsuccessfully to impose their own English bible translation on the English people, 1582, based on the Alexandrian text.
5. The Counter-Reformation nevertheless gathered momentum with the

emergence of *"higher critics"*, particularly Germans, who attacked the Received Text and exalted the Alexandrian text. Among these critics were Schleiermacher, Griesbach, Wellhausen, Lachmann, Tischendorf and Tregelles. They were the new gnostics.

6. German higher criticism invaded England in the early 19th century, resulting in the Puseyite movement to re-unite the Church of England with the Church of Rome. Cardinal Newman was one of the early defectors.

7. Romanising of the Church of England was well underway by 1870, when the Southern Convocation of the Church of England called for revision of the Text of the AV1611. The Northern Convocation refused to take part and there was no such demand from the ordinary members of the Church (7) p 23–28.

8. The Revised New Testament was published in 1881.

9. The Cambridge academics, Westcott and Hort, were strongly influenced by Pusey, Newman and Coleridge, who imported the new German gnosticism to England and by Richard Simon (14) p 131.

10. Westcott and Hort compiled the Greek text, based largely on Codices Aleph and B, which was *"secretly committed"* into the hands of the Revision Committee and used as the basis for the Revised Version (2) p 293.

11. This text differs radically from the Received New Testament Text, in 5337 places or in about 2 of every 3 verses.

12. The RV in turn differs from the AV1611 in over 36000 places. This is more than one change in every verse (2) p 294, 298, although the first working rule of the committee was that as few alterations as possible were to the introduced to the Text of the AV1611 (7) p 24.

13. Of the 25 members of the committee, only a small minority, led by Dr. Scrivener, endeavoured to abide by the rules and they were consistently outvoted by the others (2) p 293.

14. The work of Westcott and Hort can be explained by their beliefs, expressed in their own words (2) p 277–282, (12) p 400–435, (14) p 116–168. Even if clandestinely, they were servants of Satan and of Rome.

15. Hort states:

"The book which has most engaged me is Darwin . . . My feeling is strong that the theory is unanswerable."

"Evangelicals seem to me perverted rather than untrue. There are, I fear, still more serious differences between us on the subject of authority, and especially the authority of the Bible."

"Think of the vile Textus Receptus leaning entirely on late mss.; it is a blessing there are such early ones."

"I have been persuaded for many years that Mary-worship and 'Jesus'-worship have very much in common in their causes and their results."

"Moody had great sincerity . . . but in matter is quite conventional and commonplace."

"Westcott . . . and I have started a society for the investigation of ghosts . . . being all disposed to believe that such things really exist . . . our own temporary name is 'the Ghostly Guild'."

16. Westcott states:

"No one now (1890), I suppose, holds that the first three chapters of Genesis, for example, give a literal history."

"Behind a screen was a 'Pieta' the size of life (a Virgin and dead Christ) . . . Had I been alone I could have knelt there for hours."

"I never read an account of a miracle (of Christ), but I seem instinctively to feel its improbability."

"Christianity rests upon the central fact that the Word became flesh. This fact establishes not only a brotherhood of men, but also a brotherhood of nations."

Concerning Westcott and Hort's approach to the Bible, Fuller states further that: *"In spite of his brave and oft quoted words to the effect that only a thousandth part of the New Testament Text is seriously in question, Hort himself did not feel that certainty was possible"* (3) p 279.

Would God choose such men to 'revise' His Book?? *Would YOU?? Do you suppose that GOD has as much sense as YOU??*

"Have I not written to thee excellent things in counsels and knowledge, that I might make thee know the certainty of the words of truth" Proverbs 22:20, 21b.

6.2 JOHN BURGON, DEAN OF CHICHESTER

(2) p 86–105, (5) p 139

In every age God has had men who like David have **"served his own generation by the will of God"** Acts 13:36. Such a man was John

Burgon. His scholarly refutation of Westcott and Hort's revisions to the Holy Bible, entitled *The Revision Revised*, (13) stands unchallenged to this day.

17. Burgon was Fellow of Oriel College, Oxford, Gresham Professor of Divinity and Dean of Chichester 1876–1888.

18. He was described as *"a deep and laborious student . . . examining the original (i.e. extant) manuscripts on every occasion, and he himself discovered many manuscripts in his search for the truth in textual matters . . . As for his learning, even his adversaries acknowledged that it was very great"* (2) p 86–87.

19. He personally scrutinised Codices Aleph and B, concluding *"we suspect that these two mss. are indebted for their preservation; SOLELY TO THEIR ASCERTAINED EVIL CHARACTER"* (2) p 93–94.

20. Whereas Hort declared of the New Testament *"we dare not introduce considerations which could not reasonably be applied to other ancient texts"*, Burgon *"believed that the New Testament had been divinely inspired and providentially preserved . . . two basic verities which make the textual criticism of the New Testament different from the textual criticism of any other book"* (2) p 102–103.

21. Burgon readily acknowledged the hand of Satan in the corruption of New Testament mss.: *"Vanquished by THE WORD Incarnate, Satan next directed his subtle malice against the WORD written. Hence . . . the extraordinary fate which befell certain early transcripts of the Gospel"* (5) p 140–141.

22. He was a staunch defender, not only of the Received Text but of the AV1611. Of the 1881 Revision he said *"We are thoroughly convinced that the project of a rival Translation is not to be entertained for a moment. For ourselves we deprecate it entirely"* (2) p 105.

23. Burgon carefully set out 7 tests of truth for mss. readings (2) p 92:

   1. Antiquity of witnesses
   2. Number of witnesses
   3. Variety of evidence
   4. Respectability of witnesses
   5. Continuity of witnesses
   6. Context
   7. Internal considerations

He declared that "*In the balances of these seven Tests of Truth the speculations of the Westcott and Hort school, which have bewitched millions are 'Tekel', weighed in the balances and found wanting*" (2) p 92.

Of Westcott and Hort's subjective exaltation of Codices Aleph, B, D, Burgon stated "*In contrast with this sojourn in cloudland, we are essentially of the earth though not earthy. We are nothing if we are not grounded in facts: Our appeal is to facts, our test lies in facts*" (2) p 91.

8. Hort had rejected the text of the majority of mss. by assuming that it represented a standardised text compiled by Lucian of Antioch in the 4th century (11) p 32–35. This was his so-called "*conflation*" or "*recension*" theory in support of which he could cite only a mere eight verses. Hort's theory is refuted utterly by Burgon, (13) p 271–294, who states that "*not a shadow of proof is forthcoming that any such recension as Dr. Hort imagines ever took place at all*" (13) p 273.

9. Burgon vigorously defended scriptures rejected by Westcott and Hort using Aleph and B, for example:

Mark 16:9–20

Although retained by the RV, this passage was deleted from Westcott and Hort's Greek New Testament and is disputed by the NIV and other modern translations.

Burgon showed that:

"*With the exception of the two uncial mss. which have just been named (Aleph and B), there is not one codex in existence, uncial or cursive (and we are aquainted with, at least, eighteen other uncials, and above six hundred cursive copies of this Gospel), which leaves out the last twelve verses of Mark*" (18) p 60.

Burgon also cited overwhelming testimony from the ancient versions, lectionaries and church fathers in favour of these verses (2) p 168–169.

John 7:53–8:11

This passage is also omitted from the Westcott-Hort Greek text and disputed by the NIV and other modern versions.

Burgon showed that:

"*An omission which owed its beginning to a moral scruple was eventually extended for a liturgical consideration and resulted in severing twelve verses of St. John's Gospel – chapter 7:53–8:11 – from their lawful context"* (18) p 148–149. However, he states that *"Jerome, who was familiar with Greek mss.(and who handled none of later date than B and Aleph), expressly related that (the passage) "is found in many copies both Greek and Latin""* (18) p 146.

Again, Burgon cited other evidence overwhelmingly in favour of the passage, including 61 of the 73 copies of John's Gospel in the British Museum which contain the passage.

1 Timothy 3:16
The AV1611 reading **"God was manifest in the flesh"** is changed in the RV and most modern versions, including the NIV, to "He who was manifested in the flesh" or similar.

Burgon showed that ΘΕΟΣ "Theos" or "God" was invariably written ΘΣ, "THS" in the uncial mss. and could easily become ΟΣ, "OS" or "who" (13) p 425–426, as it appears in Aleph and C or "O", "which", in D. These are the only unequivocal uncial witnesses against "THS" (13) p 426–443.

Writing to Bishop Ellicott, chairman of the RV committee, Burgon states that *"The sum of the available cursive copies of S. Paul's Epistles is exactly 254 . . . Permit me to submit to your consideration as a set off against those two copies of S. Paul's Epistles which read* oς, *"os" – the following TWO HUNDRED AND FIFTY TWO COPIES which read* Θεος *"Theos""* (13) p 492. Again, Burgon provides further evidence from early citations overwhelmingly in favour of the AV1611 reading.

He warns Bishop Ellicott (13) p 430:

"It will be for you, afterwards, to come forward and prove that, on the contrary, "Theos" is a 'plain and clear error:' . . . You are further reminded, my lord Bishop, that unless you do this, you will be considered by the whole Church to have dealt unfaithfully with the Word of God" (13) p 430.

To this day, Burgon's case has never been answered. Ever **"Valiant for the truth"** Jeremiah 9:3, he sought to safeguard the Body of Christ from the peril about which the Earl of Shaftesbury gave solemn warning in 1856.

"When you are confused or perplexed by a variety of versions, you would be obliged to go to some learned pundit in whom you reposed confidence, and ask him which version he recommended;

and when you had taken his version, you must be bound by his opinion. I hold this to be the greatest danger that now threatens us. It is a danger pressed upon us from Germany, and pressed upon us by the neological spirit of the age. I hold it to be far more danger-ous than Tractarianism, or Popery, both of which I abhor from the bottom of my heart. This evil is tenfold more dangerous, tenfold more subtle than either of these, because you would be ten times more incapable of dealing with the gigantic mischief that would stand before you" (2) p 274–75.

6.3 A FLOOD OF REVISIONS – AND THE FLOTSAM OF THREE NATIONS

See Figure 4, *The Modern Versions and Their Results.*
"By their fruits ye shall know them" Matthew 7:20.

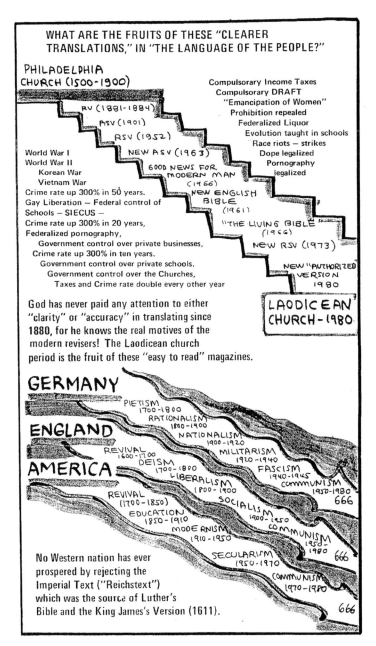

Figure 4   A Flood of Revisions

7

Flood of Revision

**"When the enemy shall come in like a flood, the Spirit of the
Lord shall lift up a standard against him"** Isaiah 59:19b

7.1 INTRODUCTION

Some differences between the AV1611 and the modern versions have
already been noted. These and others will now be examined in more
detail. It should be appreciated that the differences cited are but a small
selection of those which are NOT minor.

The AV1611 will be compared in both Testaments with four modern
translations:

1. The 'premier' evangelical translation, the NIV, New International
   Version.
2. The leading 'fundamentalist' bible, the NKJV, New King James
   Version, (JFV), either with respect to its text or its marginal notes.
3. An official bible of the Roman Catholic church, the Jerusalem Bible
   or JB, modern equivalent to the 1582 Jesuit Rheims text.
4. The bible of the Jehovah's Witnesses cult, the New World
   Translation, NWT.
5. The DR, Douay Rheims Bible, revised by Bishop Richard Challoner
   AD 1749–1752, RV, Revised Version, 1881, Ricker Berry's 1897
   Interlinear Edition of Stephanus' 1550 3rd Edition Greek Receptus
   and Nestle's Greek New Testament, 21st edition, will be included in
   the comparison for the New Testament. The two Greek New
   Testaments have been included to show that there is no such thing as
   a single, definitive Greek text.

7.2 COMPARISON OF OLD TESTAMENT READINGS

Genesis 1:21
    "whales" AV1611
    "creatures of the sea" NIV, "sea creatures" NKJV, "sea serpents" JB,
"sea monsters" NWT

Whales are the one species not named by Adam, Genesis 2:19, because they are a type of Satan, Job 41:1, Psalm 104:26, Ezekiel 29:3, 32:2, Jeremiah 51:34, Jonah 1:17, 2:2, Matthew 12:40. Note first that the term **"whales"** in Genesis 1:21 matches that of **"leviathan"** in Psalm 104:26 in that God **"created"** the former and **"hast made"** the latter. Each is then specified in distinction from **"every living creature that moveth, which the waters brought forth abundantly"** and **"the things creeping innumerable, both small and great beasts"** which teem in **"this great and wide sea"**. **"Leviathan"** is therefore typified in the physical realm by the whale but he is also **"that crooked serpent"** Isaiah 27:1, another of God's creatures whom **"his hand hath formed"** Job 26:13 and who inhabits **"the deep"** of Job 41:31. He also exists in the spiritual realm because he **"beholdeth all high things"** Job 41:34, Ephesians 6:12. He must be Satan because not only is he **"that crooked serpent"** he is a spirit being who can breathe fire, even **"the fire of God"** Job 1:12, 16, 41:21. Moreover, **"he is a king over all the children of pride"** and **"upon earth there is not his like"** Job 41:33, 34, whose heart **"was lifted up"** Ezekiel 28:17, Isaiah 14:13 but his name "livyathan" is actually **"mourning"** Job 3:8. Why? Because God has given Lucifer a new name to describe his fall, whose **"pomp is brought down to the grave"** Isaiah 14:11, who will be brought **"to ashes upon the earth"** Ezekiel 28:18, so that **"the hope of him is in vain"** Job 41:9. God has even named Leviathan's earthly type, Genesis 1:21 instead of delegating this responsibility to Adam, Genesis 2:19, because Adam, **"the son of God"** Luke 3:38, should have had a testimony equivalent to that of the Lord Jesus Christ; **"the prince of this world...hath nothing in me"** John 14:30. The modern versions now try to cover for the enemy, who was once, ironically, **"the anointed cherub that covereth"** Ezekiel 28:14.

Genesis 1:28
    "replenish" AV1611
    "fill" NIV, NKJV, JB, NWT

The opening reference to a pre-Adamic inhabited earth is lost by the modern versions. See Psalm 82:5 and Genesis 9:1.

Genesis 2:13
"**Ethiopia**" AV1611
"Cush" NIV, NKJV, NWT, JB
Which is CLEARER to the modern reader??

Genesis 3:5
"**gods**" AV1611, JB
"God" NIV, NKJV, NWT
There is a difference! Psalm 82 shows that there are "**gods**" in the universe. They were judges of nations, verses 2, 8, "**the sons of God**" of Genesis 6:2, "**the angels which kept not their first estate**" Jude 6. Their judgements corrupted the whole earth, Genesis 6:11, 12, such that God "**delivered them into chains of darkness**" 2 Peter 2:4, "**unto the judgement of the great day**" Jude 6, Isaiah 24:21, 22. This explains the significance of references to "**the gods of Egypt**" Exodus 12:12, against whom the Lord executed judgement and "**the gods of the people which are round about**" Deuteronomy 13:7, whose images God commanded Israel "**to utterly overthrow...and quite break down**" Exodus 23:24. The material images hearkened back to the time of "**gross darkness**", Isaiah 60:2, when the renegade angelic "**gods**" corrupted the earth and will do so again, according to the Lord Jesus Christ, Luke 17:26, 27. The modern versions obscure the cross-references.

Genesis 6:8
"**grace**" AV1611, NKJV
"favour" NIV, NWT, JB
This is the first appearance of the magnificent word "**grace**", which appears in the Bible 170 times, the last occasion being in Revelation 22:21. Why must it be changed?

Genesis 20:10
"**What sawest thou**" AV1611
"What was your reason" NIV
"What did you have in view" NKJV, NWT
"What possessed you" JB
The modern versions fail to recognise that "**the light of the body is the EYE**" Matthew 6:22. Abraham's sin of fear, compare Genesis 12:2,

12, arose from what he SAW. He SAW how the Egyptians regarded Sarah, Genesis 12:14, 15 and he SAW that Abimelech did the SAME. The desire to SIN, Genesis 20:9, often begins with the EYES, Matthew 6:22, 23, Mark 9:47, 2 Peter 2:14, James 1:14, 15 with 1 John 2:15, 16.

Genesis 49:6
"**digged down a wall**" AV1611
"hamstrung oxen (or similar)" NIV, NKJV, NWT, JB
The modern reading comes from the LXX. Inspection of Gen. 34:28, 29 reveals that oxen were NOT hamstrung but taken captive, along with other livestock and other mens' wives. The AV1611 reading for Genesis 49:6 therefore matches Job 24:16 exactly and the modern versions are wrong.

Deuteronomy 16:21
"**grove of any trees**" AV1611
"wooden Asherah pole (or similar)" NIV, NWT, JB
"any tree as a wooden image" NKJV
By altering "**groves**", the modern versions obscure the reference to MODERN MARIOLATRY, where a statue of 'the Virgin' is often planted in a GROVE of TREES. See 1 Kings 14:23, 2 Kings 13:6, 18:4, 23:4, 7, 14 and Section 10.6, where the word "**grove**" and its association with mariolatry is discussed in more detail with respect to 1 Kings 16:33.

1 Samuel 14:27, 29
"**enlightened**" AV1611
"brightened" NIV, NKJV, JB
"beamed" NWT
All the modern versions miss the typology with respect to the words of scripture and the wisdom or "**light**" that they give, Psalm 19:8, 10, 12, 119:130.

Job 3:8
"**mourning**" AV1611
"Leviathan" NIV, NKJV, NWT, JB
The 'Hebrew' is "Livyathan" but God HIMSELF states, in effect, that GOD ALONE is able to stir up Leviathan, Job 41:10. The modern versions, no doubt faithful to the 'original Hebrew' (!), therefore contradict God Himself!

Job 26:13

"**formed the crooked serpent**" AV1611

"pierced the gliding serpent" NIV, NWT

"pierced the fleeing serpent" NKJV

"pierced the transfixed serpent" JB

The modern versions obscure this reference to Satan as a created being.

Job 41:25

"**by reason of breakings they purify themselves**" AV1611

"they retreat before his thrashing" NIV

"because of his crashings they are beside themselves" NKJV

"due to consternation they get bewildered" NWT

"the billows of the sea retreat" JB

The modern versions obscure the cross references to 1 Kings 18:28 and 1 Corinthians 11:24, which reveal that rituals observed today in the Philippines demonstrate that Roman Catholicism is the modern heir to PHOENICIAN BAAL WORSHIP.

Psalm 39:5, 11

"**every man at his best state is altogether vanity...every man is vanity**" AV1611

"each man's life is but a breath (or similar)" NIV, NKJV, NWT, JB

The cross reference is not to James 4:14 but to Ecclesiastes, especially 1:16, 6:12 because Solomon realised man's "**best state**" more than any other.

Psalm 55:18

"**for there were many with me**" AV1611

"for there were many against me (or similar)" NIV, NKJV, NWT, JB

The modern versions contradict the cross reference to 2 Kings 6:17 and 2 Chronicles 32:7.

Proverbs 1:32

"**prosperity**" AV1611

"complacency (or similar)" NIV, NKJV, NWT, JB

PROSPERITY, not complacency, will damn most British people today, Luke 12:18–21, 1 Timothy 6:9, James 5:1–5. The Lord warned in the passage from Luke of the rich fool who laid up "**treasure for him-**

self" but was "**not rich toward God**" verse 21. Israel forsook the Lord during a time of great material abundance, Deuteronomy 32:13–16. Sodom's iniquity that led to abomination and in turn to her eventual overthrow was "**pride, fulness of bread, and abundance of idleness**" Ezekiel 16:49, 50. The modern versions therefore obscure the cross-references to "**the days of Lot**" just before the Lord's return. See Luke 17:28–30, 2 Peter 2:6–8.

Proverbs 21:27

"**wicked mind**" AV1611

"evil intent (or similar)" NIV, NKJV, JB

"loose conduct" NWT

The wicked man's problem is the MIND or HEART, Jeremiah 17:9, Mark 7:20–23. The AV1611 reading is therefore superior to both 'the Hebrew' and the modern versions.

Proverbs 23:33

"**Thine eyes shall behold strange women**" AV1611

"Your eyes will see strange things" NIV ("sights" for "things"), NKJV, NWT, JB

The context is drunkenness. A converted ex "*9th stage alcoholic*" once said "*liquor and women – always go together*".

Isaiah 5:14, 14:9, 15, 28:15, 18, 57:9

"**hell**" AV1611, each time

"grave" NIV (each time)

"sheol, Hell, Sheol (4 times)" NKJV

"sheol" NWT, JB

Hell is NOT the grave and "sheol" is a transliteration, NOT a translation. Whoever is behind the modern translations is very reluctant to use the word "hell". See also Ezekiel 31:16, 17, 32:21, 27, Amos 9:2, Jonah 2:2, Habakkuk 2:5, where of the modern versions, only the NKJV uses "hell", except in Jonah 2:2 where it resorts to "sheol".

Isaiah 9:3

"**Thou hast not increased the joy**" AV1611

"You have increased their joy (or similar)" NIV, NKJV, NWT, JB

"Not" ("al") can be found in the Masoretic Hebrew Text (19). The verse is dealing with the restoration and suffering of Israel before the

Second Advent, Zechariah 12, 13, a doctrine little understood by modern revisers.

Daniel 3:25

"**the Son of God**" AV1611, NKJV
"a son of the gods" NIV, NKJV marg., NWT, JB

As noted, the AV1611 always exalts the Lord Jesus Christ. The modern reading cannot be correct because "a son of the gods" would be a GIANT, Genesis 6:4, causing God GRIEF, Genesis 6:6.

Daniel 9:25, 26

"**Messiah**" AV1611, NKJV, NWT
"Anointed One" NIV, "anointed Prince" JB v. 25
Even the NWT has the decency to retain the precious word "Messiah" in its text.

Hosea 13:9

"**O Israel, thou hast destroyed thyself**" AV1611
"I will destroy you, O Israel (or similar)" NIV, JB
"O Israel, you are destroyed" NKJV
"It will certainly bring you to ruin, O Israel" NWT
Israel wilfully rejected the words of God, Hosea 6:5–7, 8:1, 12 and destroyed HERSELF. Hosea 13:9, 14:4–8 show that God will NOT destroy Israel, in spite of the NIV. The NKJV adopts a compromise reading, 1 Kings 18:21, Psalm 38:17.

Micah 5:2

"**whose goings forth have been from of old, from everlasting**" AV1611, NKJV
"whose origins are from old, from ancient times" (or similar) NIV, NWT, JB
The verse is a reference to the pre-existence of the Lord Jesus Christ, who does NOT have an origin, John 1:1–3. The NIV reading is therefore blasphemous.

Zechariah 13:6

"**What are these wounds in thine hands?**" AV1611, NKJV
"What are these wounds on your body?" NIV, JB

"What are these wounds (on your person) between your hands?"
NWT
Apart from the NKJV, the modern versions obscure this reference to
the crucifixion of Christ.

Malachi 1:3

"**dragons**" AV1611
"jackals" NIV, NKJV, NWT (JB has no direct equivalent)

See also Psalm 44:19, Isaiah 13:22, 34:13, 35:7, 43:20, Jeremiah 9:11,
10:22, 14:6, 49:33, 51:34 (JB "dragon"), 37, Ezekiel 29:3, Micah 1:8.
Just as there is the devil and devils, Matthew 4:1, 24, John 6:70, there is
the dragon, Isaiah 27:1, Revelation 12:3 and dragons, see above. The
modern versions obscure this fact by altering "dragon" or "dragons" in
all these verses, except for the JB in Jeremiah 51:34.

7.3 COMPARISON OF NEW TESTAMENT READINGS

Mss. evidence is included for the New Testament readings which follow. The AV1611 readings are supported by the majority of mss. unless
otherwise stated.

The following comparison will show that evidence against the
AV1611, from "*older and better*" manuscripts usually means extracts
from a few ancient corrupt uncials of Alexandrian character, e.g. Aleph
and B. Burgon (13), Burton (6), Fuller (2, 3, 18), citing Burgon and other
authors, Ray (7) and Ruckman (1, 4, 17, 20, 29 etc.) provide ample
demonstration. John Burgon's comments are, of course, directed against
the Westcott-Hort Greek text underlying the Revised Version of 1881
but since the RV is the precursor of most of the modern versions – and
like them essentially a Roman Catholic 'bible' – Burgon's remarks
apply with equal force today. Indeed, the recent book by Radmacher and
Hodges, *The NIV Reconsidered* (23), published in 1990, reaffirms that
"*Burgon's strictures on Westcott and Hort have never been responded
to . . . by any specialist in this field*" p 140 and that "*handbooks on textual criticism . . . tend to dismiss Burgon peremptorily*".

However, Radmacher and Hodges are promoters of the NKJV, which
merits special mention in that in its Preface it purports to be faithful to
the Received Text. Nevertheless, it condones the corrupt Alexandrian
text in both Preface and marginal notes. This is a sure recipe for confusion, which inevitably confers FINAL AUTHORITY on the individual,

according to which reading he happens to 'prefer.' The NKJV is thus one of the more subtle attacks against the faith of Bible believers in the Book of books and hence all the more dangerous. Note that 'NKJV marg.', shows where the NKJV has impugned the AV1611 by means of marginal notes.

The work of J.A. Moorman, see Section 1.1, should be consulted for detailed mss. lists, especially where an AV1611 reading is said not to be found in the majority of mss..

Matthew 1:25
"**firstborn**" is omitted by the RV, Ne, NIV, NKJV marg., NWT, JB to uphold catholic teaching of Mary as a perpetual virgin.

Burgon (13), p 123, states that only 3 uncials, Aleph (Sinaiticus), B (Vaticanus), Z and two cursives omit "firstborn". Ruckman (35), p 12, states that the word is found in the *"Egyptian"* family of manuscripts (e.g. C), the *"Western"* (D) and the *"Byzantine"* (i.e. the Receptus). He states that it is also found in Tatian's Diatessaron, a Syrian translation of the Gospels, circa 170 AD, (4) p 80.

Burgon cites the Latin Vulgate, Peshitta and Philoxenian Syriac, the Ethiopic, Armenian, Georgian, and Slavonian versions in favour of the AV1611 reading, (13) p 9, 123; (4) p 80–81.

Burgon, (13) p 123, also cites the following *"Fathers"* as bearing witness to the word:

2nd Century:	Tatian
4th Century:	Ambrose, Athanasius, Augustine, Basil, Cyril of Jerusalem, Chrysostom, Didymus, Ephraem Syrus, Epiphanius, Gregory of Nyssa
5th Century:	Isidorus Pelus, Proclus
8th Century:	John Damascene
9th Century:	Photius.

Matthew 2:11, 9:18, 14:33, 20:20, Mark 5:6
"Worship" has been altered to "adored" by DR (all five verses) "Kneeling down" or "knelt" or "did obeisance" by NIV (Matthew 9:18, 20:20, Mark 5:6), NKJV (Matthew 20:20), NWT (all five verses), JB (all five verses).

Ruckman (4) p 152, states that the word "proskun" for "worship" is in ALL Greek manuscripts. Note its use in Matthew 4:10, Luke 4:8, John 4:21, 23, 24, Hebrews 1:6, Revelation 4:10, 5:14, 7:11, 11:16, 14:7,

19:4, 10, 22:9. This is the word found in Berry's Greek text in all five places, although he only translates it as "worship" in Matthew 14:33.

Matthew 5:22

"without a cause" is omitted by the DR, RV, Ne, NIV, NKJV marg., JB, NWT.

The omission makes a sinner out of the Lord Jesus Christ, Mark 3:5.

Burgon, (13), p 359–360, states that the omission of these words was originally the work of Origen (184–254), preserved in a writing of Jerome. Commenting on Matthew 5:22 in relation to Ephesians 4:31, Origen assumed the text he had in front of him was wrong, indicating it included the words as found in the AV1611!

Burgon reveals that only Codices Aleph and B omit the words. ALL other uncial copies have them. Fuller (3), p 38–39, and Ruckman (36, *Matthew* p 91) state that the words are found in the Byzantine Text, embodying the majority of the Greek manuscripts. Burgon states that every extant copy of the Old Latin, Syriac, Coptic, Gothic and Armenian versions contain the words. The TBS, (37) July-September 1985 p 16, states that only about 10 Greek manuscripts omit the words, including Aleph and B and indicates that this is a very small number compared with those that include them.

Burgon, p 359–360, cites the following fathers in support of the AV1611 reading:

2nd Century:	Irenaeus, Justin Martyr
3rd Century:	Cyprian, Origen
4th Century:	Augustine, Basil, Chrysostom, Ephraem Syrus, Epiphanius, Eusebius, Gregory of Nyssa, Hilary, Lucifer
5th Century:	Cyril of Alexandria, Isidorus, Theodore of Mops, Theodoret
6th Century:	Severus
7th Century:	Antiochus the monk, Maximus
8th Century:	John Damascene
9th Century:	Photius
11th Century:	Theophylactus
12th Century:	Euthymius Zigabenus

Matthew 5:44

"bless them that curse you, do good to them that hate you, despite-

fully use you," is omitted by the RV, Ne, NIV, NKJV marg., NWT, JB. DR omits "**bless them that curse you**".

Ruckman (17) p 427, states that all the Greek uncials except Aleph and B agree with the AV1611. He adds that all the cursives – over 200 – agree with the AV1611 except 7 and (35) p 13, that the Gothic version of Ulfilas (330 AD) contains the AV1611 reading, pre-dating B by twenty years. The TBS (37) July-September 1985, p 18, states that about 12 Greek manuscripts omit the words, supported by the Sinaitic and Curetonian Syriac and Coptic versions and one 4th century Old Latin copy but that 99% of the manuscripts support the AV1611. The remaining Old Latin copies – there are about 50 in total, (38) p 42 – the Peshitta Syriac, Ethiopian and Gothic versions support the AV1611.

Burgon p 410–411, cites the following fathers in support of the AV:

2nd Century:	Athenagoras, Clemens Alexandrinus, Justin Martyr, Tertullian, Theophilus Antiochus
3rd Century:	Apostolic Constitutions, Origen
4th Century:	Ambrose, Augustine, Chrysostom, Eusebius, Gregory of Nyssa, Hilary, Lucifer
5th Century:	Cyril of Alexandria, Isidorus, Theodoret.

Burgon states that there are "*many more*" fathers in support of the AV1611, p 411.

Matthew 6:7

"**vain repetitions**" AV1611, RV, Ne, NKJV
"babbling, babble" NIV, JB
"same things over and over again" NWT
The AV1611 reading is faithful to all extant mss.. Note that the NWT is nearer to the correct reading than the NIV reading, which would enable any number of "Hail Marys" to be repeated with a clear conscience.

Matthew 6:13

"**For thine is the Kingdom, and the power, and the glory, for ever. Amen**" is omitted by the DR, RV, Ne, NIV, NKJV marg., NWT, JB.

Fuller (3) p 108, citing Burgon, states that of more than 500 relevant (Greek) manuscripts, all but nine contain the AV1611 reading. Hills (5) p 118 and (38) p 146, states that uncials B, Aleph, D, Z and 6 cursives omit the words, together with 9 manuscripts of the Old Latin and all of

Jerome's Vulgate. The TBS (37) *The Power and the Glory* have an extremely detailed compilation on this text as follows:

Evidence for the authenticity of the AV1611 reading:

1st Century:	2 Timothy 4:18b (cross reference)
2nd Century:	Didache (document of Apostolic Teaching, discovered 1875, (38) p 117), Tatian's Diatessaron, Old Syriac version (Peshitta)
3rd Century:	Coptic and Sahidic (i.e. Egyptian) versions
4th Century:	Apostolic Constitutions, Old Latin manuscript k, Gothic (Ulfilas (4) p 208) and Armenian versions
5th Century:	Uncial W, Chrysostom, Isidore of Pelusium ((5) p 147), Georgian version
6th Century:	Uncials Sigma, Phi; Ethiopic version; Palestinian, Harclean and Curetonian Syriac ((5) p 118)
8th Century:	Uncials E, L
9th Century:	Uncials G, K, M, U, V, Delta, Phi, Pi; Old Latin f, g; Cursives 33, 565, 892
10th Century:	Cursive 1079
11th Century:	Cursives 28, 124, 174, 230, 700, 788, 1216
12th Century:	Cursives 346, 543, 1010, 1071, 1195, 1230, 1241, 1365, 1646
13th Century:	Cursives 13, 1009, 1242, 1546
14th Century:	Cursives 2148, 2174
15th Century:	Cursives 69, 1253.

The TBS (ibid.) states that the majority of the *"very numerous"* Byzantine copies, including lectionaries, contain the AV1611 reading.

The evidence against the AV1611 reading is as follows:

2nd Century:	Cyprian, Origen, Tertullian, who all fail to mention the words – as do later writers listed below.
3rd Century:	Some Coptic manuscripts
4th Century:	Aleph, B, Old Latin a, Caesarius Nazarene, Cyril of Jerusalem, Gregory Nyssa, Hilary
5th Century:	Uncial D, Old Latin b, h; Chromatius, Augustine
6th Century:	Uncial Z, Cursive 0170
7th Century:	Old Latin l
9th Century:	Old Latin g2

10th-11th Centuries: Old Latin ff.
12th-13th Centuries: Cursive 1, 118, Lectionary 547, Old Latin c
14th-15th Centuries: Cursives 131, 209, 17, 130.

Clearly, the available evidence vastly favours the AV1611 reading.

Matthew 6:33

"**God**" is omitted by the RV, Ne, NIV, NWT, JB.

Ruckman (35) p 14, states that "God" appears in the Old Latin and Old Syriac of the 2nd and 3rd centuries and in the vast majority of manuscripts. "God" appears in Berry's Greek text.

Matthew 11:23

"**which art exalted unto heaven**" is altered to "shalt thou be exalted unto heaven? (or similar wording)" by the DR, RV, NIV, NKJV marg., NWT, JB.

Burgon (13) p 55, indicates that only uncials Aleph, B, C, together with copies of the Old Latin, Curetonian Syriac, Coptic and Ethiopian versions have the interrogative form. Supporting the AV1611 are 14 uncials and all the cursives, together with the Peshitta and Gothic versions. The only fathers who quote the verse, or Luke 10:15, the cross-reference, are Chrysostom (4th century), Caesarius, Cyril of Alexandria and Theodoret (all of the 5th century). These support the AV1611, as does Berry's Greek text.

Matthew 12:40

"**whale**" AV1611, RV, Ne
"huge (great) fish" NIV, NWT, NKJV, "sea monster" JB

"Ketos" is "whale", from which cetology, the study of whales, is derived. The whale is a type of Satan, Ezekiel 32:2 and as such is the only animal NOT named by Adam. See comments on Genesis 1:21. Whoever is behind the modern translations seeks to obscure this fact.

Matthew 16:3

"**O ye hypocrites**" is omitted by the DR, RV, Ne, NIV, NKJV marg., NWT, JB.

Burgon (13) p 316 cites Aleph and B as the authorities for this omission and the notes, italics or parentheses disputing the Lord's words in verses 2 and 3 in the NIV, Ne, NWT. Berry's Greek text supports the AV1611.

Matthew 17:21
"**Howbeit this kind goeth not out but by prayer and fasting**" omitted by the RV, Ne, NIV, NKJV marg., NWT, JB.

Burgon (13) p 91, 206 states that every extant uncial except Aleph and B and every extant cursive except one contain the verse. Of the versions, the Old Latin, Syriac, Coptic, Armenian, Georgian, Ethiopic and Slavonic attest to the verse, with only the Curetonian Syriac and Sahidic omitting it. He cites additional ancient authorities including:

2nd Century:	Tertullian
3rd Century:	Origen
4th Century:	Ambrose, Athanasius, Augustine, Basil, Chrysostom, Hilary, Juvencus
8th Century:	Clement of Syria, John Damascene.

Burgon also cites the Syriac version of the Canons of Eusebius and the readings of the entire Eastern Church on the 10th Sunday after Pentecost from the earliest period, in favour of the verse. Berry's Greek text supports the AV1611.

Matthew 18:11
"**For the Son of man is come to seek and to save that which was lost**" is omitted by the RV, Ne, NIV, NKJV marg., NWT, JB.

Burgon (13) p 92, states that the verse is attested by every known uncial except Aleph, B, L and every known cursive except three. Also bearing witness to the verse are the Old Latin, Peshitta, Curetonian and Philoxenian Syriac, Coptic, Armenian, Ethiopic, Georgian and Slavonic versions. Of the fathers citing the verse, Burgon lists:

2nd Century:	Tertullian
3rd Century:	Origen
4th Century:	Ambrose, Augustine, Chrysostom, pope Damasus, Hilary, Jerome, Theodorus Heracl.

Burgon adds that the verse was read in the Universal Eastern Church on the day following Pentecost, from the beginning. Berry's Greek text also contains the verse.

Matthew 19:16–17
"**Good master**" and "**Why callest thou me good**" is changed to

"Teacher" and "Why do you ask me about what is good," or similar by the RV (v. 16 as AV1611), Ne, NIV, NKJV marg., NWT, JB.

Fuller (2) p 131, citing Burgon, states that Aleph, B, D and L omit "good" in verse 16 but that the word is found in nearly 30 other sources, including a number of fathers, yielding six witnesses of the 2nd century, three of the 3rd, fourteen of the 4th, four of the 5th and two of the 6th. Hills (5) p 142–143, (38) p 119–120, states that eleven Greek manuscripts have the modern reading, which is also found in the Old Latin and Old Syriac versions and cited by Origen, Eusebius and Augustine. However, he also states that Uncial W and the vast majority of Greek manuscripts agree with the AV1611, together with the Peshitta and Sahidic versions and the 2nd century writers, Irenaeus, Hippolytus and Justin Martyr. Berry's Greek text supports the AV1611.

Matthew 20:7

"and whatsoever is right, that shall ye receive" is omitted by the RV, Ne, NIV, NKJV marg., NWT, JB.

Ruckman (35) p 14, states that AV1611 reading is found in the Byzantine, i.e. Majority, manuscripts. Berry's Greek text supports the AV1611.

Matthew 20:16

"for many be called, but few chosen" is omitted by the RV, Ne, NIV, NKJV marg., NWT, JB.

Ruckman (35) p 14, states that the words are found in the Byzantine manuscripts. Berry's Greek text supports the AV1611.

Matthew 20:22, 23

"and to be baptized with the baptism that I am baptized with" and **"and be baptized with the baptism that I am baptized with"** is omitted by the DR, RV, Ne, NIV, NKJV marg., NWT, JB.

Ruckman (35) p 14, states that the AV1611 reading for verse 22 is found in the Byzantine manuscripts and Berry supports the AV1611 in both verses.

Matthew 23:14

"Woe unto you, scribes and Pharisees, hypocrites! for ye devour widows' houses, and for a pretence make long prayer: therefore ye

shall receive the greater damnation" is omitted by the RV, Ne, NIV, NKJV marg., NWT, JB.

Ruckman (4) p 102, (35) p 15, states that the omission can be traced to Origen, whose influence is responsible for the omission of the verse in the Alexandrian manuscripts. Berry's Greek text contains verse 14, although transposing it with verse 13.

Matthew 27:4

"**The innocent blood**" AV1611

"innocent blood" RV, NIV, NKJV, JB

"righteous blood" NWT

Christ's blood differs from other innocent blood, Deuteronomy 19:10, 1 Kings 2:31, Jeremiah 19:4 etc., in that it is GOD's BLOOD, Acts 20:28. Insertion of the definite article in the ENGLISH, not 'the Greek', makes this clear.

Matthew 27:35

"**that it might be fulfilled which was spoken by the prophet, They parted my garments among them, and upon my vesture did they cast lots**" is omitted by the RV, Ne, NIV, NKJV marg., NWT, JB.

This reading is one of the few in the AV1611 which is not supported by the majority of Greek manuscripts, although it is found in the Textus Receptus editions, including Berry's Greek text. Hills (5) p 200, (38) p 197, states that the AV1611 reading is found in Uncial 1 and other manuscripts of the 'Caesarean' family, a group similar to the Byzantine manuscripts but having circulated in Egypt, (5) p 125. (See also Ruckman (20) p 4, who explains that the 'Caesarean' family was invented (1920–1930) to help disguise the fact that the vast majority of manuscripts usually do support the AV1611 Text.) Other witnesses cited by Hills in support of the AV1611 reading are the Old Latin, Harclean Syriac and Eusebius (325 AD).

Mark 1:2

"**The prophets**" is changed to "Isaiah the Prophet" in the RV, Ne, NIV, NKJV marg., NWT, JB.

The modern reading is incorrect because Isaiah did NOT write the quotation in verse 2, Malachi did. Ruckman (35) p 38, states that the AV1611 reading is found in all four families of manuscripts

(Alexandrian, Byzantine, 'Caesarean,' Western) plus citations dating from 202 AD. Berry's Greek text supports the AV1611.

Mark 6:11

"Verily I say unto you, It shall be more tolerable for Sodom and Gomorrha in the day of judgment, than for that city" is omitted by the DR, RV, Ne, NIV, NKJV marg., NWT, JB.

Burgon (13) p 137, 409, states that the AV1611 reading is attested by 11 uncials and the whole body of cursives, with only nine manuscripts in total omitting the words, including six corrupt Alexandrian uncials (p 410). The AV1611 reading is also attested (ibid.) by the Peshitta and Philoxenian Syriac versions, the Old Latin, Coptic, Ethiopic and Gothic versions, Ireneus (2nd century) and Victor of Antioch (5th century). See also Fuller (3) p 149, citing Burgon. Berry's Greek text supports the AV1611.

Mark 6:20

"he did many things" is altered to "he was greatly puzzled" or similar wording, in the RV, Ne, NIV, NWT, JB.

Burgon (13) p 69, states that the evidence against the AV1611 reading is only Aleph, B, L and the Coptic version. All other Greek copies, uncial and cursive, favour the AV1611, together with the Old Latin (2nd century), Peshitta and Philoxenian Syriac, Armenian, Ethiopic, Slavonic and Georgian versions. Burgon adds that the Thebaic, Gothic and Curetonian Syriac *"are defective here."*

More recently, the TBS (37) *Many Things*, have cited 5 uncials as the evidence against the AV1611. However, the TBS cites as favourable to the AV1611, Codices A and Bezae (D) and most other manuscripts, including the vast majority of cursives. Besides the versions listed by Burgon, they include Tatian's Diatessaron (2nd century) as supporting the AV1611. Berry's Greek text supports the AV1611. Although this passage is not of major doctrinal import, it does illustrate the lengths to which the modern textual critics will go to defy the AV1611 Text.

Mark 7:16

"If any man have ears to hear, let him hear" is omitted by the RV, Ne, NIV, NKJV marg., NWT. The JB has the reading.

Ruckman (35) p 16, cites D (6th century), Tatian's Diatessaron (180

AD) and the Gothic version of Ulfilas (320 AD) as the earliest authorities for this verse. Berry's Greek text supports the AV1611.

Mark 9:29
"and fasting" is omitted by the RV, Ne, NIV, NKJV marg., NWT, JB.

Hills (5) p 138, states that Aleph, B and the other Alexandrian manuscripts omit the words, probably owing to the influence of Alexandrian Gnostics. Berry's Greek text, reflecting the majority of manuscripts, retains the words.

Mark 9:44, 46
"Where their worm dieth not, and the fire is not quenched" is omitted by the RV, Ne, NIV, NKJV marg., NWT, JB.

Ruckman (4) p 122, states that A, D, K, X, Theta, Pi and the majority of Receptus Greek manuscripts support the AV1611. The verses were omitted in the manuscripts of Origen and Eusebius (i.e. Aleph and B). Berry's Greek text supports the AV1611.

Mark 10:24
"for them that trust in riches" is omitted by the Ne, NIV, NKJV marg., NWT, JB.

Ruckman (35) p 17, states that the words are found in all four families of manuscripts. Berry's Greek text supports the AV1611.

Mark 13:14
"spoken of by Daniel the prophet" has been omitted by the DR, RV, Ne, NIV, NKJV marg., NWT, JB.

Berry's Greek text supports the AV1611. J.A. Moorman (39) lists Aleph, B, D, L, W as the main sources for the omission.

Mark 14:68
"and the cock crew" has been omitted from Ne, NIV, NWT, JB.

Ruckman (35) p 17, indicates that the words are found in all four families of manuscripts and in the vast majority of extant manuscripts. Berry's Greek text supports the AV1611.

Mark 15:28
"And the Scripture was fulfilled which saith, And he was numbered with the transgressors" is omitted by the RV, Ne, NIV, NKJV marg., NWT, JB.

Ruckman (4) p 110, (35) p 18, states that the verse is found in the vast majority of manuscripts and in the Old Latin and Old Syriac of the 2nd and 3rd centuries respectively. Berry's Greek text supports the AV1611.

Mark 15:39

"**so cried out**" is omitted by the RV, Ne, NIV marg., NKJV marg., NWT, JB.

Burgon (13) p 72, states that Aleph, B, and L are the only manuscripts which omit these words. Berry's Greek text, representing the majority of manuscripts, supports the AV1611.

Mark 16:9–20

The NIV has a note between verses 8 and 9 stating that the most reliable early manuscripts do not contain Mark 16:9–20.

The NKJV has a marginal note stating that Aleph and B do not contain the verses, although most other manuscripts of Mark do.

The NWT has verses 9–20 as a "*long conclusion*", indicating that manuscripts A, C, D include it, while Aleph, B, the Syriac and Armenian versions omit them. NWT also has the "*short conclusion*" in its text, "And they delivered all these instructions briefly to Peter and his companions. Afterwards Jesus himself sent out by them from east to west the sacred and imperishable message of eternal salvation." The JB insists that MANY manuscripts omit the verses.

The evidence in favour of the authenticity of Mark 16:9–20 is overwhelming. The TBS publication (37) *The Authenticity of The Last Twelve Verses of . . . Mark* is an excellent summary, drawing mainly from Burgon, (13) p 36–40, 422–424 and Burgon's work cited by Fuller (18) p 25–130. See also Burton (6) p 62–63, Fuller (2) p 168–169, Hills (5) p 161–162, (38) p 133–134, Ruckman (4) p 132.

The TBS publication – see above – states that only 2 Greek manuscripts (Aleph and B) out of a total of 620 which contain the Gospel of Mark, omit the verses. See Burgon, cited by Fuller (18) p 60–61. Moreover, Burgon, ibid. p 67, states that a blank space has been left in B, where the verses should have been but where the scribe obviously omitted them.

As further evidence in favour of the verses, Burgon (13) p 423, (2) p 169, cites:

2nd Century: Old Latin and Peshitta Syriac versions, Papias, Justin Martyr, Irenaeus, Tertullian

3rd Century:	Coptic and Sahidic versions, Hippolytus, Vincentius, 'Acta Pilati' – by an unknown author, Apostolic Constitutions
4th Century:	Curetonian Syriac and Gothic versions, Syriac Table of Canons, Eusebius, Macarius Magnes, Aphraates, Didymus, The Syriac 'Acts of the Apostles', Epiphanius, Leontius, Ephraem, Ambrose, Chrysostom, Jerome, Augustine
5th Century:	Armenian version (some copies), Codices A and C, Leo, Nestorius, Cyril of Alexandria, Victor of Antioch, Patricius, Marius Mercator
6th and 7th Centuries:	Codex D, Georgian and Ethiopic versions, Hesychius, Gregentius, Prosper, Archbishop John of Thessalonica, Bishop Modestus of Jerusalem.

The TBS also cites the Philoxenian Syriac of the 5th century as containing the verses. Hills and Ruckman also cite Tatian (2nd century) as quoting the verses. Hills (5) p 162, (38) p 134, states that besides Aleph and B, the Sinaitic Syriac – from the same source as Aleph, 2 manuscripts of the Georgian version and 62 of the Armenian version omit the verses. The Old Latin manuscript k has the "*short conclusion*" instead of verses 9–20. Burgon (18) p 81–82, explains how this short ending has been obtained solely from Codex L, an 8th or 9th century manuscript "*with an exceedingly vicious text*", ibid. Hills explains the omission of verses 9–20 from the above handful of documents as indicative of the work of heretics, especially docetists who sought to de-emphasise post resurrection appearances of the Lord from the Gospel record, ibid. p 138–141, p 166–168.

Burgon (18) p 49–60 also demonstrated that the supposed adverse testimony of ancient writers is spurious, resting on a quotation from Eusebius, which does NOT deny verses 9–20. Berry's Greek text supports the AV1611.

Luke 1:28
"**blessed art thou among women**" is omitted by the RV, Ne, NIV, NKJV marg., NWT, JB.

Ruckman (35) p 18, states that the words are found in all four families of manuscripts and indicates they were quoted 170 years before the appearance of Aleph and B. Berry's Greek text supports the AV1611.

Luke 2:14

"**on earth peace, good will toward men**" is changed to "on earth peace to men on whom his favour rests" or similar wording by the RV, NIV, JB or to "towards men of good will" or similar wording by the DR, Ne, NKJV marg. and NWT.

The evidence in favour of the AV1611 against the modern textual critics is cited by Burgon (13) p 42–43, 422–423, by Fuller quoting Burgon (3) p 96 and the TBS (37) *Good Will Toward Men*. Only five codices (Aleph, A, B, D, W) support the modern textual critics, against "*every existing copy of the Gospels, amounting to many hundreds*" Fuller, ibid.

Although the Latin, Sahidic and Gothic versions support the modern textual critics, the AV1611 reading is supported by:

2nd Century:	Syriac versions, Irenaeus
3rd Century:	Coptic version, Origen, Apostolical Constitutions
4th Century:	Eusebius, Aphraates the Persian, Titus of Bostra, Didymus, Gregory of Nazianzus, Cyril of Jerusalem, Epiphanius, Gregory of Nyssa, Ephraem Syrus, Philo, Bishop of Carpasus, Chrysostom
5th Century:	Armenian version, Cyril of Alexandria, Theodoret, Theodotus of Ancyra, Proclus, Paulus of Emesa, Basil of Seleucia, the Eastern bishops of Ephesus collectively
6th Century:	Georgian and Ethiopic versions, Cosmos, Anastasius Sinaita, Eulogius, Archbishop of Alexandria
7th Century:	Andreas of Crete
8th Century:	Cosmos, Bishop of Maiuma, John Damascene, Germanus, Archbishop of Constantinople, pope Martinus.

Berry's Greek text supports the AV1611.

Luke 2:22

"**her purification**" has been altered to "their purification" or similar by the RV, Ne, NIV, NWT, JB.

Hills (5) p 221, (38) p 208, states that the modern reading is found in the majority of manuscripts and the Editions of Erasmus and Stephanus, including Berry's Greek text. The AV1611 reading is found in the Editions of Beza and Elzevir, the Complutensian Polyglot (printed at Acala, Spain, under the direction of Cardinal Ximenes and published 1522), No. 76 and a few other Greek cursives. This is one of the few occasions when the AV1611 departs from the majority of manuscripts (Hills, ibid. discusses the handful of other instances) but inspection of Leviticus 12 proves that the AV1611 reading is – as always – correct.

Luke 2:33
"**Joseph and his mother**" has been altered to "the child's father and mother" or similar by the DR, RV, Ne, NIV, NKJV marg., NWT, JB.

Ruckman (29) p 43, states that the AV1611 reading is found in an 8th century manuscript, in two from the 9th century and one from the 10th century plus "*nearly all*" the Caesarian type texts and Old Latin witnesses. Fuller (2) p 220, indicates that the modern reading which tries to make Joseph Christ's natural father, comes from Jerome, using the corrupt text (i.e. Aleph and B) of Eusebius. Berry's Greek text supports the AV1611.

Luke 4:4
"**but by every word of God**" is omitted by the RV, Ne, NIV, NKJV marg., NWT, JB.

Ruckman (35) p 18, states that the words are found in three families of manuscripts (Western, Caesarean, Byzantine) and in Tatian's Diatessaron (2nd century). Aleph and B and their associates omit the words, together with the Boharic (North African) and Coptic versions. Berry's Greek text supports the AV1611.

Luke 4:8
"**and said unto him, Get thee behind me, Satan**" is omitted by the DR, RV, Ne, NIV, NKJV marg., NWT, JB.

Ruckman (35) p 19, states that the words are found in the vast majority of Greek manuscripts. Berry's Greek text supports the AV1611.

Luke 4:18
"**to heal the brokenhearted**" is omitted by the RV, Ne, NIV, NKJV marg., NWT, JB.

Gail Riplinger, (12) p 454, states that the phrase is found in ALL extant Greek mss. containing Luke 4, except Aleph and B. Berry's Greek text supports the AV1611

Luke 6:48

The final clause "**founded upon a rock**" has been altered to "well-built" or similar by the RV, Ne, NIV, NKJV marg., NWT, JB.

1 Corinthians 10:4, 1 Peter 2:6–8 reveal that the modern reading obscures THE LORD JESUS CHRIST. Burgon (13) p 110, states that the AV1611 reading is supported by A, C, D, 12 other uncials and the whole body of cursives, the Syriac, Latin and Gothic versions. The modern reading has been derived from Aleph and B, ibid. p 315. Berry's Greek text supports the AV1611.

Luke 8:45

"**and they that were with him**" and "**and sayest thou, Who touched me**" has been omitted by the RV, Ne, NIV, NKJV marg., NWT, JB (JB includes "and his companions").

Berry's text supports the AV1611 with respect to both clauses. Burgon (13) p 401–402, states that the second clause is attested by A, C, D, P, R, X, Gamma, Delta, Xi, Lambda, Pi and every other known uncial except three "*of bad character*", every known cursive but four, by the Old Latin and Vulgate, by all four Syriac versions, by the Gothic and Ethiopic versions and Tatian and Chrysostom.

Luke 9:54–56

"**even as Elias did**", "**and said, Ye know not what manner of spirit ye are of**" and "**For the Son of man is not come to destroy men's lives, but to save them**" have been omitted by the RV, Ne, NIV, NKJV marg., NWT, JB. The DR omits "**even as Elias did**".

Burgon (13) p 316, cites Aleph and B as the authorities for the omissions, in company with a few other corrupt mss. Berry's Greek text supports the AV1611.

Luke 11:2–4

"**Our**", "**which art in heaven**", "**as in heaven, so in earth**" and "**but deliver us from evil**" have been omitted by the DR, RV, Ne, NIV, NKJV marg., NWT, JB.

Burgon (13) p 34–35, states that the modern omissions can be traced back to Marcion the heretic (150 AD). Aleph and B alone omit "**but

deliver us from evil", ibid. p 317. Berry's Greek text supports the AV1611.

Luke 11:54
"**that they might accuse him**" has been omitted by the RV, Ne, NIV, NKJV marg., NWT, JB.

Ruckman (17) p 428, states that while the AV1611 Text is rejected by Nestle, it is supported by A, C, E, F, L, M, N, P, R, S, T, Phi, Delta, Sigma and 800 cursives. Berry's Greek text supports the AV1611.

Luke 12:31
"**seek ye the kingdom of God**" has been changed to "seek his kingdom" or similar by the RV, Ne, NIV, NKJV marg., NWT, JB.

Hills (5) p 126, states that the AV1611 reading is found in the Traditional (i.e. Majority) Text and Papyrus 45 (3rd century). The modern reading is found in Aleph and B. See also remarks under **Matthew 6:33**. Berry's Greek text supports the AV1611.

Luke 17:36
"**Two men shall be in the field; the one shall be taken, and the other left**" has been omitted by the RV, Ne, NIV, NKJV marg., NWT, JB.

Hills (5) p 221, (38) p 208, states that the verse is lacking in the editions of Erasmus, in the first three editions of Stephanus and in the majority of manuscripts. Hence it is not found in Berry's Greek text. The verse is found in the 4th edition of Stephanus, in the editions of Beza and Elzevir, in D, the Latin Vulgate, the Peshitta, Curetonian and Sinaitic Syriac. Like Matthew 27:35, Luke 17:36 affords another example of the Lord's providential preservation of His words, Psalm 12:6,7.

Luke 23:38
"**in letters of Greek, and Latin, and Hebrew**" is omitted by the RV, Ne, NIV, NKJV marg., NWT, JB.

Burgon (13) p 85, states that the words are omitted by B, C, L, the Egyptian versions and the Curetonian Syriac. They are retained by Aleph, A, D, Q, R, 13 other uncials, all cursive copies, the Latin, Peshitta and Philoxenian Syriac, Armenian, Ethiopic and Georgian versions. Eusebius (4th century) and Cyril of Alexandria (5th century) also cite the words. Berry's Greek text supports the AV1611.

Luke 23:42

"**he said unto Jesus, Lord**" has been changed to "He said "Jesus"" or similar by the RV, Ne, NIV, NKJV marg., NWT, JB.

Hills (5) p 136, states that the majority text (see Berry), the Old Latin and the Sinaitic Syriac versions support the AV1611, while the modern reading is found only in Papyrus 75, Aleph, B, C, L and the Sahidic version. Ruckman (35) p 50, states that no less than 80 uncials and 70 cursives have the AV1611 reading. Both Hills and Ruckman (see also (29) p 38) explain how the modern reading is properly attributed to the corrupting influence of docetic heretics.

Luke 24:42

"**and of an honeycomb**" is omitted by the RV, Ne, NIV, NKJV marg., NWT, JB.

Fuller (2) p 131, citing Burgon, states that the words are lacking in six copies of the Gospels only, including Aleph, B, D, L. Supporting the AV1611 are all the remaining copies of the Gospels, uncial and cursive, representing by far the greater number.

John 1:3

"**by**" has been changed into "through" by the NIV, NKJV, NWT, JB.

Given that "**In the beginning God created the heaven and the earth**", Genesis 1:1, there is a big difference between "**by**" and "through". See also Revelation 3:14. Note that on this occasion, the NKJV has impugned the AV1611 in its *text* with respect to this important reference to the Deity of the Lord Jesus Christ, not just in its margin.

John 1:14, 18, 3:16, 18, 1 John 4:9

"**only begotten**" has been altered to "one and only" or similar by NIV, JB. The NKJV marg. and Ne support the Arian and NWT reading in John 1:18 that Jesus was a "begotten God".

"Monogenes" is found in the vast majority of mss. and is correctly translated "only begotten". The omission of "begotten" is obtained from Papyri 66, 75, Aleph and B. "Only begotten God" is attributable to Valentius, a 2nd century heretic, whose corrupting influence is preserved in P 66, Aleph, B, C, L. Note that the modern reading cannot be correct, according to Job 1:6, Luke 3:38 and John 1:12, which show that Jesus Christ is NOT God's "one and only son". Note also that the NWT is more faithful to the truth than the NIV in all the above verses except

1:18, demonstrating that one can find "the fundamentals of the faith" in ANY version.

John 3:13
"**which is in heaven**" is omitted by NIV, Ne, NKJV marg., NWT.

Only P 66, 75, Aleph, B, L and a few other ancient witnesses omit the words. The vast majority of witnesses, including some from the 2nd and 3rd centuries, support the AV1611 reading. Note here that the JB reading is correct. Berry's Greek text supports the AV1611.

John 5:3b, 4
"**waiting for the moving of the water. For an angel went down at a certain season into the pool, and troubled the water: whosoever then first after the troubling of the water stepped in was made whole of whatsoever disease he had**" is omitted by the RV, Ne, NIV, NKJV marg., NWT. The JB(!) retains the words but designates the angel as an angel of the Lord, thus adding to the word of God.

The excellent TBS publication (37) *The Pool of Bethesda* gives a most detailed summary of the evidence for and against the passage. Verse 3b is omitted by Papyri 66, 75, uncials Aleph, A, B, C, L, 0125, Old Latin q, Curetonian Syriac, Coptic, Sahidic, Bohairic and Diatessaron 1. Verse 3b is found in uncials D, A2, C3, K, W supp, X com, Delta, Theta, Pi*, Psi, 078; cursives F1, F13, 28, 33, 565, 700, 892, 1009, 1010, 1071, 1079, 1195, 1216, 1230, 1241, 1242, 1253, 1344, 1365, 1546, 1646, 2148, 2178, the Byzantine majority text and Lectionaries, the Old Latin a (4th century), aur (7th), b (5th), d (5th), j (6th), 1 (7th-8th), r1 (7th), c (12th-13th), e (5th), f (6th), ff2 (5th), the Syriac (Harkelian, Peshitta, Philoxenian), the Latin Vulgate, Armenian, Ethiopic and Georgian versions, some copies of the Coptic-Bohairic, Diatessaron a, Tertullian (220 AD), Ambrose (397 AD), Chrysostom (407 AD), Cyril (444 AD).

Verse 4 is omitted by Papyri 66, 75, uncials Aleph, B, C*, D, W supp, 0125, 0141, cursive 33, Old Latin d, f, l, q, Curetonian Syriac, some manuscripts of the Coptic–Sahidic-Bohairic versions, the Georgian and Latin Vulgate versions. Verse 4 is found (with variations) in uncials A, C3, K, L, Pi, X comm, Delta, Theta, Psi, 047, 063, 078, cursives 28, 565, 700, 892, 1009, 1010, 1071, 1079, 1195, 1216, 1230, 1241, 1242, 1253, 1344, 1365, 1546, 1646, 2148, 2174, Byzantine majority text and Lectionaries, Old Latin a (4th century), aur (7th), b (5th), c (12th-13th), e (5th), ff2 (5th), j (6th), r1 (7th), the Syriac (Harkelian, Peshitta,

Philoxenian, 3rd-7th centuries), some manuscripts of the Coptic-Bohairic, the Armenian version; Diatessaron a, e arm, i, n; Tertullian (220 AD), Ambrose (397 AD), Didymus (398 AD), Chrysostom (407 AD), Cyril (444 AD).

Ruckman (4) p 217, states that the Diatessaron copies (2nd century) attesting to the passage number over 200. Ruckman, ibid. and Hills (5) p 146, (38) p 122, state that the passage is virtually intact in the vast majority of Greek manuscripts. See Fuller (18) p 157–158. Berry's Greek text supports the AV1611.

John 6:69

"that Christ, the Son of the living God" has been altered to "the Holy One of God" or similar wording by the RV, Ne, NIV, NKJV marg., NWT, JB. The DR omits **"living"**.

Hills (5) p 135, (38) p 76, states that the modern reading is found in Papyrus 75, Aleph, B, C, D, L, W, the Sahidic and with the addition of "the Christ," in Papyrus 66, some copies of the Sahidic and the Bohairic version. In support of the AV1611 is the Traditional text, the Peshitta and Harclean Syriac and some copies of the Old Latin. See also Ruckman (35) p 29. Berry's Greek text supports the AV1611.

John 7:53–8:11

The NIV notes in its text that the earliest and most reliable manuscripts do not have John 7:53–8:11.

The NKJV notes in its margin that the verses are not regarded as original by the Nestle-United Bible Societies text but are found in over 900 manuscripts.

The NWT places the passage in the margin.

The JB notes in the margin that on the basis of style, the author is not John and that the oldest manuscripts do not contain the passage.

Fuller (2) p 123–124, (18) p 155, cites Burgon as stating that of 73 copies of John's Gospel in the British Museum, 61 contain John 7:53–8:11 as found in the AV1611. Burgon (18) p 155, indicates that this proportioning would be typical for any collection of manuscript copies of John. He also cites, (18) p 149, a further 60 copies, from three distinct lines of ancestry, which agree with the AV1611. He alludes to 35 of the BM copies, which contain a marginal note stating that verses 1–11 are not to be read on Whitsunday. Thus he explains how the Lectionary practice of the early church would have accounted for the omission of the verses from some of the seventy cursives from which they are absent. He also states (18) p 148, that the subject matter itself would have been sufficient for deletion of the words from many copies, including the oldest uncials, Aleph and B. The verses are also absent from A (5th century), L (8th century), T (5th century) and Delta (9th century) but Codex A has two leaves missing, which in Burgon's considered view would have contained the verses, while L and Delta exhibit blank spaces which are witnesses FOR, not against, the validity of the verses. See remarks on B in relation to Mark 16:9–20. This leaves only T in agreement with Aleph and B, both notoriously untrustworthy.

Burgon, ibid. p 156, states that the verses are to be found in the large majority of later copies (i.e. over 900 manuscripts, as the NKJV so obligingly notes.)

Hills (5) p 159, (38) p 131, states that Papyri 66 and 75 and W omit the verses, in addition to the sources cited by Burgon. D however (6th century), contains them. Burgon (18) p 145–146, 153–154, also cites in favour of the passage as found in the AV1611

Codex D and the Old Latin codices b, c, e, ff, g, h, j – see notes under John 5:3b-4 for dates. Note that the Old Latin TEXT dates from the 2nd century, (4) p 77

Jerome (385 AD), who included it in the Vulgate after surveying older Greek copies, stating it was found "in many copies both Greek and Latin", before 415 AD, (4) p 134

The Ethiopic (5th century), Palestinian Syriac (5th century), Georgian (5th-6th centuries), some copies of the Armenian (4th-5th centuries), Slavonic, Arabic and Persian versions

Ambrose (374 AD), Augustine (396), Chrysologus (433), Faustus (400), Gelasius (492), Pacian (370), Rufinus (400), Sedulius (434), Victorius (457), Vigilius (484) and others

The Lectionary practice of the Eastern Church, from earliest times (i.e. the 2nd century.)

Ruckman (4) p 134, cites in favour of the passage, the Didache (3rd century document of Apostolic Teachings), Apostolic Constitutions (4th century) and Eusebius (324 AD) citing Papias (150 AD) as recognising the passage. The Montanists (2nd century) were also aware of the passage. Ruckman (17) p 333 also cites besides D, uncials M, S and Gamma from the 5th, 8th and 9th centuries in favour of the AV1611.

Concerning authorship of the passage (see note under JB), Hills (38) p 130, states that *"arguments from style are notoriously weak."* Berry's Greek text supports the AV1611.

John 8:6

"as though he heard them not" is omitted by the DR, RV, Ne, NIV, NKJV marg., NWT, JB.

The words are in Italics in the AV1611 and hence absent from Berry's text. Hills (38) p 207, states that the AV1611 translators followed the Bishops' Bible and added the clause to the 1611 Text. The clause is found in uncials E, G, H, K and many other manuscripts, in the Complutensian Polyglot and in the first two editions of Stephanus (Berry's is the 3rd). All editions of the AV1611 since 1769 have retained the clause in Italics.

John 9:35

"son of God" has been altered to "son of man" by the NIV, Ne, NKJV marg., NWT, JB.

Hills (5) p 136–137, (38) p 76, states that the AV1611 is supported by the Traditional Text (see Berry) and the Old Latin. The modern reading is derived from Papyri 66 and 75, Aleph, B, D, and the Sinaitic Syriac and probably represents an attack on the Deity of Christ by heretics. Ruckman (35) p 31, states that the AV1611 reading is cited by Origen (200 AD) and Tertullian (220 AD) and found in Ulfilas' Gothic Bible (330 AD).

John 10:14–15

"and am known of mine. As the Father knoweth me" has been altered to "my sheep know me – just as the Father knows me" or similar by the DR, RV, Ne, NIV, NWT, JB.

The objection to the modern rendering is that it equates the knowledge of the Lord by the believer to that which is enjoyed by the Father. The result is either to deify man or humanise God, either tendency being heresy.

Burgon (13) p 220–221, states that the proportion of manuscripts of John which support the AV1611 is *"996 out of a 1000."* He states that the modern reading – unquestionably the work of heretics – is found only in Aleph, B, D, L. The AV1611 is also supported by the Syriac, Chrysostom, Gregory of Nazianzus, Macarius (4th century), Cyril of Alexandria, Theodoret (5th century) and Maximus (7th century). See also Fuller (3) p 158–159. Ruckman (17) p 418, cites only Aleph, B, D, L as against the AV1611 and A, Theta, E, F, K, M, P, Phi, Sigma, Delta in support. Berry's Greek text supports the AV1611.

Acts 2:30
"**according to the flesh he would raise up Christ**" has been omitted by
the DR, RV, Ne, NIV, NKJV marg., NWT, JB.

Dr. Ruckman states (36, *Acts* p 105) that "*The whole clause is missing in the great corrupt uncials, A, C, D.*" These are evidently the
authorities for its omission. Berry's Greek text supports the AV1611.

Acts 2:47
"**Church**" has been omitted or altered to "number" or similar by the DR,
RV, Ne, NIV, NWT, JB. The NKJV marg. indicates that "**to the
church**" is omitted from the Nestle-United Bible Societies Text.

Omission of the word "church" is objectionable on the grounds that
it eliminates the cross references to Acts 5:14, 11:24 and thus obscures
the fact that the 'Body of Christ' (Colossians 1:18, 24) began in Acts 2.
"Ekklesia" is found in Berry's Greek text, underlying its presence in the
Majority Text.

The TBS (37) *Acts 2:47* . . . states that the evidence against the
AV1611 reading is uncials Aleph, A, B, C, G, cursive 81 (1044 AD),
some manuscripts of the Old Latin, the Vulgate, the Egyptian, Armenian
and Ethiopic versions and quotations in the writings of Cyril and Lucifer.
These hostile witnesses are few and vastly offset by the evidence supporting the AV1611. Standing in favour of the AV1611 reading are
uncials D, E (both 6th century), P (9th century) 049, 056, 0142; "*the main
stream of the very numerous Byzantine manuscripts*" plus "*independent*"
copies of the Byzantine group including no's 33, 1739, 181, 436, 451,
945, 104, 88, 326, 330, 1241, 2412, 2127, 614, 2492, 1877, 629, 630,
2495. The TBS (ibid.) affirm that the Byzantine readings correspond to a
4th century text. Also in favour of the AV1611 are the Old Latin manuscripts e, d (each 4th-5th century), the Peshitta and Harkelian Syriac. The
TBS affirms that these versions represent a 2nd century text.

Acts 4:27, 30
"**child**" has been changed into "servant" by the RV, NIV, NKJV, NWT,
JB.

This is another example of how the modern translations detract from
the Deity of the Lord Jesus Christ. These verses will be discussed in
more detail later.

Acts 8:37
"**And Philip said, If thou believest with all thine heart, thou mayest.**

And he answered and said, I believe that Jesus Christ is the Son of God" is omitted by the RV, Ne, NIV, NKJV marg., NWT, JB.

Hills (5) p 201, (38) p 197, explains that the verse is absent from most Greek manuscripts because the practice of delaying baptism following profession of faith had become common before the end of the 3rd century. However, the verse is found in uncial E (6th-7th centuries), the Old Latin (2nd century), the Vulgate (5th century) and is cited by Irenaeus (180 AD) and Cyprian (250 AD). See also Ruckman (17) p 331, (35) p 19–20. Ruckman (36, *Acts* p 291) also cites Tertullian (2nd century), Pacian (370 AD), Ambrose and Augustine (4th century) as knowing of the verse.

Even though the verse is not in the Majority Text, Berry's Greek text supports the AV1611, indicating the familiarity of the 16th century editors with the ancient evidence in support of the verse.

Acts 9:5, 6
"the Lord" and **"it is hard for thee to kick against the pricks. And he trembling and astonished said, Lord, what wilt thou have me to do?"** are omitted by the RV, Ne, NIV, NKJV marg., NWT, JB. DR alters **"the Lord said"** to "he".

Hills (5) p 197, (38) p 201 and Ruckman (17) p 331–332, state that although the words are absent from most of the Greek manuscripts, they are found in uncial E, 431, the Old Latin (200 AD), the Vulgate and the Peshitta (200 AD). Ruckman (36, *Acts* p 299–300), also cites Ambrose (397 AD), Ephraem (378) and Lucifer of Cagliari (371) as quoting the passage. Berry's Greek text supports the AV1611, following the insight of Erasmus (Hills, ibid) with respect to the evidence in favour of the verse.

Note that Luke 23:42, John 9:35, Acts 8:37 and 9:5, 6 are all passages which deal with INDIVIDUAL SALVATION.

Acts 15:34
"Notwithstanding it pleased Silas to abide there still" has been omitted by the RV, Ne, NIV, NKJV marg., NWT, JB.

Ruckman (36, *Acts* p 442) states that Aleph and B omit the verse. It is found in the Syriac and Byzantine manuscripts, in D (Western family), in C (Alexandrian family) and in the Old Latin. Berry's Greek text supports the AV1611.

Acts 17:26

"**blood**" has been omitted by the DR, RV, Ne, NIV, NKJV marg., NWT, JB.

Ruckman (36, *Acts* p 505) states that "blood" is found in all four families of manuscripts, in the majority of manuscripts and cited in writings dating from the 2nd century. He shows that the modern reading is an ecumenical, political, internationalist, integrationist EXPEDIENT. Racial characteristics are not determined by blood type and would not be affected by blood transfusion, so that all humans can accurately be said to be of "**one blood**". See also Section 10:11. However, they are NOT of one race but THREE, according to Genesis 9 and 10 which list the descendants of Shem, Ham and Japheth, the three sons of Noah. Young's Concordance states that Japheth means "the extender or fair", Ham is "swarthy, dark coloured" and Shem is "renown", indicating that Noah may have had a gift of prophecy like his father Lamech, Genesis 5:29, because he later prophesied "**Blessed be the Lord God of Shem**" Genesis 9:26. Shem would therefore be conspicuous amongst Noah's descendants for his outstanding spirituality. It is very likely that he was the mysterious "**Melchizedek, king of Salem**" Genesis 14:18–20, Psalm 110:4, Hebrews 5:6, 10, 6:20, 7:1–4, 10, 11, 15, 17, 21. He blessed Abraham and declared to him "**blessed be the most high God, which hath delivered thine enemies into thine hand**" Genesis 14:20, in accordance with Noah's prophecy (36, *Genesis* p 362ff). Note that Shem lived 600 years and outlived Abraham by 33 years, Genesis 11:10–26, 25:7. Noah's prophecy has in fact been explicitly fulfilled with respect to all his sons down through the centuries, according to *Halley's Bible Handbook*, p 74:

> "*Descendants of Ham to be servant races; Shemites to preserve knowledge of the true God; Japhetic races to have largest portion of world, and to supplant Semitic races as teachers of God. It was fulfilled when Israelites took Canaan, Greeks took Sidon, and Rome conquered Carthage; and ever since Japhetic races have dominated the world, and have been converted to the God of Shem, while Semitic races have occupied a place of comparative insignificance and Hamitic races a place of servitude. An amazing forecast!*"

However, it is not 'politically correct' to make reference to racial distinctions, so the word "blood" has to go! It is then possible to infer that men are all "one" so that the national "**bounds of their habitation**" can be abolished in order to establish the one world system under the beast of Revelation 13 – who is depicted as an "integrated" animal. Observe that he is **"like unto a leopard"**, black, brown and white, verses 2, 3b, 8 but God had set up the **"bounds"** of separate nations for men so **"that they should seek the Lord"** Acts 17:27. Therefore it is not surprising that the Devil seeks to dismantle all **"bounds"**, Isaiah 10:13, whether national, racial, sociological, ideological, political, economical, educational, generational or even biological, not only between men and women but even between humans and animals. His aim is thereby to **"weaken the nations"** Isaiah 14:12, so that they can be easily absorbed into antichrist's kingdom, 1 John 2:18 – just as Britain is being steadily drained of strength by the EU, acting in concert with the traitors in Westminster. (One of these perfidious rascals has recently equated treason to patriotism, in a pre-election speech!)

Readers should note that this move to universal coalescence is akin to **"the days of Noe"** Luke 17:26 and is **"corrupt"** according to the scripture, Genesis 6:11, or as the Lord Jesus Christ said:

"That which is highly esteemed among men is abomination in the sight of God" Luke 16:15b. Once again, the inference of these interrelated passages is to the time just before the Lord's return. See comments on Proverbs 1:32.

Berry's Greek text supports the AV1611. J.A. Moorman (39) p 115 indicates that the minority of Greek mss. which omit "blood" are P74, Sinaiticus Aleph, Alexandrinus A and Vaticanus B.

Acts 23:9

"let us not fight against God" has been omitted from the DR, RV, Ne, NIV, NKJV marg., NWT, JB.

Ruckman (35) p 32 indicates that the AV1611 reading is found in the vast majority of Greek manuscripts. Berry's Greek text supports the AV1611.

Romans 8:1

"who walk not after the flesh, but after the Spirit" is omitted by the RV, Ne, NIV, NKJV marg., NWT, JB. The DR omits **"but after the spirit"**.

Ruckman (35) p 68, states that the words are found in all four families of manuscripts and in the majority of uncials and cursives. Berry's Greek text supports the AV1611.

Romans 10:15
"gospel of peace" has been omitted by the RV, Ne, NIV, NKJV marg., NWT, JB.

Ruckman (29) p 83, states that the oldest manuscripts in three families support the AV1611. Berry's Greek text supports the AV1611.

Romans 13:9
"thou shalt not bear false witness" is omitted by the RV, Ne, NIV, NKJV marg., NWT, JB.

Ruckman (35) p 21, states that Aleph, frequently used by modern translators to alter the AV1611, has the words, which are also cited by Origen (200 AD). Berry's Greek text supports the AV1611.

Romans 14:10
"judgment seat of Christ" has been altered to "judgment seat of God" or similar by the RV, Ne, NIV, NKJV marg., NWT, JB.

Hills (5) p 137, states that the AV1611 reading is not only the majority reading (see Berry's Greek text) but it is cited by Polycarp (1st-2nd centuries), Tertullian and Marcion (both 2nd century). The modern alteration comes from Aleph, B, D2 plus other Western and Alexandrian texts and is almost certainly a deliberate heretical substitution.

1 Corinthians 5:4
"Christ" is omitted TWICE by the RV, Ne, NIV, NWT, JB. The DR omits **"Christ"** once.

Ruckman (4) p 98 states that the bases for the omissions are B (4th century), A and D (each 5th century) against Papyrus 46 (3rd century), Aleph (4th century), G (10th century), the majority of remaining uncials, the Receptus (see Berry's Greek text), the Old Latin and Old Syriac (a dozen 3rd-5th century copies.)

1 Corinthians 10:28
"for the earth is the Lord's and the fullness thereof" is omitted by the DR, RV, Ne, NIV, NKJV marg., NWT, JB.

Ruckman (35) p 32, indicates that the AV1611 reading is found in the vast majority of manuscripts, in all four families and in citations from Origen (200 AD). Berry's Greek text supports the AV1611.

1 Corinthians 11:24

"**broken**" is omitted by the RV, Ne, NIV, NKJV marg., NWT, JB. The DR has "shall be delivered".

The Lord's body had to be BROKEN, so that His blood could be SHED for the purpose of INDIVIDUAL SALVATION, Ephesians 1:7, 2:13, Colossians 1:14, 1 Peter 1:19, 1 John 1:7.

The TBS (37) *Broken For You* has produced an excellent summary of the evidence for and against the AV1611 Text.

"Broken" is omitted by Aleph, B (4th century), A, C (5th century), cursives 33 (9th century), 1739 (10th century). Also omitting the word are citations by the Armenian of Zohrab, Origen (3rd century), Cyril of Alexandria, Pelagius (both 5th century) and Fulgentius (6th century).

"Broken" is reinserted by correctors of Aleph and C and retained by the 'Abschrift' (9th century copy of D), G, K, P (all 8th-9th centuries), the majority of the Byzantine manuscripts, the majority of ancient Lectionary copies and a considerable number of "*independent*" Byzantine cursives: 81, 88, 104, 181, 326, 330, 436, 451, 614, 629, 630, 1241, 1739 mg. (i.e. margin), 1877, 1881, 1962, 1984, 1985, 2127, 2492, 2495. "Broken" is also found in copies of the Peshitta and Harclean Syriac, the Old Latin (Claromontanus and Palatinus of the 5th century, Boernerianus of the 9th), in Ulfilas' Gothic version (4th century) and in the Armenian of Uscan. The word is cited by Ambrosiaster, Basil and Chrysostom (all 4th century), Euthalius and Theodoret (both 5th century) and John of Damascus (8th century). The TBS states that these writers had access to manuscripts older than any now in existence. Berry's Greek text supports the AV1611. See also Hills (5) p 138 and Ruckman (29) p 80.

1 Corinthians 11:29

"**unworthily**" has been omitted by the RV, Ne, NIV, NKJV marg., NWT, JB.

See comments under 1 Corinthians 10:28.

1 Corinthians 15:47

"**the Lord**" has been omitted by the DR, RV, Ne, NIV, NKJV marg., NWT, JB.

See comments under 1 Corinthians 10:28. Ruckman affirms (17) p 429 that "the Lord" is in the texts of Aleph, B and Origen.

2 Corinthians 4:6
"**Jesus**" has been omitted by the NIV, Ne, NWT, JB.

Ruckman (29) p 78 states that Origen and Marcion (i.e. the HERETIC) were responsible for the omission, perpetuated only in A (5th century) and B (4th century). Papyrus 46 (3rd century, i.e. MORE ANCIENT even than B) and Aleph (contemporaneous with B) both support the AV1611. Berry's Greek text supports the AV1611.

Ephesians 3:9
"**by Jesus Christ**" has been omitted by the DR, RV, Ne, NIV, NKJV marg., NWT, JB.

Berry's Greek text supports the AV1611. J. A. Moorman (39) indicates that P46, Aleph and B are among the few mss. which omit this phrase.

Ephesians 3:14
"**of our Lord Jesus Christ**" has been omitted by the RV, Ne, NIV, NKJV marg., NWT, JB.

Ruckman (36, *Ephesians* p 257) indicates that Aleph and B omit the phrase. J.A. Moorman (39) indicates that P46 is also among the few mss. which omit the phrase. Berry's Greek text supports the AV1611.

Ephesians 5:9
"**the Spirit**" has been changed to "(the) light" (2 Corinthians 11:14!!) by the DR, RV, Ne, NIV, NKJV marg., NWT, JB.

Berry's Greek text supports the AV1611. Ruckman (29) p 82 indicates that the authority for the modern alteration was B. Papyrus 46 (3rd century) supports the AV1611. See also Ruckman (36, *Ephesians* p 302).

Colossians 1:2
"**and the Lord Jesus Christ**" has been omitted by the RV, Ne, NIV, NKJV marg., NWT, JB.

Ruckman (36, *Colossians* p 470–471) states that B and D (6th century) have omitted the words, which are found in all families of manuscripts and in the majority of manuscripts. Berry's Greek text, representing this majority, supports the AV1611.

Colossians 1:14

"through his blood" is omitted by the RV, Ne, NIV, NKJV marg., NWT, JB.

The omission makes redemption equal to forgiveness – which it is NOT, Romans 3:25 – and encourages the abomination of auricular confession. See *The Priest, the Woman and the Confessional* by Charles Chiniquy. The omission is attributed to Origen but citations for the AV1611 reading date from the 2nd century (36, *Colossians* p 473–475). Berry's Greek text supports the AV1611.

1 Timothy 3:16

"God" has been altered to "He" or "Who" by the RV, Ne, NIV, NKJV marg., NWT, JB. The DR has "which".

The alteration of "God" to "He" or "Who" obviously constitutes an attack on the Deity of Jesus Christ by the modern textual critics. This alteration has been discussed exhaustively by Burgon (13) pp 101–105, 424–504, whose researches have been summarised by the TBS (37) *God was Manifest in the Flesh*. See also Fuller, citing the TBS, (3) p 24–41. The TBS, ibid. state that all the early Greek editions of the New Testament (Ximenes, Erasmus, Beza, Stephens – see Berry's Greek text, the Elzevirs) read "God was manifest" and hence this must have been the reading of the manuscripts available to those editors. The wording of their editions is reflected in all the early English translations (Tyndale 1534, Great Bible 1539, Geneva 1557, Bishops' 1568) except the surviving copies of Wyclif (1380) derived in part from the Vulgate. Moreover, the European versions associated with true Bible believers (Italian (Diodati), French (Osterwald), Spanish (Valera), German (Luther), Portuguese (Almeida)) all concur with the AV1611.

However, the 19th and 20th century Greek editions of the New Testament, culminating in those of Westcott and Hort and Nestle, all rejected "God" in 1 Timothy 3:16 in favour of "who." These corrupt texts form the basis for most of the modern translations. According to Burgon, p 443, the only ancient witness in support of "who" is Aleph (4th century), while D (6th century) has "which". C (5th century) and F and G (9th century) are indistinct in this place and their testimony therefore equivocal, while Codex B does not contain 1 Timothy. In addition, Burgon p 99, cites only one cursive copy of Paul's Epistles, designated 'Paul 17', as reading "who" in 1 Timothy 3:16. ('Paul 73', a second copy, was thought to be possibly in agreement with 'Paul 17' but Burgon, p 99, states it is actually an abridgement of Ecumenius' citation – see later, which reads "God"). Burgon p 483 states that of the ancient versions, only the Gothic (4th century) unequivocally witnesses to "who". Agreeing with D in exhibiting "which" in 1 Timothy 3:16 are the Old Latin (2nd century), Vulgate (4th century), Peshitta Syriac (2nd century) Coptic and Sahidic (3rd and 4th centuries) and Ethiopic (6th-7th centuries) versions. The Armenian and Arabic versions are indeterminate in this place (Burgon, ibid. p 454).

The only fathers in opposition to "God" are Gelasius of Cyzicus (476 AD), who cites "which" and an unknown author of uncertain date, who also cites "which." The TBS ibid. p 8 state that the Latin, Peshitta and other versions may well have been influenced by the erroneous reading in D, of the 'Western' family. Later copies of the Peshitta (4th century) may have been influenced by the views of Nestorius, who evidently denied that Christ was both God and man. It is probable therefore, that the earliest copies of the Peshitta, now non-extant, in fact read "God", rather than "who". The most ancient Greek uncial in favour of "God" in 1 Timothy 3:16, is Codex A (5th century). Burgon (p 432–436) cites in detail the witnesses who attest to the horizontal stroke of "Theta" in "Theos" being clearly visible up to the mid-18th century. The TBS pamphlet provides an excellent summary. In support of A are uncials K, L and P, ('Mosquensis', 'Angelicus' and 'Porphyrianus') all of the 9th century. The extant cursive copies of Paul's letters number 300, of which 254 (designated 'Paul 1' to 'Paul 301') contain 1 Timothy 3:16. Of these, no less than 252 read "God", in agreement with the AV1611. (The two exceptions, which have already been discussed, are 'Paul 17' and 'Paul 73' of which the latter is a doubtful witness.) Added to this favourable testimony are 29 out of 32 Lectionary copies from the Eastern Church, reaching back to earliest times, i.e. before Aleph, which support the reading "God". (Burgon p 478, declares the 3 exceptions to be *"Western documents of suspicious character."*). Burgon p 450, 454, 489–490, also cites the Georgian (6th century), Harkleian Syriac (616 AD) and the Slavonic (9th century) versions as reading "God". The fathers in support of the AV1611 are as follows (Burgon, p 486–490):

1st Century:	Barnabus, Ignatius (90 AD)
2nd Century:	Hippolytus (190 AD)
3rd Century:	Apostolic Constitutions, Epistle ascribed to Dionysius of Alexandria (264 AD), Gregory Thaumaturgus
4th Century:	Basil the Great (355 AD), Chrysostom (380 AD), Didymus (325 AD), Diodorus (370 AD), Gregory of

Nazianzus (355 AD), Gregory of Nyssa (370 AD). 'Euthalian' chapter title of 1 Timothy 3, attesting to "God in the flesh."

5th Century: Anon. citation in works of Athanasius (430 AD), Cyril of Alexandria (410 AD), Euthalius (458 AD), Macedonius II (496 AD), Theodoret (420 AD)

6th Century: Severus, Bishop of Antioch (512 AD)

8th Century: Epiphanius of Catana (787 AD), John Damascene (730 AD), Theodorus Studita (790 AD)

10th Century: Ecumenius (990 AD)

11th Century: Theophylact (1077 AD)

12th Century: Euthymius (1116 AD).

See also Fuller (2) p 110–111, (3) p 98, 260 (summarising Burgon's final findings as 300 Greek manuscripts (uncial, cursive, lectionary), reading "**God**" in 1 Timothy 3:16, vs. 7 which do not), Hills (5) p 137–138, Ruckman (17) p 330, (35) 46–48.

1 Timothy 6:20

"**science**" has been altered to "knowledge" by the DR, RV, NIV, NKJV, NWT, JB.

The alteration clearly stems from a refusal to accept the word "**science**" in ANY negative context, 'science' being one of the 'gods' of the modern age.

2 Timothy 2:15

"**study**" has been altered to "give diligence" or "do your best" or similar by the RV, NIV, NKJV, NWT, JB.

The Lord's command is to "**search the Scriptures**", John 5:39 and those who did so were commended by the Holy Spirit, Acts 17:11. To "**search the Scriptures**" one must become, primarily, a STUDENT of THE WORD OF TRUTH – THE BIBLE, see context, NOT 'the Hebrew' or 'the Greek'.

Hebrews 3:6

"**unto the end**" has been omitted by the NIV, NKJV marg., JB.

Ruckman (36, *Hebrews* p 70) states that B and Papyrus 46 are the "*authorities*" for the omission. The words are found in all four families of manuscripts – including Aleph, the old Itala (i.e. Latin), the Vulgate (oldest copies), three families of the Syriac and in the Armenian, Coptic and Ethiopic versions. Berry's Greek text supports the AV1611. The NWT has the reading.

James 5:16

"**faults**" has been altered to "sins" or similar by the DR, RV, Ne, NIV, NKJV ("trespasses"), NWT, JB.

The alteration is ready made for the abominable Roman Catholic 'confessional' – see comments on Colossians 1:14 – and shows how modern revisers will alter the word of truth to accommodate the whore of Revelation 17, 18.

Gail Riplinger in her book *Which Bible is God's Word?*, Hearthstone Publishing, Ltd., 1994, p 102, confirms that mss. Aleph, B, A, P, Scrivener's a, c, d and Tregelles 13 read "harmatias", ("sins"). She adds that the majority of Greek mss., including uncials K, L, 049 and cursives 322, 323, 1846 and 2298 read "paraptomata" ("faults") and explains that the minority ms. reading is a corruption which was discarded by the early church. It is therefore preserved in only a few mss. and has no unbroken testimony down through history. The reader should note that this is in complete contrast to the few AV1611 readings such as Acts 8:37 and 1 John 5:7, 8 which are not found in the majority of extant mss. but nevertheless enjoy considerable support from many other sources, dating from the 2nd century. See also J. A. Moorman, (39).

Ne contains "harmatias" and Berry reads "paraptomata" but translates it as "offences".

1 Peter 1:22

"**through the Spirit**" and "**pure**" have been omitted by the DR (changes "**pure**" to "sincere"), RV, Ne, NIV, NKJV marg. ("**through the Spirit**" only), NWT, JB.

Ruckman (29) p 82, indicates that the authority for the omissions is B. However, the AV1611 readings are found in Papyrus 72, written 80 years before B, as well as in the Receptus – see Berry's Greek text.

2 Peter 1:20

"**private interpretation**" has been altered to "prophet's own interpretation" or similar by the NIV, JB. The NKJV and NWT read with the AV1611.

The alteration would still allow THE CHURCH to engage in 'private interpretation'!

1 John 4:3
"Christ is come in the flesh" has been omitted by the DR, RV, Ne, NIV, NKJV marg., NWT, JB.

J.A. Moorman (39) cites A, B, Psi and some copies of the Old Latin as the main sources of this omission. Berry's Greek text supports the AV1611.

1 John 5:7, 8
"in heaven, the Father, the Word, and the Holy Ghost: and these three are one. And there are three that bear witness in earth" is omitted by the RV, Ne, NIV, NKJV marg., NWT, JB.

This passage, known as the 'Johannine Comma', is lacking from most of the 500–600 extant Greek mss. which contain 1 John, although Dr. Gill stated in the 18th century that *"out of sixteen ancient copies of Robert Stephens', nine of them had (the passage)"* (40) p 25.

Citing Nestle's 26th Edition as the source, J. A. Moorman (41) lists nine Greek mss. in his work which contain the Comma, four in the text and five in the margin.

The former include Codex 61 of the 15th-16th century, kept in Dublin and known as the Montfort manuscript, Codex Ravianus and Codex 629 (Wizanburgensis). The latter include Codex 88 (3), (17), (42), (37). J. A. Moorman (41) designates Codex 629 as a 14th century ms., citing Metzger, although Dr. Ruckman locates it in the 8th century (42).

The main authorities for the passage are the Old Latin Text of the 2nd century, including manuscript r, written in the 5th-6th century and the *Speculum*, a treatise containing the Old Latin Text, written, according to Moorman, early in the 5th century and several fathers. Fuller (2) p 213, citing Wilkinson, states that the passage was found in the Old Latin Bibles of the Waldenses, whose text pre-dated Jerome's Vulgate. See also Ray (7) p 98, who states that this Italic Bible dates from 157 AD. The Old Latin text carried sufficient weight to influence the later copies of the Vulgate, most of which from 800 AD onward incorporated the passage.

The fathers who cite the passage include Tatian, Tertullian (both 2nd century), Cyprian (250 AD), Priscillian (385 AD), Idacius Clarus (385 AD), several African writers of the 5th century and Cassiodorus (480–570 AD). The combined influence of these authorities, together with grammatical difficulties which arise if the Comma is omitted, was sufficient to ensure its place in most editions of the Textus Receptus – see Berry's text – and hence in the AV1611, where it undoubtedly belongs. For more detailed discussion see Hills (5) p 209, (38) p 210, the

TBS (37) *Notes on the Vindication of 1 John 5:7* (available from Bible
Baptist Bookstore, Pensacola Florida.), Ruckman (4) p 128–129, (17) p
334 (42). The TBS have produced a more recent version of their notes,
entitled *Why 1 John 5:7, 8 is in the Bible*. The omission of the Comma
from the majority of the manuscripts most likely stems from the influence of Origen and some of his supporters, who did not accept the doctrine of the Trinity.

Revelation 22:14
"**do his commandments**" has been altered to "wash their robes," or similar wording, by the DR (adding "in the blood of the Lamb") RV, Ne,
NIV, NKJV marg., NWT, JB.

The TBS (37), Article 38 *Revelation 22:14* . . . have provided an
excellent resume of the evidence. In favour of the modern textual critics
are Aleph (4th century), A (5th century), about 15 cursives including
104 and 1006 (11th century), 2053 (12th) and 2020 (15th), the Coptic
(Sahidic), Ethiopic and Latin Vulgate versions of the 4th-6th centuries
and 5 Old Latin copies of the 9th-13th centuries. The following fathers
also support the modern reading: Athanasius (373 AD), Fulgentius (533
AD), Apringius (551 AD), Primasius (552 AD), a 6th century Ambrose
and Haymo (841 AD).

The manuscripts which read "do his commandments" consist of the
vast majority, including uncial 046, cursives 1, 82, 94, 1611, 1854,
1859, 2042, 2065, 2073, 2138, 2329, 2432 and more than 150 others.
Also supporting the AV1611 are the Coptic (Bohairic) 3rd-4th centuries,
the Harkelian and Philoxenian Syriac (6th-7th centuries) and the
Armenian (5th century) versions. Fathers in support of the AV1611
include Tertullian (220 AD), Cyprian (258 AD), Tyconius (380 AD),
Andrew (614 AD) and Arethas (914 AD). Obviously the weight of evidence vindicates the AV1611 reading, which is supported by Berry's
Greek text.

Revelation 22:19
"**book of life**" has been altered to "tree(s) of life" by the RV, Ne, NIV,
NKJV marg., NWT, JB.

Hills (5) p 202, (38) p 198, indicates that the AV1611 reading is
found only in one or two Greek manuscripts, including Codex 141. All
the remaining Greek manuscripts read with the modern textual critics,
although Ruckman (36, *Revelation* p 606) refers to the modern reading
as a non-existent "*Alexandrian Conjecture.*" Hills states that the

AV1611 reading is supported by the Latin Vulgate, including a very old manuscript designated F, the Bohairic version, Ambrose (397 AD) and the commentaries of Primasius (6th century) and Haymo (9th century). Ruckman (35) p 70, states that the reading "book of life" is found in the Bibles of the Waldenses, Albigenses and Gothic Christians (2nd-4th centuries). J.A. Moorman (41) summarises the evidence favouring the AV1611 reading. This evidence indicates a varied and unbroken testimony to the AV1611 reading down through history.

7.4 IN SUMMARY...

132 New Testament verses have been listed. The Majority mss. support 123 of the AV1611 readings, or 93%, which appears to be typical, Section 1.3. Of these verses, the NIV agrees with the JB in 126, with the NWT in 123 and with BOTH in 119, or 95%, 93% and 90% respectively, AGAINST the AV1611.

In addition, 60 Old Testament verses have been listed, including those cited under Deuteronomy 16:21, Isaiah 5:14 and Malachi 1:3. Of these verses, if one includes avoidance of the word "hell" in Isaiah 5:14 etc. the NIV agrees with the JB in 57, with the NWT in 55 and with BOTH in 52, or 95%, 92% and 87% respectively AGAINST the AV1611. Even this brief survey shows how the modern versions approved by fundamentalists, the NIV and NKJV, repeatedly:

1. Weaken or cast doubt on the testimony of Scripture to MAJOR DOCTRINES.
2. Agree, with only few exceptions, with bibles declared by fundamentalists to be corrupt, the NWT, JB and often the DR, AGAINST the AV1611.
3. Follow or support the corrupt Alexandrian text of Westcott and Hort.
4. Detract from the Person and Deity of the Lord Jesus Christ.
5. Fail to improve on many important truths revealed by the AV1611 and indeed tend to obscure such truths.
6. In particular, obscure many verses which deal with HELL, ROME and DEVILS.

Dr. Ruckman provides a fitting assessment of the NIV. See Figure 5.

More searching surveys, particularly that of Gail Riplinger (12) will abundantly confirm these results.

Figure 5 The NIV Unmasked

7.5   CONCLUSIONS

1. The answer to the question **"whence comest thou?"** concerning the Bible reveals:
   2 lines of bibles,
   2 lines of Greek mss.,
   2 lines of church history,
   2 lines of men.
2. Of each of these 2 lines, one is honouring to God, one is not.
3. Of each of these 2 lines, one is honoured BY God, one is not.

   "Choose you this day whom ye will serve; . . . as for me and my house, we will serve the Lord" Joshua 24:15.

7.6 PRACTICAL SUGGESTIONS

1. Be guided by conscience, Acts 24:16. No one should be forced to abide by any bible against the dictates of conscience.
2. Be aware of the facts in the selection of a bible. **"The prudent man looketh well to his going"** Proverbs 14:15.
3. Be honest. If NO bible is inerrant, then NO bible should be declared 'the word of God' for **"God is light, and in him is no darkness at all"** 1 John 1:5.
4. Be consistent. If A bible IS the pure word of God, then it must be ENTIRELY the pure word of God. **"But as God is true, our word toward you was not yea and nay"** 2 Corinthians 1:18.
5. **"Be ready always to give an answer to every man that asketh you a reason of the hope that is in you with meekness and fear"** 1 Peter 3:15. Don"t correct the BOOK, it will correct YOU.

Additional Note: Since this work was compiled, the author has become acquainted with two UK sources on Bible versions that are extremely informative, supplying material that is freely available. These are:
   Bible Versions – Which is the Real Word of God?
   Author: *David B Loughran*, July 1999
   Stewarton Bible School, Stewarton, Scotland
   Internet: http://atschool.eduweb.co.uk/sbs777/vital/kjv/index.html
   email:sbs777@rmplc.co.uk
   Dr. Rev. Ian Paisley's web page:
   http://www.ianpaisley.org/main.asp, with articles *Foundation of the KJV*, 9/5/01 and *History of the KJV*, 14/5/01. It is possible that these arti-

cles may be the first two in a series. If so, future instalments are awaited with eagerness.

Other extremely valuable sources with available on-line material on Bible versions are:

A.V. Publications, http//www.avpublications.com/
Chick Publications,
http://www.chick.com/information/bibleversions/comparison.asp
Dial-the-Truth Ministries, News and Views,
http://www.av1611.org/othpubl.html
Fundamental Baptist Site Index,
http://www.thebaptiststandard.org/kingjamesbible.html

Epilogue:
A former local pastor levelled detailed criticisms at the AV1611 after having read an earlier version of Chapters 1 to 7 of this work, which contained much the same material as the present version. This cleric, a saved man, is a graduate of the Universities of Oxford, London and Belfast. He has an M.A., B.D. and M. Th., did his doctoral research in the New Testament and taught New Testament Greek to theological students for twenty years. Chapter 8 of this work and those following address these and related criticisms of the Holy Bible.

Post Script, May 2001:
The gentleman made his criticisms of the Holy Bible in September 1994 and forwarded them to this author. A few years later, the gentleman, now in his sixties, suffered ill health and retired late last year to the south of England. Was it really a coincidence, or had he overlooked the "**jot**" and "**tittle**" (*Matthew* 5:18–19) and *Revelation* 22:18–19?

Interim References

Volume 1 made use of the following references. See Volume 5 for the complete list of references and a bibliography.

1. *The Christian's Handbook of Biblical Scholarship* Dr. Peter S. Ruckman, Bible Baptist Bookstore, P.O. Box 7135, Pensacola FL. 32504, 1988.
2. *Which Bible?* 5th Edit. David Otis Fuller, D.D., Grand Rapids International Publications, P.O. Box 2607, Grand Rapids, Michigan 49501, 1984.
3. *True or False?* 2nd Edition, Edit. Dr. David Otis Fuller, D.D., Grand Rapids International Publications, 1983.
4. *The Christian's Handbook of Manuscript Evidence* Dr. Peter S. Ruckman, Pensacola Bible Press, P.O. Box 86, Palatka, Florida 32077, 1976.
5. *The King James Version Defended* 3rd Edit. Edward F. Hills, ThD, Christian Research Press, P.O. Box 2013, Des Moines, Iowa 50310, 1979.
6. *Let's Weigh the Evidence* Barry Burton, Chick Publications, P.O. Box 662, Chino, CA 91710, 1983.
7. *God Only Wrote One Bible* Jasper James Ray, The Eye Opener Publishers, P.O. Box 7944, Eugene, Oregon USA 97401, 1980. See also *New Eye Opener* leaflet.
8. *Perfected or Perverted?* Norman Ward, Which Bible? Society Inc., 605 Deeming, S.E., P.O. Box 7096, Grand Rapids.
9. *The Answer Book* Dr. Samuel C. Gipp, Th.D., Samuel C. Gipp, 1989.
10. *Supplement to The Inheritance Paper No. 9* J. Coad, Totnes, Devon.
11. *Famine In The Land* Norman Ward, Which Bible? Society Inc.
12. *New Age Bible Versions* Gail Riplinger, Bible and Literary Missionary Foundation, 1993.
13. *The Revision Revised* Dean John William Burgon, Centennial Edition, 1883–1983, A.G. Hobbs Publications, P.O. Box 14218, Fort Worth TX76117, 1983.
14. *An Understandable History Of The Bible* Rev. Samuel C. Gipp Th.D., Samuel C. Gipp, 1987.

15. *The Inheritance Paper 9* J. Coad, Totnes, Devon.
16. *The History of the New Testament Church Vol. 1* Dr. Peter S. Ruckman, Bible Baptist Bookstore, 1982.
17. *Problem Texts* Dr. Peter S. Ruckman, Pensacola Bible Institute Press, P.O. Box 7135, Pensacola, Florida 32504, 1980.
18. *Counterfeit or Genuine? Mark 16? John 8?* 2nd Edition, Edit. Dr. David Otis Fuller, D.D., Grand Rapids International Publications, 1984.
19. *Interlinear Hebrew/English Old Testament*, 3 Vols. Jay P.Green, (edit.) The Eye Opener Publishers, 1983.
20. *The Monarch of the Books* Dr. Peter S. Ruckman, Bible Baptist Bookstore 1980.
21. *The History of the Waldenses* Rev. J.A. Wylie, LL.D., reprinted by Church History Research and Archives, 1985.
22. *A Brief History of English Bible Translations* Dr. Laurence M. Vance, Vance Publications, 1993.
23. *The NIV Reconsidered* Earl Radmacher and Zane C. Hodges, Kerugma, Inc. 1990.
24. *John Wycliffe The Dawn of The Reformation* David Fountain, Mayflower Christian Books, 1984.
25. *William Tyndale, His Life and Times* S. M. Houghton, M.A., FOCUS Christian Ministries Trust, 6 Orchard Road, Lewes, East Sussex, BN7 2HB, 1985.
26. *The Newe Testament by William Tyndale (1526)* John Wesley Sawyer, The Martyrs Bible Series Volume 1, 1989.
27. *Pioneers of the Reformation in England* Marcus Loane, Church Book Room Press, Ltd., 1964.
28. *The Newe Testament of Matthew's Bible 1537 AD* John Wesley Sawyer, The Martyrs Bible Series Volume 2, 1989.
29. *The Bible Babel* Dr. Peter S. Ruckman, The Bible Baptist Bookstore, 1981.
30. *Why I Believe the King James Version is the Word of God* Dr. Peter S. Ruckman, Bible Baptist Bookstore, 1988.
31. *Desecrating God's Word* William A. De Jonge, Bible Truth Society.(tract), obtained from FOCUS.
32. *A Bible Word List and Daily Reading Scheme* The Trinitarian Bible Society, London.
33. *A Treasury of Evangelical Writings* Edit. Dr. David Otis Fuller, D.D., Kregel Publications, Grand Rapids, Michigan 49501, 1980.
34. *Differences in the King James Version Editions* Dr. Peter S. Ruckman, Bible Baptist Bookstore, 1983.
35. *The New ASV-Satan's Masterpiece* Dr. Peter S. Ruckman, Bible Baptist Bookstore, 1983.
36. *The Bible Believer's Commentary Series, Genesis, Exodus, Job, Proverbs, Minor Prophets (Hosea-Nahum), Matthew, Acts, Gal-Eph-Phil-Col.,*

Hebrews, Revelation Dr. Peter S.Ruckman, Bible Baptist Bookstore, 1970–87.

37. Articles and Reprints from *The Quarterly Record* The Trinitarian Bible Society, London:

Topics: *The Bible-A Sure Foundation, Common Bible?, Divine Inspiration of the Holy Scriptures, English Bible and Apocrypha, Excellence of the AV, Good Will Toward Men, Holding Fast the Faithful Word, The Holy Bible, Holy Trinity, The Image of God, Important Omissions, Italic Type, Plain Reasons Why We Keep the AV, Of the Resurrection of Christ, Rome and Reunion, Standing on a Rock, The Only Begotten Son, Who is the Rock?, The Word Baptism in the KJV, What is Wrong with the Modern Versions? etc.*

Verses: Gen. 37:3, 2 Sam. 15:7, Matt. 6:13, Mk. 6:20, 16:9–20, Jn. 1:1, 5:3, 4, 17:24, Acts 2:47, 13:48, Rom. 8:14–16, 9:5, 1 Cor. 11:23, 24, 1 Tim. 3:16, 2 Tim. 2:24–26, 3:16, 17, Heb. 1:6, 2 Pet. 1:20, 21, 1 John 5:7, Rev. 22:14.

Versions: NIV, NKJV, RSV, GN, LB, AMP, NASV, NEB, NWT, JB, NJB, etc. See references 43–45 for particular articles.

38. *Believing Bible Study* Edward F. Hills, Th.D, Second Edition, the Christian Research Press, 1977.

39. *Early Manuscripts and the Authorized Version* J. A. Moorman, B.F.T. #1825, 900 Park Avenue, Collingswood, N.J. 08108. Also obtainable from A.V. Publications Corp. P.O. Box 280, Ararat, VA 24053.

40. *The Providential Preservation of the Greek Text of the New Testament* Rev. W. Maclean M.A., Westminster Standard, 1983.

41. *When the KJV Departs from the "Majority" Text* J. A. Moorman B.F.T. #1825, 900 Park Avenue, Collingswood, N.J. 08108.

42. *1 John 5:7* Dr. Peter S. Ruckman, Bible Baptist Bookstore, 1990.

8

Fundamental Errors

8.1 INTRODUCTION

I hope that the preceding chapters and the list of suggested essential references will provide an adequate summary of the Bible translation issue. However, it should come as no surprise that the material in those chapters proved to be an offence to some of the enemies of the Holy Bible. Academic theologians have voiced many criticisms of the Holy Bible. See Chapter 5 for some of the more common, general criticisms. In addition to these, I have received many more specific objections to the AV1611, aimed at subverting both the words of God and the faith of the ordinary Bible believer in these words. The following sections address these particular criticisms, which must be answered for at least three very good reasons.

1. I believe that the AV1611 is the true word of God and the FINAL AUTHORITY in ALL matters of faith and practice.
2. I believe that it should be restored to the minds and hearts of the British people, from whom it was stolen by Christian scholarship.
3. I believe that there is no issue more important than that of FINAL AUTHORITY in ALL matters of faith and practice. If the Christian cannot put his hand on ONE book and state unequivocally that "this is my FINAL AUTHORITY", he has NO authority which he can read, preach, teach, believe and memorise, other than his own subjective opinion or 'scholarship'.

Such 'scholarship' is a far cry from **"the words of the living God"**, Jeremiah 23:36, **"the word of his grace, which is able to build you up,**

and to give you an inheritance among all them which are sanctified"
Acts 20:32.

8.2 ACADEMIC CRITICISMS

I will therefore answer the detailed criticisms of the Holy Bible from the
scholarly gentleman mentioned at the end of Chapter 7. These criticisms
have been cited in ***bold Italic*** as received and are followed by detailed
responses, point by point where necessary. Although I have referred to
this gentleman as 'our critic', singular, repeatedly in the text, I believe
that his criticisms are typical of the genre.

8.2.1 *"You should become acquainted with the standard scholarly works"*

1. Who sets the standard and on what basis? It appears that the basis is
   to alter the AV1611 at all costs.
2. One's time and financial resources are limited. I prefer to invest mine
   into what will reinforce fidelity to the Holy Bible, not weaken it.
3. Whatever *"the standard scholarly works"* are, the EFFECT of
   following them is to become a Bible rejecting destructive critic. I
   prefer to remain a Bible believer.

8.2.2 *"You have an attitude which is constantly looking for papal plots, which repeatedly attributes the lowest possible motives to textual critics and translators"*

1. It is a realistic attitude. In addition to the works by Edmond Paris and
   Avro Manhattan, The reader should consult:

   Jesuit Plots from Elizabethan to Modern Times Albert Close, The
   Protestant Truth Society, London,

   The Babington Plot J.E.C. Shepherd, Wittenburg Publications,
   Toronto,

   The British Monarchy and the See of Rome Michael McCarthy, The
   Protestant Truth Society, London,

   Is Alberto for Real? Sid Hunter, Chick Publications, Chino,
   California, a vindication of the testimony of the late Dr. Alberto
   Rivera, ex Jesuit priest,

All Roads Lead to Rome? Michael de Semlyen, Dorchester House Publications, Bucks..

2. Academia has yet to show that papal plots aimed at overthrowing the word of God and replacing it with the authority of Rome are not in operation even now.

8.2.3 *"You do not take into account evidence that is inconvenient"*

This charge is false. Chapters 1 to 7 constitute a summary document but even then it originally ran to over 60 pages of text and figures. I have included evidence which is essential, with references which the reader can check. In doing so I have sought to maintain the right balance, which shows that the evidence is overwhelmingly favourable to the AV1611.

I have also included evidence which, at face value, DOES appear "*inconvenient*". For example, Chapter 1 shows that the majority of manuscripts do not uniformly support the Text of the AV1611. There is an up to 10% discrepancy. I included the Vulgate in Figure 2 as the basis in part of Wycliffe's Bible and discussed several important AV1611 readings which are not supported by the Majority Text. Moreover, in the 100+ verses cited I included several where some modern versions have RETAINED AV1611 readings. See Chapter 7. I also mentioned differences between various editions of the AV1611. See Chapter 5.

8.2.4 *"You overlook the fact that the critics . . . leave so much in the text which stands in complete contradiction to their alleged purposes"*

1. Dr. Ruckman (4), p 211, answers as follows: "*90% of Sinaiticus and Vaticanus . . . have to read with the Byzantine Family IN ORDER TO PASS OFF AS BIBLES*". Gail Riplinger (12), p 499, states: "*a large part of even new versions must contain the traditional bible readings in order to be sold as 'bibles'*".

2. 1 Corinthians 5:6 states that "**a little leaven leaveneth the whole lump**". How many words of the 'Divinely inspired original' did Mother Eve have to change in order to damn the entire human race? Genesis 2:16, 17; 3:2, 3. These observations also answer in part the excuse for the mutilation of Holy Scripture, that doctrine does not depend on one verse, etc.. Spurgeon stated in his final manifesto to his students, April 1891: "*It is sadly common among ministers to add a word or subtract a word from the passage, or in some way debase*

the language of sacred writ . . . Our reverence for the Great Author of Scripture should forbid all mauling of His Words."

"Thus saith the LORD; Stand in the court of the Lord's house, and speak unto all the cities of Judah, which come to worship in the LORD's house, all the words that I command thee to speak unto them; diminish not a word:" Jeremiah 26:2.

8.2.5 *"Your cartoons and diagrams (are) . . . nonsensical and puerile . . . inaccurate (and) offensive"*

1. Figures 1 to 3 merely summarise the main aspects of ms. evidence, Bible ancestry and the passage of church history as the Gospel moves east to west. Academia has NOT demonstrated that such an approach is inaccurate.
2. Figure 4 IS offensive, at least to Bible critics. They are meant to be. Dr. Ruckman has said *"my pictures aim to find out if a man wants the truth at any cost. If he doesn't, I aim to kick him into hell if he's unsaved and kick him to Rome if he's saved!"*

8.2.6 *"You use irresponsible language about the text of Hitler and the IRA"*

1. **"The mother of harlots and abominations of the earth"**, Revelation 17:5, the Roman Catholic church, brought Hitler and the Nazi party to power. The detailed works by Edmond Paris, *The Secret History of the Jesuits* and *The Vatican Against Europe* will amply bear this out. The corrupt text of Alexandria was and is the official text of the Roman Catholic 'church'.
2. The work by Avro Manhattan, *Catholic Terror in Ireland*, shows the IRA to be another abomination of 'mother church' and hence inextricably linked to the corrupt text of Alexandria.
3. I have a photograph of Desmond Tutu preaching from a Jerusalem 'bible', an Alexandrian stable-mate of the NIV. This photograph is part of a 'Christian Aid' document compiled by several Catholic organisations agitating for the overthrow of the former legally constituted government of South Africa. The ANC and the IRA are *"blood brothers"* in terror, providing a direct link between the IRA and the corrupt Alexandrian text. See the very informative leaflet *The IRA and the ANC*, from Open Bible Publications, Belfast. **"Wherefore by their fruits ye shall know them"** Matthew 7:20.

8.2.7 *"Your claims that the KJV is superior to the original Hebrew and Greek . . . the God breathed originals are unacceptable"*

1. 7 specific verses substantiating these *"claims"* have been cited. See Chapter 5. A total of 60 examples can be obtained from Ruckman (1), Appendix 7 plus issues March, April 1989 and November 1991 of the *Bible Believers' Bulletin.*
2. I repeat several reasons why the AV1611 is superior to *"the originals"* (29) p 118.

The AV1611:

2.1 can be READ, the originals CANNOT and were NEVER collated into one volume. The verse usually quoted in support of *"the God-breathed originals"*, 2 Timothy 3:16, refers to copies of the scriptures, NOT the original.

2.2 has chapter and verse divisions, which even the modern translations must follow. The oldest manuscripts do NOT.

2.3 has word separation so that it can be more easily understood. The oldest manuscripts do NOT.

2.4 is arranged in Pre-millennial order which the Masoretic text is NOT and even though the translators were NOT Pre-millennial. Again, the modern translations must follow this order.

2.5 is rhythmical and easy to memorise which Greek and Hebrew are NOT.

2.6 has been responsible for the conversion of more souls than any original autograph or any copy made within 5 centuries of the original autographs.

2.7 is in the universal language which Greek and Hebrew are NOT. Hebrew is spoken by approximately 1% of the world's population. New Testament Greek is a DEAD language, not even spoken in Greece, which incidentally is one of the most spiritually impoverished nations in Europe, according to the Trinitarian Bible Society.

3. The following quotations may be of interest, the first from *John Bunyan, The Immortal Dreamer,* by W. Burgess McCreary, copyright 1928, Gospel Trumpet Company, cited in the *Bible Believers' Bulletin*, March 1994: *"A university man met Bunyan on the road near Cambridge. Said he to Bunyan, "How dare you preach, not having the original Scriptures?" "Do you have them – the copies written by the apostles and prophets?" asked Bunyan. "No," replied*

the scholar. *"But I have what I believe to be a true copy of the original".* *"And I,"* said Bunyan, *"believe the English Bible to be a true copy too".* The second quotation is from Dr. Ruckman's *History of the New Testament Church*, Vol. 2, p 110, citing Billy Sunday:

"When the Bible (AV1611) says one thing and scholarship says another, scholarship can go plumb to the Devil!"

Despite his highly unorthodox attitude and offensive manner, *"Billy Sunday saw over 1,000,000 men and women "hit the sawdust trail" in open profession of faith in our Lord Jesus Christ"*, according to the paper *How Great Soul winners Were Endued with Power*, Martyrs Memorial Free Presbyterian Church, Belfast.

4. It will be shown that to confine inspiration to *"the God breathed originals"* is actually to detract from inspiration.

8.2.8 *"Your position seems to assume . . . the KJV is always right . . . This in effect means that any meaningful discussion of linguistic, textual and exegetical matters is quite impossible."*

1. The academic's position is the same as mine, except that he insists that SCHOLARSHIP is always right and is capable of correcting the AV1611. I maintain that the AV1611 is always right and is quite able to correct the dogma of fundamental scholarship. The academic also insists that *"a knowledge of what the original writers actually said"* is necessary to avoid error and that *"all versions must be subject to the original languages"* which should be constantly consulted. Neither assertion has any scriptural foundation. John 16:13 shows that it is **"the Spirit of truth"** Who guides the believer into **"all truth"**, not *"the original languages"*. *"A knowledge of what the original writers actually said"* cannot be gained unless (like Bunyan or Timothy, 2 Timothy 3:15) one has *"a true copy of the original"* because the 'original' record, Jeremiah 36:18, does not exist! There is absolutely NO scripture that limits such knowledge, first hand, to Greek and Hebrew linguists, transforming them into a special privileged 'priest class' who are supposed to dictate to uneducated initiates that constitute the rest of the Body of Christ. The Bible shows that the *reverse* is true, Luke 10:21, Acts 4:13!

2. Far from being impossible, a very large amount of *"meaningful discussion of linguistic, textual and exegetical matters"* may take place when the AV1611 is upheld as the FINAL authority in ALL matters of faith and practice. The bibliography included in this work,

bears witness to this fact. Such discussion is not only possible, it is also "**profitable**" 2 Timothy 3:16 and COMMANDED BY GOD, Deuteronomy 6:6, 7, Colossians 3:16. However, for it to take place, one must believe the scripture, John 2:22, love the scripture, Psalm 119:97, 140, hear the scripture, Luke 11:28, Romans 10:17, read the scripture, Deuteronomy 17:19, Nehemiah 8:8, Isaiah 34:16, Revelation 1:3, study the scripture, Proverbs 2:1–5, Acts 17:11, 2 Timothy 2:15, memorise the scripture, Joshua 1:8, Psalm 119:9, 11, Matthew 4:4, 7, 10, Acts 2:17–21, 25–28 and meditate upon the scripture, Joshua 1:8, Psalm 1:2, 3, 119:15, 23, 48, 78, 97, 99, 148 in order to OBEY the scripture, Ezra 7:10, John 14:21, 23, James 1:22, 1 John 3:22. By its own profession Academia can do none of these things because it does not have "*the God-breathed originals*"!

8.2.9 *"If you later become open to the weight of evidence . . . that the case for the KJV is not as watertight as you imagine . . . the results could be devastating"*

1. I was in bondage to Bible-rejecting 'fundamentalism' for 17 years and the results WERE devastating, certainly in regard to inner peace, Biblical understanding, concern for lost souls and genuine submission to the Lord Jesus Christ.

2. As a Bible believer submitting to the BOOK for the last 17 years, I have found this to be the best defence against "**the sleight of men and cunning craftiness, whereby they lie in wait to deceive**" Ephesians 4:14.

3. There is no "*imagination*" about the case for the AV1611 as the following pages will show. "*Imagination*" is a symptom of "*scholarship only-ism*". "**Because that, when they knew God, they glorified him not as God, neither were thankful; but became vain in their imaginations, and their foolish heart was darkened**" Romans 1:21.

4. This criticism really means that when a Christian student caves in under the pressure applied at theological college to disbelieve the Book by which in all probability he was saved and called to the ministry, it is a great tragedy. I agree. Christian educators will have a lot to answer for at the Judgement Seat of Christ, Romans 14:10.

8.2.10 *"I am willing to explain orally my position on a number of texts"*

1. I am not interested in any academic "*position*" on these verses. I am

interested only in GOD's position and am very aware of the fact that He has vindicated the readings for the past four centuries as they stand in ANY edition of the AV1611 since 1611.

2. No amount of discussion will alter the evidence which I cited concerning the verses and which I will in this document enlarge upon, notably with respect to Luke 2:33, John 1:18, Acts 8:37, 1 Timothy 3:16 and 1 John 5:7. These verses are prominent amongst the God honoured readings in the AV1611 that academia would alter to conform to the demands of "s*cholarship only-ism*".

8.2.11 *"This version like every other must be subject to the original languages"*

1. This statement means that the Holy Bible must be made subject to the demands of linguistic scholarship, an assumption for which there is no scriptural basis whatsoever. See comments above. I base belief in the AV1611 as the final authority in all matters of faith and conduct upon Psalm 138:2, **"For thou hast magnified thy word above all thy name"**.

2. By contrast, academia is persistently vague about WHERE it consults "*the original languages*" and about what the pure word of God is TODAY and WHERE a copy can be obtained. It cannot lay claim to any ONE book on the face of this earth as being genuinely and unequivocally THE WORD OF GOD and hence the FINAL AUTHORITY in ALL matters of faith and practice. In short, it has NO 'Bible'.

9

"The Text of the New Testament"

9.1 GENERAL OBSERVATION

The scholarly gentleman mentioned earlier forwarded to me a 20+ page document containing detailed criticisms of the Holy Bible. The first portion of the document has the above title. It appears to have been copied from some other work. If so, our critic ought to have cited the source of information but this section, like his entire document, is very poorly referenced. As an academic, I would judge it to fall short of the standard I would expect from an undergraduate student for a literature survey. Nevertheless, the first section appears to match very closely the gist of a book entitled *Which Version Now?* by Bob Sheehan, who thinks it "*reprehensible*" for Dr. David Otis Fuller to use the title *Which Bible?* (10). Titles of the following sub sections have been taken from our critic's document.

9.2 "GETTING THINGS INTO PERSPECTIVE"

Para 1 of this sub-section states "*All Greek manuscripts are in essential agreement in at least 95% of the NT text and in the remaining 5% none of the variant readings pose any threat to the basic doctrines of the Bible*".

Chapter 1 and Figure 1 show the essential aspects of manuscript evidence. The figure of 95% refers to the manuscripts of Antioch, of which about 90% agree with the Text of the AV1611. Chapter 1 also includes information on the discrepancies between Aleph and B, the most prominent of the "5%" manuscripts. Chapter 5, Section 5.7 notes the 50% departure of B from the Received Text. Our critic ignored this evidence.

Chapter 5, Section 5.7 and Chapter 7, Section 7.3 list over 25 passages of scripture with manuscript evidence, where basic doctrines were omitted or weakened mainly by the 5% manuscripts. A total of 200 examples may be found in the *New Eye Opener* leaflet published by missionary J.J. Ray (7), where modern translations have distorted or omitted scriptures, again mainly by means of the 5% manuscripts. The NIV is guilty in this respect in 195 instances out of 200. See also Dr. Ruckman's detailed study (43), a copy of which I could have forwarded to our critic upon request.

Moreover, it is not for Greek scholars, saved or lost, to dictate to Bible believers about whether or not variant readings affect "*basic doctrines*". The Lord Jesus Christ said to the father of all Bible critics, Genesis 3:1, that "**Man shall not live by bread alone, but by every word that proceedeth out of the mouth of God**" Matthew 4:4. Jealous of every word, Bible believers will not stand to lose even one of them to "**the fowls of the air**" Mark 4:4, whether scholars think it is "*basic*" or not.

Dr. Ruckman states (44), p 8 "*Ninety percent of the Textus Receptus manuscripts agree. The Alexandrian manuscripts not only disagree with these but have very little agreement between themselves: in many cases less than fifty percent*".

Para 2 states: "***The measure of agreement between (the Received Text, the Westcott and Hort text and the United Bible Societies text) . . . is as much as 97%. The real issue for the translator is which of the variants for the 3% of disputed text he should follow***".

A concerned layman, J. Coad of Totnes, Devon makes some penetrating observations (10) about the 97%-3% thesis, as it applies to the AV1611 and the NIV, which our critic has failed to appreciate:

> "*Is it true that there is only a 3% difference, as Bob Sheehan claims? Yes! It is true. And that 3% makes all the difference! It is "the jam in the sandwich!" It means, for certain, that 17 complete verses belong to the New Testament, as in the Received Text (AV) or otherwise they don't, as in the NIV. It means, again, the 147 part verses missing from the NIV should be missing – or they should not be missing. It means that a certain 169 names of Our Lord God, retained in the AV are correct, or that they should be omitted, as in the NIV! It means that the words* "**The Son of Man is come to save that which was lost**" *was either spoken by the Saviour Himself, as*

*recorded in the AV (Matt. 18:11) or otherwise were not spoken by
Him, as is missing in the NIV!*

*"Yet wait . . . consider these NIV 3% short measures. They are not
short measures of any secular book out of Egypt. They are part of
the sacred measures of the* "**shekel of the Sanctuary**"*! . . . we
demand full measure after* "**the Shekel of the Sanctuary**"*! A 97%
salvation is no salvation, and a 97% Bible is not God's Book. It has
no place in the Sanctuary!"*

Our critic slights Dr. Fuller's book in para 3 but gives no indication of
even having read it, let alone being able to refute it. One should note the
shift in para 3 which states that no variant affects the *"total message"* of
the Bible. This is less reassuring than *"no threat to basic doctrines"* in
para 1 and is similar to the statement in the preface to the RSV, 1952 that
*"The Bible carries its full message . . . to those who read it that they may
discern and understand God's Word".* The RSV attacked the virgin birth
of the Lord Jesus Christ in Isaiah 7:14, completely omitted Mark 16:9–20
from its text and demoted the Lord Jesus Christ to "a son of God" in
Matthew 27:54. The NIV continues to dispute Mark 16:9–20 and retains
the RSV reading for Matthew 27:54 in its margin. See Chapters 1 and 6.

Dr. Ruckman (4), p 36 warns *"We are dealing with committees who
announce publicly that the "word of God" is NOT the Bible, but some
message you are supposed to get THROUGH THE BIBLE".*

Similar remarks apply to the assertion of F.F. Bruce, given in para 8,
that *"even . . . the most incompetent . . . translation of the most uncritical
edition of the Hebrew or Greek . . . cannot effectively obscure the real
message of the Bible or neutralize its saving power".*

Is the *"real message of the Bible"* the pure word of God? If so, why
not call it that? If not, what is it and where is it FOR TODAY? Neither
F.F. Bruce nor our critic are prepared to say so. As for the *"saving power"*
of *"the most incompetent translation . . . "*, our critic blithely dismissed
the content of Figures 3 and 4, without refuting ANY of it.

Para 4 states *"The fact is that theologically the NT is the same in all
the manuscripts and in all the versions".* This sentence really summarises
the remainder of this section. The statement itself is very similar to that
of Dr. Custer (44), p 9, who says: *"The important thing to note is that
each of these four types of texts is theologically conservative".*

Chapter 1 lists the so-called *"text types"*. Dr. Ruckman has this reply.
*"Not according to Zane Hodges, Donald Waite, Otis Fuller, Burgon,
Miller, Scrivener, Edward Hills, Wilkinson, Pickering or Hoskier. Custer*

just gave you his own personal, unscholarly opinion and expected you to think he was talking about FACTS. He dreams up his "facts". He expected you to accept that statement above without questioning it. We say he is a DECEIVED FOOL and we will document WHY we say that".

Also matching the statement from para 4, Dr. Custer (44) says *"Not one of these texts can be called heretical or apostate as Mr. Ruckman alleges"*, to which Dr. Ruckman replies:

"Flim-flam. ACCORDING TO TWO DOZEN BIBLE-BELIEVING CONSERVATIVES, Custer is an uneducated fool. Any knowledgeable person who has investigated the hundreds of pages of documented evidence on the Alexandrian manuscripts (patterns, family, pattern of texts, "niceties", idiomatic expressions, wording, etc.) knows of the HERETICAL and HETERODOX nature of those manuscripts (we will document)."

Chapter 1, Section 1.6 summarises the corrupt nature of the major Alexandrian manuscripts behind the NIV and most modern versions. See also Chapter 6 for Dean Burgon's comments. Our critic ignored this information.

Before citing Dr. Ruckman's evidence, it will be helpful to consider the credentials of some of the men he mentioned.

Zane C. Hodges: A.B. Th.M., Assistant Professor of New Testament Literature and Exegesis, Dallas Theological Seminary (2) Acknowledgements. Professor Hodges is co-author of the recent book *The NIV Reconsidered*, which highlights many of the defects of the NIV, with respect to doctrinal errors, misleading translation of important prophetical passages and poor style.

John Burgon: See Chapter 6, Section 6.2.

Edward F. Hills: A.B., (Yale and Westminster Theological Seminary (5)), Th.M., Columbia Seminary (5), Th.D., Harvard (2) Acknowledgements.

Herman C. Hoskier, understudy of Burgon and author of *Codex B and Its Allies – A Study and an Indictment*, described by Dr. Fuller as *"a vast amount of convincing documentary evidence in a volume of nearly 500 pages demonstrating the unreliability of the group of manuscripts headed by The Codex Vaticanus and Codex Sinaiticus"* (2), p 134.

Wilbur Pickering (12), p 467 is the author of *The Identity of the New Testament Text*, holds a Th.M in Greek Exegesis from Dallas Theological Seminary and an M.A. and Ph.D. in linguistics from the University of Toronto.

Dr. Frederick H.A. Scrivener, author of four editions of the

Introduction to the Criticism of the New Testament and the *Authorised Edition of the English Bible*, described by Dr. Hills as a *"definitive history of the King James Version"* (5), p 117, 217. Dr. Scrivener catalogued almost 3000 New Testament manuscripts.

Benjamin G. Wilkinson, Ph.D., author of *Our Authorised Bible Vindicated*, with copyrights in both England and the USA, described by Dr. Fuller as *"a scholar of the first rank with a thorough knowledge of the subjects about which he wrote"* (2) p 174.

Would our critic consider these men to be "*scholarly*"? If not, why not?

Of Dr. Fuller himself, Dr. Ruckman wrote in the Bible Believers' Bulletin, May 1990 an article entitled *Ich Hatte Eine Kameraden, I Had a Comrade*: "*February 21, 1989, David Otis Fuller died . . . this comrade was a graduate of Wheaton College and Princeton Theological Seminary, who had an honorary Doctor of Divinity degree from Dallas Theological Seminary . . . although at times he had his doubts about some of the wording in the King James Bible, he would not correct it and did not correct it and believed it until the day he died. Bible believers lost a real comrade when they lost David Otis Fuller*".

I can testify to this. Dr. Fuller sent me this word of encouragement in a letter dated 25th September 1985. "*so many Christians are being blinded in the glare of scholarship . . . Satan hates the KJV and he will raise unshirted hell to try and deceive Christians . . . NO OTHER VERSION HAS EVER TRIGGERED A MIGHTY REVIVAL OR EVEN A SMALL ONE*".

Our critic is unable to allude to ANY revival stemming from a modern version. So much for their "*saving power*".

Dr. Ruckman cites the findings of Dr. Hills (5), pp 135–137, (38), pp 76–78.

> "*(a) Heretical Readings in Codex Aleph*
>
> '*some of the scribes who copied some of the ancient manuscripts were heretics, probably Gnostics, who altered the texts that they were copying rather freely in order to tone down the teaching of the New Testament Scriptures concerning Christ's deity. One of the manuscripts in which this heretical tendency shows itself most strongly is Codex Aleph . . . The following Aleph readings seem beyond all doubt heretical.*

Mark 1:1   "the Son of God", is omitted by Aleph, Theta, 28, 255 . . . Westcott and Hort.

Luke 23:42   according to . . . P75, Aleph, B, C, L and the Sahidic, the thief said, "Jesus, remember me when thou comest in thy kingdom" . . . this prayer has been tampered with by the docetists who believed that the divine "Christ" returned to heaven just before the crucifixion.

John 1:34   Instead of "son of God", Aleph, P4, 77, 218, two Old Latin manuscripts, the Old Syriac version . . . read "God's Chosen One".

John 3:13   "who is in heaven" is omitted by Aleph, P66, P75, B, L, the Diatessaron, Westcott and Hort".

John 6:69   Instead of "the Christ, the Son of the living God", Aleph, P75, B, C, D, L, W, Westcott and Hort . . . read "the Holy One of God".

John 9:35   Instead of "son of God", Aleph, P66, P75, B, W, . . . Westcott and Hort read, "son of Man".

John 9:38–39   "And he said, Lord, I believe. And he worshipped Him. And Jesus said" are omitted by Aleph, P75, W, Old Latin manuscripts b, l.

Roman 14:10   Aleph, B, D2 . . . (substitute) "judgment seat of God" for "judgment seat of Christ". It is difficult to believe that this substitution was not also made by heretics".

Dr. Hills includes John 1:18 and 1 Timothy 3:16 in the above context. These verses will be discussed when our critic's manuscript 'evidence' is considered.

"Here we have (ten) readings which either deny the deity of Christ or in some way detract from it. All (ten) of them are found in Aleph. All (ten) of them are supported by other ancient New Testament documents. (Six) of them occur in Papyrus 75 . . . The longer we ponder the evidence of these important passages, the more obvious it becomes that the texts of Papyrus 75 and of Aleph were the work of heretics who for some reason were reluctant to acknowledge Jesus to be the Son of God. And the same seems to be true of B and the other manuscripts of the Alexandrian type. Long ago Burgon and Miller pointed out this heretical trait in Aleph and B, and their observations have never been refuted."

Our critic has not refuted their observations either, in spite of his endorsement of the NIV. Note that the NIV New Testament, which claims

Aleph and B are the "*most reliable early manuscripts*" p 70, 127 retains 7 of the 10 heretical readings. Chapter 7, Sections 7.3 to 7.6 consider 6 of these readings.

Moreover, he has expressed a high regard for the Bodmer Papyri. Yet Dr. Hills has documented more heretical readings in these (38), p 77:

> "*Traces of Gnosticism seem clearly discernible in Papyrus Bodmer III . . . E. Massaux (1959) points out the following instances of the false intellectualism which characterised the Gnostics, namely, their preoccupation with the notion of truth and the substitution of truth for righteousness.*

John 5:33   "and he testified to you through the truth", instead of, "and he testified to the truth".

John 8:34   "Whosoever does not do the truth is a servant of sin," instead of, "Whosoever does sin is a servant of sin".

John 16:8   "He will convict the world because of sin, because of truth, and because of judgment," instead of, "He will convict the world concerning sin, concerning righteousness, and concerning judgment".

John 16:10 "because of truth", instead of, "concerning righteousness".

John 18:37 "that I should bear witness through the truth," instead of, "that I should bear witness to the truth".

> "*In John 7:52 also Papyrus Bodmer III reads* "search and see that the Christ or the Prophet shall not arise out of Galilee." *Papyrus 66 reads* "the Prophet". *All the other New Testament documents read* "a prophet" *. . . This insistence on 'the' prophet could again indicate a contact with Gnosticism. In short, the texts of all the Bodmer Papyri give evidences of having been tampered with, partly by heretics. Hence one wonders why certain scholars say that these Bodmer Papyri "support" the texts of B and Aleph. One might better say that these papyri drag the closely related B and Aleph texts down. Since the papyri are heretical and error ridden, B and Aleph must be heretical and error ridden too.*"

Dr. Hills states under the heading *Errors in the Bodmer Papyri* p 48–49:

> "*In Papyrus 66 we find instances of this tendency of the Alexandrian scribes continually to tamper with the New Testament text . . . the number of corrections in this manuscript is unusually large, totalling 269. At least 35 of them are of significance to textual critics, and these have been listed by Klijn (1957). Most of these*

*corrections are from the Western reading to the Alexandrian
reading, but some are the other way round, and in several either the
original reading or the correction is of the Traditional type.
Certainly these corrections give the impression that the Alexandrian
scribes worked haphazardly rather than methodically.*

*"There are serious errors also in Papyrus 66. For example, in John
19:5 Papyrus 66 omits the following famous sentence,* "And he saith
unto them, Behold the Man". *Four Old Latin manuscripts and one
Coptic manuscript also omit this reading. This omission seems to be
a mutilation of the sacred text at the hands of heretics, probably
Gnostics. They seem to have disliked the idea that Christ, whom they
regarded as exclusively a heavenly being, actually became a man
and was crucified.*

*"Likewise, the ending of Papyrus 66 constitutes a problem for
students of the New Testament text. This manuscript has preserved
the last chapter of John's Gospel in only a few fragments, the last of
which ends at John 21:9. In John 21:6, however, Papyrus 66 adds
the following words to the text:* "and they said, we have toiled the
whole night through and have taken nothing, but in thy name we
will cast (the nets)". *This addition to the text is found in Aleph as a
correction, in Cyril, in the Ethiopic versions, and in certain Old
Latin manuscripts. It is obviously a harmonisation taken from Luke
5:5 . . . the fact that Papyrus 66 contains such an error cannot fail to
diminish our confidence in the general trustworthiness of this
ancient document.*

*"Papyrus 75 also has its share of false readings. For example, in the
parable of the rich man and Lazarus . . . Papyrus 75 says that the
rich man's name was Neves . . . this reading was taken into the
Neutral text of Papyrus 75 from the Sahidic version. And if the
Neutral text of Papyrus 75 was influenced by the Sahidic version in
this passage, why not in many other passages also? Hoskier (1914)
accused the Neutral text of B* "of being tremendously influenced" *by
the Sahidic version and the evidence of Papyrus 75 seems to
indicate that he was at least partly right. For the text of Papyrus 75
was undoubtedly the ancestor of the text of B."* (Note that our critic
agrees with Dr. Hills on this point, para 10 of the next sub section.
However, Dr. Hills reveals the true nature of B's alignment with
P75.)

"Another Sahidic reading that found its way into the text of Papyrus 75 occurs in John 8:57. Here the majority of the New Testament documents read "Hast thou seen Abraham?" *But Papyrus 75, Aleph, T, Sahidic....* "Hath Abraham seen thee?"

"In John 10:7 Papyrus 75 agrees with the Sahidic version in reading, "I am the shepherd of the sheep", *instead of,* "I am the door of the sheep".

"In John 11:12 Papyrus 75 agrees with the Sahidic version against all the rest of the New Testament documents. In the other documents the disciples say . . . "Lord, if he hath fallen asleep, he will be saved," *Papyrus 75 and the Sahidic version, however, read,* "he will be raised"."

Our critic insists that *"those who favour the Byzantine family do not discuss seriously the implications of a papyrus like 75"*. On the contrary, it is the opponents of the Byzantine Text who do not discuss the contents of the papyri and Dr. Hills has shown why.

9.3 "THE BASIC ISSUES CONCERNING THE TEXT" – "OLDEST IS BEST"

Para 1 states that *"There is no unambiguous evidence that the Byzantine text type was known before the middle of the 4th century"*. This assertion is qualified by a second in para 2. *"Though there are readings in the Byzantine text type found in the Ante Nicene period almost all of them are found in the other text types . . . the other three textual traditions – Western, Caesarean and Alexandrian undoubtedly stretch far back into the Ante Nicene period"*.

Just in case evidence should be produced to the contrary, our critic is careful to add *"even if the Byzantine text were proved to be Ante Nicene that would not prove its superiority"*. His 'proof' for the inferiority of the Byzantine text consists of the bald statement in para 4 that *"The fact that most extant mss. attest this text type proves nothing . . . in assessing (a) reading manuscripts are weighed not counted – in other words quality is of far more importance than quantity"*.

He continues in para 7 with *"The Byzantine text type is seen to be a demonstrably secondary text . . . by the presence of harmonization and conflation"* and in para 9 with *"The Alexandrian text type has better credentials than any other now available"*.

He has not given any indication of how the *"quality"* of a manuscript or the *"credentials"* of a text are to be judged, apart from age. The information given in Chapter 6, Section 6.2 on Burgon's 7 *"tests of truth"* is ignored, as is the evidence cited for the corrupt nature of Aleph and B. See Chapter 1, Section 1.6. Also, his knowledge of the contents of the papyri and of the Alexandrian mss. as a whole, appears lamentably deficient compared to that of Dr. Hills.

He has also ignored the painstaking research of Burgon, who utterly refuted the *"recension"* theory of Hort, Chapter 6, Section 6.2, which is the basis for the supposed *"harmonisation"* and *"conflation"* of the Byzantine Text by which it is deemed *"demonstrably secondary"*. Our critic has provided no such *"demonstration"* at all.

All he has demonstrated so far is a marked tendency to avoid facts, distort facts and contradict facts.

Further to the alleged inferiority of the Byzantine Text, Hodges states (2), p 32–34,37:

> *"The view popularised by Westcott and Hort before the turn of the century, that the Majority text issued from an authoritative, ecclesiastical revision of the Greek text, is widely abandoned as no longer tenable. Yet it was this view of the Majority text which was largely responsible for relegating it to a secondary status in the eyes of textual critics generally . . .*
>
> *"Some critics now wish to posit the idea of a "process" drawn out over a long period of time . . . (but) the Majority text . . . is relatively uniform in its general character with comparatively low amounts of variation between its major representatives"*. (Hodges notes here that although *"individual members of the Majority text show varying amounts of conformity to it . . . the nearness of its representatives to the general standard is not hard to demonstrate in most cases . . . in a study of 100 places of variation in John 11, the representatives of the Majority text used in the study showed a range of agreement from around 70% to 93% . . . the uncial codex Omega's 93% agreement with the Textus Receptus compares well with the 92% agreement found between P75 and B."* (Note the comments in Section 9.2 by Dr. Hills on P75 as *"undoubtedly the ancestor . . . of B"*.) *"Omega's affinity with the TR is more nearly typical of the pattern one would find in the great mass of minuscule texts. High levels of agreement of this kind are (as in the case of P75 and B) the result of a shared ancestral base . . . the Byzantine manuscripts*

together form . . . a rather closely knit group, and the variations in question within this entire large group are relatively minor in character".)

Brake, (18) p 211, wrote his thesis for Master of Theology at Dallas Theological Seminary on *The Doctrine of the Preservation of the Scriptures.* He states *"Although there are variants within the Textus Receptus these are extremely few and often trivial, which demonstrates the highly stable character of the manuscript tradition."* Hodges continues, ibid.

"No one has yet explained how a long, slow process spread out over many centuries as well as over a wide geographical area, and involving a multitude of copyists, who often knew nothing of the state of the text outside of their own monasteries or scriptoria, could achieve this widespread uniformity out of the diversity presented by the earlier forms of text. Even an official edition of the New Testament . . . would have great difficulty achieving this result as the history of Jerome's Vulgate demonstrates."

Here Hodges notes *"the more than 8000 Vulgate manuscripts which are extant today exhibit the greatest amount of cross contamination of textual types".* He continues.

"But an unguided process achieving relative stability and uniformity in the diversified textual, historical, and cultural circumstances in which the New Testament was copied, imposes impossible strains on our imagination.

"Herein lies the greatest weakness of contemporary textual criticism. Denying to the Majority text any claim to represent the actual form of the original text, it is nevertheless unable to explain its rise, its comparative uniformity, and its dominance in any satisfactory manner. All these factors can be rationally accounted for, however, if the Majority text represents simply the continuous transmission of the original text from the very first. All minority text forms are, on this view, merely divergent offshoots of the broad stream of transmission whose source is the autographs themselves . . . "

The analogy of textual transmission as a flowing stream is described by Grady (45), p 60–61, citing the work of Pickering and Scrivener to refute the notion that the oldest texts are automatically the best.

"The "oldest is best" advocate will often resort to the analogy of a flowing stream. This line of reasoning assumes . . . that the closer one gets to the stream's source, the purer the water MUST be . . . Pickering throws in the proverbial monkey wrench:

"This is normally true, no doubt, but what if a sewer pipe empties into the stream a few yards below the spring? Then the process is reversed – as the polluted water is exposed to the purifying action of the sun and ground, THE FARTHER IT RUNS THE PURER IT BECOMES (unless it passes more pipes). That is what happened to the stream of the New Testament transmission. Very near to the source, by 100 A.D. at least, THE POLLUTION STARTED GUSHING INTO THE PURE STREAM".

Grady continues *"the available manuscript evidence supports this conclusion by exhibiting both an excessive corruption in the earliest manuscripts and an exceptional coherence in the latter. While Colwell affirms, "The overwhelming majority of readings were created before the year 200," Scrivener summarises his research as follows:*

"It is no less true to fact than paradoxical in sound, that the worst corruptions to which the New Testament has ever been subjected, originated within a hundred years after it was composed; that Irenaeus and the African Fathers and the whole Western, with a portion of the Syrian Church, used far inferior manuscripts to those employed by Stucia, or Erasmus, or Stephen thirteen centuries later, when moulding the Textus Receptus"."

Our critic supposes that the Alexandrian text has "***better credentials***" than any other and is of superior "***quality***", to be "***weighed not counted***" and of which B and Aleph "***are not the only exemplars***", paras 4, 9. However, Pickering (3), p 265 states:

""Witnesses are to be weighed and not counted" is an axiom to those who work within Hort's framework. The fallacies . . . are basic and need to be considered closely. How are witnesses to be weighed? This weighing has been done by Hort, etc. on the basis of SUBJECTIVE CONSIDERATIONS . . . " He adds the observation of Burgon:

"In the very form of the maxim, – 'NOT to be counted BUT to be weighed,' – the undeniable fact is overlooked that "number" is the most ordinary ingredient of weight and indeed, even in matters of human testimony, is an element which cannot be cast away."

Pickering (3), p 269 continues *"The great majority of pastors . . .
speak confidently of the "best manuscripts," repeating uncritically
what they were taught. Upon inquiry, the enumeration of the "best"
often gets no further than codices B and Aleph – even if the list is
longer, these two usually head it. Yet it is generally recognised that
this small handful of "best" witnesses represents but one area.*

*"When the textual critic looks more closely at his oldest
manuscript materials, the paucity of his resources is more fully
realised. All the earliest witnesses, papyrus or parchment, come
from Egypt alone. Manuscripts produced in Egypt, ranging between
the third and fifth centuries, provide only a half – dozen extensive
witnesses (the Beatty Papyri, and the well-known uncials, Vaticanus
(B), Sinaiticus (Aleph), Alexandrinus (A), Ephraem Syrus (C), and
Freer Washington (W))."*

Codex W is thought to be either a 4th or 5th century document.
Pickering has therefore cited W instead of D, which is of the 5th or 6th
century, (1) p 315, (13) p 11 and *"the only real Greek representative of
the "Western" text"* (23) p 142. W was discovered in 1906, (5) p 170,
nearly 20 years after Burgon's death and therefore not listed by him
amongst the oldest uncials.

Attention has already been drawn to the importance of the Fathers and
Versions which testify to the nature of the text in other parts of the world
AT A TIME CONTEMPORARY WITH AND PRIOR TO that of the
"best manuscripts". (On p 265–269 Pickering states, citing Burgon,
*"Taking the year 400 A.D. as an arbitrary cut-off point, "ANTIQUITY"
WOULD INCLUDE OVER SEVENTY FATHERS, Codices Aleph and B,
the early papyri, and the earliest versions.) BY AND LARGE THEY (the
fathers and the versions) DISAGREE WITH EGYPT."*

On the *"quality"* of the older manuscripts, Pickering, p 270, cites
Burgon:

*"The five Old Uncials' (Aleph A B C D) falsify the Lord's Prayer as
given by St. Luke in no less than forty-five words. But so little do
they agree among themselves, that they throw themselves into six
different combinations in their departures from the Traditional Text;
and yet they are never able to agree among themselves as to one
single various reading: while only once are more than two of them
observed to stand together, and their grand point of union is no less
than an omission of an article. Such is their eccentric tendency, that*

in respect of thirty-two out of the whole forty-five words they bear in turn solitary evidence."

Mark 2:1–12 is another example:

"In the course of those 12 verses . . . there will be found to be 60 variations of reading . . . Now, in the present instance, the 'five old uncials' CANNOT BE the depositories of a tradition, – whether Western or Eastern, – because they render inconsistent testimony IN EVERY VERSE. It must further be admitted, (for this is really not a question of opinion, but a plain matter of fact,) that it is unreasonable to place confidence in such documents. What would be the thought in a Court of Law of five witnesses, called up 47 times for examination, who should be observed to bear contradictory testimony EVERY TIME?"

Dr. Ruckman (44), p 29 cites Pickering and Hoskier: *"There are more disagreements within the Alexandrian family of manuscripts in four Gospels than there are in all the published editions of twenty-seven Receptus New Testament books as found in Beza, Colinaeus, Erasmus, Elzevir and Stephanus". He continues "Custer (says) "There is not a single manuscript of the Byzantine text that AGREES COMPLETELY with any one of these editions" . . . Why, sonny boy, there is not one single manuscript in the Alexandrian family that even agrees with any one of TWENTY ALEXANDRIAN MANUSCRIPTS in the SAME FAMILY!"* Pickering (12) p 476 states that *"We are not judging between two text forms, one representing 80% of the MSS. and the other 20%. Rather, we have to judge between 80–90% and a fraction of 1%."*

Our critical cleric regards as an ***"insoluble problem"*** the fact that ***"no two mss. in the Byzantine or T.R. tradition agree perfectly."*** He therefore maintains that ***"this tradition is not better off than any other"***. Dr. Hills (38) p 196 compares *"the printed Textus Receptus to the Traditional New Testament text found in the majority of the Greek New Testament manuscripts."*

"These two texts are virtually identical. Kirsopp Lake and his associates (1928) demonstrated this fact . . . they came to the conclusion that in the 11th chapter of Mark "the most popular text in the manuscripts of the tenth to the fourteenth century" differed from the Textus Receptus only four times. This small number of differences seems almost negligible in . . . that in this same chapter

Aleph, B and D differ from the Textus Receptus 69, 71, and 95 times
respectively . . . in this same chapter B differs from Aleph 34 times
and from D 102 times and . . . Aleph differs from D 100 times". Dr.
Hills states further (5) p126–128:

"Luke 10:41–42	"Few things are needful or one" B Aleph WH. This Alexandrian alteration makes Jesus talk about food rather than spiritual realities.
Luke 12:31	"seek ye the kingdom" P 75, "seek ye His kingdom" B Aleph WH. ("God" has been omitted.)
Luke 23:45	P75, Aleph B C L Coptic WH read "the sun having been eclipsed." This rationalistic explanation . . . is impossible, because at Passover time the moon was full.
John 10:29	"That which My Father hath given unto Me is greater than all" B Aleph, WH. This alteration is of great doctrinal importance, since it makes the preservation of the saints depend on the Church rather than on God."

Hodges concludes his evaluation of the Majority text (2) p 37: *"The*
manuscript tradition of an ancient book will, under any but the most
exceptional circumstances, multiply in a reasonably regular fashion
with the result that the copies nearest the autograph will normally
have the largest number of descendants. The further removed from
the history of transmission a text becomes from its source the less
time it has to leave behind a large family of offspring. Hence, in a
large tradition where a pronounced unity is observed between . . .
eighty percent of the evidence, a very strong presumption is raised
that this numerical preponderance is due to direct derivation from
the very oldest sources. In the absence of any convincing contrary
explanation, this presumption is raised to a very high level of
probability indeed. Thus the Majority text, upon which the King
James Version is based, has in reality the strongest claim possible to
be regarded as an authentic representation of the original text. This
claim is quite independent of any shifting consensus of scholarly
judgment about its readings and is based on the objective reality of
its dominance in the transmissional history of the New Testament
text. This dominance has not and – we venture to suggest – cannot
be otherwise explained."

9.4 "THE BASIC ISSUES CONCERNING THE TEXT" – "RECENSIONS" AND "FAMILIES"

Our critic subscribes to the *"recension"* theory of Westcott and Hort. See Chapter 6. Hills (5), p 175, states *"Westcott and Hort found proof for their position that the Traditional Text was a "work of attempted criticism performed deliberately by editors and not merely by scribes" in eight passages in the Gospels in which the Western text contains one half of the reading found in the Traditional Text and the Alexandrian text in the other half. These passages are Mark 6:33, 8:26, 9:38, 9:49, Luke 9:10, 11:54, 12:18, 24:53 . . . Dean Burgon immediately registered one telling criticism of this hypothesis of conflation in the Traditional Text . . . "Their theory has at last forced them to make an appeal to Scripture and to produce some actual specimens of their meaning. After ransacking the Gospels for 30 years, they have at last fastened upon EIGHT."*

Hills reinforces the point: *"If the Traditional Text was created by 4th-century Antiochan editors . . . surely more examples of such conflation ought to be discoverable in the Gospels than just Hort's EIGHT."*

Burgon's analysis continues (3) p 192: *"Drs. Westcott and Hort require us to believe that the authors of the (imaginary) Syrian Revisions of A.D. 250 and A.D. 350, interpolated the genuine text of the Gospels with between 2877 (B) and 3455 (Aleph) spurious words; mutilated the genuine text in respect of between 536 (B) and 839 (Aleph) words, substituted for as many genuine words, between 935 (B) and 1114 (Aleph) uninspired words, licentiously transposed between 2098 (B) and 2299 (Aleph); and in respect to number, case, mood, tense, person, etc., altered without authority between 1132 (B) and 1265 (Aleph) words . . . "The illustrious professor invites us to believe that the mistaken textual judgment pronounced at Antioch in A.D. 350 had an immediate effect on the text of Scripture throughout the world. We are requested to suppose that it resulted in the instantaneous extinction of codices like B Aleph, wherever found; and caused codices of the A type to spring up like mushrooms in their place, and that, in every library of ancient Christendom . . . We read and marvel!"*

Therefore, despite our critic's unsubstantiated opinions, the Majority or Byzantine Text is NOT secondary, NOR is it the result of any "*recension*". Its variations are "*extremely few and often trivial*", certainly compared to those of the minority manuscripts. Moreover, as Professor Hodges explains in considerable detail, the NUMBER of manuscripts is of GREAT significance when assessing the form of the original text.

What of the so-called "*text types*" or "*families*" of manuscripts, in which our learned pastor has such great confidence? Dr. Ruckman states (4) p 89–91: "*Griesbach (1796) hit upon the novel idea of dividing the manuscripts into three families – Western, Syrian and Alexandrian*". Dr. Ruckman notes "*some make a fourth family "Caesarean," which of course, is the corruptions of Origen and Eusebius (both at Caesarea), inserted into the correct text of the N.T.*

> "*Having done this, [Griesbach] assigned ALL THE EARLY MANUSCRIPTS TO THE ALEXANDRIAN FAMILY (!), leaving the Syrian text standing like a cold cat in the snow, with nothing but LATE MANUSCRIPTS TO SUPPORT IT . . . From the "family" idea, W&H (1884) agreed with Griesbach (1796) that "B" was a "remarkably pure text" . . . "When this was done, the arguments in the Seminaries . . . no longer revolved around the Syrian text at all, but were continually revolving around Western, or Alexandrian authority. Clark (1926) said that the Western type was first and the Alexandrian scholars copied it, omitting some of the Western readings. Ropes (1926) said that the Alexandrian type was first, and that the Western copied it, and ADDED to it . . . " There is a third theory, propounded in 1881 by* Dean *Burgon . . . which matches ALL THE FACTS OF HISTORY, ALL THE EVIDENCE OF THE PAPYRUS, ALL THE EVIDENCE FOUND IN THE UNCIALS, AND ALL THE EVIDENCES OF SOUL WINNING AND REVIVAL, AND ALL THE EVIDENCES OF COMMON SENSE AND REASON, THAT THE SYRIAN TEXT WAS FIRST, AND THE ALEXANDRIAN SCRIBES SUBTRACTED FROM IT (ASV, RSV) AND THE ROMAN SCRIBES ADDED TO IT (VULGATE, DOUAY-RHEIMS). This theory, supported by Scrivener, Miller, and Hills, tallies perfectly with EVERYTHING.*"

Dr. Ruckman therefore (44), p 8, 21, concludes that the "*Family Classification*" is a HOAX.

Our critic does not show otherwise.

Pickering (3), p 225 ff states: "*Hort's mistaken perspective led him to bring over into the textual criticism of the N.T. the family-tree method, or*

*genealogy, as developed by students of the classics . . . (Burgon)
concludes:*

> *"High time however is it to declare that . . . all this talk about
> 'Genealogical evidence', when applied to manuscripts, is –
> MOONSHINE. The expression is metaphorical, and assumes that it
> has fared with mss. as it fares with the successive generations of a
> family; and so, to a remarkable extent, no doubt, it HAS. But then, it
> happens, unfortunately, that we are unacquainted with ONE
> SINGLE INSTANCE of a known ms. copied from another known ms.
> And perforce all talk about 'Genealogical evidence,' where NO
> SINGLE STEP IN THE DESCENT can be produced, – in other
> words, WHERE NO GENEALOGICAL EVIDENCE EXISTS, – is
> absurd."*

Pickering continues, p 227

> *"Recent scholarship has agreed with Burgon. Colwell's treatment of
> the subject is very thorough."*
> *"As the justification of their rejection of the majority Westcott and
> Hort found the possibilities of genealogical method invaluable . . .
> That Westcott and Hort did not apply this method to the manuscripts
> of the New Testament is obvious. Where are the charts which start
> with the majority of late manuscripts and climb back through
> diminishing generations of ancestors to the Neutral and Eastern
> texts? The answer is that they are nowhere . . . Note, for example,
> the diagrams and discussions in Kenyon's most popular work on
> textual criticism . . . All the manuscripts referred to are imaginary
> manuscripts."*

Pickering adds, p 228–229, that Westcott and Hort, like our critic,
"nevertheless championed the genealogical method."

> *"Hort felt that the genealogical method enabled him to reduce the
> mass of manuscript testimony to four voices – "Neutral,"
> "Alexandrian," "Western", and "Syrian". Though such
> classifications have been generally "recognised" since Hort's day,
> they have never been demonstrated to be valid. The Papyri have
> obliged recent scholarship to reconsider them and have increasingly
> vindicated Burgon's remonstrance. M.M Parvis complains:*
> > *"We have reconstructed text-types and families and sub-families
> > and in doing so have created things that never before existed on
> > earth or in heaven . . . "*

> *"Allen Wikgren shows that sweeping generalizations about text-types in general, and the "Byzantine" text and lectionaries in particular, should no longer be made. Colwell affirms:*
> *"The major mistake is made in thinking of the "old text-types" as frozen blocks, even after admitting that no one manuscript is a perfect witness to any text-type. IF no one ms. is a perfect witness to any type, then all witnesses are mixed in ancestry . . . ""*

Our critic notes that all so-called text-types exhibit variations, para 11 but still maintains that the family classification method is valid. Pickering continues:

> *"Burgon, the only man, living or dead, who ever personally collated all five of the old uncials (Aleph, A, B, C, D) throughout the Gospels, asserted that it is actually easier to find two consecutive verses in which B and Aleph differ from each other than two consecutive verses in which they entirely agree."* Pickering also shows that, although the Byzantine manuscripts overwhelmingly bear witness to the Traditional TEXT, see above, the manuscripts themselves cannot be grouped as a *"family"*. Fuller (2), p 264, states *"It would be difficult to find even two "identical" manuscripts."*

Of the Papyri as a group, Pickering quotes Aland:

> *"It is impossible to fit the papyri, from the time prior to the fourth century, into these two text-types (Alexandrian and Byzantine) . . . the simple fact that all these papyri, with their various distinctive characteristics, did exist side by side, in the same ecclesiastical province, that is, in Egypt, where they were found, is the best argument against the existence of any text types . . . including the Alexandrian and the Antiochan . . . the increase of the documentary evidence and the entirely new areas of research which were opened to us on the discovery of the papyri, mean the end of Westcott and Hort's conception"."*

The upshot of this highly technical material is that Westcott and Hort were wrong to try to drown out the Traditional Text on the basis of *"families"* and *"text-types"*. So is our critic.

Pickering (3), p 264ff gives a detailed discussion on Burgon's 7 *"Notes of Truth"* and cites Burgon on *"Variety of evidence, or catholicity"*, p 267–268:

> *"The combined testimony of the Uncials and of the whole body of*

the Cursive Copies (shows) They are (a) dotted over at least 1000
years; (b) they evidently belong to so many divers countries, –
Greece, Constantinople, Asia Minor, Palestine, Syria, Alexandria,
and other parts of Africa, not to say Sicily, Southern Italy, Gaul,
England and Ireland: (c) they exhibit so many strange
characteristics and peculiar sympathies: (d) they so clearly
represent countless families of mss., being in no single instance
absolutely identical in their text, and certainly not being copies of
any other Codex in existence . . . The advocates of the Traditional
Text urge that the Consent without Concert of so many hundreds of
copies, executed by different persons, at diverse times, in widely
sundered regions of the church, is a proof presumptive of their
trustworthiness, which nothing can invalidate . . . "

And Pickering concludes:

'since Hort it has been customary to assert and assume that
"Genealogy" has invalidated the witness of the many. As we saw in
the previous chapter, "genealogy" HAS NOT BEEN (and probably
CANNOT BE) applied to the New Testament. As Colwell says, "It is
clear that in a field where no manuscripts have parents, where
centuries and continents separate witnesses, the genealogical
method is not of primary importance."'

Having shown that the Byzantine Text is NOT inferior to the older
manuscripts and that the family classification of manuscripts is invalid, I
return to our critic's unproven assertion that the Byzantine Text was
unknown before the 4th century.

9.5 "The Basic Issues Concerning the Text" – "The Late, Mixed, Secondary Text"

In para 3 of this sub-section, our critic states categorically that the Ante
Nicene Fathers did not cite the Byzantine Text. According to Kenyon, (3)
p 236, this was *"Hort's contention, which was the cornerstone of his*
theory" of a *"late and mixed, and therefore secondary text"*.

Pickering (3), p 237ff gives a detailed rebuttal of this blatant falsehood.
He cites the work of Miller, who examined *"Burgon's massive index of*
patristic quotations from the New Testament". Kenyon summarised
Miller's findings:

"Taking the Greek and Latin fathers who died before A.D. 400, their

quotations are found to support the Traditional Text in 2630 instances, the "neologian" in 1753". (Dr. Ruckman explains that the "Neologian text" includes both "neutral" and "Western" readings, (44) p 22. Both are supposedly earlier than the "Byzantine", the "Neutral" text being that of the Alexandrian Codex B, according to Hort (3), p 114.) Kenyon continues:

"Nor is this majority due solely to the writers who belong to the end of the period. On the contrary, if only the earliest writers be taken, from Clement of Rome to Irenaeus and Hippolytus, the majority in favour of the Traditional Text is proportionately even greater, 151 to 84. Only in the Western and Alexandrian writers do we find approximate equality of votes on either side." (Dr. Ruckman (44) p 22, cites Miller who found that "Origen sided with THE TRADITIONAL TEXT (in 200 A.D.!) 460 times while siding with the 'Neologian' text 491 times".)

"Further", says Kenyon, "if a select list of thirty important passages be taken for detailed examination, the preponderance of early patristic evidence in favour of the Traditional Text is seen to be no less than 530 to 170."

Kenyon, however, has an 'explanation' for these results. It is identical to the opinion of our critic, stated in para 2 of this sub-section: "(Of) the readings found in the Ante Nicene period almost all of them are also found in the other text types". (Note that the concept of "text types" as upheld by the opponents of the Received Text, has been shown to be invalid, so that Our critic's statement is meaningless anyway.) Kenyon's 'explanation' is as follows:

"The thirty "traditional" readings, which (Miller) shows to be so overwhelmingly vindicated by the Fathers, are not what Hort would call pure "Syrian" readings at all. In nearly every case they have Western or Neutral attestation". Kenyon lists as examples Matthew 17:21, 19:16, 23:38, Mark 16:9–20, Luke 24:40, John 21:25.

Dr. Ruckman (44) p 32, has an incisive comment: "The WESTERN FAMILY . . . conflates in John 5:37, and the ALEXANDRIAN "family" conflates in Colossians 1:12 and 2 Thessalonians 3:4. Who didn't know that the WESTERN TEXT again "conflates" neutral and Syrian readings in Matthew 4:13, John 5:37, and Acts 10:48, while VATICANUS "conflates" in Mark 1:28, Mark 1:40, and John 13:24, Revelation 6:1,2,5,7,8 and 17:14, and ALEPH "conflates" B with a BYZANTINE TEXT in 1

*Corinthians 7:34. This would make the WESTERN and
ALEXANDRIAN texts CONFLATE TEXTS DERIVED FROM THE
BYZANTINE TEXT."*

Yet our critic insists, para 10, "**the Alexandrian text shows no signs
of being recensional**". Kenyon concludes his "explanation".

*"According to Hort, the traditional text is the result of a revision in
which old elements were incorporated; and Mr. Miller merely points
to some of those old elements, and argues therefrom that the whole
is old. It is clear that by such arguments Hort's theory is
untouched."*

Pickering (3), p 239 replies:

*"It is hard to believe that Kenyon was precisely honest here. He had
obviously read Miller's work with care. Why did he not say anything
about "unto repentance" in Matt. 9:13 and Mark 2:17, or "vinegar"
in Matt. 27:34, or "from the door" in Matt. 28:2, or "the prophets"
in Mark 1:2, or "good will" in Luke 2:14, or the Lord's prayer for
His murderers in Luke 23:34, or "some honeycomb" in Luke 24:42,
or "they" in John 17:24 . . . these instances are also among "the
thirty." They would appear to be "strictly Syrian" readings, if there
really is such a thing. Why did Kenyon ignore them? The cases
Kenyon cites fell within the scope of Miller's inquiry because they
are Traditional readings, whatever other attestation they may also
have, and because the English Revisers of 1881 rejected them.
Kenyon asserted that Miller's figures "cannot be accepted as
representing in any way the true state of case," but he has not shown
us why.*

*"It is commonplace among the many who are determined to
despise the "Byzantine" text to dodge the issue, as Kenyon did
above. The postulates of Hort's theory are assumed to be true and
the evidence is interpreted on the basis of these presuppositions.
Apart from the imaginary nature of the "Alexandrian" and
"Western" texts, as strictly definable entities, their priority to the
"Byzantine" text is the very point to be proved and may not be
assumed."*

With reference to two of the early and most prominent fathers,
Pickering states (3) p 242, "*Metzger affirms: "Origen knows of the
existence of variant readings which represent each of the main
families of manuscripts that modern scholars have isolated." How*

then could Hort say, "(Origen's) quotations to the best of our belief
exhibit no clear and tangible traces of the Syrian text"?
"What about Irenaeus, does he really represent the "Western"
text? Miller found that Irenaeus sided with the Traditional Text 63
times and with the "Neologian" text 41 times."

Hills (5) p 170–172 discusses the antiquity of the Traditional Text with
respect to Origen, the early versions, the early manuscripts A and W and
the papyri. This evidence not only refutes our critic's opinion, para 1,
about the lateness of the Byzantine text, Section 9.3. It reveals the true
nature of the papyri readings, with respect to so-called "*text-types*", which
our critic avoided, although he insists that the papyri support the "*better
credentials*" of the Alexandrian text, para 6, 10 of this sub-section.

Hills says of Origen: "*The distinctive readings of the Traditional . . .
Text were known to Origen . . . in the first 14 chapters of the Gospel
of John (that is, in the area covered by Papyrus 66 and Papyrus 75)
out of 52 instances in which the Traditional Text stands alone
Origen agrees with the Traditional Text 20 times and disagrees with
it 32 times. These results make the position of the critics that Origen
knew nothing of the Traditional Text difficult indeed to maintain . . .*
*"It is argued that these Traditional readings are not really
Origen's but represent alterations made by scribes . . . The evidence
of the Bodmer papyri, however, indicates that this is not an
adequate explanation of the facts. Certainly, it seems a very
unsatisfactory way to account for the phenomena which appear in
the first 14 chapters of John. In these chapters 7 out of 20
"distinctly" Traditional readings which occur in Origen occur also
in Papyrus 66 and/or Papyrus 75. These 7 readings at least must
have been Origen's own readings . . . "*

Of the ancient versions, Hills states:

"*The Peshitta Syriac version . . . agrees closely with the Traditional
text found in the vast majority of Greek New Testament manuscripts.
Until about one hundred years ago it was almost universally
believed that the Peshitta originated in the 2nd century and hence
was one of the oldest New Testament versions. Hence because of its
agreement with the Traditional Text the Peshitta was regarded as
one of the most important witnesses to the antiquity of the
Traditional Text. In more recent times, however, naturalistic critics*

have tried to nullify this testimony . . . Burkitt (1904), for example, insisted that the Peshitta did not exist before the 5th century but "was prepared by Rabbula, bishop of Edessa (the capital city of Syria) from 411–435 A.D., and published by his authority."

"Now scholars are realising that the Peshitta must have been in existence before Rabbula's episcopate, because it was the received text of both of the two sects into which the Syrian Church became divided. Since this division took place in Rabbula's time and since Rabbula was the leader of one of these sects, it is impossible to suppose that the Peshitta was his handiwork, for if it had been produced under his auspices, his opponents would never have adopted it as their received New Testament text."

Hills says of the Sinaitic Syriac Manuscript: "Critics assign an early 3rd-century date to the text of the Sinaitic Syriac manuscript. If they are correct in this, then this manuscript is remarkable for the unexpected support which it gives to the Traditional Text. For Burkitt (1904) found that "not infrequently" this manuscript agreed with the Traditional text against the Western and Alexandrian texts."

Of the Gothic Version, Hills says: "This New Testament translation was made from the Greek into Gothic shortly after 350 A.D. by Ulfilas, missionary bishop to the Goths. "The type of text represented in it," Kenyon (1912) tells us "is for the most part that which is found in the majority of Greek manuscripts." The fact, therefore, that Ulfilas in A.D. 350 produced a Gothic version based on the Traditional Text proves that this text must have been in existence before that date."

Of Codices W and A, Hills states: "Codex W is a very ancient manuscript. B.P. Grenfell regarded it as "probably fourth century". Other scholars have dated it in the 5th century. Hence W is one of the oldest complete manuscripts of the Gospels in existence, possibly of the same age as Aleph. Moreover, W seems to have been written in Egypt, since during the first centuries of its existence, it seems to have been the property of the Monastery of the Vinedresser, which was located near the third pyramid. If the Traditional Text had been invented at Antioch in the 4th century, how would it have found its way into Egypt and thence into Codex W so soon after? Why would the scribe of W, writing in the 4th or early 5th century, have adopted this newly fabricated text in Matthew and Luke in preference to the other texts which (according to Hort's hypothesis) were older and more familiar to him? Thus the presence of the Traditional Text in

W indicates that this text is a very ancient text and that it was known in Egypt before the 4th century.

"*Another witness to the early existence of the Traditional text is Codex A . . . which dates from the 5th century . . . In Acts and the Epistles Codex A agrees most closely with the Alexandrian text of the B and Aleph type, but in the Gospels it agrees generally with the Traditional Text. Thus in the Gospels Codex A testifies to the antiquity of the Traditional Text. According to Gregory (1907) and Kenyon (1937), Codex A was probably written in Egypt. If this is so, then A is another witness to the early presence of the Traditional text upon the Egyptian scene.*"

The most important papyri (Hills (5) p116), are the Chester Beatty Papyri, including Papyrus 45 (Gospels and Acts, c. 225 A.D.), Papyrus 46 (Pauline Epistles, c. 225 A.D.), and Papyrus 47 (Revelation, c. 275 A.D.) and the Bodmer Papyri, Papyrus 66 (John, c. 200 A.D.) and Papyrus 75 (Luke and John 1–15, c. 200 A.D.).

Our critic states in para 10 of this sub-section: "***The Greek papyri of the 3rd and 2nd Centuries have a mixed Alexandrian/Western text. It is very important to notice that the Byzantine family is not found in any of the papyri.***"

Note, however, the existence of the 7 Traditional readings in Origen, cited above, which match those of P66 and/or P75. I quote from Hills (5) p 171:

"*The Evidence of the Papyri*

"*When the Chester Beatty papyri were published (1933–37), it was found that these early 3rd century fragments agree surprisingly often with the Traditional (Byzantine) Text against all other types of text. "A number of Byzantine readings," Zuntz (1953) observes, "most of them genuine, which previously were discarded as 'late', are anticipated by Pap. 46." And to this observation he adds the following significant note, "The same is true of the sister-manuscript Pap. 45; see, for example, Matt. 26:7 and Acts 17:13." And the same is true also of the Bodmer Papyri (published 1956–62). Birdsall (1960) acknowledges that "the Bodmer papyrus of John (Papyrus 66) has not a few such Byzantine readings." And Metzger (1962) lists 23 instances of the agreements of Papyri 45,46 and 66 with the Traditional (Byzantine) Text against all other text-types. And at least a dozen more such agreements occur in Papyrus 75.*"

Reviewing the above statement of Zuntz, Pickering (3) p 242ff says:

> *"(Colwell) had said of the "Byzantine New Testament", "Most of its*
> *readings existed in the second century.""* In case our critic or
> anyone else should think of Professor Colwell as 'unscholarly', Gail
> Riplinger (12) p468, writes:
> *"The late E.C. Colwell, past president of the University of*
> *Chicago and THE premier North American New Testament Greek*
> *scholar, authored scores of books, such as* Studies in Methodology
> in Textual Criticism of the New Testament. *He confesses his*
> *'change of heart' concerning the reliability of readings in the new*
> *versions (circa 1950)".* See also Pickering (3) p 224:
> *'scholars now believe that most errors were made deliberately.*
> *The majority of the variant readings in the New Testament were*
> *created for theological or dogmatic reasons. Most of the manuals*
> *and handbooks now in print (including mine!) will tell you that these*
> *variations were the fruit of careless treatment which was possible*
> *because the books of the New Testament had not yet attained a strong*
> *position as 'Bible'. The reverse is the case. It was because they were*
> *the religious treasure of the church that they were changed.""*

Colwell reveals that the basic problem in the rejection of the
Traditional Text is not a problem of scholarship. It is a HEART problem.

"The heart is deceitful above all things, and desperately wicked:
who can know it? I the LORD search the heart, I try the reins,
even to give every man according to his ways, and according to
the fruit of his doings" Jeremiah 17:9, 10.

Pickering (3) p 243 also cites Dr. Hills:

> *"E.F. Hills claims that the Beatty papyri vindicate 26 "Byzantine"*
> *readings in the Gospels, 8 in Acts and 31 in Paul's epistles. He says*
> *concerning P66: "To be precise Papyrus Bodmer II contains*
> *thirteen percent of all the alleged late readings of the Byzantine text*
> *in the area which it covers (18 out of 138). Thirteen percent of the*
> *Byzantine readings which most critics regarded as late have now*
> *been proved by Papyrus Bodmer II to be early readings."*

Pickering again cites Colwell:

> *"It may be well to repeat Colwell's statement noted above:*
> *"The Bodmer John (P66) is also a witness to the early existence of*

many of the readings found in the Alpha text-type (Hort's "Syrian").
Strangely enough to our previous ideas, the contemporary
corrections in that papyrus frequently change in Alpha-type reading
to a Beta-type reading (Hort's "Neutral"). This indicates that at this
early period readings of both kinds were known, and the Beta-type
were supplanting the Alpha-type – at least as far as this witness is
concerned.""

Pickering notes, (3) p 244, that *"there do appear to be certain*
instances where copyists altered the Fathers' wording to conform to
the "Byzantine", but such instances do not justify a widespread
generalization. The generalization is based on the presupposition
that the "Byzantine" text is late – but this is the very point to be
proved and may not be assumed."

Pickering then cites H.M. Breidenthal who *"gives the following*
results of a complete collation of B, Aleph, and the Textus Receptus
against P66 in the 615 verses where it is extant. "The total number
of variants from P66 for the manuscripts in increasing progression
are, B with 589, Textus Receptus with 695, and Aleph with 864."
P66 is closer to the Textus Receptus than to the average of B and
Aleph. Collating P66, Aleph, A, B, D with the Textus Receptus
against P45 (Kenyon's edition) in the 76 verses where all are extant,
Breidenthal found the order based on number of variants in
increasing progression to be – the T.R., B, Aleph, A, P66, D. In this
small area P45 is closer to the T.R. than to B, Aleph, etc. All of this
places quite a strain upon the view that the "Byzantine" text is late."

Of the papyri, Grady (45) p 27–28, notes *"these overrated*
"ancient authorities" actually owe their unnatural survival to a
continuous abandonment by God's people . . . Notice the conflict
between two of the oldest and most revered of the papyrus
manuscripts in existence – the Chester Beatty (P45, P46) and the
Bodmer papyri (P66, P75). Dated from approximately 200 A.D.,
they have about seventy verses in common. In just this brief stretch
alone, they are found to differ with one another over seventy-three
times, not including simple copyists' mistakes. Predictably, such
demonstrable logic and evidence is ignored by the desperate
Nicolaitanes."

A "**Nicolaitan**", Revelation 2:6, 15, according to Grady, p 8, is a
"*cleric*" who aims "*to conquer*", nikao, "*the laity*" or "*the people*", laos,
by asserting his own opinion as the Final Authority. Our critic's document
is riddled with "**Nicolaitan**" doctrine.

Citing the work of Klijn, who compared Aleph and B readings with the papyri in his book *A Survey of the Researches into the Western Text of the Gospels* and that of Pickering, Gail Riplinger (12) p 481, 482 provides a detailed comparison of the texts of the papyri, the old uncials and the Textus Receptus TR.

It is found that where these texts are all extant:

P45 has:

TR	33 places	41.8%
B	25 places	31.6%
Aleph	21 places	26.6%
Total		100.0%

P66 has:

TR	38 places	44.2%
B	32 places	37.2%
Aleph	16 places	18.6%
Total		100.0%

P75 has:

TR	33 places	41.2%
B	36 places	45.0%
Aleph	11 places	13.8%
Total		100.0%

These figures appear to reflect the places where each of the three texts reads AGAINST the other two. Note that they are proportional figures. Dr. Ruckman (1) p 325, states *"P66 . . . agrees with the Textus Receptus 315 times out of 633 in John 1–14, which is (50) % RECEPTUS AGAINST ALL THREE OF THE OTHER "FAMILIES"."*

Gail Riplinger also gives the level of agreement in John 1–14 between P75, the TR and the oldest uncials:

P75 agrees with W 45%, D 38.9%, C 48.5%, A 45.6%, Aleph 44.6%, B 50.4%, TR 51.2%.

She comments *"Note: Even P75 which is touted as the great ally of Aleph and B, agrees here with the TR to a GREATER extent."*

Our critic *"touts"* for P75 in para 10: *"**P75 . . . is remarkably close to Vaticanus (B)**"*. (Note that the 92% agreement between B and P75 in John 11, see Section 9.3, does not seem to be typical over the first 14 chapters of John.)

It is worth recalling here that the so-called *"recensional"* nature of the

Traditional Text has been disproved in some detail. Our critic's allegation that "*unambiguous*" readings of the Traditional Text did not exist in the writings of the Fathers before 350 A.D. has also therefore been disproved. His assertion that the TR is not found in the papyri is likewise shown to be fallacious. It is also worth recalling Pickering's comment (3) p 239, 244 that the "*lateness*" of the Byzantine Text is the very point to be proved and may NOT be assumed.

Rlplinger (12) p 483, states Pickering's conclusion from the evidence of the papyri: "*The TR has more early attestation than B and twice as much as Aleph – evidently the TR reflects an earlier text than either B or Aleph.*"

> She cautions, however, (12) p 581–582 "*The papyri that have been discovered are intact because they are such POOR manuscripts. The fragility of papyrus causes its disintegration if used, as normal scriptures would be. Since there was no printing, many people would use one ms.. Many of the recent discoveries were from the city garbage heaps, accompanied by such New Age apocryphal material as the "Gospel of Thomas" and the "sayings of Jesus"* . . . *The weak character of the papyri is indicated below in E.C. Colwell's article,* Scribal Habits in Early Papyri: A Study in the Corruption of the Text. . . ."

I have enlarged upon Pickering's comments from Grady (45) p 62. See also the more detailed comments of Pickering, edited by Fuller (3) p 283ff.

P66:   (900 errors in John)
        200 nonsense readings
        400 itacistic (incorrect) spellings
        216 careless readings
        482 singular readings
        269 correctors
        54 leaps forward; 22 backward

> *Pickering notes it has "Roughly two mistakes per verse . . . a very poor copy – and yet it is one of the earliest!"*

P75:   145 itacisms (misspellings)
        257 singular readings
        27 leaps forward; 10 backward
        57 careless readings

Pickering notes, " . . . scarcely a good copy . . . If you were asked to write out the Gospel of John by hand, would you make over 400 mistakes? Try it and see!"

P45:   90 itacisms
         275 singular readings
         20 careless readings

P46: *Zuntz says, "In spite of its neat appearance . . . P46 is by no means a good manuscript. The scribe committed very many blunders . . . My impression is that he was liable to fits of exhaustion."*

Gail Riplinger ends her chapter on a chilling note:

"The errors in these ancient manuscripts are important to note, because liberal scholars hope to recast the bible in a mold CLOSER to these manuscripts Comfort hopes: "It is my HOPE that future editions of the Greek text will incorporate even more of the readings found in the early papyri . . . "

"The NIV translators say, Preface vii, " . . . the work of translation is never wholly finished." The New Age boasts of their plans for a new bible from the "archaeological archives." The stage is set for the Antichrist to pull back the veil and launch HIS FINAL VERSION of the story."

I draw attention to Gail Riplinger's mention of the papyri as having survived because they are POOR manuscripts. This matches Burgon's observation concerning the survival of B and Aleph, see Chapter 6, Section 6.2. In Chapter 1, Section 1.3, I listed 6 reasons why the Alexandrian mss. are earlier than the Majority mss. but not BETTER. Our critic alluded to just one of them, para 3, then only by way of a scornful dismissal: ***"The usual ingenious but completely unproved response is that the exemplars of the Byzantine text were worn out from constant use."***

Why is this response *"completely unproved"*? Surely it is attested by common experience that any book which receives frequent and heavy use deteriorates in a few years. There was once a poster in our critic's church with the caption:

"Bibles that are falling apart are usually read by people who AREN'T" (my emphasis).

Hills (2) p 93–94, gives a more detailed explanation:

"Burgon regarded the good state of preservation of B and Aleph in spite of their exceptional age as a proof not of their goodness but of their badness. If they had been good manuscripts, they would have been read

to pieces long ago. *"We suspect that these two manuscripts are indebted for their preservation, SOLELY TO THEIR ASCERTAINED EVIL CHARACTER; which has occasioned that the one eventually found its way, four centuries ago, to a forgotten shelf in the Vatican Library; while the other, after exercising the ingenuity of several generations of critical Correctors, eventually (viz. in A.D. 1844) got deposited in the wastepaper basket of the Convent at the foot of Mount Sinai. Had B and Aleph been copies of average purity, they must long since have shared the inevitable fate of books which are freely used and highly prized; namely, they would have fallen into decadence and disappeared from sight."*

"Thus the fact that B and Aleph are so old is a point against them, not something in their favour. It shows that the Church rejected them and did not read them. Otherwise they would have worn out and disappeared through much reading. Burgon has been accused of sophistry in arguing this way, but certainly his suggestion cannot be rejected by naturalistic critics as impossible. For one of their "own poets" (Kirsopp Lake) favoured the idea that the scribes "usually destroyed their exemplars when they had copied the sacred books."

"If Lake could believe this, why may not orthodox Christians believe that many ancient Byzantine manuscripts have been worn out with much copying and reading? And conversely, why may we not believe that B, Aleph and the other ancient non-Byzantine manuscripts have survived unto the present day simply because they were rejected by the Church and not used?"

9.6 "THE BASIC ISSUES CONCERNING THE TEXT" – "ERASMUS USED THE VULGATE!"

I turn now to the *"even greater problem"* that our critic raises, namely that *"the Textus Receptus has to face"* than the *"insoluble problem"* of no two identical Byzantine manuscripts. See para 12 of this sub-section. (Dr. Hills and others have solved our critic's *"insoluble problem"* – see Section 9.3.)

This *"problem"* is stated as follows: *"**A dozen or so readings in the KJV find no support in any Greek mss. In the last few verses of Revelation half a dozen such inventions occur. They can be traced to the fact that Erasmus had to prepare a Greek manuscript from these verses by translating back from the Vulgate . . . his self-made Greek text contained readings found in no known Greek manuscript. But they are still perpetuated in the printing of the Textus Receptus . . . if it is wrong to**"* *omit or change God's Words it must be equally wrong to add to God's Words. So should not the KJV (be) thrown away with all the other alleged "perversions"?"* Our critic further states under the heading of *"The Defects of the KJV"*, see Chapter 10, *"parts of Revelation and passages like Acts 9:6 . . . cannot be found in any Greek manuscript at all. They are simply translations by Erasmus of verses in the Latin Vulgate."*

In para 1 of this sub-section, our critic attempted to dispose of the Textus Receptus by referring to *"versions in other languages"*. He also refers to *"8000 Latin mss."*, which must include the Vulgate, in his summary on manuscript evidence available to his church members. He now does an about-face to dispose of the Textus Receptus by IGNORING the ancient versions! He has also ignored the list given in Chapter 4, Section 4.3 of the materials that were used for the AV1611, indicating that the translators had several sources to complement the testimony of the Greek manuscripts. These sources included the Latin Bibles of the Waldenses, which had preserved the pure scriptures from the 2nd century A.D. (2) p 212.

Since our critic neglected to list in para 12 the verses that are absent from the Greek mss., I will do so, together with their manuscript support, using Hills (5) p 200–202. Dr. Hills' explanation for the inclusion of these verses in the TR and the AV1611 should make sense to any Bible believer:

"Are the readings which Erasmus thus introduced into the Textus Receptus necessarily erroneous? By no means ought we to infer this. For it is inconceivable that the divine providence which had preserved the New Testament text during the long ages of the manuscript period should blunder when at last this text was committed to the printing press . . . Erasmus, we may well believe, was guided providentially by the common faith to include these readings in his printed Greek New Testament text. In the Textus Receptus God corrected the few mistakes of any consequence which yet remained in the Traditional New Testament text of the majority of the Greek manuscripts.

"The following are some of the most familiar and important of those relatively few Latin Vulgate readings which, though not part of the Traditional Greek text, seem to have been placed in the Textus Receptus by the direction of God's special providence and therefore are to be retained . . .

Matt. 10:8   "raise the dead" . . . in Aleph B C D1, the Latin Vulgate, and the Textus Receptus. (Burgon's redoubtable scholarship failed him here (13) p 108. He rejected the above reading, simply demonstrating that he wasn"t infallible.)

Matt. 27:35   "that it might be fulfilled which was spoken by the prophet, They parted My garments among them, and upon My vesture did they cast lots" . . . in Eusebius (c.325), 1 and other "Caesarean" manuscripts, the Harclean Syriac, the Old Latin, the Vulgate, and the Textus Receptus.

John 3:25   "Then there arose a questioning between some of John's disciples and the Jews about purifying". Pap 66, Aleph, 1 and other "Caesarean" manuscripts, the Old Latin, the Vulgate, and the Textus Receptus read "the Jews" . . . the majority of the Greek manuscripts read "a Jew".

Acts 8:37   (This is one of several Scriptures that our critic wishes to excise from the Bible, Jeremiah 36:23. It will therefore be discussed with them subsequently.)

Acts 9:5   "it is hard for thee to kick against the pricks" . . . in Old Latin manuscripts and in the Latin Vulgate known to Erasmus . . . E, 431, the Peshitta. In Acts 26:14, however, this reading is present in all the Greek manuscripts. In his notes Erasmus indicates that he took this reading from Acts 26:14 and inserted it here.

Acts 9:6   "And he trembling and astonished said, Lord, what wilt thou have me to do? and the Lord said unto him," . . . in the Latin Vulgate and in other ancient witnesses . . . Erasmus indicates that this reading is a translation made by him from the Vulgate into Greek. (Dr. Ruckman (1) p 237, (17) p 331–332, cites the Peshitta and the Old Latin, c, h, l, p, ph, ar (200 AD) for both verses 5 and 6. In his commentary on Acts p 299–300, he also cites Ambrose (397 AD), Ephraem (378) and Lucifer of Cagliari (371) as quoting Acts 9:5, 6. The passage therefore has variety, respectability and antiquity of witnesses, according to Burgon's tests of truth, Chapter 6, Section 6.2.)

Acts 20:28   The majority of the Greek manuscripts read, "Church of the Lord and God." The Latin Vulgate . . . and the Textus Receptus read "Church of God", which is also the reading of Aleph, B and other ancient witnesses.

Rom. 16:25–27   In the majority of manuscripts this doxology is placed

Rev. 22:19

at the end of chapter 14. In the Latin Vulgate and the Textus Receptus it is placed at the end of chapter 16 and this is also the position it occupies in Aleph, B, C and D "And if any man shall take away from the words of the book of this prophecy, God shall take away his part out of the book of life." According to Hoskier, all the Greek manuscripts, except possibly one or two, read, "tree of life." The Textus Receptus reads, "book of life", with the Latin Vulgate . . . Ambrose (d. 397), and the commentaries of Primasius (6th century) and Haymo (9th century). This is one of the verses which Erasmus is said to have translated from Latin into Greek. But Hoskier seems to doubt that Erasmus did this, suggesting that he may have followed Codex 141."

Note that of the eight passages above which are absent from most of the Greek manuscripts, five are stated as being extant in the Old Latin. It is highly likely, therefore, that the translators of the AV1611 were influenced – rightly – by the Waldensian Bibles for most, if not all of these passages.

The Bible believer, therefore, would be wise to heed Dr. Hills' advice and retain ALL the passages. Dr. Hills (5) p 202–203, discusses Erasmus' ending on Revelation as follows:

"The last six verses of Codex 1r (Rev. 22:16–21) were lacking . . . According to almost all scholars, Erasmus endeavoured to supply these deficiencies in his manuscript by retranslating the Latin Vulgate into Greek. Hoskier, however, was inclined to dispute this on the evidence of manuscript 141. In his 4th edition of his Greek New Testament (1527) Erasmus corrected much of this translation Greek (if it was indeed such) on the basis of a comparison with the Complutensian Polyglot Bible (. . . published in 1522), but he overlooked some of it, and this still remains in the Textus Receptus. These readings, however, do not materially affect the sense of the passages in which they occur . . . The only exception is "book" for "tree" in Rev. 22:19, a variant which Erasmus . . . must have retained purposely. Critics blame him for this but here he may have been guided providentially by the common faith to follow the Latin Vulgate.

"There is one passage in Revelation, however, in which the critics, rather inconsistently, blame Erasmus for NOT moving in the direction of the Latin Vulgate. This is Rev. 22:14a, "Blessed are they that do His

commandments, etc." *Here, according to Hoskier, Aleph and A and a few Greek minuscule manuscripts read* "wash their robes", *and this is the reading favoured by the critics . . . The Latin Vulgate reads,* "wash their robes in the blood of the Lamb." *But the Textus Receptus reading . . .* "do His commandments," *is found in the majority of the Greek manuscripts . . . and is undoubtedly the Traditional reading."*

This illustrates how the critics will attack the TR and AV1611 by ANY means whatsoever, even if, upon examination, they are found to be 'rather inconsistent', Mark 14:56. Our critic makes no mention of the critics' preference for half of the Vulgate reading in Revelation 22:14a. The reading is found in the NIV and Nestle's 21st edition.

Dr. Ruckman (44) p 30–31, also discusses *"Those "Spurious Words" of Erasmus"*:

"The Greek text in this passage contains 135 words, of which Nestle (and Aland and Metzger) omits 17 words, adds 5 and alters 13, making a total of 35 words affected. Of these 35 words, 26 make no perceptible difference in an English translation, and most of the remaining 9 are of very small significance.... "them" (vs. 18), "paper" (vs. 19), "tree" (vs. 19), "and" (vs. 19), "even so" (vs. 20), "our" (vs. 20), "Christ" (vs. 21), "you" (vs. 21), and "amen" (vs. 9). (Trinitarian Bible Society, Oct.-Dec., 1964, Vol. 449, p. 14, 15) *... On each one of those words Erasmus NOW has been supported by recent editors and translators.*

"The Trinitarian Bible Society wisely noticed that if "Erasmus had consulted certain copies of the Fifth Century Armenian Version he would now read quite WRONGLY 'the root and offspring of Adam'" (vs. 16). That is, the OLDER manuscript this time WAS NOT THE BEST! Again, if Erasmus had been able to read Sinaiticus, it would not only have confirmed his final "amen" (see above), but would have "misguided" him in verse 19. "It is too often ASSUMED that when consulting ancient manuscripts of the Bible, the nearer we approach to the date of the original writing the nearer we get to the purest obtainable text. This is VERY FAR from being the case as some of the OLDEST surviving copies contain some of the least defensible variations from the true text . . . a good LATE copy is to be preferred over a BAD EARLY COPY . . . even when all the manuscripts, versions and "fathers" have been assembled and consulted and the most penetrating textual criticism of the last hundred years has been directed to this passage, the correctness of a very large proportion of the text of Erasmus is CONFIRMED and in the case of the few exceptions it cannot be shown with CERTAINTY that the modern CRITICS are RIGHT and Erasmus was WRONG."

So much for our critic's *"greater than insoluble problem"* of Erasmus' *"self made Greek text"*. An appropriate conclusion would be to retain the Holy Bible (AV1611 – any Edition will suffice, see later) and throw out the ACTUAL perversions (any "bible" published for the first time since 1800.)

9.7 "THE BASIC ISSUES CONCERNING THE TEXT" – "THE INERRANT, INFALLIBLE ORIGINALS"

Para 13 of this sub-section states *"Inerrancy and infallibility are found only in the original documents"*. What is our critic's proof for this statement? He has no proof for this statement whatsoever. The church of which he was pastor has as part of its first doctrinal basis of faith 2 Timothy 3:16, 17 as a reference for the *"inerrancy and infallibility"* of the originals. It was noted in Chapter 5, Section 5.7, that this passage is NOT a reference to *"the originals"*. The context, verse 15, shows that it is a reference to the scriptures by which Timothy was saved and which were taught to him by his mother and grandmother, 2 Timothy 1:5. These could hardly have been *"the originals"*.

Para 13 continues: *"Only 60 words (one in a 1000) are in doubt."* This statement is similar to Hort's opinion that *"only a thousandth part of the New Testament is seriously in question."* See Chapter 6, Section 6.1. If this is the case, our critic has not explained why Hort's Greek text differs from the Received Text in 5337 places, Section 6.1. Nor has he explained why the NIV omitted 195 out of 200 important readings (7) in the Greek Textus Receptus. Over 60 alterations and/or omissions by the NIV New Testament were cited in Chapter 7, Section 7.3, together with their significant doctrinal implications. See also J. Coad's penetrating observations on the omissions and alterations in the NIV, Section 9.2 . The total alterations in the wording of the NIV, with respect to the AV1611 are 5615 words omitted and 1090 words added, *Bible Believer's Bulletin* May 1993.

Even allowing for the updating of supposed *"archaic"* words, which our critic claims to be approximately 300 – see next section, surely this amount of alteration cannot be explained by a mere 60 doubtful words.

Our critic tries to reassure the reader that *"not one article of faith or one moral precept depends entirely for its support on a disputed reading."* He does NOT state what they DO entirely depend on, nor does he adduce even ONE verse of Scripture in support of this supposed reassurance. The Lord Jesus Christ said **"Man shall not live by bread** alone, but by **EVERY WORD** that proceedeth out of the mouth of God" Matthew 4:4. See also Luke 4:4, where the NIV omitted the phrase "**but by every word of God**".

The contrast between the Lord's admonition and our critic's 'reassurance' could not be greater. Evidently the Lord Jesus Christ did not recognise scholarly opinion about "*disputed readings*". Nor did He appear to recognise the scholar's dictum that so long as SOME verses can be found to support the 'articles of faith' and the 'moral precepts', it is all right to obliterate others which would provide the same support.

I believe that such an unholy teaching must be Satanic. It certainly has NO foundation in EITHER Testament of the Holy Bible. It is important to emphasise that here because our critic resorts to this "teaching" later in order to justify some of the mutilations in the NIV. It should be appreciated that the number of mutilations has, overall, been gradually increasing with the proliferation of new translations. Reviewing 162 New Testament Scriptures in 45 versions, Ray (7) shows that the Douay 1582, omitted 75. The Revised Version of 1881 omitted 135. The Revised Standard Version 1946, omitted 158 but the NIV 1973, exceeded this with 160.

One wonders how many the ultimate 'New Age Version' will omit, with a text even closer to the early papyri than the NIV (12) p 583–584, especially if Sir Frederick Kenyon's "*hope*" of unearthing "*more discoveries . . . awaiting in the sands of Egypt*" is realised.

One notes in passing that "*1 in a 1000*" is actually 180 words in the English New Testament of the AV1611, given that the New Testament contains 181,253 words, according to *The Oxford Bible Reader's Dictionary and Concordance*, p 29. Even this number is appreciably different from the 3% variation, or over 5400 words, mentioned in the earlier sub-section entitled "***Getting Things Into Perspective***". The discrepancy suggests that the critics are themselves in doubt about how much of the Bible IS in doubt.

This para concludes on the optimistic note that "***despite the variants Christian doctrine and practice can still be authoritatively defined.***" The statement begs the question which our critic does NOT answer ANYWHERE in his entire document. WHO or WHAT is 'the authority' by which Christian doctrine etc. is defined? Para 14 has the amazing statement that "***nothing we believe to be doctrinally true and nothing we are commanded to do is in any way jeopardized by the variants. This is true of any textual tradition – even the Byzantine and Textus Receptus!***"

Why, then, is so much scholarly effort expended to downgrade the TR into a *"demonstrably secondary text and a late development"* and to exalt the supposedly *"better credentials"* of the Alexandrian text? Would it not be much simpler and a more efficient use of the Lord's time, Colossians 4:5, to keep on believing and preaching the Book which He has blessed with soul-winning and revival for over three centuries? Even our critic is unable to deny the FRUITS of fidelity to this Book. Surely they are more important than any scholarly prestige which accrues from trying to discredit it?

9.8 "The Position in Textual Criticism Today"

Paras 1 and 2 of this sub section exhibit a contradiction. In para 1, our critic states that *"codices Vaticanus and Sinaiticus and . . . the opinions of Westcott and Hort"* no longer dominate.

However, in para 2, he insists that *"almost universal opinion sees the Byzantine text still as a later conflation of earlier manuscripts."* If this is not Hort's opinion, coupled with his subjective exaltation of Aleph and B, Chapter 6, Section 6.1, then what else is it?

More importantly, as the previous pages show, the truth is almost the reverse of our critic's material in para 2. The evidence of the papyri actually support the TR MORE than the Alexandrian text, see Section 9.5. In particular, recent scholarship REJECTS Hort's *"conflation"* theory and vindicates Burgon. See Section 9.3 and note Brake's thesis (18) p 206, reviewing the whole scene:

"The view presented by Westcott and Hort, of an authoritative ecclesiastical revision (i.e. the origin of the Syrian text) has widely been abandoned. Colwell writes concerning the deficiency of this view:

"Many years ago I joined others in pointing out the limitations in Hort's use of genealogy, and the inapplicability of the genealogical method – strictly defined – to the textual criticism of the N.T. Since then many others have assented to this criticism, and the building of family trees is only rarely attempted.""

This section of our critic's document ends with some comments on *"eclecticism"*, paras 3, 4, *"in which the translators (of the modern versions) follow no text type slavishly but examine each reading in turn on its own merits."*

The list of materials available to the AV1611 translators, Chapter 4, Section 4.3, which our critic ignored, makes it clear that this is exactly what those translators did! Moreover, if Erasmus occasionally used the Vulgate or other ancient sources in the preparation of his Greek text, why is he criticised, para 12 of the previous section, for doing precisely what modern translators do?

For a final word on *"eclecticism"*, I cite Dr. Ruckman (29) p 64–65: *"The little pitch used for the suckers . . . is that the new bibles are not from Nestle's or Westcott and Hort; THEY ARE FROM AN "ECLECTIC TEXT".*

"This pipe man's pitch has been chosen "by faith," hoping two things:

1. *The reader will not understand the word and think, therefore, that Hort and Nestle were not involved, which they were.*
2. *The reader will not find out that ALL TRANSLATIONS ARE FROM ECLECTIC TEXTS. Luther did not use Erasmus for every reading any more than he used Beza, and the AV translators did not use the Geneva Bible for every reading any more than they used Stephanus or Erasmus.*

""Eclectic" was just a jaw breaker . . . which was part of the tradesman's terminology for derailing the truth. "Eclectic," in the case of Bible translating, simply means you use a number of Greek texts from which to translate. However, the ASV and NASV (as the RSV and NRSV) are basically Nestle or Hort or combinations of both."

Note therefore that, although our critic gives some of the truth about *"eclecticism"*, there are further important truths which should be disclosed.

The departures of NIV from the AV1611 are also based largely upon Nestle and Hort. I cited over 20 examples in Chapter 7, Section 7.3, to illustrate this, which our critic saw. More examples will be cited when I address our critic's section on the NIV. Ray (7), *Eye Opener* leaflet, lists 195.

To continue with getting the truth back on the rails – see Dr. Ruckman above – I turn now to our critic's comments about the Authorised Version. Chapter and Section headings have been taken from our critic's document. His remarks have been quoted as necessary.

10

"The Defects of the KJV"

10.1 "URGENT REASONS" FOR OVERTHROWING THE AV1611

Our critic charges the Holy Bible with so many "*defects*" that in his opinion it must be replaced as a matter of urgency. I begin therefore with a quote from a sermon published in 1880 by Thomas DeWitt Talmage, 1832–1902, a minister of the Dutch Reformed Church, of whom Fuller (33) p 390, writes "*He attracted large crowds whenever he preached . . . Three times his churches were demolished by fire. Around the world, over three thousand newspapers carried his sermons. He lectured on an average of fifty times a year.*" Talmage writes (46) p 293:

"*Now let us divide off . . . Let those people who do not believe the Bible and who are critical of this and that part of it, go clear over to the other side. Let them stand behind the devil's guns . . . Give us the out-and-out opposition of infidelity rather than the work of these hybrid theologians, these mongrel ecclesiastics, these half-evoluted people who BELIEVE the Bible and do NOT believe it. I TAKE UP THE KING JAMES TRANSLATION; I CONSIDER IT TO BE A PERFECT BIBLE*" (Vol. 4, p187; Vol. 18, p255).

Our critic wrote this to me in an introductory letter to his document. "**What troubles me most are your claims that the KJV is superior to the original Hebrew and Greek. This stance is totally impossible for me to accept and I find it unbelievable that anyone should hold it . . . it seems to me a most serious spiritual matter when a manifestly fallible translation . . . is preferred to the God breathed originals.**"

Yes, it certainly is "*a most serious spiritual matter*", especially when one compares the ministries of Bunyan, Sunday and Talmage with that of our critic. In para 2 of his section on "*defects*" of the Holy Bible, our critic states "***The discovery of many additional and very early manuscripts since 1611, the rise of the study of Biblical archaeology, the development in comparative Semitics and . . . changes in the English language over the centuries all provide urgent reasons for using 20th Century versions of the Bible.***"

The phrase "*many additional and very early manuscripts*" is rather misleading, because it implies that the additional manuscripts discovered since 1611 are ALSO the very early ones. Even our critic's document denies this. See Chapter 1, Section 1.3 and Chapter 9, Section 9.3. The last twenty or so pages of this work have dealt in detail with the "quality" of "*the very early manuscripts*" discovered since 1611.

Our critic adds in this para "***I believe the KJV translators would have . . . approved of modern translations.***"

He has obviously ignored the information given in Chapter 4, Section 4.3 that the AV1611 translators had the same selections of readings as the modern translators.

Wilkinson (2) p250, states:

"*It is an exaggerated idea, much exploited by those who are attacking the Received Text, that we of the present have greater, as well as more valuable, sources of information than had the translators of 1611.*"

"*It is true that thousands of manuscripts have been brought to life since 1611, but it must be emphasised that the great majority of these are in substantial agreement with the Traditional Text underlying the Reformers' Bibles and the King James Version.*"

He continues: "*The Reformers themselves considered their sources of information perfect. Dr. Fulke (writing circa 1580) says:*

"*But as for the Hebrew and Greek that now is, (it) may easily be proved to be the same that always hath been; neither is there any diversity in sentence, however some copies, either through negligence of the writer, or by any other occasion, do vary from that which is commonly and most generally received in some letters, syllables, or words.*"

"*We cannot censure the Reformers for considering their sources of information sufficient and authentic enough to settle in their minds the infallible inspiration of the Holy Scriptures, since we have a scholar of repute today rating their material as high as the material of the present. Dr. Jacobus thus indicates the relative value of information available to Jerome, to the translators of the King James, and to the Revisers of 1900:*

"*On the whole, the differences in the matter of the sources available in 390, 1590 and 1890 are not very serious.*"

Dr. Ruckman (1) p124, states: *"The AV translators were acquainted with every textual problem anyone was acquainted with on the ASV committee of 1901 or the NASV committee of 1960 . . . The AV translators had the VATICANUS and SINAITICUS readings ON THE TABLES IN 1604 WHEN THEY SAT DOWN."*

As Dr. Ruckman points out p 120, the AV1611 translators had the Latin Vulgate and the Douay-Rheims bible among their sources.

Grady says (45) p 112:

"At this juncture, it would behove us to address the Nicolaitane fallacy that the King James translators were deprived of the Aleph and B readings. Beale writes:

'*Since the publication of the King James Version in 1611, numerous manuscript discoveries have contributed to a vastly increased knowledge of the original Scripture" (47).*

"The hypocrisy of (this statement) is unbelievable when one realizes that these same readings of Sinaiticus and Vaticanus were very much before the scholars of the 1611 Authorised Version as represented IN THE LATIN VULGATE."

No doubt our critic would defend the supposed advanced knowledge of the modern revisers on the basis of the papyri, the contents of which were not published until 1933. However, the dubious nature of these sources has already been considered in detail, together with the fact that they do NOT unequivocally support the modern revisions.

Note that although Erasmus may have used the Vulgate in the few places listed by Hills, see Section 9.6, it was known by the scholars of 1611 to contain many errors (2) p 188, 221. (Dr. Ruckman attributes Erasmus' *"guesswork"* on Revelation to his use of the Old Latin (1) p 67.)

Dr. Ruckman writes (1) p 96: *"Jerome's New Testament is basically Vaticanus and Sinaiticus, although . . . he occasionally retains the correct Old Latin Receptus readings against the Alexandrian corruptions from Egypt."*

In another work, (48) p 6, Dr. Ruckman states: *"ninety eight percent of these "updatings" (of the modern translations) came from the Roman Catholic text that brought in the DARK AGES (Jesuit Rheims, 1582, from Jerome's Alexandrian New Testament Vulgate)."*

In other words, for all practical purposes, the AV1611 translators had access to *"all the knowledge which has come to light since their day."* Contrary to our critic's opinion, they would NOT *"have approved of modern translations"* because the Bible they produced DOES NOT MATCH the modern translations.

Our critic does not list the Greek and Hebrew words of which the AV1611 translators *"did not understand the meaning"*, so I am unable to discuss them here. (Neither does he demonstrate that modern revisers DO.)

He quotes the statement *"nothing is begun and perfect at the same time"* from *The Translators To the Readers* by Dr. Miles Smith, p 15. The full sentence is: *"Yet for all that, as nothing is begun and perfited at the same time, and the later thoughts are thought to be the wiser: so, if we building upon their foundation that went before us, and being holpen by their labors, do endeavour to make that better which they left so good; no man, we are sure, hath cause to mislike us; they, we persuade ourselves, if they were alive, would thank us."*

Dr. Smith is commending the translators of the previous century, such as Tyndale and Rogers – see Chapter 3, Sections 3.2, 3.3. He writes on p 14 *"And to the same effect say we, that we are so far off from condemning any of their labors that travailed before us in this kind, either in this land or beyond sea, either in King Henry's time, or King Edward's (if there were any translation, or correction of a translation in his time) or Queen Elizabeth's of ever renowned memory, that we acknowledge them to have been raised up of God, for the building and furnishing of his Church, and that they deserve to be had of us and of posterity in everlasting remembrance . . . Therefore blessed be they, and most honoured be their name, that break the ice, and giveth the onset upon that which helpeth forward to the saving of souls. Now what can be more available thereto, than to deliver God's book unto God's people in a tongue which they understand?"*

Dr. Smith is speaking of the translation of the Received Text into English, which was achieved by the labours of Tyndale and others. He is NOT giving carte-blanche to the enemies of the Received Text to replace it with the Dark Age text of Sinaiticus and Vaticanus of the Roman Catholic church, which our critic's partial quotation tries to imply. This is not the only time in his document that he delivers a carefully edited quotation which is misleading, as will be shown.

10.2 "THE HEBREW AND THE GREEK TEXT USED IN 1611"

This sub-section refers largely to matters which have been discussed in the previous chapter, namely: the *"late"* manuscripts for the KJV, *"**the five uncials . . . crucial for the purity of the NT**"*, the papyri and the *"translations by Erasmus"*. See Sections 9.3–9.6, especially the findings of Burgon, with respect to the above "*crucial*" Codices Aleph, A, B, C and D. When our critic stated that Aleph and B "*are not the only exemplars of (the Alexandrian) family as seems to be alleged at times*", he failed to mention there that A, C and D are – apparently in his view – the most important of the other exemplars.

The reader is urged once again to review the findings of Burgon about the "*purity*" of these "*crucial*" codices, Section 9.3.

The absence of early Masoretic manuscripts posed no difficulty for the AV1611 translators, as Wilkinson, above, has shown. Dr. R.D. Wilson, M.A., Phd., Princeton, 1856–1930, has affirmed (2) p 47–48: "*For forty-five years continuously since I left college I have devoted myself to the one great study of the Old Testament in all its languages, in all its archaeology, in all its translations, and, as far as possible, everything bearing upon its text and history . . . The evidence in our possession has convinced me that* "at sundry times and in divers manners God spoke unto our fathers through the prophets," *and that the Old Testament in Hebrew,* "*being immediately inspired by God,*" *has* "*by His singular care and providence been kept pure in all ages.*""

Our critic provides nothing to contradict Dr. Wilson's conclusions. He does, however, make reference to the Dead Sea Scrolls, implying that their discovery serves to overthrow the Received (Hebrew) Text of the Authorised Holy Bible. He does not discuss the contents of the Dead Sea Scrolls but Dr. Hills (5) p 101–102, gives a detailed description of the documents yielded up by the Qumran caves.

Those of greatest interest, no doubt, to the opponents of the AV1611 are the manuscripts from Cave 4, which showed that "*many other text-types*" of the Old Testament existed in ancient times, according to some scholars, in particular F.M. Cross (1964). However, another scholar, "*G.R. Driver (1965), disagreed with . . . Cross. According to him, the Dead Sea Scrolls were written in the first and early second centuries A.D.*" In other words, the other 'ancient' text-types were merely 'modern (A.D.) revisions'.

Dr. Hills concludes "*Despite the new discoveries, our confidence in the trustworthiness of the Old Testament text must rest on some more solid foundation than the opinions of naturalistic scholars. For as the Qumran studies demonstrate, these scholars disagree with one another. What one scholar grants, another takes away. Instead of depending on such inconstant allies, Bible believing Christians should develop their own type of Old Testament textual criticism which takes its stand on the teachings of the Old Testament and views the evidence in the light of these teachings.*

Such a believing textual criticism leads us to full confidence in the Masoretic Hebrew text which was preserved by the divinely appointed Old Testament priesthood and the scribes and scholars grouped around it."

Dr. Ruckman writes concerning the Dead Sea Scrolls, *Bible Believer's Bulletin* April 1983:

"Having surveyed the contents of forty or fifty caves in the "Qumran community" and having discussed the . . . Biblical and non-Biblical materials found in them, we have learned that if there is one thing the Dead Sea Scrolls do NOT do it is to shed "light" on any BIBLICAL TRUTH in either Testament from ANY translation. We have also learned that they bear no witness whatsoever to any Greek Old Testament (LXX) translated in 250 B.C. under the Ptolemies in Egypt."

Interestingly enough Dr. Fuller (2) p 9–11, reports on the findings in the 1950's of Old Testament manuscripts in the fortress of Masada, which fell in the year 73 AD. The manuscripts, which had been written *"perhaps twenty or thirty years earlier"* included Psalms 81–85, Leviticus 8–12, Deuteronomy 33–34 and parts of Ezekiel, including Chapter 37, the vision of the dry bones. All these portions were found to be *"virtually identical with the traditional Biblical texts"*.

So why does our critic attach such great importance to the Dead Sea Scrolls in his opposition to the Hebrew text of the AV1611? He does not say – because in reality there is nothing to say.

10.3 "OMISSIONS IN THE KJV"

Our critic has omitted to mention the sources for these *"omissions"*. Berry's edition of Stephens' Greek text of 1550 (49) shows that the modern sources are mainly the editions of the Greek New Testament by Griesbach, Lachmann, Tischendorf, Tregelles and Alford and therefore their Alexandrian mss. sources in turn. With the exception of Alford, these individuals were listed in Chapter 6, Section 6.1 as the *"higher critics"*, who instigated the Puseyite movement to re-unite the Church of England with Rome. Ne, Nestle's 21st Edition and the RV (Hort) include many of these *"omissions"*.

Since our critic has ignored all of this, it will be helpful to give a brief sketch of these *"higher critics"*.

Dr. Hills (5) p 65, states:

"J.J. Griesbach (1745–1812), pupil of Semler (who believed that "the Scriptures were not inspired in the traditional sense") and professor at

Jena, early declared himself a sceptic regarding the New Testament text. In 1771 he wrote "The New Testament abounds in more glosses, additions, and interpolations purposely introduced than any other book". And during his long career there is no indication that he ever changed this view. He was noted for . . . the comprehensive way in which he worked out a classification of the New Testament manuscripts into three "rescensions" or ancestral groups. He also developed the thought implicit in Bengel's rule, "The hard reading is to be preferred to the easy reading." Like Bengel he interpreted this rule to mean that the orthodox Christians had corrupted their own New Testament text. According to Griesbach, whenever the New Testament manuscripts varied from each other, the orthodox readings were to be ruled out at once as spurious. "The most suspicious reading of all," Griesbach wrote, "is the one that yields a sense favourable to the nourishment of piety (especially monastic piety)." And to this he added another directive: "When there are many variant readings in one place, that reading which more than the others manifestly favours the dogmas of the orthodox is deservedly regarded as suspicious."

Fuller (3) p 66–67, citing Philip Mauro, barrister to the Supreme Court of the United States, says of Carl Lachmann, 1793–1851:

"This editor appears to have been the first to act upon the theory or principle that the more ancient the manuscript the more worthy of credence. The extent to which this idea has been allowed to control in the settling of disputed readings, without regard to other weighty considerations whereby the credibility of the contradictory witnesses should properly have been determined, is very extraordinary.

"Lachmann seems to have conceived a prejudicial dislike for the Received Text, and . . . to have "set to work to form a text independent of that, right or wrong. He started with the theory of ancient evidence only, thus sweeping away many copies and much evidence, because they dated below his fixed period." In fact he did not seek to arrive at the original inspired Writings, but merely "to recover the Text as it was in the fourth century".

Mauro then cites the conclusion of Scrivener, about the inferiority of the texts of Irenaeus compared to those of Erasmus and Stephens. See Section 9.3. Mauro continues:

"Lachmann proceeded to disregard this fact, and no doubt because ignorant of it. He thus set a bad example; and unfortunately his example has been followed by editors who came after him, men of great learning unquestionably, and having accurate knowledge of early Greek, but apparently knowing little of the history of the various Greek manuscripts,

and nothing at all of the laws of evidence, and how to deal with problems involving the investigation of a mass of conflicting testimony."

Of Constantine Tischendorf 1815–1879, Mauro states:

"This scholar . . . has had a dominating influence in the formation of the modern Text. Tischendorf proceeded upon a plan which we give in his own words: *"The text is to be sought only from ancient evidence and especially from Greek Mss., but without neglecting the testimonies of Versions and Fathers."*

"From this we see that Tischendorf thoroughly committed himself to the principle of giving the "ancient evidence" the deciding voice in all disputed readings. That he should have adopted this principle was specially unfortunate because of the circumstance that Tischendorf himself was the discoverer of the famous Codex Sinaiticus (and) . . . the most serious of the many departures of the R.V. from the A.V. are due to the unhappy conjunction of an unsound principle of evidence and the fortuitous discovery, by a scholar who had accepted that principle, of a very ancient Greek Ms. of the N.T., a Ms. which, despite its unquestioned antiquity, turns out to be about the worst and most "scandalously corrupt" of all the Greek Texts now known to exist."

Of Samuel Tregelles 1813–1875, Mauro states:

"As stated in his own words his purpose was "to give the text on the authority of the oldest Mss. and Versions, and with the aid of the earlier citations, so as to present, so far as possible, the text commonly received in the fourth century." This . . . is substantially the plan proposed by Lachmann; and these are the precedents which seem to have mainly influenced Westcott and Hort in the compilation of their Text, which is virtually the Text from which the R.V. was made.

"Dr. Scrivener says . . . "Lachmann's text seldom rests on more than four Greek Codices, very often on three, not infrequently on two, sometimes on only one." His fallacy, which was adopted by Tregelles, necessarily proved fatal to the text prepared by the latter, who in fact acted upon the astounding assumption that "eighty-nine ninetieths" of our existing manuscripts and other authorities might safely be rejected, in order that we might be free to follow a few early documents of bad repute."

Of Henry Alford 1810–1871, Mauro states:

"This editor . . . is rated high as a Greek scholar, though we know not how competent he was to decide questions of fact where there was conflict of testimony . . . Alford's text was constructed – to state it in his own words – "by following in all ordinary cases the united or preponderating

testimony of the most ancient authorities." Later evidence was taken into consideration by him only when "the most ancient authorities did not agree or preponderate."

"It seems not to have occurred to this learned man, any more than to the others, that mere antiquity was not a safe test of reliability where witnesses were in conflict, and that a late copy of a correct original should be preferred to a corrupt Ms. of earlier date."

Later in his document, under the heading of *Westcott Hort and Burgon*, para 6, our critic takes me to task for not having **"troubled to find out about the work of modern textual critics and the principles on which they arrive at their conclusions."**

That this statement is a blatant lie is demonstrated by the material in Chapter 6, Section 6.2 in relation to Hort's *"conflation"* theory, which is still the basis for modern textual criticism – it is, after all, upheld by our critic! It is further demonstrated by the comparison of New Testament readings, Chapter 7, Section 7.3, which show the continuing heavy reliance of modern revisers on Aleph and B – in spite of our critic's opinion to the contrary. The subjective nature of modern textual criticism and *"eclecticism"* will be discussed later but for now I again draw attention to the work of Philip Mauro. As an experienced trial lawyer for the U.S. Supreme Court, it was his professional calling and responsibility to evaluate conflicting evidence. He could therefore be considered an 'authority' in this respect. His conclusion was that the editors who pioneered the modern Greek texts did so by means of unsound principles and corrupt sources.

In the light of this evidence, our critic is in no position to admonish anyone about disregarding the *"work of modern textual critics"* who have followed in the wake of Griesbach, Lachmann, Tischendorf and company.

Moreover, none of these editors appear to have left behind any clear testimony of salvation, or of having led anyone to a saving knowledge of the Lord Jesus Christ, any more than Westcott and Hort (45) p 214.

In fact, none of them appear to have had any significant Christian ministry. Yet they were contemporaries of John Wesley (1703–1791), William Carey (1761–1834), Robert Murray McCheyne (1813–1834), Adoniram Judson (1788–1850), Billy Bray (1794–1868), Charles Finney (1792–1875), George Mueller (1805–1898), David Livingstone (1813–1873), Dwight L. Moody (1837–1899) and Charles Haddon Spurgeon (1834–1892). See Dr. Ruckman's *History of the New Testament Church* p 62–101. All of the men listed in the last paragraph built their ministries on ONE Book and it was NOT *"the God breathed originals"* or ANY of the critical editions of Griesbach and those who followed him. I will deal later with Spurgeon and Wesley's occasional defections from the AV1611, which our critic uses as an alibi for sin.

According to our critic, these "*omissions*" in the AV1611 stemmed from "*defective*" manuscripts. Actually, the "*omissions*" are additions to the word of God which stemmed from the defective scholarship of the "*higher critics*" listed above. The additions are listed as follows, with the Greek texts and modern versions which contain them:

Matthew 24:36 "nor the Son" is added by NIV, JB, NWT, Ne, L (Lachmann), T (Tischendorf, 8th Edition).

Dr. Ruckman, in his Commentary on *Matthew* (36), p 555ff, states: "*Aleph and B have added* "neither the son" . . . *the majority of all Greek manuscripts do not contain the reading; furthermore, (neither do) the Old Latin and the Old Syriac . . . the old Sahidic (2nd and 3rd century BEFORE "Vaticanus"!) does not have it; furthermore, Ambrosius (397) and Heironymus (420) do not recognise it as authoritative . . . The ASV, RSV, RV, and Catholic Bible assume that the passage* "neither the Son", *was removed by orthodox scribes because they resented the inference it had that Christ was not omniscient; therefore, they accept the* "Vaticanus" *which has the addition as the authentic reading. But here, all logic, common sense, reason and honesty falls apart; for if this was done, why did not the scribe remove it from Mark also? (Mark 13:32). If the Textus Receptus of the King James was derived by conflating two other type manuscripts, how is it that here BOTH TYPES WERE IGNORED?*

1. *If Western "D" has it and Egyptian "B" has it, and the Textus Receptus is a combination (conflation) of Western and Egyptian, then the Textus Receptus HAS TO HAVE IT.*
2. *If (the true Text) had it, and it was taken out, why was it not taken out of Mark 13:32, where it is also found in the Western (D) and the Egyptian (B)?*
3. *Is it not more reasonable . . . to suppose that the corrupt Italian manuscripts of "D" (West – Rome) and "B" (Egyptian but written in ITALY according to W&H) added to the original text a favourite verse they found in Mark, hoping to emphasise the fact that Jesus was not omniscient?*
4. *If this is supposed, what happens to W&H's theory that Vaticanus is a PURE text and the Syrian is a later corruption?*

Matthew 24:36 reveals the Western and Egyptian MSS. for what they are – illegitimate corruptions from forged manuscripts written for the purpose of BROWBEATING the soul-winning Christians of 70–400 A.D. who were using the Syrian text of the Apostles (written in Asia Minor and Palestine)."

John 19:3 "and went up to him again and again" or similar is added by NIV, JB, NWT, Ne, L, T, Tr (Tregelles), A (Alford). NIV, JB, NWT alter "**they smote him with their hands**" to "they struck him in the face" or similar.

Note first that the "scholars" are not united over the "*omissions*" discussed so far. Four of them support this one but that of Matthew 24:36 is found only in two of them. Griesbach has abstained each time so far.

The addition is superfluous because the Lord's assailants would have to have come up to within arm's reach of Him in order to strike Him "**with their hands**", as the AV1611 reads. The repetitive nature of the mockery in these circumstances is self-evident and the NIV's "again and again" is unwarranted and clumsy by comparison with the AV1611's more economical style.

Concerning the altered reading from "**their hands**" AV1611, to "in the face" NIV, JB, NWT, none of the Greek New Testaments, TR (Berry), Ne, G, L, T, Tr, A appear explicitly to support the change. The reading "**they struck him on the face**" is found in Luke 22:64 of the AV1611 and the TR but it is OMITTED by NIV, JB, NWT, Ne, T, Tr, A and treated as doubtful by L. Our critic has not seen fit to justify this "*omission*" from the NIV etc..

Acts 4:25 "by the Holy Spirit" and "our father" referring to David, or similar, is added by NIV, JB, NWT, Ne, L, T, Tr, A.

The additions detract from the nature of the Godhead, Romans 1:20.

Although the Bible says that "**God . . . hath in these last days spoken unto us by his Son**" Hebrews 1:2, as He did "**by the prophets**", verse 1, nowhere does the Bible say that God "speaks" by the Holy Spirit because God speaking IS the Holy Spirit speaking! Isaiah 6:8,9 says "**I heard the voice of the Lord, saying . . . Go, and tell this people, Hear ye indeed, but understand not;**". Yet when Paul quotes this passage in Acts 28:25–26, he says "**Well spake the Holy Ghost by Esaias the prophet unto our fathers, Saying, Go unto this people, and say, Hearing ye shall hear, and shall not understand;**"

Moreover, when Agabus speaks in Acts 21:11, he says "**Thus saith the Holy Ghost**", instead of "**Thus saith the Lord,**" which is used for prophetic utterances over 200 times in the Old Testament. Further, Acts 1:16 shows that it was in the Person of the Holy Ghost that God spoke through David. 2 Samuel 23:2, 3 makes this clear:

"The Spirit of the Lord spake by me, and his word was in my tongue. The God of Israel said, the Rock of Israel spake to me, He that ruleth over men must be just, ruling in the fear of God."

The words of the Spirit of the Lord and the God of Israel are one and the same – because the Spirit of the Lord and the God of Israel are one and the same, even though distinct Persons of the Godhead. The Holy Spirit is not merely an intermediary through whom God speaks, as the addition in the NIV etc. implies.

The addition of "our father" to Acts 4:25 is inappropriate because the apostles are PRAYING and the Lord taught them to pray! See Matthew 6:9, Luke 11:2.

"Now the Lord is that Spirit" 2 Corinthians 3:17.

Our critic here shows that he is rather inconsistent in two respects. First, he criticises the AV1611 for supposedly omitting a phrase which has "*a bearing on important doctrine.*" Yet he strenuously objects to the same criticism being applied to the NIV in its omissions or distortions of 1 John 5:7, 1 Timothy 3:16 and Acts 8:37 on the grounds that the doctrines embodied in these verses "*(are) taught repeatedly in the N.T.*". See Chapter 14, "**Disputed Texts(?)**" where our critic's objections to these verses will be answered.

Second, he regards the addition of "by the Holy Spirit" in the NIV etc. as being important for the particular doctrine of "*the work of the Holy Spirit in inspiration.*" Yet he fails to criticise the NIV for having removed the word "**inspiration**" from each of the only two places in the Bible where it occurs, namely Job 32:8 and 2 Timothy 3:16.

No doubt instead of "**inspiration of God**" he would "prefer" the literal rendering of "theopneustos" which is "God-breathed", which our critic insists applies only to the "*originals*". However, the term "**inspiration**" means "breathing in". When it is used in association with God, it means GOD breathing IN, or INTO or UPON, Ezekiel 37:9, which is much more specific than simply "God-breathed". Dr. Ruckman (1) p 250ff states

"*In the Bible, God breathes into an army of DEAD men, and they become alive (Ezek. 37). They are present in substance before they have life. In the Bible, God breathes into the body of a lifeless man (Psalm 139:15,16), and the body, already formed, becomes alive (Gen. 2:7). If the word "**inspiration**" . . . means "God-breathed", then someone has done the body of Christ a great injustice in not pointing out all four of these references. Someone has privately interpreted the term "**inspiration**" to mean that some WRITINGS were inspired because they were "God-breathed". The same class of people forgot that BREATH was* *something that came out of a man's MOUTH (2 Peter 1:21) and had to do with what someone SPOKE: not what he WROTE.*

*"Computers have shown that Paul did not WRITE some of the Pauline Epistles, and this was common knowledge anyway: Paul used an amanuensis when he wrote, and he mentions this matter in Romans 16:22. We assume that if only what Paul WROTE (2 Peter 3:15) is "*scripture,*" (2 Peter 3:16), and his writings are "*scriptures,*" Romans could not be inspired. This is the Satanic mess that Fundamentalists get into when they go charging madly along through "historic positions" . . . For 100 years, apostate Conservatives have been saying "since the Authorised Version translators did not CLAIM to be inspired, they could NOT have been inspired," unaware . . . that by saying this, they had erased the mark of "inspiration" from Genesis, Joshua, Judges, Ruth, Esther, Ecclesiastes, Matthew, Mark, John, and a dozen other canonical scriptures.*

*"The AUTHORISED VERSION says, "***ALL SCRIPTURE IS GIVEN BY INSPIRATION OF GOD.***"*

*"Question one: What does the word "***scripture***" mean?*

*"Question two: What does "***given by inspiration***" mean?*

"Answer (from the Alexandrian Cult): "The word 'scripture' is a reference to the verbally inspired original autographs and therefore has no application to TRANSLATIONS or COPIES OF THE ORIGINALS. The word "inspiration" means that the words written down on a sheet of paper were "GOD BREATHED" THE FIRST TIME THEY WERE WRITTEN DOWN: the verse was MISTRANSLATED and should have been 'All scripture WAS God-breathed' "

"There. That is the standard "historical position" of the Alexandrian Cult. "There are three things wrong with it that label it as a Catholic HERESY.

1. *The word* **"scripture"** *in the Bible is ALWAYS used of COPIES OR TRANSLATIONS (Mark 12:10; Acts 8:32; Acts 17:11; etc.), and NEVER ONCE is referring to "original autographs". Christ READ the scriptures, the Bereans STUDIED the scriptures (Acts 17:11), the Ethiopian eunuch had them OPEN on his lap (Acts 8:32), and Christ rebuked people for not READING them (Matt. 21:42).*

2. *The word* **"scripture"** *was defined in the context (2 Tim. 3:15) as something that Timothy had known all of his life, and he didn"t have ONE "original autograph" . . . THE HERETICS TOOK A TEXT OUT OF THE CONTEXT . . .*

3. *Paul ascribes FOREKNOWLEDGE and SPEECH to copies of the*

scripture (Rom. 9:17; Gal. 3:8), since he never had an ORIGINAL of Exodus 9:16 or Genesis 22:18 a day in his life . . .

"WE believe the Bible we QUOTE, and use it to prove what we BELIEVE. There is no tortuous circuit around the facts or the truth; we aren"t quoting scriptures to prove that some lost pieces of paper were **"given by inspiration of God.**" *We are quoting THE SCRIPTURES to prove that THE SCRIPTURES (as THE SCRIPTURES use the term) were* **"given by inspiration of God.**" **"ALL SCRIPTURE.**" *If it is* **"SCRIPTURE",** *God gave it; if God gave it, the method He used was by inspiration: HE BREATHED ON IT. "That is what put LIFE into the Scriptures (see Gen. 2:7 and Ezek. 37:1–14).*

"(Missed it, didn"t you, you God-forsaken Fundamental Greek scholars and Conservative Hebrew scholars and Evangelical textual critics – all of you orthodox Bible teachers. Missed it by a mile, didn"t you? Do you know why you did? Because God won't bless a LIAR.)"

The next *"omission"* in the AV1611 is in **Acts 16:7**. Instead of **"the Spirit"**, "the Spirit of Jesus" is found in the NIV, JB, NWT, Ne, G (Griesbach), L, T, Tr, A, W (Bishop Wordsworth, who published an edition of the Greek New Testament. in 1870.)

This addition is inappropriate for two reasons:

1. The Bible uses the term **"spirit of Christ"**, Romans 8:9, 1 Peter 1:11, **"spirit of his Son"**, Galatians 4:6 and **"spirit of Jesus Christ"** Philippians 1:19 specifically in the context of the indwelling presence of the Lord in the believer. See also Philippians 1:20. This is NOT how "spirit of Jesus" is used in Acts 16:7 in the NIV etc..

2. The Bible does not use the term "spirit of Jesus" anywhere. The name **"Jesus"** was bestowed upon Him at his birth by Joseph at the behest of the angel of the Lord and is therefore strongly associated with his humanity, Matthew 1:21. It is surely inappropriate to detach the name **"Jesus"** from his humanity – even though it is SUPER humanity, Acts 9:3–8 – and give it a spiritual association only. Moreover, Jesus, as a man, 1 Thessalonians 5:23, has a spirit, Luke 2:40, 10:21, 23:46, John 11:33, 13:21. It is wrong to suggest that His spirit has somehow become detached from Him, as the NIV addition implies.

Our critic fails to mention that "**Christ**" has been omitted from Paul's salvation message in Acts 16:31 by the NIV, JB, NWT, Ne, L, T, Tr, A.

Is it not *"IMPORTANT DOCTRINE"* for a man DESIRING TO BE ETERNALLY SAVED to believe on the Lord Jesus CHRIST?

Our critic's next *"omission"* is in **Luke 10:21**, where **"in spirit"** has been altered to "through the Holy Spirit" by the NIV, JB, NWT, Ne, L, T, Tr, A.

As it stands in the AV1611, this verse simply shows that Jesus, as a man, has a spirit. See comments above, where the NIV follows the AV1611 in Luke 23:46 and John 13:21. *"The relationship of the Son to the Spirit"* is explained by the Son Himself in exact detail in John 14:16–17, 26; 16:7–15, so our critic's objection here is nonsense. Obviously, the Lord's spirit is holy, as He is, Luke 1:35, Acts 4:27, 30.

The next *"omission"* is **Romans 8:28**, where **"all things work together for good"** has been altered to "in all things God works for the good", or similar by the NIV, JB, NWT, Ne, L. T, Tr, A are absent on this occasion, demonstrating once again that scholars are not unanimous in their attacks on the AV1611.

Given Psalm 72:18 and Proverbs 10:22, no Christian would ever need reassurance that God would neglect to do GOOD. The test of faith is whether ALL THINGS can be received as the agents for good. Nevertheless, in the Bible **"all things"** are used to encourage rejoicing IN THE LORD, Habakkuk 3:17, 18; Philippians 4:4, to strengthen faith, Psalm 112:7, 1 Peter 1:6,7, to develop character, Job 23:10, to deepen intimacy with the Lord, Job 42:5, 6, and to reveal more of one's real self, Job 42:5, 6 again, 2 Chronicles 32:24–26,3 1. Note that in the last reference, God is not "working" at all. He simply lets events take their course – for Hezekiah's admonition. See Isaiah 39:5–8.

Furthermore, the NIV reading implies that God may not always be able to control circumstances but must work in spite of them. This, of course is not so, Isaiah 10:5–15.

The next *"omission"* is in **1 Thess. 4:1**, where "as in fact you are living" or similar, has been added by the NIV, JB, NWT, Ne, L, T, Tr, A, W.

Since Paul is actually exhorting the Thessalonians to **"abound more and more"** in godly living and pleasing God, it is obvious that they HAD put into practice his earlier exhortation and therefore the clause added by the Bible-rejecting *"higher critics"* above is superfluous.

In **1 Peter 2:3** **"if so be"** has been changed to "now that" by the NIV, JB. The NWT has "providing" and Ne, L, T, Tr retain **"if"** but omit "so be".

The question is, HAD all of Peter's readers **"tasted that the Lord is gracious"**? Verse 2:1 indicates that perhaps some of them had NOT. Peter was therefore right to encourage his readers, tactfully, to make sure that they HAD been "**born again . . . by the word of God, which liveth and abideth for ever**", verse 1:23, to ensure that they could grow in graciousness themselves, especially in their dealings with one another. See also his exhortations in 2 Peter 1:1–11, 3:18. One of the practical aspects of a pastorate is in allowing for the fact that not everyone in the congregation may be born again. Paul makes the same allowances in 1 Corinthians 15:2 and 2 Corinthians 13:5.

The NIV and JB miss the practicality of the verse.

Our critic fails to mention that instead of "**the sincere milk of the word**" 1 Peter 2:2, AV1611, the obscure reading "crave pure spiritual milk" is found with minor variation in the NIV, JB, NWT (which adds "belonging to the word"). He also neglects to mention the addition "unto salvation" found, with variation, in the NIV, JB, NWT, Ne, G, L, T, Tr, A, W.

Dr. Ruckman states (43) p 38, of the NIV reading in 1 Peter 2:2, *"you just "grow up in your salvation", IMPLYING YOU MIGHT ALREADY HAVE IT. In the AV you simply grow by feasting on the sincere milk AFTER you are saved. "eis soterian" has been ADDED to the text by "conflation" (Aleph, P72, A, B and C) and this time, going completely contrary to Griesbach's "canons", the "SHORTER READING" WAS REJECTED. The "shorter reading" was the TEXTUS RECEPTUS."*

It is ironic that in the morning service on October 30th 1994, our critic quoted once, if not twice, the words "**the sincere milk of the word**" with respect to the requirements for Christian growth. In his introductory letter he assures me that *"if a translation from the KJV is for some reason preferable I am always prepared to say so."*

However, he was not, on this occasion. Like many of the quotations in his document, this one remained anonymous.

1 Peter 5:2 in the AV1611 supposedly omits "as God wants you to be", found in the NIV, JB, Ne and in L, T, Tr as "according to God". The NWT does not have this addition.

The essence of willingness is that it is voluntary, Leviticus 1:3, according to the INDIVIDUAL. The addition tends to obscure this fact. However, granted that God would desire true willingness on the part of a pastor, is there any need for this addition given that it is GOD's flock, verse 2 and GOD's heritage, verse 3, of which GOD HIMSELF is the CHIEF Shepherd, verse 4?

Concerning *"the will of God in pastoral care"*, the NIV, JB, NWT and ALL the Greek texts miss the FIRST priority in *"pastoral care"* as expressed succinctly in the AV1611:

"FEED the flock of God which is among you" 1 Peter 5:2.

This exhortation matches perfectly the Lord's promise in Jeremiah 3:15:

"And I will give you pastors according to mine heart, which shall FEED you with knowledge and understanding." Note that in the NIV, the pastors only "lead" and do NOT "**feed**"!

Note that the Lord is INDIGNANT when the sheep are NOT fed, Ezekiel 34:2:

"Should not the shepherds FEED the flocks?" Yes, they should but in this verse in the NIV, which reads "take care" instead of "feed", they evidently should NOT!

The AV1611 is accused in **1 John 3:1** of having omitted "And that is what we are", found with variation in the NIV, JB, NWT, Ne, L, T, Tr, A and therefore detracting from *"assurance"*, according to our critic. The clause is superfluous in verse 1 for two reasons:

1. **"Sons of God"** in verse 1 is obviously a term applied by the Father to those who have believed in the Lord Jesus Christ, in order to show the **"manner of love"** which He, the Father **"hath bestowed"** on them. If **"the sons of God"** are **"called"** such, it follows immediately that that is what they ARE, because God CANNOT lie, Titus 1:2. (Note here that the NIV and JB have only that "God DOES not lie.")
2. The statement **"now are we the sons of God"** follows in verse 2, so that the extra clause in verse 1 adds NOTHING by way of *"assurance"*. By contrast, the omission of **"that ye may believe on the Son of God"** from 1 John 5:13 by the NIV, JB, NWT, Ne eliminates one of the main reasons why John wrote his letter, to instil, encourage and consolidate faith in the Lord Jesus Christ. See also John 20:30, 31. (The omission no doubt stems from G, L, T, Tr, A, W, although these editions actually omit **"that believe on the name of the Son of God"**.)

Can our critic prove that the converts of the soul-winners of the past, who were faithful to the AV1611, Moody, Finney, Sunday etc., lacked ASSURANCE, compared to those who are "the fruits" of ministries based on the NIV etc.?

Our critic's next *"omission"* is in **Jude 25**, where "through Jesus Christ our Lord", or similar, found in the NIV, JB, NWT, Ne, G, L, T, Tr, A, W, has to do with Christ's *"mediation"* according to our critic.

Christ's *"mediation"* is described in 1 Timothy 2:5, 6. **"Majesty"**, **"power . . . and glory"** and **"dominion"** also belong to the Lord Jesus

Christ, 2 Peter 1:16, Luke 9:26, Revelation 5:12, 11:15, 1:6. He is not merely an agent by which they are bestowed upon God the Father, as the NIV etc. imply.

Returning to the list of omissions of and alterations to 162 important Scriptures (7) p 33ff with respect to the AV1611, one finds that, overall, the number increases as higher criticism progresses through the 18th and 19th centuries: Griesbach's New Testament 61, Lachmann's 121, Alford's 134, Tregelles" 140, Tischendorf's 150, Westcott & Hort's 151, Nestle's (prior to the 26th edition) 155. Wordsworth was not among the "*higher critics*" and his New Testament has only 47 changes. I believe Griesbach was also the editor of the Diaglot New Testament, which has 128.

Turning to the Old Testament., our critic accuses the AV1611 of omitting "Let's go out into the field", from **Genesis 4:8**, found in the NIV, JB (less "into the field"), NWT (in brackets). The NIV footnote reveals that the reading is obtained from the Samaritan Pentateuch, Septuagint (Brenton's has "plain" instead of field), Vulgate and Syriac.

Anderson (50) p 7, states "*The New International Version . . . seems to hold these other translations (see above), particularly the Septuagint, on an equal level with the Masoretic Text. This is done (citing NIV Preface, p vii)* "*where accepted principles of textual criticism showed that one or more of these textual witnesses appeared to provide the correct reading.*" *It should be noted that not all scholars . . . accept these principles of textual criticism; and the matter of providing a correct reading can be extremely subjective.*"

The TBS also states (51) p 5, "*Every such change (from the above sources) is debatable, and the process of reconstructing obscure passages of the Hebrew, with the aid of Greek, Latin and Syriac translations of the Hebrew, is precarious and uncertain. These versions themselves have suffered in the course of transmission, and there is no evidence that their Hebrew sources were more reliable than those now available to us.*"

Our critic then attacks **Isaiah 53:11**, where the AV1611 reading "**He shall see of the travail of his soul**" has been altered to "After the suffering of his soul, he will see the light (of life)" in the NIV, the brackets indicating that the words are UNCERTAIN (NIV Preface p viii). See Proverbs 22:21! Both the JB and NWT change the sense of Isaiah 53:11 with the NIV. The JB also adds "the light" and the NWT has "Because of the trouble of his soul he will see." The AV1611 is correct because the Lord Jesus Christ IS "**the Light**" John 1:7–9. He does not need to "see" it. However, He 'saw' "**the travail of his soul**" Matthew 26:38, John

12:27, even to the extent of His bloody sweat, Luke 22:44. The NIV, JB, NWT overlook all of this.

The sources for the NIV reading are the *"Dead Sea Scrolls"* and the Septuagint, where Brenton has the rather garbled reading "the Lord also is pleased to take away from him the travail of his soul, to shew him light and to form him with understanding." The unsavoury character of the Septuagint or LXX, was outlined in Chapter 1, Section 1.2.

Our critic's last *"omission"* for the AV1611 is in **Psalm 145:13,** where the NIV adds "The Lord is faithful to all his promises and loving towards all he has made" on the basis of *"One manuscript of the Masoretic Text, Dead Sea Scrolls, Septuagint and Syriac."* Brenton's LXX reads "The Lord is faithful in his words, and holy in all his works."

The addition, found also in the JB, is apparently necessary to complete the Hebrew alphabet for the Psalm. Based therefore on mere conjecture and a few mostly dubious sources, it was rightly discarded by the AV1611 translators.

Moreover, the NIV addition is misleading. The Lord does NOT have to be "faithful" in keeping any promises to **"the froward"** 2 Samuel 22:27, Psalm 18:26 and is NOT "loving to all he has made". See Psalm 5:5, 6, 11:5, Proverbs 16:4, 22:14, Ezekiel 28:15–19.

10.4 "INCORRECT RENDERINGS OF THE HEBREW AND GREEK"

Unfortunately, our critic does NOT specify what *"the Hebrew and Greek"* ARE, whether words, texts, languages, manuscripts, *"original autographs"* or critical editions. His terminology is not very precise.

However, he begins this section with the statement *"**These are innumerable.**"* Yet in the previous section *The Text of the New Testament*, in the sub-section *Getting things into perspective*, para 3, he maintains that *"**Bibles differ for 3% of the text and agree for 97%.**"*

Does this mean that the NIV has 97% of these *"innumerable errors"* or that our critic has lost some of his *"perspective"*? For a proper "perspective", I quote from Dr. Ruckman (29) p 47–48: *"It is surpassingly strange that I have not been able to find fault with the Holy Bible . . . after reading the AV through carefully about eighty times (from 1949–1981), I have been unable to find an error in it – NOT ONE REAL ERROR."*

I would add that Dr. Ruckman has taught Greek and Hebrew at his Pensacola Bible Institute for well over twenty years. To this day he maintains the position quoted above, having now read through the AV1611 at least one hundred and twenty seven times.

The essential point here is that anyone CAN KNOW FOR CERTAIN what Dr. Ruckman's 'final authority' is, in ALL matters of faith and PRACTICE. This is NOT true in regard to our critic.

One should note that he does not give examples of incorrect Hebrew renderings here. Apart from his objection to the word "**charity**", neither does he state explicitly WHAT the supposed errors in the AV1611 ARE or HOW they are corrected or by WHAT authority.

Our critic's first "error" is **Mark 6:20**, where instead of "**observed him**" and "**he did many things**" AV1611, "protected him" and "he was greatly puzzled" or similar, are found in the NIV, JB, NWT, Ne. All the Greek editions, including the TR, are rendered as the NIV etc. for the first phrase. The second phrase is found only in T, besides Ne.

The reading "protected him" is said to be "*ridiculous*" by Dr. Ruckman (4) p 220, who poses the extremely pertinent question "*Wouldn"t John have been safer in the wilderness with his converts?*" Herod's "*protection*" was extremely dubious. It consisted of INCARCERATION, verse 17, followed by DECAPITATION, verse 16.

However, (4) p 148–149, "**observed**" matches the rest of the verse: "**when he heard him, he did many things, and heard him gladly.**" Herod certainly kept John under observation and put into practice – or "**observed**" – his teachings.

The TBS article 33, *Many Things* says of the AV1611 reading "**he did many things**": "*According to the "critical apparatus" in the first and second editions of the Greek text published by the United Bible Societies, the "Received Text" EPOIEI is supported by the Codex Alexandrinus, Codex Bezae, most of the other manuscripts, the Vulgate and Old Latin versions, and most of the Syriac versions, the Gothic, Armenian and Georgian, and the Diatessaron – a witness from the 2nd century. Against this torrent of favourable testimony the textual critics quote the Codex Sinaiticus, Codex Vaticanus, Codex Freerianus, and two 9th century copies of the Gospels . . . L and theta. One of these has EPOREITO, and four have EPOREI, which by the variation of two letters (I, R) lays the foundation for the changed rendering of this verse found in the modern versions . . .*

"The new reading violates the "laws of Textual Criticism" which the critics themselves have propounded and sometimes seem disposed to accept only when favourable to their case. One of the rules of internal evidence is . . . that where the manuscripts differ, the more difficult reading is more likely to be genuine . . . One would think that the present case was one in which the critics might be prepared to apply their own

acknowledged rule of criticism... "**He did many things**" *is certainly the harder reading, and it is difficult to imagine that a copyist would find in his original document the simple phrase* "was much perplexed" *and deliberately alter it to* "**did many things**" . . .

"*Why then did the critics forsake their own law? . . . There is one answer. Namely that since the middle of the 19th century many who have pursued the "science of textual criticism" have allowed their judgement to be ruled by a small group of ancient and defective manuscripts, akin to Codex Vaticanus and Codex Sinaiticus, which the Church as a whole wisely and rightly rejected in the 4th century as being not truly representative of that Divine Revelation which was first given,* "**not in words which man's wisdom teacheth, but which the Holy Ghost teacheth**"" 1 Corinthians 2:13.

Our critic's next "*error*" is in **Mark 9:18**, where the AV1611 readings "**teareth him**" and "**and pineth away**" are replaced by "throws him to the ground" and "becomes rigid", or similar, in the NIV, JB, NWT ("loses his strength" instead of "pineth away"). The English renderings in the TR, Ne, G, L, T, Tr, A, W all support the first alteration but not the second.

Two books which deal extensively with demon possession are *War on the Saints* by Jesse Penn-Lewis and *He Came to Set the Captives Free* by Rebecca Brown, M.D. Dr. Brown, p 247, states: "*Demons tear apart a physical body on the molecular level. They do this in such a way that devastating damage can be done to the various organs without altering the appearance of the cellular structure under our microscopes.*"

It would appear that the AV1611's "*error*" here has yielded medical information IN ADVANCE of subsequent scientific research.

Mrs. Penn-Lewis confirms the other AV1611 reading in this verse. She writes of individuals under demonic influence, p 151: "*Such persons lose their flesh, for demoniac possession is very wearing on the vital forces and produces a terrible strain on the heart and nervous system.*"

Note that whereas the AV1611 uses the simple word "**tare**" in verse 20, the NIV uses the more complex expression "threw into a convulsion". See Gail Riplinger's detailed analysis of the complexities of the NIV's wording (12) p 209. This information was given in Chapter 5, Section 5.7 but our critic chose to ignore it.

Our critic's next "*error*" is in **John 18:1** where "**garden**" in the AV1611 should be changed to "olive grove" as in the NIV. The JB, NWT, Ne and the other Greek New Testaments all have "garden" here. "Kepos" is given uniformly as "garden" in Berry's Greek-English Lexicon, as does the *Expository Dictionary of Bible Words* by W.E. Vine (52), who is no friend of the AV1611.

The AV1611 shows that Gethsemane was on the mount of OLIVES, Matthew 26:30, 36 but adds that the Lord's "**hour**", John 17:1, was "**at hand**" Matthew 26:45 in "**a garden**". WHY WOULDN"T IT BE AT HAND IN A GARDEN, WITH AN ADVERSARY, John 18:3 and GENESIS 3? The NIV 'correction' destroys the cross reference. It may be that our critic prefers "finished praying" in the NIV to "**had spoken these words**" in the AV1611 but the latter reading shows explicitly that the Lord had prayed ALOUD.

The next "*error*", according to our critic, is in **Acts 2:6**, where "**this was noised abroad**" in the AV1611 should be changed to "they heard this sound", as in the NIV, JB, NWT, Ne. Berry's translation of the TR has "rumour".

Dr. Ruckman's Commentary on *Acts*, p 70–71, states: *"The reading "sound" instead of "**noised abroad**" was the reading of the Roman Catholic version of 1941, and the word was translated as "voice" in the Jesuit Bible of 1582 . . . But look at the context! Wasn"t there a NOISE in the context (vs. 2)? And after reading through page after page of corrections on a "**rushing mighty wind**" and being told that it was a "violent wind being borne along," or "like a hurricane," or "like a tornado," are we then to suddenly assume that only a "sound" was heard and that this sound was only the "twelve" speaking in tongues? . . .*

"The "**THIS**" *of* "**Now when THIS was noised abroad . . .** " *plainly refers to the whole transaction mentioned in verses 2, 3 and 4. The noise of the wind was heard and those who heard spread the news like wildfire (Acts 2:22)."*

Our critic's next "*error*" is in **Acts 5:30**, where the AV1611 reading "**whom ye slew and hanged on a tree**" should be changed to "whom you had killed by hanging him on a tree" in the NIV. The JB, NWT, Ne and the renderings of all the other Greek texts follow suit, with minor variation. However, the NIV alone has the additional words "from the dead" which do not appear in any of the Greek editions.

Of this alteration, Dr. Ruckman states, ibid p 213: *"The idea behind the juggling (of verse 30) is that the "first aorist middle indicative" and the "first aorist active participle" are supposed to indicate the slaying took place AFTER the hanging. But, of course, all of this grammatical twaddling does nothing for the text; "**YE**" in the text is aimed at men who did not even touch a nail, spear, rope, mallet, cross, or hammer. They did not "SLAY" Christ BEFORE or AFTER. He was hung on a tree, and*

Peter's remark is going behind the bare act to the INTENTION of the elders of Israel when they delivered Jesus over to Pilate. First Aorists and Middle participles are about as relevant to proper exposition of the text as first basemen and middle line-backers." John 11:53 states **"they took counsel together for to put him to death"** *and 1 John 3:15 states* **"Whosoever hateth his brother is a murderer."**

Our critic's next *"error"* is in **Acts 19:2** where *"since"* in the AV1611 should apparently be "when" as found in the NIV, JB, NWT. Ne has "if" and the English rendering of the other Greek texts is "having believed".

Dr. Ruckman, ibid p 548–552, states: *"The New ASV (as the old one) has inserted* "WHEN" *for* **"SINCE"** *in verse 2. Then this necessitates altering* **"HAVE YE?"** *to* "did you?" *And just to make sure the verse no longer bears any resemblance to the hated King James Bible, the word* **"GHOST"** *has been altered to* "spirit" . . . *The* **"baptism of repentance"** *(vs. 4) which John preached (vs. 4) was NOT the baptism of the Holy Ghost (Acts 1:5), and John told his audience that when they quizzed him (Matthew 3:11).*

"They had NOT received the HOLY GHOST "since" *they believed for they were in the same position that the Samaritan converts were in Acts 8.* **"We have not so much as heard whether there be any Holy Ghost"** *(vs. 2)...* **"Unto what then were ye baptized?"** *(vs. 3). Well, John was baptizing in his own name so they were baptized unto John, just as Israel was baptized* **"unto"** *Moses (Cf. 1 Corinthians 10:1–4, Matthew 3:7, 21:25, Mark 11:30, Luke 7:29). It is* **"John's Baptism,"** *NOT CHRIST's . . . Not a word about John's statement which he made on the baptism of the Holy Ghost (Matthew 3:11), and therefore, these "interim" converts, halfway between Matthew 3 and Acts 2:38, match their master (Apollos) who was caught in the same transitional place (18:25)."*

Dr. Ruckman comments on how these men speak in tongues after the laying on of Paul's hands, verse 6: *"In the Corinthians Epistle, the Bible believer was first told that tongues were a* **"Sign"** *(1 Corinthians 14:22) to ISRAEL (Isaiah 28:11,12); then he was told that prophecy (1 Corinthians 14:22) served the BELIEVER. Paul is a believer, hence the double notice of Acts 19:6:* **"they spake with tongues, AND prophesied . . . "** *the passage was interpreted in 1 Corinthians 14:22 more than 18 centuries before any British scholar (or American scholar) changed* **"since"** *to* "when". *Obviously Apollos' converts had not been baptized according to Matthew 28:19, 20 or Acts 2:38, for the HOLY GHOST is mentioned in connection with both baptisms! The only fair question to ask then is,* **"Unto what then were you baptized?"** "

"The AV (1611) text is infallible, absolute truth as it stands, and no "God-breathed originals" would shed any more light on it than the light it already has in the God-honoured Reformation text of 1611."

Our critic's's next *"error"* is in **Romans 3:25**, where "**remission of sins that are past**" in the AV1611 should supposedly read "sins committed beforehand unpunished" as in the NIV, JB. The NWT and all the Greek texts appear to match the AV1611 here, with only minor variation.

Dr. Ruckman states (43) p 30–31: *"Romans 3:25. Case E: (Where the reviser doesn't believe the verse or can't understand it.) Forgetting that when they perverted Exodus 34:7 to match their theory (that "people in the Old Testament were saved by looking forward to the cross"), they had said* "he does NOT leave the guilty unpunished". *Now the wretched apostates crash into Romans, dealing with the sins of Exodus 34, and say,* "He had left the sins committed beforehand UNPUNISHED".

"You never saw a grosser contradiction in any book in the Library of Congress. There was nothing in Romans 3:25 about anyone punishing or not punishing anyone's sins. The verse had to do with the FINISHED, COMPLETED BLOOD ATONEMENT OF JESUS CHRIST, which was the "**REDEMPTION** *(look at v. 24)* **OF THE TRANSGRESSIONS WHICH WERE UNDER THE FIRST TESTAMENT**" *(Heb. 9:15). God did not* "**forebear**" *to punish Cain, Abel, Abraham, Isaac, Jacob, Noah, David, Moses, Jehoshaphat, Josiah, Elijah, or Elisha. His* "**forbearance**" *(AV) was REMITTING sins without REDEEMING them (Heb. 9:15). The irreverent, stupid, blundering blockheads who believed in* "verbal, plenary inspiration" *couldn't actually understand Hebrew, Greek, or English. Furthermore, they couldn't read THEIR OWN TRANSLATION when they got through messing it up.*

"This is the NEW INTERNATIONAL VERSION (1978)."

Our critic's next *"error"* is in **Galatians 3:24** where "**our schoolmaster**", AV1611, should – apparently – be changed to the NIV's "put in charge." The JB has "guardian", Ne has "trainer" and the NWT with the English renderings of the other Greek editions have "tutor".

The supposed error here is described by Vine (52) in his *Expository Dictionary of Bible Words*: *"The paidagogus ("schoolmaster") was not the instructor of the child; he exercised a general supervision over him and was responsible for his moral and physical well-being. Thus understood, paidagogus is appropriately used with 'kept in ward' and 'shut up,' whereas to understand it as equivalent to 'teacher' introduces an idea entirely foreign to the passage, and throws the Apostle's argument into confusion.*"

The English word 'pedagogue' is from 'paidagogus' and means 'schoolmaster' or 'teacher', although usually in a derogatory sense, implying pedantry. Nevertheless, *"pedagogy"* is *"science of teaching"* in the normal sense.

However, could either W.E. Vine or our critic seriously believe that the Law was not there to TEACH, especially in regard to the Lord Jesus Christ?

'**Search the Scriptures; for in them ye think ye have eternal life: and they are they which testify of me**" John 5:39.

"**And beginning at Moses and all the prophets, he expounded unto them in all the scriptures the things concerning himself**" Luke 24:27.

"**All things must be fulfilled, which were written in the law of Moses, and in the prophets, and in the psalms concerning me**" Luke 24:44b.

"**I have more understanding than ALL MY TEACHERS: for THY TESTIMONIES are my meditation**" Psalm 119:99.

"**The law of the Lord is perfect, CONVERTING the soul: the testimony of the Lord is sure, Making WISE the simple**" Psalm 19:8.

Is the pedantic (!), literal, 'original' sense of 'pedagogue' as "put in charge," likely to be 'clearer' to the modern reader than SCHOOLMASTER? For every one child who had the former, there must be untold thousands who have had the latter. Moreover, how could the law "lead us to Christ", NIV, if it was simply "put in charge"? In Acts 16:24, a JAILOR was "put in charge" of Paul and Silas and did not "lead" them anywhere. (He THRUST them into the inner prison.)

In his Commentary on *Galatians*, p 103, Dr. Ruckman states: *"The law was a teacher, and everyday it taught the same lesson – "YOU ARE A SINNER." It kept this curriculum through 1400 years (or more) of history and absolutely prevented any man from justifying himself (Luke 16:15). Even those who walked blameless in the Law (Luke 1:6, Phil. 3:3–6) still had to trust the shed blood of the lamb; and all the lambs in Asia, Africa, and Europe could not REDEEM the* "**transgressions**" (Rom 3:25) *which were under the first covenant. There is only one door out of the classroom, and the class will not dismiss until Revelation 21. Christ is* "**THE DOOR.**" *You can no more* "*go home for recess*" *through Buddha, Lao Tse, and Mohammed than you can bust your way out of a Bank Vault with a toothbrush.*"

Our critic's next *"error"* is in **Galatians 6:11** where "**how large a**

letter", AV1611, should be "what large letters", as in the NIV, JB, NWT, Ne and the English renderings in all the other Greek texts.

Dr. Ruckman states in his Commentary on *Galatians*, p 180: "*The Jesuits have always objected to this translation because their fabrication of 1582 (Rheims) . . . has written* "what manner of LETTERS I have written to you" . . .

"*But again the entire body of Catholic, Protestant, and Atheistic scholarship is "fudging." Why all the "accuracy" this time about the dative plural of "gamma" (Gk., "letter") after omitting WHOLE WORDS (Gal. 5:21* "**murder**" *omitted by NIV, JB, NWT, Ne, T; L, Tr, A regard as* "doubtful"*) and PHRASES (Gal. 3:1* "**that ye should not obey the truth**" *omitted by NIV, JB, NWT, Ne, G, L, T, Tr, A, W)* . . .

"*After tearing out an admonition to* "**obey the truth**" *(3:1), now who are you to go around babbling about* "singulars and plurals"*? Having swallowed the camel, are you going to expect us to give you audience while you strain the gnat? If it was* "large letters", *what would it mean? . . .*

"*Paul is plainly saying:* "*This is a long letter for me to write because writing is tough on my eyes (4:15), but I am taking the time out to do it so you can see how concerned I am. I am not waiting for an* 'amanuensis.' *And if the RV or the ASV or the New ASV (or any other ASV or the NIV, JB, NWT) translators put an* 's' *on this here word* 'letter,' *ASK THEM WHY THEY FORGOT TO PUT ONE ON* "**SABBATH**" *IN MATTHEW 28:1. If there is anything I can't stand it's an inconsistent hypocrite!!*"

Our critic concludes this sub-section by objecting to the AV1611's use of the word "**charity**". The Dictionary meaning of "**charity**" is "*Christian love of fellow men,*" which certainly matches the description given in 1 Corinthians 13. "**Charity**", therefore, cannot be regarded as an "*incorrect rendering,*" whatever reasons the translators had for this rendering of "agape."

The contexts where "**charity**" is used show that it is intimately associated with actions that affect others, Romans 14:15, 1 Corinthians 13,16:14, should characterise Christian fellowship, Colossians 3:14, 2 Thessalonians 1:3, 2 Peter 2:7 and can be OBSERVED, 1 Thessalonians 3:6, 1 Timothy 4:12, 3 John 6. Moreover, use of "**charity**" in 1 Corinthians 13:3 eliminates any confusion arising from 'modern' connotations of the word. The AV1611 translators, therefore, were quite justified in translating "agape" in this way, in spite of Our critic's opinion.

Paine (53) p 125 states: "*Many have discussed the use, in 1 Corinthians 13, of the word* "**charity**" *for the Greek agape. We have no light on how*

170 *O BIBLIOS*

the learned men came to prefer this word to the word "love" *which appears in some older versions . . . But if we can, as we read 1 Corinthians, divest the word* "**charity**" *of rather smug later readings, we can sense a fitness in its rhythm.*

"*Rhythm in the days of King James was important not merely as a source of pleasure to the ear, but as an aid to the mind. Generations to come would learn to read by puzzling out verses in the Bible that for many families would be a whole library. But at the time of translation, a Bible* "*appointed to be read in churches*" *was made to be listened to and remembered. Its rhythms were important as a prompting for memory. For that reason, in the words of their own Bible, it is evident that the learned men learned to use their ears as they worked – "the ear trieth words as the mouth tasteth meat."*

NO modern version even comes close to the AV1611 for the ease with which its words can be REMEMBERED. See the discussion in Chapter 5, Section 5.7, which our critic also chose to ignore. Rhythmic words like "**charity**" are part of that process of enabling the child of God to HIDE GOD's WORD IN HIS HEART, Psalm 119:11 in order to have AN HONEST AND GOOD HEART, Luke 8:15.

On that basis, which our critic seems to have overlooked, use of the word "**charity**", where it occurs, is MORE than justified.

10.5 "NUMEROUS ERRORS IN TEXTS WHICH CONCERN SALVATION"

Our critic's first "*error*" here is the AV1611 reading of "**such as should be saved**" in **Acts 2:47**, where "*a present participle passive*" demands that the "*correct*" reading should be "were being saved," as in the NIV, NWT and the English renderings of Ne and the other Greek texts. The JB has "destined to be saved."

Dr. Ruckman (17) p 339–340, prints John 3:16 beside Acts 2:47 to show "*how the word* "**SHOULD**" *is used.*" He adds "*Obviously, the word* "**should**" *in neither place is a five-point Calvinistic word and in neither place does it carry any doubtful connotation (such as* "*You SHOULD go downtown, but MAYBE you won't*"*). The word* "**should**" *in John 3:16 is the same simple future found in Matthew 26:35 –* "**Though I should die with thee.**" *Note John 6:71,* "**He it was that should betray him.**" *There is no* "*if*" *to it. The simple future is found throughout the AV text (*'**shut up unto the faith which SHOULD after . . .** " *(Gal. 3:23),* "**unto those that after SHOULD live ungodly**" *(2 Peter 2:6). The word* "**should**" *in*

Acts 2:47 is used in the sense of "as many as would trust Christ did it, and those that did it were added to the Church."'

Note that both the AV1611 and the NIV have the simple future in Romans 6:6, "**should not serve sin**" and "**should no longer be slaves to sin**" respectively.

Our critic states that "***the Greek construction***" of Acts 2:47 is the same as in 1 Corinthians 1:18 where "are being saved" is the reading of the NIV, NWT and the English renderings of the Greek editions. The JB has "on the way to salvation."

He also states that **Romans 6:6, 8:24** and **Galatians 2:20** are wrong in the AV1611, which has "**is crucified**", "**are saved**" and "**am crucified,**" respectively. The "*correct*" readings are "was crucified," "were saved" and "have been crucified" as in the NIV and partly in the JB ("shall be saved" in Romans 8:24) and NWT ("was impaled" in Romans 6:6, "am impaled" in Galatians 2:20). The English renderings of Ne and the other Greek texts follow the NIV readings. The basis for the alterations are the "***aorist indicative passive,***" Romans 6:6, 8:24 and the "*perfect indicative passive,*" Galatians 2:20.

Gail Riplinger (12) p 242ff and John Burgon (13) p 154ff have some penetrating comments on the modern alterations:

Mrs Riplinger writes:

"The Church of Cain"

"Clement, the second century core of the new versions, contrived a system in which "baptism is decidedly more prominent than redemption by the blood of Christ," since he had been "initiated by the laver of illumination into the true mysteries." His formula for salvation became fixed in print at the Council of Constantinople and later by the Council of Trent. The foundation, "One baptism for the remission of sins," was framed on a fault line extending back to Cain, the father of false creeds. New version editors have built their churches and versions on this volcanic rock. Westcott writes of "initiation in the Mysteries . . . deep in mystic rites . . . purified with holiest water." Elsewhere he says,

"The remission of sins has always been connected with Baptism, the sacrament of incorporation . . . (We are) placed in relation to God by Baptism."

"Philip Schaff, at the hub of the "New" Greek and ASV, was tried for heresy by his denomination for his belief in baptism/initiation regeneration. From his hub, spokes like the Living Bible and NASV moved this creed into the next century. Hort peddled the same heresy:

"I am a staunch sacerdotalist . . . Paul connected the state (salvation)

with a PAST COMPLETED act (baptism) by which it was formerly taken possession of."

'See this "past completed" action of baptism in the NASV, NIV and all new versions. Their verbs are mistranslated, as even the preface of the NASB Interlinear Greek-English New Testament admits:

"The Authorized Version is idiomatically correct."

"Christians "are saved" (present tense) when they receive Jesus as Saviour. The new versions present baptism/initiation views as intended by their editors, a past completed act that does not necessarily follow into the present."

Mrs Riplinger then presents a table of readings from the new versions vs. the AV1611 to substantiate this statement. I have listed the readings from the NIV, with additions, including the so-called *"corrections"* given by our critic:

NIV	Verse	KJV
has been baptised, NASV	Mark 16:16	is baptised
has died	Rom. 6:7	is dead
has been freed	Rom. 6:7	is freed
have been enriched	1 Cor. 1:5	are enriched
has been crucified	Gal. 2:20	am crucified
have been saved	Eph. 2:8	are saved
have been given fullness	Col. 2:10	are complete
have been raised	Col. 3:1	be risen
have been born again	1 Pet. 1:23	being born again
have come to know him	1 John 2:3	know him
sanctified	1 Cor. 1:2	are sanctified
died	Rom. 6:8	be dead
died	Col. 2:20	be dead
died	Col. 3:3	are dead
died	2 Tim. 2:11	be dead
were buried	Rom. 6:4	are buried
was crucified	Rom. 6:6	is crucified
were washed	1 Cor. 6:11	are washed
were sanctified	1 Cor. 6:11	are sanctified
were justified	1 Cor. 6:11	are justified
were called	1 Tim. 6:12	art also called

Dr. Ruckman (1) p 332–333 has a detailed analysis of Galatians 2:20:

"The tense of the Greek word "sustauroo" in Galatians 2:20 in any family of manuscripts is a past perfect indicative passive ("I have been crucified"), and so it is translated in the NIV, ASV, NASV, RSV, RV, NRSV,

*etc. (To save time and space, we will hereafter refer to these versions and others like them simply as "the Laodicean washouts.") The English scriptures have quite a comment to make about this "tense." The comments will be found in scriptures where Paul dies "***DAILY***" *(1 Cor. 15:31), where the outward man is presently perishing (2 Cor. 4:16, not past tense), in Luke 9:23, where a man is to take up his cross "***DAILY***", not in THE PAST, and where being made conformable to Christ's death on Calvary (Phil. 3:10) is A PRESENT AND FUTURE OPERATION: not just in THE PAST. The AUTHORISED VERSION here has the correct translation, "I AM CRUCIFIED" (present not perfect tense), and the scriptures ALREADY DREW JUDGMENT ON THE GREEK GRAMMARS AND LEXICONS. All of the Laodicean washouts missed it, because their authors got down off the cross and paraded their stinking, fleshly natures in public before the body of Christ."*

Our critic has a comment that "***Luke 9:23 is dealing with a quite different concept***" from that of Galatians 2:20. He does not state what that difference is but of course there COULD be a difference if the wording of either verse was changed. However, the Bible believer can thank the Author of the Book that he has the RIGHT wording for BOTH verses and therefore the RIGHT "*concept*", as set out by Dr. Ruckman above.

Mrs Riplinger continues: "*sounding like the scribes in the synagogue* "**who laughed him to scorn**" *(Mark 5:40), Calvin Linton, NIV Committee member refers to those who disagree with the alterations in the new versions as "uninitiated" and "amusingly uninformed."*

"**The just upright man is laughed to scorn**" *Job 12:4.*

"*Hort and the new version editors who,* "*have been saved*" *at baptism, have a spokesman today in Alan Schreck, author of "Catholic and Christian".*

""*Evangelical Protestants will sometimes ask a Catholic acquaintance, "Have you been saved?" . . . The question seems to suggest that a person's salvation is a once-and-for-all event that happens in a single moment, rather than a process . . . I believe that a Catholic can adequately answer the question. The Catholic can say that, "I have been saved (Catholic baptism); I am being saved" (works, obedience, perseverance)."*

"*The new versions echo Schreck saying,* "have been saved" *(Eph 2:8) and* "are being saved" *(1 Cor. 1:18 et al.). In both of these verses the KJV says* "**are saved**", *which clearly describes the once-for-all-event that occurs when Jesus Christ is received as Saviour. One can only ask, are*

*the new versions Catholic or Christian? Notice how the new versions
present the process theology of the New Age and apostate Christianity
where initiation commences an incessant course conveying one to
salvation.*

NIV	Verse	KJV
were being saved	Acts 2:47	should be saved
are turning to God	Acts 15:19	are turned
are being saved	1 Cor. 1:18	are saved
are being saved	2 Cor. 2:15	are saved
are perishing	2 Cor. 4:3	are lost
is being renewed	Col. 3:10	is renewed
is passing	1 John 2:8	is past

"Dean Burgon, noted Greek scholar, comments on the "are being
saved" *and* "have been saved" *rendition of the Greek verbs.*

"*The schoolboy method of translation is therein exhibited in constant
operation throughout. We are never permitted to believe that we are in
the company of scholars . . . the idiomatic rendering of a Greek author
into English is a higher achievement by far . . . Examples of their
inconsistency reduces the whole matter to a question of Taste . . . The vast
number of cases in which they have forsaken their own rule shows that it
could not be followed without changing elements of the original.. They
virtually admit that they have been all along unjustly forcing on an
independent language an alien yoke.*"

See *The Revision Revised* (13) p 154ff. The NIV translators appear to
have heeded Burgon's admonitions in Matthew 2:6, 7, 9, 23. However
they retained the un-idiomatic RV readings in Matthew 2:1, 2, 12
(omitting "**of God**"), 13, upon which Burgon comments in detail.

Mrs Riplinger concludes "*Foster of the NIV and NKJV committees
agrees, (with Burgon) admitting, "This in itself results in an unnatural
straining of the tenses of the English." However, the doctrinal bend of the
translator tends toward a progressive kind of salvation and this is
reflected in their versions.*"

Our critic's next "*error*" in the AV1611 is in **Romans 5:11** where
"**atonement**" should be "reconciliation," as in the NIV, JB, NWT and the
English renderings of the Greek texts.

Unger's Bible Dictionary defines "**atonement**" as "*the reconciliation
between God and man, accomplished by the Lord Jesus Christ,*" which
is suggested by the word itself, at-one-ment. It is difficult, therefore to see
anything in our critic's objection other than an irrational prejudice against
the AV1611.

Moreover, the word "**atonement**" in Romans 5:11, which occurs NOWHERE ELSE in the New Testament IMMEDIATELY associates the work of the Lord Jesus Christ at Calvary with the sacrifices under the Mosaic Law, Exodus, Leviticus, showing that the Law was indeed our SCHOOLMASTER TO BRING US UNTO CHRIST, Galatians 3:24, 25.

Our critic's next "*error*" in the AV1611 is in **Hebrews 2:17**, where "**make reconciliation**" in the AV1611 should be "make propitiation" as in the NKJV, NWT ("propitiatory sacrifice") and the English renderings of the Greek texts.

In spite of our critic's confidence that the NIV is "**correct each time**" in the verses he lists in this sub-section, the NIV has "make atonement" in Hebrews 2:17 and a similar reading is in the JB. The NIV here is obviously the same as the AV1611 reading.

However, given our critic's concern for the word "**propitiation**", why does he not criticise the NIV which OMITS it EACH TIME it occurs in the New Testament, substituting "sacrifice of atonement," Romans 3:25 and "atoning sacrifice," 1 John 2:2, 4:10? The JB does likewise with "reconciliation," Romans 3:25 and "sacrifice," 1 John 2:2, 4:10. (The NWT has "propitiation," Romans 3:25 and "propitiatory sacrifice," 1 John 2:2, 4:10.)

The key to the correct reading, as usual preserved in the AV1611, is that the Lord Jesus Christ IS the propitiation who thus can MAKE RECONCILIATION. In Romans 3:25, He is "**set forth to be A PROPITIATION,**" in 1 John 2:2, He IS THE PROPITIATION FOR THE SINS OF THE WHOLE WORLD – not just "the elect" and in 1 John 4:10, "**God . . . sent his Son to be THE PROPITIATION FOR OUR SINS.**" The Lord Jesus Christ does not just MAKE "a specific payment to appease or placate an offended party," which is propitiation, He IS that specific payment, which is then the basis FOR reconciliation. This is surely the sense of 2 Corinthians 5:19, 20.

Our critic's last "*error*" in this sub-section is in **2 Timothy 2:8**, where "**was raised from the dead**" in the AV1611 should be "raised from the dead" in the NIV, JB ("risen from the dead") and the English renderings of the Greek texts. The NWT has the AV1611 reading here.

The basis for this "*error*" is that 'the Greek' is a "*perfect participle passive*" which means that the Lord "*continues now in his risen state*", rather than "*was raised*", which is only (!) "*a historical fact*".

Is the Lord's resurrection an historical fact or isn"t it? If so, is it not an IMPORTANT historical fact, for which there should be BIBLICAL

DOCUMENTATION?? See also Romans 1:4 and 1 Corinthians 15:3, 4. Could anyone miss the fact that The Lord "*continues now in his risen state*" if they read verses 1, 7, 10, 11, 12, 13, 14, 22 IN THE SAME CHAPTER of 2 Timothy??

Our critic is gnat-straining, Matthew 23:24.

Concerning the Lord continuing "*in his risen state,*" should not our critic object to the NIV in Romans 6:9 with "was raised" and 1 Corinthians 15:20 with "has been raised," where the AV1611 has "**being raised,**" Romans 6:9 and "**is risen,**" 1 Corinthians 15:20?

One should note that upon examination of the verses in this subsection, it is THE NIV which is guilty of FALSE DOCTRINE with respect to SALVATION, not the AV1611.

10.6 "INACCURACIES OF TRANSLATION CORRECTED BY ARCHAEOLOGY"

One is here to suppose that somebody, somewhere – our critic does not elaborate – dug up some things which should make the child of God dispense with the Book God gave him and submit to "*scholarship only-ism.*"

The first "*inaccuracy,*" according to our critic, is in **Joshua 11:13**, where "**strength,**" AV1611, should be "Tells," the latter word, which is a Hebrew word, being translated as "mounds" in most of the modern versions.

The verse as it stands indicates that the cities which had not been damaged by the ravages of war, were preserved as dwelling places for the people of Israel. This would be the fulfilment of Deuteronomy 6:10, with a precedent having been set in Deuteronomy 3:12. The modern reading adds NOTHING to an understanding of the verse.

Dr. Ruckman has an interesting comment (48) p 69: "*All of this sudden "light on the originals," . . . had to come from some cold, dead, back-slidden, non-Pauline type of bookworm without the common sense of a muskrat . . . As near as I can remember from my five years of Greek and three years of Hebrew, it went something like this:*

"*The translators of the Authorised Version, not in possession of the light archaeology has shed on the passage in Joshua 11:13, ERRONEOUSLY rendered the text "*but as for the cities that stood still in their strength.*" It should have been "s*tood on their mounds" – because some blockhead found out they built cities on mounds.*"

If "mounds" is "preferred" it must be because cities built on such would
have had a good field of vision, Matthew 5:14 but this was true of Ai, which
was located on a ridge overlooking a valley. Yet Ai was destroyed; Joshua
8:11, 28. The modern reading therefore cannot be correct.

Our critic's next *"error"* is in **1 Kings 16:33**, which should not read
"**grove**," AV1611 but "asherah pole" as in the NIV. The JB, NWT have
"sacred pole."

In his Commentary on the *Minor Prophets* p 438, Dr. Ruckman states:
*""***Groves***" (Micah 5:14) has been altered to "s*acred poles*", in keeping
with the contemporary bull-shooting of the "scholars" that the GROVES
were really not "***groves***" – they were really "*images*".*

*"(Since ALL of the [modern] Bibles resort to this last alteration of text,
it might be a blessing for the believing student of the scripture to observe
how the Holy Spirit has corrected the stupid blundering of these
recognized scholars by giving us the material of Deuteronomy 16:21,
"***PLANT . . . a grove of any TREES***"; 2 Chronicles 31:1, "***Brake the
IMAGES in pieces, AND cut down the groves***"; 2 Chronicles 33:19,
"***And set up groves AND graven images***"; 2 Chronicles 34:3, "***And the
groves, AND the carved images, AND the molten images***"; and 2 Kings
23:14 "***and he brake in pieces the IMAGES, and cut down the
GROVES***." Don't you find it rather interesting to notice that bones are
buried in a PLACE where a grove was? And isn't it enlightening to notice
that "***NEITHER***" (Deut. 16:22) has been set in opposition to "***A grove
of any trees***" (Deut. 16:21), and the "***neither***" is a reference to "***ANY
IMAGE***"? Interesting, isn't it? An "asherim" (see comments by any
Hebrew scholar) CAN BE an image cut out of wood that came from a
GROVE, but a GROVE is a GROVE, exactly as you find it growing around
statues of Mary on the campus of every Catholic school in America.)*" Dr.
Ruckman states further in *Modern Ecology And the Oak Tree*, Part 2,
Bible Believers' Bulletin March 1999 "*[The Catholic Church] sports more
than eighty statues standing in literal "groves" by Catholic schools and
hospitals throughout the United States*".

A brief comment to this effect was included in Chapter 7, Section 7.2,
which our critic also chose to ignore.

Our critic's next *"error"* in the AV1611 is in **Matthew 5:15**, which
should not read "**candle**", AV1611 but "lamp", as in the NIV, JB, NWT
and the English renderings of the Greek texts.

However, "**candlestick,**" to which one attaches "candles" occurs in
Exodus 25:31 and in verse 37 the "candles" are called LAMPS, which
"**give LIGHT**", like the "**candle**" in Matthew 5:15. Another

'enlightening' reference is Zechariah 4:2, where the "**candlestick all of gold**" has "**seven LAMPS thereon.**"

Moreover CANDLEpower is still used as a unit of light measurement, so the word is entirely appropriate for the modern reader. Our critic is gnat-straining, again, Matthew 23:24.

10.7 "OLD TESTAMENT VERSES QUOTED IN NT PASSAGES IN DIFFERENT WORDS BY KJV, THOUGH THEY ARE IDENTICAL IN GREEK"

The first examples given are **Romans 12:19** and **Hebrews 10:30**, where the AV1611 readings are: "**Vengeance is mine; I will repay**" and "**Vengeance belongeth unto me, I will recompense.**" The NIV, JB, NWT and the English renderings of the Greek texts all have uniform readings in these verses. The Old Testament reading in Deuteronomy 32:35 is "**To me belongeth vengeance, and recompence**" AV1611.

In this case the AV1611 English 'sheds light' on the "*original Greek*" by showing that a "**recompence**" is a "repayment." This 'additional light' on "*the original*" is lost in the modern uniformity. Note too the greater force of the AV1611 readings "**Vengeance is MINE**", "**Vengeance BELONGETH UNTO ME**" compared to the milder tone of the NIV "It is mine to avenge", in which God can inflict vengeance like a human authority but it is not necessarily His, Romans 13:4, as in the AV1611. The NIV reading, in BOTH Testaments, is thus a subtle attack on God's omnipotence. This helps to reveal the Satanic nature of the modern versions, Isaiah 14:13.

The next example is that of **Romans 4:3, 22** and **Galatians 3:6**, where the AV1611 has "**it was counted unto him for righteousness**", "**it was imputed to him for righteousness**" and "**it was accounted to him for righteousness.**" Genesis 15:6, the underlying Old Testament passage, reads "**he counted it to him for righteousness**" AV1611. The NIV, JB, NWT and the Greek texts translate uniformly in each passage.

Once again the AV1611 demonstrates its superiority to the "*original Greek.*" The first reading, Romans 4:3, associates all three verses with Genesis 15:6 and when taken with verse 22 shows that "imputation" is a "counting", or attributing, of righteousness to the believer. Galatians 3:6 shows that this righteousness is entered on the believer's ACCOUNT with God. Although he will still give "**account**" for "**the things done in his body**", Romans 14:12, 2 Corinthians 5:10, he will not have to give "account" like an UNbeliever, 1 Peter 4:4, 5, who has only HIS OWN righteousness in which to trust, Isaiah 64:6. The modern versions do not yield this "additional light" on "*the original*".

Unless our critic can produce a verse of scripture which commands that readings which are identical in Greek MUST have identical renderings in English, I am inclined to dismiss his objections. His insistence on this point is too reminiscent of the schoolboy pedantry rightly denounced by Burgon (12) p 245, even if in a different context.

If he is really concerned about 'uniform translating' he should examine the NIV's translation of "mashal" in Numbers 24:3, Psalm 49:4 and 78:2, of "alma" in Genesis 24:43, Leviticus 21:13 and Song. 1:3, 6:8 and of "ouranos" in Luke 4:25 and 2 Corinthians 12:2 (29) p 53 and (48) p 24–25.

10.8 "FAILURE TO RENDER THE SAME HEBREW AND GREEK WORD BY THE SAME ENGLISH EQUIVALENT – RESULTING IN CONFUSION TO THE READER"

This is the first sub-section where "*confusion*" allegedly results from "*defects*" in the AV1611, the last of which is entitled "*Confusion created by variety in the spellings of Names of Persons and Places*". Similar comments apply in each of these sub-sections, so I will consider them together.

Our critic takes the AV1611 translators to task for seeming "*to scorn the idea that the same word in Hebrew and Greek should be always rendered by the same English equivalent where possible since it would "savor more of curiosity than wisdom.*"" He does not, however, take modern revisers to task for exercising identical scorn. See above.

He continues "*The concern to please the ear rather than be as strictly accurate and unambiguous as possible has had disastrous consequences.*"

He insists that "*Readers are misled by imagining two different words in the original underlie two different English words when in fact they do not. A few examples are "creation and creature," "soul and life," "Blessed and happy," "serve and worship," "covenant and testament," "eternal and everlasting," "authority and power," "love and charity," "appearing and revelation," "servant and son or child.*""

Examples of different spellings of names include "*Jeremiah, Jeremias and Jeremie,*" "*Noah and Noe,*" "*Jonah, Jona and Jonas,*" "*Elijah and Elias,*" "*Joshua and Jesus,*" "*Timothy and Timotheus,*" "*Elisha and Eliseus,*" "*Tyrus and Tyre,*" *Areopagus and Mars Hill,*" "*Kidron and Cedron.*" Our critic insists that "*This lack of uniformity only creates perplexities and confuses many readers. Modern versions of the Bible helpfully simplify the matter by adopting one form throughout.*"

Our critic has still not cleared up any confusion over what is "*the Bible*". It appears that only "*versions*" of "*the Bible*" are available to the reader.

Upon examination of Dr. Miles Smith's preface to the AV1611, from which the above quote was taken, it is fair to say that he has quoted Dr. Smith out of context.

Dr. Smith states: "*Another thing we think good to admonish thee of (gentle Reader) that we have not tied ourselves to an uniformity of phrasing, or to an identity of words, as some peradventure would wish that we had done, because they observe, that some learned men somewhere, have been as exact as they could that way. Truly, that we might not vary from the sense of that which we had translated before, if the word signified the same thing in both places (for there be some words that be not of the same sense everywhere) we were especially careful, and made a conscience, according to our duty.*

"*But, that we should express the same notion in the particular word; as for example, if we translate the Hebrew or Greek word once by* Purpose, *never to call it* Intent; *if one were* Journeying, *never* Traveling; *if one were* Think, *never* Suppose; *if one were* Pain, *never* Ache; *if one were* Joy, *never* Gladness, *etc. Thus to mince the matter, we thought to savor more of curiosity than wisdom, and that rather it* would breed scorn in the Atheist, than bring profit to the godly Reader. For is the kingdom of God become words and syllables? Why should we be in bondage to them if we may be free, use one precisely when we may use another no less fit, as commodiously?*" *That is, pedantic "*wisdom*"

Dr. Smith's explanation indicates that the AV1611 translators:

1. Did not tie themselves "*to a uniformity of phrasing*".
2. Recognised that some words were "*not of the same sense everywhere*".
3. Were "*especially careful*" not to "*vary from the sense*" of the underlying Greek and Hebrew word. Dr. Smith gave specific examples.
4. Were constrained to "*bring profit to the godly reader*".
5. Were fully aware that "*schoolboy pedantry*", as denounced later by Burgon, Section 10.5, would only "*breed scorn in the atheist*" INSTEAD OF ENCOURAGING HIM TO READ THE BOOK AND GET SAVED.

Our critic's criticisms are therefore unfounded because Dr. Smith and his fellow translators were obviously fully aware of having to maintain the right sense in translation, whatever English word they chose, whatever Greek or Hebrew word they had to translate. Our critic has furnished NO EVIDENCE that they failed in this responsibility.

He gives NO INDICATION WHATSOEVER of WHO was "*confused*", of WHO was "*misled*", of WHAT the "*disastrous consequences*" were or what the RESULTS were of anyone having been "*confused*" or "*misled*". Neither does he indicate who was "*perplexed*" by the "*lack of uniformity*" in the spellings of names or what were the consequences of such "*perplexity*". Nevertheless, I am supposed to accept WITHOUT QUESTION his unsubstantiated opinion that all this "*confusion*" and "*perplexity*" has arisen "*for MANY readers*", with "*disastrous consequences*".

One is reminded of the comments of Burgon (13) p xxvi, with respect to the "*recension theory*" of Westcott and Hort:

"*It dispenses with proof. It furnishes no evidence. It asserts when it ought to argue. It reiterates when it is called on to explain... "I am sir Oracle.""*

Apart from his own misleading comments on Matthew 12:18 and Acts 3:13, 26, 4:27, 30, our critic gives no explanation anywhere of HOW these pairs of "*different English words*" gave rise to ANY confusion, except in the minds of the opponents of the "*God-breathed*" AV1611. See Section 10.3.

Our critic criticises the AV1611 translators in this sub-section for their use of 84 English words to render one Hebrew word and of 17 English words for one Greek word. WHO was "*confused*" by this variety and HOW? Moreover, aren't the champions of 'the Greek and the Hebrew' continually reminding the poor, ignorant "*KJV-onlyists*" about how the 'feeble English' can never attain the 'depth of meaning' of the "*trusty Greek*" and of how words in the AV1611 were repeatedly mistranslated and should have been translated differently? This very section of our critic's document certainly testifies to this. Surely the AV1611 translators would have been RIGHT some of the time, after 84 attempts in one case and 17 in another? Why doesn't our critic list these instances?

See Dr. Gipp's analysis (9) p 124ff about so-called "*nuggets*" from "*the Greek*" and the incident with Dr. Kilbye in Chapter 4, Section 4.2.

Dr. Ruckman (4) p 148, comments: "*It is objected that the word* **Jeremiah** *has been transliterated three different ways in the AV1611 (Matt. 27:9, 16:14, 2:14). This is "confusing to the reader." It didn't* *confuse Moody, Torrey, Finney, Sunday, Spurgeon, Scofield, Carey, Goforth, Livingstone, DeHaan, Fuller, Ironsides, Rice, or anyone else who believed the Bible and PUT IT INTO PRACTICE. WHOM DID IT "CONFUSE?"*

*"If the new bibles are going to clear up these "inconsistent practices," how is it that they have translated the word "Alma" (Hebrew) three different ways, while spelling Jeremiah the same way every time? Are we supposed to be so stupid as to imagine that the word for "***Virgin***" (Alma), referring to the Virgin birth of Jesus Christ, is of LESS IMPORTANCE than the transliteration of a proper name given to a prophet?"*

The only set of *"confusing"* words which our critic actually discusses are *"servant and son or child"*, found in Matthew 12:18 "**servant**", Acts 3:13, 26 "**son**" and Acts 4:27, 30 "**child**", in the AV1611. The NIV, JB, NWT and all the English renderings of the Greek texts have "servant" in each place AND THE NIV, JB, NWT UNIFORMLY OMIT "**JESUS**" IN ACTS 3:26, along with Ne, Gr, L, T, Tr, A! The NIV, JB, NWT alter "**judgment**" to "justice" or "faith" in Matthew 12:18 and obscure God's righteous judgment at the Second Advent, Psalm 98:9.

Our critic states: *"**Your claim that modern renderings in these Acts passages...deny the deity of Christ should also be applied in consistency to the KJV in Matt. 12:18 since the underlying Greek phrase "**Pais Theou" *is exactly the same...The word "***servant***"...is a clear reference to the servant passages in Isaiah. The apostles had heard the Lord many times especially during the later part of his ministry, identify himself with the suffering servant figure. They were merely following him when they used the word "***servant***".*

*"***"Pais Theou"*** means "***servant of God***" and it is not to be confused with "***Huios Theou*** *which means "***son of God***"". A detailed discussion of these passages is found in Dr. Ruckman's Commentary on *Matthew* p 206, Commentary on *Acts* p 146ff, 185ff and in his book *King James Onlyism In Action* (54).

For Matthew 12:18, he states: *"The quotation turns out to be a description of a silent first coming, as a suffering servant, who will save not only Jews but Gentiles; but where the quotation occurs (Isa 42:1–4), there is no way to tell whether it is an individual (as in Isa 41:8) representing Israel (Isa 45:4), or whether it is the individual Messiah (Isa 49:6;41:25) representing Jehovah (Isa 53). Again, we see the subtlety and shrewdness of the Divine mind. The prophecies are so placed that they can apply to Israel or to Jesus Christ, depending upon what ISRAEL DOES WITH JESUS CHRIST WHEN HE SHOWS UP. This is the mystery* that baffled the prophets (1 Pet 1:10, 11). The modern-day Gentile expositor misses the doctrine of the Second Coming now, exactly as the Pharisee missed the first coming then; he refuses to recognise the divisions which set prophecy into dispensations."

For Acts 3:13, 26 he states: "The word paida (Greek) has been translated "SERVANT" instead of "**SON**" (The King James text – "**SON**" – is found in Tyndale, Geneva, and the Bishop's Bible, so the word was not changed until 1881–1884 (RV) by Philip Schaff, Ellicott, Lightfoot, Sanday, Westcott and Hort.)

"The first alibi given is that the word pais is translated in the Authorised Version as "**servant**" ten times; therefore why not here? The second alibi is that since the LXX...used paida for "servant" in Isaiah 42:1 and 52:13, the word should be inserted here. The third excuse given is that it would have to be huios (Greek), here, to be translated as "SON." And the fourth excuse is that it must ALWAYS MATCH ISAIAH'S DESIGNATION of the Messiah and, therefore, it has to be "servant."

1. *NOT ONE TIME IN TEN...has the word* pais *been translated as* "servant" *where it was connected with JESUS CHRIST. Every one of the ten references was a reference to ISRAEL, or DAVID, or a HIRED SERVANT – Matthew 8:6, 8, 13; 12:18; 14:2, Luke 1:54, 69; 7:2; 15:26, and Acts 4:25.*

2. *How do we know that Origen, Philo, Symmachus, Aquila, Theodotian, etc., used the right Greek word in translating "servant" from Isaiah? And if they decided on pais, what of it? THEY HAD THE GREEK TEXT OF THE KING JAMES BIBLE (Acts 4:27, 30) ON THE TABLE WHEN THEY MANUFACTURED THEIR SEPTUAGINT. You can't find any "Isaiah Scroll" in GREEK, written before 100 A.D...What dunce couldn't write pais in Isaiah 42 and 52 after reading pais in Acts 4:27 and 3:13?*

   *$10,000 reward for any accredited jackrabbit who can find any DIRECT REFERENCE to the "**servant**" of Isaiah 42 and 52 in Acts 3:13 or 4:27. Simon Peter isn't quoting one passage from Isaiah; SHOW IT TO US, SON!*

3. *And why would it have to be huios to be "son"? Didn't the (NIV translators) translate teknon (Greek for "child") as "son" in Matthew 21:28? YES, THEY DID. And did they not do it again in Luke 2:48? YES, THEY DID...If you don't keep YOUR OWN RULES, who is going to play by them? DO YOU THINK THAT GOD THE HOLY SPIRIT WILL?*

4. *Why did you pick* "servant", *as Peter's designation for the Messiah, when Isaiah has also said* "**SON**" *(Isaiah 7:14, 16) and* "**CHILD**" *(Isaiah 9:6) RIGHT IN THE SAME BOOK?* "**HAVE YE NOT READ?**" *Have ye never read? Have ye never read? (Can ye READ!?) If Peter was quoting Isaiah, which he was NOT, how do you know he wasn't talking about the* "**son**" *and the* "**child**" *of Isaiah 9:6?*

"But the Lion of the Tribe of Judah is not through with the Conservative field mice yet. Notice the "clincher," please! Romans 1:3, 4!

"The context of Acts 3:13 is the Resurrection; look at verse 15. Christ was declared to be "**THE SON of God**" *(not* "the SERVANT of God"*) by this transaction. Therefore, the substitution...is not merely unreasonable and inconsistent: IT IS NON-BIBLICAL.*

Of Acts 3:26, Dr. Ruckman states:

"Again we must note that the raising up of Christ from the dead (vs 26, "**having raised up his Son Jesus...**"*) is connected with Christ's SONSHIP, not His servitude. The word* "servant" *is out of place in either context (vss 13, 26), and you may disregard the scholarship of any man, college, institute, church, or university that recommends this kind of textual clap-trap."*

Concerning Acts 4:27, 30, Dr. Ruckman writes (54) p 5ff: *"Five Bibles before 1611 translated the Greek word as* "CHILD" *or* "SON" *(Tyndale, The Great Bible, The Geneva Bible, The Bishop's Bible, and the Douay-Rheims). All five were wrong, were they? And only AFTER 1880 did you get the* "true light" *on the text? A light that DENIED the Deity of Christ and the incarnation?...Well, let's just see about that* "Greek"...

""Ton hagion paida sou" is "THE" Greek text printed in any Greek New Testament...Now if a man were reasonable – "good men are always reasonable" (Bob Jones Sr.) – and were a Christian, he would begin to look here for a way to justify a translation that honours the Deity and Virgin Birth of Christ...We will document.

"Consider: does "paida" *mean* "CHILD" *or* "SERVANT"*?...*

"Consider: Could "paida" *mean either* "CHILD" *or* "SERVANT"?

"Would "servant" *or* "child" *be proper ways to translate it? Would both be proper HERE?...*

"In keeping with all traditional "historical" *canons of textual criticism, how does the author (Dr. Luke) usually use the word* "PAIDA"? *After all, he IS the author of Acts 4:27,30...*

"Here is a single problem in "selected readings" with "alternate possibilities," with no translator claiming to be inspired and no grammatical or exegetical problems involved except the POSSIBILITY of one or both translations ("child" and "servant") being permissible. Are both of them permissible and possible with "paida" as the source? What have you done with the Virgin Birth and the Deity of Christ if one ('servant") is used to the exclusion of the other ("child")?

"Is it possible that this is the "suffering servant" of Isaiah 42:1, 19; 43:10, and 49:5, 6? With DAVID as a servant, right in the context (vs. 25), as "PAIDOS", why shouldn't you reduce Jesus Christ to his level? Isn't the same Greek word used both times? Why all the fuss about the power and authority of the Authorised Version if the same Greek word is used for David and Christ, albeit Christ is in the context (vs. 26) of **"THOU ART MY SON; THIS DAY I HAVE BEGOTTEN THEE"**? *You see, the quotation from David was from Psalm 2 – NOT ISAIAH – and the context of verse 24, 25, and 26 is a Davidic Psalm – NOT ISAIAH – concerning the Incarnation and Virgin Birth (Psa. 2:7, 12) of Jesus Christ...*

"The men who recommended this blatant perversion of content, context, subject matter, Greek and Hebrew, and English texts – in order to avoid "King James Onlyism" – were Nestle, Aland, Metzger...R.A. Torrey, Bishop Pike, Pope Paul VI...Pope Pius XII, J. Gresham Machen, A.T. Robertson, Stewart Custer, Benjamin Warfield, and the faculties and staff of every major, recognized seminary and college in the United States.

"Now watch how documented evidence dealing with the scriptural truths involved shows how KING JAMES ONLYISM is not a "heresy," but is the greatest corrective and purgative for Nicolaitanism that the world has ever seen...

1. *PAIDA is* "**a little CHILD**" *or* "**young lad**" *in Matthew 14, 15; Mark 7, 9, 10; Luke 7,11; John 21; 1 Corinthians 14; Hebrews 2, and Matthew 2 and 21. (This word is given in the plural as* "**children**"...)
2. *In the singular, PAIDA is translated as* "**child**" *(or* "**young lad**") *in Mark 9; Luke 1, 2, 9; John 4:16; Matthew 17; Acts 7; Revelation 12, as well as Matthew 18, 19; Mark 10, Luke 18; 1 John 2, etc.. PAIDION is used for a* "**child**" *in Matthew 2 EIGHT TIMES IN A ROW, and PAIDION is used by the author of Acts as* "**CHILD**" *TEN TIMES IN HIS GOSPEL.*

"In connection with Christ's virgin mother, the medical doctor (Luke), who knew all about the Virgin Birth (Luke 1–2), never says "SERVANT"

one time in ANY Greek text or ANY English text, translated from ANY Greek text, for the word in Luke 1:59, 66, 76, 80; 2:17, 21, 27; or 9:47 ,48. In Luke 2:43, it is "**THE CHILD JESUS**" – not anyone's "servant." The word "teknon" can be translated as "child," and so can the word "huios"; see for example Matthew 10:21, Luke 1:7, Acts 7:5, Matthew 23:15, Acts 13:10, and Revelation 12:5, but PSALM 2 IS NOT ABOUT A "SERVANT," it is about a SON and the SON is the "**CHILD**" of the "**MOST HIGH**" (Luke 8:28) AND A "**KING**" (Psa. 2:6).

"Here is the Greek layout: PAIDOS: "A child in relation to PARENTS, or in respect to age; a boy, youth, girl, maiden, a servant or slave, an attendant or minister." PAIDION: "An infant or babe." PAIDARION: "A little boy or child or lad." PAIDEIA: "Correction, instruction or nurture of children" – not "servants." PAIDEUTES: "A teacher or instructor of boys." PAIDEUO: "To educate, teach, learn or instruct." PAIDIOTHEN: "From a child or childhood – not "servanthood".

"This word (pais) is only translated as "SERVANT" in ten out of more than ONE HUNDRED AND TWENTY PLACES in the New Testament. One of these places is Luke himself, the author of Acts, who calls David a "**servant**" (pais) in Luke 1:69. Luke will use "pais" for ISRAEL and DAVID, but not when speaking of JESUS CHRIST. When Luke says "**SERVANTS**" right in the context of Acts 4:27, 30 he uses DOULOS (Acts 4:29).

"When you hit PAIS in Kittel's Theological Dictionary of the New Testament you get only a passing mention that the word could mean a "servant" on occasion. Instead, you get eighty pages on "The CHILD from natural and Ethico-Religious standpoint...The CHILD in Antiquity...The Rediscovery of the CHILD in Hellenism...The CHILD in the Cultus...The CHILD in the Old Testament and Judaism...The Estimation of the CHILD...The Participation of the CHILD in religious exercises...The CHILD in the New Testament...The Affirmation of the CHILD as a creature of God, etc." The only other thing that is mentioned is "SONSHIP."

'so could "paida" in Acts 4:27, 30 really be translated as "servant"? Yes, it could, if you deny five things:

1. The style and INTENTION of the author.
2. The basic root MEANING of the word it came from.
3. The CONTEXT of the passage and the OLD TESTAMENT SCRIPTURE it was based on.

4. The MATHEMATICAL ODDS against it being "servant" (eleven to 1).
5. The DIFFERENCE between David as a mortal sinner (vs. 25) and Jesus Christ, who was "**God manifest in the flesh**".

"Could "paida" be translated as "**CHILD**"? Yes, if one goes by the context, the quotation, the author, the basic meaning of the word, the Old Testament passage it is from, the mathematical odds, and one is zealous for the FUNDAMENTALS of the Christian faith.

"There is ONE English Bible that obeys these laws of common sense, maths, reason, grammar, history, scripture, and faithfulness to the scriptures…a KING JAMES 1611 AUTHORISED VERSION.

10.9 "FAILURE TO RECOGNISE DISTINCTIONS IN THE ORIGINAL BY USING THE SAME WORD OR PHRASE FOR DIFFERENT GREEK WORDS"

Once again, our critic's terminology is not very precise. He fails to define "the original".

He also fails to explain WHY the "distinctions in the original" should be preserved in English.

The first "failure" is in **John 1:11**, where a distinction should supposedly be drawn between the two occurrences of "**his own,**" the first being "that which was his own" NIV or "his own domain" JB or "his own home" or "his own things" Ne. Berry's English rendering agrees with the AV1611.

Two observations can be made.

1. Verse 10 covers ALL the possibilities raised by drawing a distinction in "the Greek" for verse 11.
2. The point of verse 11 is surely that He must have come to "**his own**", second occurrence, when He came to "**his own**", first occurrence, because the former are reproached by the Scripture for NOT receiving Him! How could they have "**received him not**" unless He had come "**unto them**" in the first place?

Our critic's next "failure" is in **Philippians 2:6, 7** where the AV1611 has "**form**" in each verse. The NIV has "nature" in each place and although there is a spelling change in the Greek word "morphe" (form) from verse 6 to 7, Ne and Berry give each word as "form." Young's Concordance (55) lists "form" as "morphe" for both verses and Vine –

no friend of the AV1611 – states *"The true meaning of* morphe *in the expression* 'form of God' *is confirmed by its recurrence in the corresponding phrase,* 'form of a servant.' *It is universally admitted that the two phrases are directly antithetical, and that* 'form' *must therefore have the same sense in both."*

Our critic's next "failure" is with respect to the word "**hell** (many places in the Gospels)" in the AV1611.

He has obviously ignored the discussions on this matter in Chapter 5, Section 5.7 and Chapter 7, Section 7.2. The AV1611 consistently translates "hades" as "**hell**" in Matthew 11:23, 16:18; Luke 10:15, 16:23; Acts 2:27, 31; Revelation 1:18 ,6:8, 20:13, 14. It translates "geena" as "**hell**" in Matthew 5:22, 29, 30, 10:18, 18:9, 23:15, 22; Mark 9:43, 45, 47; Luke 12:5; James 3:6 and "tartaroo" as "**hell**" in 2 Peter 2:4.

For "hades", the NIV has "depths, Hades, depths, hell, grave (twice), Hades (4 times)". The JB has "hell, underworld, hell, Hades (3 times), underworld, Hades (3 times)".

Although the word "geena" has been translated as "hell" by the modern versions, their reluctance to express "hades" as "HELL" is all too apparent. They have a distinct tendency not to translate at all but to TRANSLITERATE.

It is hardly reasonable for our critic to criticise the AV1611 for doing what the modern versions often do not even ATTEMPT! He then has the nerve later to blame the AV1611 with *"Unintelligibility due to the presence of archaic and obsolete words"* – as if "**hell**" is *"unintelligible"* and "hades" is NOT!!

Dr. Ruckman (4) p 147–148 states: *"It is objected that* "**Hell**" *(for* "hades" *and* "gehenna") *is improper. To correct this* "error," *the new bibles read* "Hades" *for* "Hell" *in (ten) places, and the guileless Christian is told this is a better* "translation." *But Hades is not a translation; it is a TRANSLITERATION. By the use of this transliteration, the word* "HELL" *has been all but taken out of the Bible, much to the delight of Christ-rejecting, self-righteous* "Christians." *If the revisers had been honest men would they not have transliterated* "Heaven" *as well and called it* "Ouranos" *instead of* "Heaven?" *Again, if they wanted to put the Bible* "in the language of 20th century people," *why did they not invent a NEW word for* "hades"? HADES *IS NOT AN ENGLISH WORD."*

See also Mrs. Riplinger's extensive discussion (12) p 290ff.

Our critic's last *"failure"* in this sub-section is in **Matthew 28:19, 20**, where the AV1611 has "**teach**" and "**teaching**" respectively. "**Teach**", verse 19, should evidently be "make disciples" as in the NIV, JB, NWT.

Ne's English rendering is "Going therefore disciple ye all the nations" and Berry's TR rendering is identical, except for the omission of "ye." The sense of *"the Greek"* in this passage is therefore closer to the AV1611 reading than that of the NIV etc.

However, the Bible believer never has to rely on *"the Greek"* in a stand-off between the AV1611 and the *"Laodicean washouts"* – see Section 10.5. Leaving aside doctrinal matters which stem from the distinctly Jewish nature of the passage, see Dr. Ruckman's Commentary on *Matthew*, p 732, one need only compare "**spiritual things with spiritual**" 1 Corinthians 2:13.

The Apostle Paul in 1 Corinthians 11:1 exhorts not only the Corinthians but all Christians to "**Be ye followers of me, as I also am of Christ.**"

What did the great Apostle DO that Christians are to FOLLOW? "**(Him) we preach, warning every man, and TEACHING every man in all wisdom; that we may present every man perfect in Christ Jesus**" Colossians 1:28.

Even the NIV has "teaching" in this verse but the AV1611 is consistent in both Matthew 28:19 and Colossians 1:28.

The child of God who seeks to be 'consistent' according to the Apostle to the Gentiles, Romans 15:16 and THE LORD JESUS CHRIST should go by THE BOOK. Never mind *"the Greek"*.

10.10 "CONFUSION CREATED BY THE WRONG USE OF THE PREPOSITION"

This is the second of the three sub-sections in which *"confusion"* allegedly arises through *"defects"* in the AV1611. See Section 10.9.

Once again, it should be noted that our critic gives NO INDICATION WHATSOEVER of WHO was confused, precisely HOW they were confused and what the RESULTS of such *"confusion"* were. Neither does he indicate which preposition was *"wrongly used"* nor how.

Our critic's first *"wrong use of the Preposition"* is in **Luke 16:9**, where "**make to yourselves**", AV1611, should be "for yourselves" as in the NIV, NWT. The JB has "to win you friends." The English renderings of Ne and Berry read as the AV1611.

The AV1611 is perfectly clear as it stands. The Lord is saying to His followers 'Use worldly riches to make people well disposed or friendly TO YOU.' He had just given a detailed illustration of this tactic in the eight verses immediately preceding verse 9!

The 'fruit' of this tactic is that if the friends thus made are drawn to the Lord and go to be with the Lord first, they will provide the reception when the soul winner eventually follows. The NIV, JB, NWT MISSED this simple truth by changing "**ye fail**" to "it fails" or similar and created a NONSENSE reading.

Our critic's next "*wrong use*" is in **Luke 23:15** where "**nothing worthy of death is done unto him**", AV1611, should be "he has done nothing to deserve death" as in the NIV, JB, NWT with minor variation. The NWT has "nothing deserving of death has been committed by him", "by" instead of "to" evidently corresponding to our critic's "*correct*" reading. The English renderings of the Greek texts this time side with the modern versions.

The modern reading misses the fact that Herod's mockery of Jesus, verse 11, signified that He was simply to be disregarded, "**set at nought**", NOT executed. Herod did nothing to the Lord to show that He was an "**evil doer**", 2 Timothy 2:9 who was "**worthy of death**". For example, the Lord was not "**bound**", 2 Timothy 2:9 but "**arrayed...in a gorgeous robe**". Note that Pilate testifies to the Lord's innocence in verse 22 and so the modern reading provides no additional information at all.

The RV, NIV, JB, NWT, Ne also miss the cross reference in verse 15 to verse 10 by changing "**I sent you to him**" to "he sent him back to us". The alteration is from Tischendorf and removes the explanation of the Jews' presence in verse 10. Verse 11 of the AV1611 contains the information found in the altered reading, which therefore adds nothing to the text.

Our critic fails to mention that the RV, NIV, JB, NWT, Ne remove verse 17 from the chapter and the words "**in letters of Greek, and Latin, and Hebrew**" from verse 38. Berry indicates that T, Tr omit these scriptures while L, A regard them as "*doubtful*", although the modern versions all retain the verse numbering sequence of the AV1611. Tischendorf further omits "**and of the chief priests**" from verse 23 followed by the RV, NIV, JB, NWT, Ne.

Burgon (13) p 85–86 writes concerning the words omitted from verse 38: "*The incident is omitted by B, C, L, the corrupt Egyptian versions, and Cureton's depraved Syriac...this little band of disreputable witnesses is entirely outweighed by the positive evidence of Aleph, A, D, Q, R with 13 other uncials, – the evidence of THE ENTIRE BODY OF CURSIVES, – the sanction of the Latin, – the Peschito and Philoxenian Syriac...besides Eusebius – whose testimony (which is express) has been hitherto strangely overlooked, – and Cyril. Against the threefold plea of*

Antiquity, Respectability of witnesses, Universality of testimony, – what have our Revisionists to show?"

All our critic has had "*to show*" is some more gnat-straining, about prepositions.

Burgon then shows how codices A, B, C, D give the Title in verse 38 "*IN FOUR DIFFERENT WAYS*". This is "*the Greek*" which one is to substitute for belief in the AV1611 as the final authority,

Our critic's next "*wrong use*" is in **Romans 6:23** where "**through Jesus Christ**", AV1611, should be "in Jesus Christ" as in the NIV, JB and the English renderings of the Greek texts. The NWT has "by Jesus Christ".

Eternal life is not simply "in" Jesus Christ. He IS Eternal Life, 1 John 1:2. Anyone who receives Jesus Christ receives eternal life THROUGH Him because He indwells whoever receives Him by an act of faith, John 1:12, Romans 8:9–11, 1 John 5:11, 12, 13.

There is NO CONFUSION IN THE AV1611 WHATSOEVER.

Our critic's last "*wrong use*" is in **1 Corinthians 4:4** where "**I know nothing by myself**", AV1611, should be "my conscience is clear" or similar according to the NIV, JB, NWT and the English renderings of the Greek texts. The NWT and Ne have "against myself" and Berry has "in myself". Either or both of these I take to be our critic's "*correct reading*".

That the AV1611 reading is correct and needs no modification is revealed in Psalm 19:12, 13 "**Who can discern his errors? Cleanse thou me from secret faults. Keep back thy servant also from presumptuous sins…**" Like David, Paul did not have sufficient wisdom to know himself perfectly. He therefore looked to the Lord "**that judgeth me**", verse 4, to "**bring to light the HIDDEN things of darkness**", such as "s**ecret faults**" so that he could confess and forsake them, Proverbs 28:13, 1 John 1:9.

The NIV etc. reading is misleading because conscience DOES indicate guilt or innocence, unless it is weak, defiled or seared. See Romans 2:15, 1 Corinthians 8:7, 1 Timothy 4:2. Moreover, a conscience "**void of offence**" was Paul's lifelong objective, which cost him effort, Acts 24:16 – AS EVEN THE NIV ADMITS!

I must admit to some difficulty with the NIV's rendering of "*the Greek*" in 1 Corinthians 4:4. "Conscience" in the form of the noun "suneidesis" is not present in either Ne or the TR, although our critic could probably justify translation of the verb "know", "sunoida" in this fashion. However, "clear", which is "agnos" in 2 Corinthians 7:11, is entirely absent from 1 Corinthians 4:4 in both Ne and the TR. Outright additions to the Scripture by the NIV certainly occur in 1 Corinthians 4:9, according to the TBS *Quarterly Record,* No. 501, Oct.-Dec. 1987, (37), (56), which states:

"The words "procession" *and* "arena" *(found in the NIV) do not occur here in Paul's Greek, and it is not certain that Paul is even indirectly referring to these ideas. By exercising their imagination in this way, the NIV translators here overstep the boundary between translating and explaining."* See also Radmacher and Hodges, (23), Chapters 3 and 4, for example with respect to the NIV expression "Dear woman" in John 2:4 and 19:26 and merely "woman" in John 4:21 and 8:10, even though the underlying Greek text is the same in all four verses. Moreover, the NIV has "heart" for "pneuma" in Romans 1:9 although neither Vine nor Young give such a meaning. The word is that for "**spirit**" as given in the AV1611.

Dr. Ruckman (48) p 27 speaks of *"The approved legitimacy of the AV – by its enemies; those who tried to take it out of the hand of the student who enrolled – in choosing ANY way to translate a preposition, in view of the fact that most of them have five to ten meanings."* That is, even critics of the AV1611 have to concede that a Greek preposition may have several English equivalents.

Dr. Ruckman then illustrates, p 31–33 how the AV1611 translators were much wiser in their choice of preposition in Acts 2:38 than the modern revisers. He first cites A.T. Robertson:

"A case like Acts 2:38...can mean either "ON THE BASIS OF FORGIVENESS OF SINS"...or 'WITH A VIEW TO FORGIVENESS OF SINS' (prep. "eis"). One will interpret it according to HIS THEOLOGY.'

The NIV has the latter interpretation with "so that your sins may be forgiven" which is the sense of Ne, although Berry, JB and NWT have "for the remission of sins" as the AV1611. Dr. Ruckman continues:

*"A.T. Robertson was a deceived liar...He just told you that the meaning of the Greek preposition ("eis") would be determined by the meaning of the words and the context. The context of Acts 2:38 is God ANSWERING the prayer of His Son on the cross ("**Father, forgive them, for they know not what they do**"), and is confirmed by Acts 3:17 and 1 Corinthians 2:8.*

*"The expression "**for the forgiveness of sins**"...occurs only FOUR times in the New Testament, and not ONE time does it ever have any reference to "with a view to, or to obtain, forgiveness of sins." In all four cases it was a reference to sins that HAD BEEN FORGIVEN, and in all four cases the expression was explained by Exodus 34:7 and Hebrews 9:15, 10:4.*

"The English text of 1611 determined how the Greek preposition ("eis") was to be interpreted in Acts 2:38, and it allowed no leeway of interpretation at all, no matter what any lexicon said.

"If the Greek meant "in order to obtain forgiveness of sins" (I said "IF"), then the Greek was WRONG, and THE ENGLISH was correct. It could not mean "either," as Dr. Robertson said: not in Acts 2:38. Dr. Robertson simply LIED. He referred you to the subjective opinions of your own theological preferences as the FINAL AUTHORITY for interpreting a preposition the Holy Bible had already "interpreted.""

10.11 "DEFECTS CAUSED BY WRONG USE OF THE ARTICLE OR ELSE ITS OMISSION"

Our critic states at the end of this sub-section that "***Clearly doctrine is affected by the wrong use or omission of the article.***" However, he does not explain anywhere in this sub-section just HOW any doctrine was "*affected*" by any of these supposed "*defects*" in the AV1611, or even what that doctrine was.

His objections here are not new. Robert Young has a list of "*injurious*" additions and omissions of the definite article in the AV1611 Text in his Concordance. Like our critic, Young does NOT say WHY these additions or omissions are injurious.

Dr. Ruckman has some detailed comments about "*articles*". He states (4) p 118 "*For the gnat-strainers who worry about Greek "articles," the Lord has placed the definite "o" before the name of Jesus, about 40 times (Matthew 18:22, 19:1, 14, 18, 23, 26 etc.) Not ONE OF THE NEW TRANSLATIONS translates it.*"

He also states (29) p 61 "*The NASV and ASV (and NIV) certainly do NOT translate the Greek articles in Luke 1:8, 20, John 2:1, 9:16, Acts 1:14, 10:2, 3, Rom. 1:9, etc., and they certainly do ADD them in Luke 1:25, 32, Acts 7:35, 10:1, Heb. 1:10, 2:4. Fundamentalists who complain about the "translation of the article in the AV"...stimulate, propagate, and increase false impressions in the mind of the public.*"

Dr. Ruckman adds (17) p 404 "*Places in the grossly corrupt NASV (and old ASV) where the translators refused to translate the articles in their own corrupt Greek text which they used:*"

I have listed the places in the "*grossly corrupt*" NIV where this occurs, together with the NIV readings:

"Matthew 18:17: THE pagan and THE tax collector; 1 Corinthians 16:12: THE brother; John 16:21: THE joy; Titus 1:9: THE sound

doctrine; James 1:15: THE desire, THE sin; James 3:11: THE fresh and THE salt; Hebrews 12:9: THE human fathers plus...Matthew 17:1, 16:13, 15:29, 12:28, 18, 1:2, 3, 4, 5, 6, 7, 8; Romans 11:2; Philippians 1:5, 7...

Dr. Ruckman then lists *"Places in the grossly corrupt NASV (and old ASV) where the translators have added articles to suit themselves without regard for any Greek text."*

I have listed the places in the *"grossly corrupt"* NIV where this occurs: *"Luke 1:17; Acts 10:6 (twice); 1 Corinthians 2:16 (three times); Hebrews 2:12 (twice)."*

The first of our critic's *"wrong inclusions"* is in **Daniel 3:25**, where the AV1611 has **"the Son of God"**, in contrast to "a son of the gods", NIV, JB, NWT. Our critic has ignored the discussion of this verse in Chapter 7, Section 7.2. He has also ignored Proverbs 30:4, which revealed that God had a Son with a special name Genesis 32:29, Judges 13:18, 400 years before the incident in Daniel 3.

Our critic attempts to justify the modern perversion by reference to Daniel 3:28. He infers, without saying so, that the reading **"his angel"** in verse 28 refutes the reading **"the Son of God"** in verse 25.

Of course it does nothing of the kind but actually reinforces the AV1611 reading. Dr. Ruckman states in his Commentary on *Matthew*, p 17–18 *"The Angel of the Lord occupies a unique position...for the term is found in both Testaments as applying to the Lord Jesus Himself (note Gal. 4:14, Acts 27:23, Gen. 32:27, Jud. 13:18). The word "angelos" is used in classical Greek, as meaning "messenger"; however...In the Bible, it has a definite meaning of "an appearance," or "apparition,"...Christ Jesus, as a Spirit, has a bodily shape (Gal. 4:19, Phil. 3:10, 1 Cor. 4:15), and this bodily shape is the bodily shape ascribed to HIM; and He is* **"the Angel of the Lord."** *An angel is an "appearance," not merely a "messenger," as we find it in classical Greek."*

Dr. Ruckman further states in his Theological Study Book 18, on *Angelology* p 3: *"There are many angels who bring no message at all...You will notice the children's angels in heaven are not messengers. They are appearances of the children. You will notice the famous angels or powers that represent Greece and Persia, with whom Michael and Gabriel fought in the Book of Daniel, are not messengers. They are appearances."*

In his Commentary on *Revelation* p 33–34, Dr. Ruckman states: *"The meaning that confines the word* **"angel"** *to messenger will NOT meet about twenty verses; therefore it should be discarded immediately and ignored...Revelation 2:1 is written to the appearance (angel) of this* *church; that is, God has before His face (in Heaven) a representative spiritual condition of every local church on the face of this earth."*

Obviously then, "**his angel**" in Daniel 3:28 is an APPEARANCE of the Lord and matches the term "**Son of God**" in verse 25.

Our critic's next *"wrong inclusion"* is in **John 4:27** where "**the woman**", AV1611 should be "a woman" as in the NIV, JB, NWT and the English renderings of the Greek texts. The AV1611 reading follows "**the woman**" in verses 9, 11, 15, 17, 19 and 25 so that there could be no possible confusion about whom the Lord was speaking to. Moreover, the AV1611 reading indicates that the Bible views the conversation from GOD's perspective, NOT the disciples'.

Our critic's next *"wrong inclusion"* is in **Acts 17:23**, where "**THE UNKNOWN GOD**", AV1611, should be "AN UNKNOWN GOD" as in the NIV, JB, NWT, Ne and the English renderings of the other Greek texts.

However, in his Commentary on *Acts* p 502–503, Dr. Ruckman explains why the AV1611 reading is correct. *"The* "**Unknown God**" *turns out to be the God and Father of our Lord Jesus Christ (vs. 31), and He is just as* "unknown" *in the Faculty Smoking Room today as he was when Pharaoh made the classic statement for Thomas Huxley (Exodus 5:2). The Greeks worshipped this God in ignorance, in the sense that they left room for Him in case He was there. And this, of course, is the* "lee-way" *that is given by a modern educated Liberal when religious discussions get heated...Western Education usually admits that there is some God somewhere who started things, but He has no name, no revelation, no Book, no Son, no plan for the saving of sinners, not even any purpose in letting things operate as they do. The Greeks threw a kiss in the right direction – and then went on with the PHILOSOPHERS."*

The NIV, JB, Ne and Berry translate two different Greek words the same way in Acts 17:22 and James 1:27, "deisdaimonesterous" and "threskaia", as "religious" and "religion". Young gives "superstitious" as the only use of the former and Berry has a note that the literal meaning is "very reverent to demons." Vine admits to this meaning but is anxious to show, by means of Deissmann *Light from the Ancient East* and others, that *"the context (of Acts 17) suggests that the adjective is used in a good sense."* At this point, Vine is rather lacking in *"good sense"* himself.

Earlier our critic had charged the AV1611 with *"Failure to recognise distinctions in the original by using the same word or phrase for different Greek words."* See Section 10.9. Yet he neglects to mention the same *"failure"* on the part of the NIV etc., which in this case is a failure to distinguish between worship of GOD and worship of the DEVIL!

Our critic also failed to mention that **"blood"** has been omitted from **Acts 17:26** by the RV, NIV, JB, NWT, Ne, L, T, Tr with A regarding the word as *"doubtful."*

Dr. Ruckman states in his Commentary on *Acts*, p 503–505 ""ONE BLOOD" *is found in ALL FOUR FAMILIES of manuscripts and in the majority of manuscripts, and is cited in writings that ante-date the corrupt Alexandrian Uncials by 200 years."*

So why was the term left out? Dr. Ruckman continues:

"IT IS NOT SOCIALLY, OR POLITICALLY EXPEDIENT...All men have the same blood, but the RACIAL CHARACTERISTICS come from the genes and chromosomes, NOT FROM THE BLOOD."

In other words, the term is 'politically incorrect' for racial integration and so it was omitted. As Dr. Ruckman states *"Real FIDELITY TO THE WORD OF GOD is not even a side issue."*

Our critic's next *"wrong inclusion"* is in **1 Timothy 6:10**, where **"the root of all evil"**, AV1611, should be "a root of all kinds of evil" as in the NIV, NWT, Ne and the renderings of the other Greek texts. The JB has "the root of all evils".

The modern alteration is not surprising because like all modern versions, the NIV is bound by Copyright. Gail Riplinger states (12) p 171–172 *"At the root of all the rhetoric about the need for new versions lies the true cause – covetousness...The KJV is the only version not bound by a copyright. No author or publisher receives a royalty because God is the author. However,* **"God is not the author of confusion"** *(1 Corinthians 14:33) or of "commercial ventures." The latter term was used to describe the ASV (NASB, Living Bible), RV (RSV) and "New" Greek Text by Philip Schaff the chairman of their American Committee...*

"The autobiography of J.B. Phillips (NASB Interlinear Greek-English New Testament Forward, J.B. Phillips Translation, Living Letters et al) likewise lays bare his beliefs (about his billfold). He not only expects to receive royalties from the sale of these versions but those who use "extended quotes"...must expect to pay a proper copyright fee."

"Is it any wonder new version editors twist or water down verses which warn of seeking wealth?" 1 Timothy 6:10 is just such a verse.

Pastor Rockwood of Halifax, N.S., Canada cited *The Wall Street Journal*, Nov. 16th, 1978 in his review of the NIV: *"Zondervan Corp. believes it has struck a new vein of gold in an ancient and well-mined lode: the Bible. Accordingly, it told analysts here, it raised its already-*

gleaming sales and earnings forecasts...Zondervan raised its earnings prediction 10 cents a share, to $1.85, and its sales prediction $3 million to $41 million, for the year."

Our critic was rather put out in his letter that I had attributed *"the lowest possible motives to textual critics and translators."* In view of the above, how could their motives be any lower?

Our critic's next *"wrong inclusion"* is in **Revelation 1:13**, where "**the Son of man**", AV1611 should be "a son of man" as in the NIV, JB, NWT, Ne. Berry has "the" enclosed in brackets.

Dr. Ruckman states in his Commentary on *Revelation* p 24: *"Readers of the gospels immediately recognise who this is. This is the Lord Jesus Christ, the Son of Man."* The modern alteration is therefore an attack on the Lord's humanity.

Comparison of verses 8 and 11 also confirm the Lord's identity. However, the NIV AFFECTS DOCTRINE and CAUSES CONFUSION by OMITTING "**I am Alpha and Omega, the first and the last**" from verse 11 without even a footnote, along with the JB, NWT, Ne, Gr., L, T, Tr, A, W.

Our critic failed to mention this attack on the Lord's Deity in almost the same passage as his complaint about *"the article"*.

His next and last *"wrong inclusion"* is in **Revelation 14:10** where "**the same**", AV1611, should be "he" or similar as in the NIV, JB, NWT, Ne and the English renderings of the other Greek texts.

Comparing verses 9 and 10 shows that our critic is gnat-straining, again. Yet he neglects to mention that in the very same verse, the NIV leaves one article untranslated and inserts an article before "holy angels" from the TR, this article being absent from Ne. 'Eclecticism' at work!

Our critic then accuses the AV1611 of wrongly omitting the article, the first instance being in **Matthew 2:4**, where "**Christ**", AV1611, is given as "the Christ" in the NIV, JB, NWT and all the Greek texts.

Given that the Lord's full Name has already been given in Matthew 1:1, 18, our critic really has no basis for complaint.

However, Mrs Riplinger (12) p 318 states *"T-H-E Christ: Antichrist Bob Larson's lifelong familiarity with the cults and the New Age prompted this warning: "By using the definite article (the) when referring to Christ, mind sciences distinguish between Jesus the man and the divine idea of Christ-realization attainable by men."*

"Liberty University's Dean Norman Geisler adds: "We should be particularly wary when someone refers to Jesus Christ as "the Christ"."

"Real references to Jesus as "the Christ" are rare; however new versions literally paint their pages with this pawn."

Mrs Riplinger then lists:

Matthew 1:17; 2:4; 22:42; 24:5, 23;

Mark 12:35;

Luke 4:41; 20:41; 23:35; 39; 24:26, 46;

John 1:25; 7:26, 27 ,31; 12:34;

Acts 3:20; 5:42; 8:5; 9:22; 17:3; 18:28; 26:23; all of which contain "the Christ" in the NIV, where the AV1611 has "**Christ**" in every place except John 7:26, which reads "**the very Christ**".

Our critic's next "*wrong omission*" is in **John 3:10** where "**a master**", AV1611, should be "Israel's teacher" as in the NIV or "the teacher of Israel" as in Ne and the other Greek texts. The JB, NWT have "a teacher".

The Bible shows that GOD is THE teacher of Israel. See Section 10.4. See also:

Exodus 4:12; 24:12;

Deuteronomy 4:9, 14, 15; 5:31; 6:1, 6, 7;

Judges 13:8;

Job 34:32;

Psalm 25:4, 5, 8, 9, 12; 27:11; 32:8; 71:17; 86:1; 90:12; 119:12, 26, 33, 64, 66, 68 ,102, 108, 124, 135, 171; 143:10;

Isaiah 2:3; 28:9, 26; 54:13.

The modern alteration is therefore incorrect, both with respect to the article and substitution of the word "teacher".

The definite article would be incorrect with respect to "**master**" in the AV1611 because the Lord Jesus Christ is THE Master of Israel, whether Israel recognised Him as such or not. See Matthew 10:25, 23:8, Mark 5:35, 10:17, 18, Luke 8:49, John 11:28.

See Riplinger (12) p 322ff for a detailed discussion of the sinister alteration of "**master**" to "teacher" by the modern versions with respect to the Lord Jesus Christ.

One observes that, according to our critic, the Lord Jesus Christ should only be "A son of man" in Revelation 1:13 but Nicodemus should be "THE teacher" in John 3:10.

Our critic's next "*wrong omission*" is in **Revelation 7:14** where "**great tribulation**", AV1611, should be "the great tribulation" or similar as in the NIV, JB, NWT, Ne and the other Greek texts.

The AV1611 reading matches Matthew 24:21. The NIV and JB miss the cross reference. The AV1611 inserts two articles into this verse. It must be correct because the NIV does too!

The AV1611 reading of Revelation 7:14 emphasises the PERSONAL suffering of the Tribulation saints. The Church-Age saint must "**suffer tribulation**" 1 Thessalonians 3:4 but the Tribulation saint will suffer GREAT tribulation. The NIV etc. obscure this fact.

Our critic's last "*omission*" is in **John 5:35** where "**A burning and A shining light**", AV1611, should be "the lamp burning and shining" as in the Ne and the English renderings of the other Greek texts. The NIV, JB, NWT read as the AV1611, with minor variation, as our critic acknowledges. However, the NIV, JB, NWT insert "lamp" into the reading. This obscures the cross reference to Philippians 2:15, which the NIV, JB, NWT obscure anyway by changing "**lights**" to "stars" or "illuminators".

One should note that the article before "burning and shining" in the Greek texts is left untranslated in ALL the English texts.

The article is NOT appropriate in John 5:35 because it would contradict John 1:4, 5, 7, 8, 9 which show that the LORD JESUS CHRIST is "**the true Light.**"

Our critic then claims that "*The indefinite article is wrongly inserted by the KJV in John 4:24.*" Not only is the article omitted by the NIV, JB but they use a small "s" for "spirit", where the AV1611 reads "**God is a Spirit**", capital "S". The NWT reads with the AV1611 and Berry includes the indefinite article but uses a small "s" for "spirit". All the English texts omit the definite article before "God" in the verse.

Dr. Ruckman states (4) p 118 "*In John 4:24 the A.V. says* "**God is a Spirit.**" *The* "*New Bibles*" *going by the* "*original Greek*" *(!) say* "God is spirit"...*But is this the right reading?*

"*The Devil is "spirit" (Eph. 2:2). Angels are spirit (Heb. 1:14). Demons are spirit (1 Tim. 4:1, 2).*

"*That is, a translation that ignores the rest of the body of Revelation is inaccurate. This time, the criteria for judging the translation is not found in the grammars published by Machen, Robertson, Davis, Moulton, or Milligan. The translation has already been judged by the other Bible verses. It is a false translation, for God is not "spirit". God is A Spirit, in distinction from other spirits. The AV1611 reading, here, is superior to ANY Greek text.*"

Our critic's last "*insertion*" is in **1 Timothy 3:11**, where "**their wives**", AV1611, should simply be "wives" as in Ne or "Women" as in JB, NWT, Berry. The NIV has "their wives are to be women." Although our critic criticises the NIV for inserting "their", he does not mention that "gunaikos" or "**wives**", is found only once in the Greek texts. The NIV has therefore made an unwarranted addition to the word of God here.

The insertion of "**their**" is by no means unwarranted. Verse 11 is set in the context of qualifications for bishops and deacons, verses 1–10,12–13. "**Their**" clearly refers to the wives of BISHOPS or DEACONS. If it is removed, verse 11 then appears OUT of context.

The AV1611 shows that "**their**" is an insertion by placing it in italics. The NIV does NOT.

Our critic concludes this section with his assertion about "*doctrine affected by the wrong use or omission of the article.*" See the beginning of this section.

Doctrine certainly is affected, IN THE MODERN VERSIONS, when one considers the attack on the Deity of Christ in Daniel 3:25, the cover-up for the covetousness of modern revisers in 1 Timothy 6:10, the attack on the humanity of Christ in Revelation 1:13, the subtle promotion of Antichrist in Matthew 2:4 AND ELSEWHERE, equating God with a human teacher in John 3:10, ignoring the suffering of Tribulation saints in Revelation 7:14, equating John the Baptist with Jesus Christ in John 5:35 and equating God with angels, demons and THE DEVIL in John 4:24.

Section 10.9 addresses our critic's next sub-section, which concerns the variety of spellings of proper names. It could be argued that if the different spellings reflect the changing nature of language, then the AV1611 is only following the procedure which the modern versions all insist is the reason for their existence! Even our critic acknowledges this in his summary of this section where he states "*There is no valid reason why God's word should be frozen in 17th Century English.*" Just as the meaning of "*archaic*" words could be placed in the margin, a single spelling could be noted in the margin, WITHOUT changing the Text.

Alternatively, has it ever occurred to the 'uniformitarians' that the different spellings MIGHT be beneficial in prompting the reader to SEARCH THE SCRIPTURES, John 5:39, to resolve the apparent confusion?? I doubt it.

10.12 "UNWARRANTED PARAPHRASING IN THE KJV"

Our critic states "*This is very evident when the following texts are seen in the original.*" Again, his terminology is not very precise because once again, he does not specify what the original is. Moreover, he does not explain why such *"paraphrasing"*, if indeed it is, is *"unwarranted"* and why a literal rendering would be superior.

His first examples are in **1 Samuel 10:24** and **2 Kings 11:12**, where "**God save the king**", AV1611, should be "Long live the king" or similar as in the NIV, JB, NWT.

Regardless of any complaints about *"paraphrasing"*, 1 Timothy 2:1–4 IN THE BIBLE, not *"the Greek"*, shows that the AV1611 is perfectly in order and SUPERIOR TO THE LITERAL HEBREW.

Moreover, I am just old enough to remember when the National Anthem was literally "**God save the King**". It is hardly surprising that the Roman Catholic 'bibles', NIV etc. would object to the reading. It would appear therefore, that our critic seeks not only to deprive me of the words of the Bible but also the words of the National Anthem, which were engraved on the hearts of school children for generations across the world wherever the Union Jack floated on the breeze. (Even the flag of the British nation is now threatened with extinction by the 12 pentagram Romish, demonic circle of the EU banner. See *The Principality and Power of Europe*, by Adrian Hilton, 2nd edition, 2000, Dorchester House Publications, p 55, 165–166 and *The Tower of Eurobabel*, International Currency Review 23, 4, p 46.)

Such sentiments are doubtless *"old hat"* now – our critic's phrase, see later – thanks to the "new bibles".

Our critic's next *"paraphrase"* is in **Romans 6:1**, actually verse 2, where "**God forbid**", AV1611, should be "By no means" or similar, as in the NIV, JB, NWT and the English renderings of the Greek texts.

Dr. Ruckman (48) p 33–34 states "*"The expression* "me genoito" *is a fairly common Pauline locution" (Carson,* The King James Version Debate, *p. 92). This is translated by the "King's men" as "**God forbid**" (Rom. 3:4, 1 Cor. 6:15). On the grounds that the word "God" is not found in any Greek text...Carson says the NIV rendering translates the expression PERFECTLY (ibid). How does this Jesuit, Dark Age revision translate "me genoito"? It says, "not at all" the first time (Rom. 3:4), but "never" the second time (1 Cor. 6:15).*"

The NIV gives "me genoito" as "by no means" in Romans 6:2. Yet our critic complains about the AV1611's *"Failure to render the same Hebrew or Greek word by the same English equivalent"*, Section 10.8. Dr. Ruckman continues:

"Well, is "oudepo", "me pote", "oudepote" ("NEVER") found anywhere, in any Greek text used by the NIV? No, it isn't. They added "never" after saying you couldn't add "God." Did they translate the

Optative (genoito)*? No, they didn't even attempt to. They just ignored it…so, presuming himself to be the final authority, (Carson) says the NIV catches the expression "PERFECTLY."*

"It does? Well, WHO is it that lets things "be, or not be?" WHO is it that can let a thing happen, or prevent it from happening? Are we to assume a converted Orthodox Jewish rabbinical scholar (Phil. 3) wouldn't have THAT in mind when he said "Let it not be!"?…

"If you were a Bible-believing Christian, you would know it was a prayer as well as a denial. Paul is asking God to forbid such a thing from happening. (This is where the NIV got "NEVER" from). God is going to forbid it from "being" (happening). But without God as the source for letting some things happen, while stopping other things from "becoming," the expression is not translated at all. It is missing its most essential element: THE ONE WHO FORBIDS."

Our critic's next *"paraphrase"* is in **Matthew 26:15**, where **"covenanted"**, AV1611, should be "counted" or similar, as in the NIV, JB, NWT and the English renderings of the Greek texts.

Vine – no friend of the AV1611 – gives "covenanted" as one of the meanings of "histemi" in a metaphorical sense. Even he does not consider it an *"unwarranted paraphrase"*. Interestingly, he does not list the NIV's "count" as one of the meanings of "histemi".

Aside from *"the Greek"*, comparison of Mark 14:11 and Luke 22:5 shows that the AV1611 reading is ENTIRELY WARRANTED. It is difficult to see how the Jews could have "counted" the money unless they had "made a deal" or a "covenant" first.

One also wonders whether the rather casual expression "hand him over" in verse 16 of the NIV is an appropriate substitute for **"betray"**, AV1611, with respect to the Lord Jesus Christ.

The use of the word **"covenant"** with respect to Judas and the Jews, in two places, Matthew 26:15, Luke 22:5, associates the betrayal of Jesus to another betrayal, also following a covenant with the Jews. See Isaiah 28:15–18 and Daniel 9:27. This association has deep doctrinal implications beyond the scope of this work but the cross references are lost by the modern alterations.

Our critic's last *"paraphrase"* is in **Matthew 27:44** where **"cast the same in his teeth"**, AV1611, should be "heaped insults on him" or similar as in the NIV, JB, NWT and the English renderings of the Greek texts.

The AV1611 reading is found in the *Concise Oxford Dictionary* with the meaning *"REPROACH"*. Our critic is gnat-straining and Dr. Ruckman has an appropriate comment (1) p 227:

"*THE BOOK is the real author of all controversies among the Biblical Scholars; all their gimmicks are invented for one purpose only – to get rid of THE BOOK.*

"*Observe! If the AUTHORISED VERSION says* "**cast the same in his teeth**" *(Matt. 27:44), it obviously is a very poor translation because it does not CORRESPOND (formally) to* "*the Greek text.*" *Alter it. Make it FORMAL.*

"*If the AUTHORISED VERSION says,* "**by many infallible proofs**" *(Acts 1:3), it is TOO FORMAL, for the word* "tekmerion" *(infallible proofs) is found to mean* "*demonstrative proofs*" *in Aristotle and* "*convincing proofs*" *in Plato. (Lysias says in his* "*Oration against Erastosthenes*" *that it is* "*CERTAIN PROOFS.*")

"*But, this* "*should be*" *DYNAMIC EQUIVALENCE this time instead of FORMAL CORRESPONDENCE; so every English translation on the market since 1881 DIVESTED JESUS CHRIST OF THE INFALLIBLE PROOFS OF HIS RESURRECTION and gives you* "dynamism" *instead of* "formalism": *i.e.,* "many proofs."

"*See how it's done? Do you see WHY it is done?*"

10.13 "INCONSISTENCY IN THE USE OF ITALICS"

Our critic shows here that he has largely ignored the information given in Chapter 5, Section 5.3 He states that "***The use of italics has been fluid in the various printings of the KJV.***" I alluded to this fact in Chapter 5, Section 5.7. I also stated that Dr. Blaney's Edition of 1769 is the standard AV1611 Text of today. Our critic ignored this information as well.

He continues "***Since they have at present an entirely different significance, their use can cause serious misunderstandings.***" As usual, he does NOT state WHAT were the "*serious misunderstandings*", nor WHO "*misunderstood*", nor HOW their lives, ministries etc. were affected. Nor does he indicate how the significance in the use of italics differs between now and 1611.

He says that italics are "***not always consistently applied***" in the AV1611, meaning only that they vary between editions – see above. However, he does NOT cite even ONE genuine case where "*inconsistent*" use of italics confused ANYONE about ANYTHING in ANY Edition of an AV1611.

He maintains that **Matthew 6:2** contains an unnecessary un-italicised addition. He obviously did not check the verse in a contemporary

AV1611. The extra word "**thine**" IS in italics. It is not in italics in the 1611 Edition but neither the wording nor the sense of the verse is affected.

As for his objection that "**thou doest thine alms**" in **Matthew 6:2** AV1611 contains an unnecessary "**thine**", the NIV has the same construction "they have received their reward" IN THE SAME VERSE. Why did not our critic draw attention to the "*unnecessary*" addition of "their" in the NIV? He is gnat-straining, not for the first time.

The TBS article on italics, cited Chapter 5, Section 5.7, reveals that "*In the editions of 1611 and 1613 there were many inconsistencies in the use of italics*" and that "*considerable improvement*" was achieved in the editions of 1629 and 1638. This improvement was "*carried further*" in the editions of 1762 and 1769.

Grady states (45) p 171 that "*over 72 percent of the textual variations were already cleared up by 1638.*"

The TBS article clearly outlines why words are placed in italics in an AV1611, giving six distinct reasons, with GENUINE examples. This information is readily available to ANYONE who desires to know more about this aspect of the English Text. There is no excuse for any "*confusion*" about the matter. If a Christian is "*confused*" about italics in an AV1611, it is because he is either lazy, Proverbs 26:16, or wilfully ignorant, 1 Corinthians 14:38, or both.

The TBS article does maintain that the AV translators did not always achieve consistency in use of italics and suggests where additional use of them should be made in the AV1611. However, Dr. Gipp has a more scriptural verdict on italicised words (9) p 52ff.

"*Read below, please, Deuteronomy 8:3*"
"**...man doth not live by bread only, but by every WORD that proceedeth out of the mouth of the LORD doth man live.**"

"*You will note that the word "**word**" is in italics, meaning of course, that it was not in the Hebrew text. Upon examination of Deuteronomy 8:3 in Hebrew one will find that the word "dabar" which is Hebrew for "**word**" is not found anywhere in the verse.*"

"*Yet in His contest with Satan we find Jesus quoting Deuteronomy 8:3 as follows in Matthew 4:4.*"

"**...Man shall not live by bread alone, but by every word that proceedeth out of the mouth of God.**"

"*While quoting Deuteronomy 8:3 Jesus quotes the entire verse INCLUDING THE KING JAMES ITALICIZED WORD!*"

The simple answer to the question of 'why the KJV uses italics' is that

GOD WANTS THEM IN HIS BOOK, our critic's opinions notwithstanding.

The main reason why I mentioned italics in Volume 1 was to demonstrate the HONESTY of the preservation of the AV1611 Text. Inspection of an NIV shows it to be a DISHONEST translation because "word" in Deuteronomy 8:3 is NOT in italics.

10.14 "UNINTELLIGIBILITY DUE TO THE PRESENCE OF ARCHAIC AND OBSOLETE WORDS AND ALSO MISUNDERSTANDINGS CAUSED BY WORDS WHOSE MEANING HAS CHANGED OVER ALMOST 400 YEARS"

One cannot pass by that title without noting its verbosity and poor style, especially when one is accustomed to the concise elegance of the AV1611.

Our critic states in this sub-section that "*There are more than 300 words in the KJV which are entirely obsolete or used in a sense substantially different from that which they now convey. It does the KJV translators no honour and is indeed quite unfair to them and to the truth which they understood to retain these words which now convey meanings they did not intend.*"

Does our critic discuss any of the 300 "*archaic and obsolete words*"? No.

Does our critic give any examples of "*Unintelligibility*" and "*misunderstandings*" caused by these words? No.

Does our critic refer specifically to ANYONE who "*misunderstood*" the AV1611 because some words were "*archaic and obsolete*" and what the RESULTS of that "*misunderstanding*" were? No.

Does our critic give any examples of "*words whose meaning has changed over the last 400 years*"? No.

Does our critic even ATTEMPT to discuss ANY of the material on "*archaic*" words in Chapter 5, Section 5.7, where dictionaries, glossaries, marginal notes and BIBLICAL PRINCIPLES were recommended as aids to understanding? No.

Does our critic even ATTEMPT to discuss the MODERN terms found in the AV1611, Chapter 5, Section 5.7 and the OBSCURE terms in the NIV, Section 5.7, which are CLEAR in an AV1611? No.

Does our critic refute or even ADDRESS the material provided by Gail Riplinger (12) and cited in Section 5.7 which showed the AV1611 to be the EASIEST Bible to read? No.

Does our critic discuss the BIBLE VERSES which provide the key to "*intelligibility*" and "*understanding*" of the Scriptures? No.

What our critic does is to repeat the 'party line' – WITHOUT referring to its source. I quote from p viii of the Preface to the 1946 edition of the RSV, a translation little in use today, if at all.

"There are more than three hundred such words which are used in the King James Version in a sense substantially different from that which they now convey. It not only does the King James translators no honor, but is quite unfair to them and to the truth which they understood and expressed, to retain these words which now convey meanings they did not intend."

The RSV was one of A HUNDRED attempts to "update" the "*archaic*" words of the AV1611 in the last 100 years. See the list by Dr. Vance (22). As William Grady says (45) p 166:

"The "archaic" words of the King James Bible have already been "updated" more than 100 times in as many years for an average of one modern version per year. NOW, WHO's KIDDING WHOM? Can the English language be changing that fast?

Dr. Ruckman's assistant pastor, Brian Donovan, states in his tape series *Our Amazing English Bible* that the AV1611 uses approximately 10,000 English words. Our critic's objection applies therefore to approximately 3% of the words in an AV1611. (The comprehensive list given by the TBS numbers about 650 words but many of these are little changed from their modern equivalents – see Section 5.7.)

However, is the number even as high as 300? Dr. Ruckman (4) p 22, p 180 asks *"Are there really "857 archaic words" in the AV1611?...There are about 100 and they are all listed in the Glossary of the Cambridge Interleaved Bible (Cambridge University Press, England), pp. 290–296, and 1/3 of these can be understood without a high school education. (I personally tried them out on three classes of ministerial students in which there were some students having only an 8th grade education (up to 14 years old.)) Any "archaic" words could be printed in the margin without disturbing the text, and those who desire to disturb the text always PERVERT the text before they are through."*

Has our critic ever conducted such a test? If so, why doesn't he discuss the RESULTS?

Dr. Ruckman further asks (4) p 22 *"What is "archaic" or "Elizabethan" about the A.V. English of Deuteronomy 24:5* **"cheer up"**, *Numbers 24:14* **"advertise"**, *Genesis 19:10* **"shut to the door"**, *Psalm 107:25, 27* **"stormy wind"**, **"wits" end"**, *Mark 15:2* **"thou sayest it"** *("you said it"), Luke 15:27* **"fatted calf"**, *1 Samuel 24:14, 27:11* **"a dead** dog", "**tell on us**", *1 Peter 4:5* "**the quick and the dead**", *Joshua 14:15* "**a great man**", *Exodus 32:3* "**brake off**", *Jeremiah 13:10, 31:29* "**good for nothing**", "**sour grape**", *Numbers 14:34* "**breach of promise**"*?*"

The NIV equivalents are "bring happiness", "warn", "shut the door", "tempest", "wits" end", "It is as you say", "fatted calf", "a dead dog", "inform on us", "the living and the dead", "the greatest man", "completely useless", "sour grapes", "what it is like to have me against you".

There does not seem to have been much 'updating' in 400 years. In fact, the TBS (50) p 12 states "*Many modern versions tend to replace the simple short words of the Authorised Version with more difficult words, and the New International Version does so in hundreds of places. The following twenty examples are all found in the Epistle to the Hebrews:*"

Verse	AV1611	NIV
1:2	worlds	universe
1:3	brightness, image, upholding, purged	radiance, representation, sustaining, provided purification
1:4	better than	superior to
2:3	spoken	announced
2:10	are	exists
4:2	mixed	combine
4:15	be touched	sympathise
5:7	he feared	his reverent submission
5:10	called	designated
5:13	unskilful	not acquainted
6:6	put him to	subjecting him
7:16	endless	indestructible
8:13	old	obsolete
10:26	wilfully	deliberately
10:27	looking for	expectation
11:5	see death	experience death
11:22	departing	exodus

See also Gail Riplinger's findings (12) p 195–214. She gives the above NIV 'updatings' as containing 108 syllables versus 54 for the AV1611 and concludes "*Double trouble for memorizers or meditation...The NIV's vocabulary evades young and old alike.*"

Our critic also states in this sub-section "***Insistence on the supremacy of the KJV is a reversal of the Holy Spirit's action by insisting that the best idiom for the Word of God should not be the modern living colloquial idiom but the classical language of Shakespeare.***"

I set aside the clumsy and verbose nature of that last sentence and draw attention to the term "*the Holy Spirit's action.*" One is surely entitled to ask for '*Chapter and verse*' with respect to such "*action*". Unfortunately, our critic does not provide any. Moreover, one can judge from the examples given above just how "*colloquial*" the NIV actually is.

His assertion is answered by G.W. Anderson, Editorial Manager of the TBS:

"*The Authorised Version – following its predecessors, including Tyndale – was written in the common language of its time, although in a literary rather than colloquial style. It was not written in "the classical language of Shakespeare". The literary style used by the translators is what has enabled the Authorised Version to stand the test of time. It must also be remembered that the edition of the Authorised Version which is used today is the 1769 revision, which is indeed closer to us than it is to Shakespeare.*"

The literary style of the AV1611 was discussed in Chapter 5, Section 5.2.

Our critic concludes this sub-section with the statement "***The sound of the KJV on 20th Century ears makes an impression which the original inspired Scriptures did not make on the first readers.***"

Does our critic substantiate this statement in any way? No.

Even if the statement is taken at face value surely no-one could seriously belittle the effect of the AV1611 on the 1,000,000 plus converts of Billy Sunday. See Chapter 8.

The Bible Believers' Bulletin, March 1994 has this article from a Mrs. Delfa Roberts: "*In 1959, at the First Baptist Church, Olive Branch, Mississippi, I was asked to order Bibles to give to children in the Junior Department of Sunday School...The following Sunday I read some familiar Psalms from the KJV, then from the RSV, explaining that they were to select either 'the Bible we have been using, or this book that some people call a Bible.' Each child chose the KJV and when I asked 'Why?', a ten year old girl said, 'Because this one (KJV) sounds like what God said – and that one (RSV) sounds like what some man wishes God had said.' More profound than what I have heard from the professors.*"

What did the Preface of the largely defunct RSV say, together with our critic? "***It not only does the King James translators no honor, but is quite unfair to them...to retain these words...***" The Lord said "**Out of the mouth of babes and sucklings thou hast perfected praise**" Matthew 21:16.

The Roman Catholic F. W. Faber, 1814–1863, (53) p vii, had this evaluation of the AV1611. See the TBS Article No. 24 *The Excellence of the Authorised Version* (37).

"*Who will not say that the uncommon beauty and marvellous English of the Protestant Bible is not one of the great strongholds of heresy in this country? It lives on the ear like music that can never be forgotten, like the sound of church bells. Its felicities often seem to be things rather than words. It is part of the national mind, and the anchor of national seriousness.*"

Since 1881, the strongholds have clearly been broken down and laid waste, Proverbs 25:28b.

10.15 'SUMMARY'

Our critic states "***This has by no means been an exhaustive treatment of the subject. Not only could I have given many more examples to illustrate my points…***"

The "*examples*" which our critic did give to "*illustrate*" his "*points*" consisted mainly of the 72 verses in the AV1611 which he attacked:

Genesis 4:8, Joshua 11:13, 1 Samuel 10:24, 1 Kings 16:33, 2 Kings 11:12, Psalm 145:13, Isaiah 53:11, Daniel 3:25	8 verses
Matthew 2:4, 5:15, 6:2, 12:18, 24:36, 26:15, 27:44, 28:19, 20	9 verses
Mark 6:20, 9:18	2 verses
Luke 10:21, 16:9, 23:15	3 verses
John 1:11, 3:10, 4:24, 27, 5:35, 18:1, 19:3	7 verses
Acts 2:6, 47, 3:13, 26, 4:25, 27, 30, 5:30, 9:6, 16:7, 17:23, 19:2	12 verses
Romans 3:25, 4:3, 22, 5:11, 6:1, 6, 23, 8:24, 28, 12:19	10 verses
1 Corinthians 1:18, 4:4	2 verses
Galatians 2:20, 3:6, 24, 6:11	4 verses
Philippians 2:6, 7	2 verses
1 Thessalonians 4:1, 1 Timothy 3:11, 6:10, 2 Timothy 2:8	4 verses
Hebrews 2:17, 10:30, 1 Peter 2:3, 5:2, 1 John 3:1, Jude 25	6 verses
Revelation 1:13, 7:14, 14:10	3 verses

This total does not count the 26 verses containing the word "**charity**" or the 10 verses where "hades" has been translated "**hell**" in the AV1611.

The facts concerning each of the verses listed above have been discussed, with specific references. In each case, the AV1611 has been shown to be RIGHT and our critic to be WRONG. Many of the alterations which he recommends have been introduced into the English texts by

UNSAVED HERETICS who disagreed even amongst themselves. See Section 10.3.

Of these 72 verses, the NIV:

stands alone in 2	John 3:10, 18:1
agrees with the NWT alone in 1	Luke 16:9
agrees with the AV1611 in 3	John 5:35, 1 Timothy 3:11, Hebrews 2:10. According to our critic, the JB, NWT are "*correct*" in 1 Timothy 3:11 and the NWT is "*correct*" in Hebrews 2:10.
agrees with the JB alone in 9	Psalm 145:13, John 1:11, 4:24, Romans 3:25, 6:23, Galatians 3:24, 2 Timothy 2:8, 1 Peter 2:3, 5:2.

In the remaining 57 verses, the NIV reads with BOTH the JB and the NWT with minor variation, AGAINST THE AV1611.

It follows therefore, that of the 72 changes in the AV1611 that our critic recommends,

60 would be approved by the Jehovah's Witnesses, 67 by the Vatican and 57 by BOTH!

In other words, in at least 90% of the so-called "*defects of the KJV*", our critic is in perfect agreement with the Pope and in 80% with BOTH Watchtower and the Pope.

In addition, listing verses in the order in which they appear in the text, the NIV has been shown to either wrong or 'inconsistent' in:

Luke 22:64, Acts 16:31, 1 Peter 2:2, 5:2 (again), Titus 1:2, 1 John 5:13	Section 10.3
Exodus 34:7, Matthew 28:1, Galatians 3:1, 5:21	Section 10.4
Romans 6:4, 6, 7, 8, 1 Corinthians 1:2, 5, 6:11, Ephesians 2:8, Colossians 2:10, 20, 3:1, 3, 1 Timothy 6:12, 2 Timothy 2:11, 1 Peter 1:23, 1 John 2:3, Acts 15:19, 1 Corinthians 1:18, 2 Corinthians 2:15, 4:3, Colossians 3:10, 1 John 2:8, Matthew 2:1, 2, 12, 1 John 2:2, 4:10, Romans 6:9, 1 Corinthians 15:20	Section 10.5
Genesis 24:43 vs. Leviticus 21:13, Song of Solomon 1:3 vs. 6:8, Numbers 24:3 vs. Psalm 49:4 vs. 78:2, Luke 4:25 vs. 2 Corinthians 12:2	Section 10.5
Matthew 11:23 vs. 16:18 vs. Luke 16:23 vs. Acts 2:27	Section 10.9
Luke 23:17, 23, 38, 1 Corinthians 4:9, John 2:4, 19:26, Acts 2:38	Section 10.5

Romans 1:9, Acts 17:22, 26, Revelation 1:11, John 5:35   Section 10.11
   ("lamp" inserted) Philippians 2:15, 1 Timothy 3:11
   ("women" inserted)
1 Corinthians 6:15 vs. Romans 3:4   Section 10.12
Deuteronomy 8:3   Section 10:13

This list adds a further 69 verses to the 72 above, 141 in all, not counting the "**charity**" verses and 6 of the "hades" vs. "**hell**" verses.

Moreover, *"Inconsistent"* inclusions and omissions of Greek articles have been found to occur in more than 40 verses in the NIV, Section 10.11. A further 24 verses in the NIV have been shown to include the term "THE Christ", which is a subtle reference to ANTIchrist, Section 10:11. See also the 20 terms used by the NIV in the Book of Hebrews which prove to be more DIFFICULT to read, understand and MEMORISE than those of the AV1611 which they are supposed to have "updated", Section 10:14.

It is fair to say that this work has *"given many more examples to illustrate MY points"* i.e. the author's. The above results appear to be fairly typical for the NIV. I have carried out a separate study on 1218 verses where the NIV departs from the AV1611. This is approximately 15% of the 7959 verses of the New Testament. The NIV departs with the JB in 1026 verses, 84% of the total, with the NWT in 1094 verses, 90% of the total and with both in 958 verses, 79% of the total. These percentages are not as high as those given for the list of verses in Section 7.3 but nevertheless show overwhelmingly that the NIV, JB, NWT are truly ecumenical translations, united in error.

To *"illustrate"* HIS *"points"* further, our critic made some more vague and misleading references to *"The Hebrew and Greek text used in 1611"*, which have been answered in detail. See Section 10.2. He also referred to *"confusion"* arising from variations in spelling of proper names, without giving even ONE example of such *"confusion"* and of how it affected anyone. He criticised the AV1611 for its use of italics, while ignoring the total LACK of ANY indication in the NIV where words have been inserted into the English text. He plagiarised the Preface of a well-nigh defunct translation, the RSV, in order to attack the *"archaic and obsolete"* words of the AV1611, again without discussing even ONE example.

Nevertheless, our critic continues *"**there are some topics I have not even touched on e.g. cases where the KJV misses the meaning of the text, mistranslations, meaningless coinage, the printing of each verse as a separate paragraph, imperfect punctuation, untranslated Semitisms – many of which in turn have doctrinal implications.**"*

One observes that he does not specify ANY 'final authority', or even 'higher authority' by which the AV1611 may be judged to be at fault in the above respects. One would have thought that he could have at least done this, even if he did not choose to discuss the topics listed. For that reason, his criticisms here are really no more than vague innuendoes, designed to unsettle the Bible believer into abandoning the Book in favour of 'scholarly' conjecture."

"*The printing of each verse as a separate paragraph*" is actually an advantage of the AV1611. It enables the reader to locate a reference much more easily than when the verse numbers are scattered through a passage of prose, as in the NIV. I have found that this feature of the AV1611 is particularly helpful when reading the scriptures aloud and in expository preaching.

As for the AV1611 missing the meaning of the text, Dr. Ruckman has an interesting comment (48) p 35–36 "*The AV is supposed to have "missed the point of the Greek text" in 3 John 2, for it should have apostatized with the NIV to produce the degenerate* "Dear friends, I pray that you may enjoy good health and that ALL MAY GO WELL WITH YOU" . . . *Here a literal rendering would have produced* "Beloved, concerning all things, I am wishing thee to prosper and be in health, even as it prospers, thy (the) soul."

"*The AV took* "peri" *to mean* "**above all**", *instead of* "concerning" *(see notes on prepositions above). This was because* "peri," *when attached to other stems, means* "over and above," "extraordinary," "much," "abundantly," "more abundantly," "exceedingly," "to be over and above," *hence* "I wish above all things."

"*Down in the Greek class, where the Greek teacher is busy destroying the ministerial candidate with* "THE ORIGINAL GREEK TEXT" . . . *he is told that the NIV corrects this* "gaff" *in a King James Bible (see Carson, op cit. p. 94) by altering* "peri panton" *to an accusative used in indirect discourse:* "I wish THAT all things . . . etc." *In doing this, the NIV eradicated* "things" – *which is plural* – *whereas* "all" *is a singular* – *ignoring the first wish (*"thee to prosper"*) because it was in the Accusative case (not the Genitive plural as* "panton"*), and then paraphrased the rest of the verse* "even as your soul is getting along well." *The verb (*"euodoutai"*) is not a reference to anyone just* "getting along well." *It is a reference to someone PROSPERING, or succeeding in accomplishing something.*

"*The NIV is a better rendering than your KING JAMES BIBLE?*"

Our critic then states that *"The urgent need for new translations lies in the inadequacies of the KJV."*

Does he seriously believe that after ONE HUNDRED translations in AS MANY YEARS, see Grady's comment Section 10.14, *"the inadequacies of the KJV"* are still a problem? Does he mean that after the flood of 'bibles' over the last century, that MORE are needed to overcome these *"inadequacies"*? To paraphrase Dean Burgon, Chapter 10, Section 10.4, I *"read and marvel."*

Why, indeed, does he even bother to make the *"KJV"* the standard for comparison? Why not the RV, or the RSV, or the NEB, or the NASV, or one of the interlinear Greek or Hebrew editions? Surely ANY of these must have been an improvement over that *"manifestly fallible translation made by men . . . not wholly orthodox"* – a description of the Holy Bible found in our critic's introductory letter to me. It is astounding that the AV1611 even exists today, let alone gives rise to an *"URGENT need for new translations"* 383 YEARS AND OVER 100 TRANSLATIONS AFTER IT WAS FIRST PUBLISHED! Here is this *"archaic"* piece of work from a *"late"* and *"demonstrably secondary text"* based on *"defective manuscripts"*, which causes so much *"confusion"* and *"unintelligibility"* with respect to *"important doctrines"* and contains *"incorrect renderings of the Hebrew and the Greek"* which are *"INNUMERABLE"*.

For all this, the AV1611 has not yet been eliminated, in spite of 100 translations in 100 years from *"new discoveries of manuscripts"* and *"all the Dead Sea Scrolls"* and the *"eclectic principles"* wherein *"manuscripts are weighed not counted"*. Surely the survival of the AV1611 must be the eighth wonder of the world.

In fact, *"the urgent need for new translations"* arises from the need of publishing companies like Zondervan and Thomas Nelson Inc. to maintain their profit margins. See Section 10.11.

"And through COVETOUSNESS shall they with FEIGNED WORDS make MERCHANDISE of you . . . " 2 Peter 2:3.

Our critic continues *"The KJV is not the original Bible."* Nowhere in my first document did I say that it was. There never was on the face of this earth such a thing as *"the original Bible"*, consisting of all the original autographs collated into one volume. Our critic cannot prove otherwise.

He continues *"its translators did not work by inspiration or special divine approval."* Does our critic even attempt to substantiate that statement? No.

Whether or not the AV1611 translators worked *"by inspiration"* – I am surprised that our critic retained the AV1611 term – is NOT and has NEVER been the issue. The issue is whether or not a BOOK available TODAY is 'The Holy Scriptures.' If there is such a Book and I believe that it is ANY Edition of the AV1611, then IT (the BOOK) is GIVEN BY INSPIRATION OF GOD. See Dr. Ruckman's analysis, Section 10.3.

As for our critic's second point, I believe that even modern revisers *"work by special divine approval."* Unfortunately, it is the WRONG kind of *"approval"*. Dr. Ruckman explains (16) p 166:

"The Dark Ages, from a SCRIPTURAL standpoint, ARE THE RESULTS OF AN OFFICIAL CHURCH-STATE ADOPTING A DEVIL'S BIBLE. For a counterpart in history one may study the history of England SINCE 1884 when that same Bible was adopted, or the history of America SINCE 1901 when that Bible was adopted. The **"writing of divorcement"** *given to the woman in Matthew 19:7, in every Greek text, says* "Biblion apostasion" *– an apostate Bible. A nation gets its walking papers when it steps out on God."*

"For them that honour me I will honour, and they that despise me shall be lightly esteemed" 1 Samuel 2:30.

Our critic continues *"It is not a mark of orthodoxy to use it (the "KJV")."*

I never said that it was. I am not interested in *"USING"* the AV1611. Even our critic and the local church he pastored occasionally USE the AV1611. I am interested in BELIEVING the AV1611 and SUBMITTING it. Nowhere in his document does he lay claim to BELIEVING or SUBMITTING to ANY Bible, where it contradicts his theology, his opinion or his interpretation of the *"original languages."*

He then states that *"There is no valid reason why God's word should be frozen in 17th Century English."*

I have shown that the AV1611 is NOT written in *"17th Century English"*. See Chapter 5, Section 5.2 which our critic has ignored. See also Section 10.14 where his assertion has been answered by Mr. Anderson of the TBS.

However, once again, I *"read and marvel."*

In his introductory letter, our critic speaks reverently of *"the God-breathed originals"* and assures me that *"EVERY version . . . must be subject to THE ORIGINAL LANGUAGES."*

It follows, therefore, that although God's word must NOT *"be frozen in 17th Century English"*, it MUST be frozen in Old Testament Hebrew and New Testament Greek, the former being spoken only by less than 1%

of the world's population and the latter being a DEAD language, SPOKEN BY NO-ONE, NOT EVEN IN GREECE.

Our critic refers to the question posed in the Preface to the AV1611, "*how shall men meditate in that, which they cannot understand?*", to quote the exact words. He neglects to mention the question which immediately follows, "*How shall they understand that which is kept close in an unknown tongue?*"

The only way that our critic could answer that question would be to say "*Come to me for understanding because I can subject your English version to the ORIGINAL LANGUAGES which I constantly consult but which are UNKNOWN to YOU!*"

He continues "*Much progress has been made since 1611 and we can be profoundly grateful to Almighty God that we can now possess more accurate and readable translations than the KJV.*"

Not any that our critic has been able to identify, certainly not any of the "*Laodicean washouts*" derived from the unregenerate 'scholarship' of Griesbach and company.

He concludes his summary with a quotation from E.H. Palmer, "*the coordinator of all the work on the NIV*", (12) p 230ff. The essence of it is as follows:

"*Do not give them a loaf of bread, covered with an inedible, impenetrable crust, fossilised by three and a half centuries . . . to allow that Word to go on being misunderstood because of the veneration of an archaic, not-understood version of four centuries ago is inexcusable . . .*"

This quotation seems to have come from an article by a certain Brad Allman entitled *The KJV – Can It Be Totally Trusted?* (Our critic does not give the source of the quotation.)

The article has been reviewed by Dr. Ruckman in Part 8 of his series on *The Alexandrian Cult* p 15ff.. He writes:

"*The purpose of Allman's article is to destroy the faith of the reader in the AV text; this is sheepishly worded as "to respond to claims made by those who hold the erroneous view of the KJV as the only accurate and trustworthy version of the Holy Scriptures"* . . .

"*Allman begins by listing "archaic words" which can easily be updated in the margin of any King James Bible and often are . . . Allman's alibi for listing these words is that he and a man named Edwin Palmer think that the word of God is covered by an "INEDIBLE, IMPENETRABLE CRUST" in the AV. Sunday, Torrey, Moody, Finney, Spurgeon, Larkin, Paton, Carey, Goforth, etc., evidently never found that much trouble with it. Neither have I . . . We had no trouble "penetrating the crust" and feeding our souls and the souls of 400,000 people from the "fossilized text" (citing Edwin Palmer) . . .*

*"(Allman) concludes his paper by calling the Holy Bible "AN ARCHAIC LOAF OF BREAD." Little cuties like "***crown***" should have been* "diadem" *(Rev. 19:12) are to make you think that* "diadem" *is easier to understand – not "archaic," remember? – like* "**CROWN**" *. . . "*

I note in passing that the NIV has regressed to the *"archaic"*, *"fossilized"* reading "CROWNS", found in the AV1611.

Dr. Ruckman concludes *"Allman bases his cockeyed position on the opinions of Robert Sumner . . . Newman and MacRae . . . D.A. Carson . . . F.F. Bruce . . . Ralph Earle . . . H. Dennett . . . and other members of the Alexandrian Cult. THERE ISN'T A BIBLE BELIEVER IN THE ENTIRE LIST. Birds of a feather flock together."*

I turn now to our critic's next section, entitled "***The Character of the KJV***"

11

"The Character of the KJV"

11.1   "A TYPICAL ANGLICAN COMPROMISE"

Our critic begins this section of his document by asserting that the KJV
was not a "***Protestant Reformers' Bible***", although later he acknowledges
that the AV1611 New Testament is 90% that of Tyndale, who WAS a
Protestant Reformer. So was Rogers and so was Stephanus who was
largely responsible for the AV1611's verse numbering sequence. So was
Beza whose Greek Textus Receptus underlies the New Testament of the
AV1611. See Chapters 2 and 3. The AV1611 at least has a Protestant
pedigree, more so than ANY modern translation.

He then states that the AV1611 was "***essentially a Church of England
version . . . a typical Anglican compromise***" and insists that "***It was
Anglicanism which secured its triumph and that became complete after
the Restoration of 1660.***"

Not according to Gustavus Paine (53) p 163, who says "*The Puritans
fought their way forward. The 1611 Bible by its own worth was making
itself welcome throughout the country, for those on both sides needed the
best modern texts with which to fight their doctrinal skirmishes. High
churchmen in greater numbers began to use the 1611 version, which in
centuries to come would be the sole bond uniting the countless English-
speaking Protestant sects.*

"*In 1629 the Bible was again revised, but only in small ways, and once
more in minor respects in 1638. The last issue of the Geneva Bible was
in 1644. By then the King James Version was ahead of all others, and
now the strife over forms and doctrine helped it on.*"

So far from being "***an Anglican compromise***" relying on the Church of England for its survival, the AV1611 appealed to ALL factions within English Christianity *"by its own worth."*

Paine continues p 181 *"Though the new translation captured readers slowly, in the long run it appealed to High Church, Low Church, and chapel alike. Though it was never merely a Puritan work, Cromwell and his fellow Roundheads pushed it forward. George Fox, Milton, Bunyan, and Defoe used it. Boswell quoted it roughly. An early Plymouth Elder William Brewster appears to have had only a Great Bible, yet soon Roger Williams, Increase Mather, Cotton Mather, the New Lights, Wesley, all made their teachings comport with the King James text . . . it suited nearly all Protestant sects. In the United States it has been the standby not only of "the Bible belt" but of all other regions."*

Writing in the 1950's, Paine's comments are somewhat dated but Dr. Ruckman states (1) p 123 *"We are reminded ten times a year that (the translators) were baby-sprinkling Anglicans under a King who had no use for Baptists; you are NOT told they produced THE BOOK that built the NORTHERN AND SOUTHERN BAPTIST CONVENTION IN AMERICA and produced the ten largest Sunday Schools the world has ever seen. NO WRITER ON THE SUBJECT OF THE KING JAMES BIBLE GIVES YOU HALF THE "FACTS." He deals only with the bare substance: the number of translators (54), the number of companies (six – at Oxford, Cambridge, and Westminster), the effeminacy of King James, Hugh Broughton's criticism of the translation, King James' "anti-Presbyterianism," and the archaic language of the "original." This is the stock-and-trade of twentieth century apostate scholarship.*

"No mention is usually made of the Jesuit plot TO KILL THE KING AND BOMB THE PARLIAMENT THAT HAD CALLED FOR THE TRANSLATION (1604). No mention is made of the fact that the Dedicatory identifies the Pope as the "man of sin" (2 Thess. 2:3), though NO TRANSLATION SINCE HAS DARED TO BRING UP THE SUBJECT.

"No mention is found of a supernatural chapter and verse numbering system that would astound a professional gambler in Las Vegas, although the SCHOLAR's UNION simply ignores it as "verse numbers made while riding horseback." No mention is made of an order of Books that is AGAINST the Hebrew original manuscripts (scholar's cliché: more properly "ANY set of Hebrew manuscripts making up the Orthodox Hebrew canon"), so that the PREMILLENIAL COMING OF CHRIST is indicated by the order of those Books – ALTHOUGH THE TRANSLATORS WERE NOT PREMILLENIAL.

"Finally, no mention is made of the amazing fact that, to this day, this

Book can be taught to children 4, 5, 6, 7, 8, 9 and 10 years old without ANY OTHER VERSION, and they can get saved, called to preach, live separated lives, and grow up as NON-BABY SPRINKLING, PREMILLENIAL ANTI-CATHOLICS."

"**By their fruits ye shall know them**" *(Matt. 7:20)."*

Alexander McClure (57) p 60 states *"It (the AV1611) speedily came into general use as the standard version, by the common consent of the English people; and required no act of parliament nor royal proclamation to establish its authority. Some of the older versions continued to be reprinted for forty years; but no long time elapsed ere the common version quietly and exclusively occupied the field."*

Although Paine says "s*lowly*" and McClure says "s*peedily*", both of these men arrive at the same conclusion about the general acceptance of the AV1611. McClure cites Dr. Lee, Principal of the University of Edinburgh; *"I do not find that there was any canon, proclamation, or act of parliament, to enforce the use of it."* He also cites a Dr. Symonds, who states *"The present version appears to have made its way, without the interposition of any authority whatsoever; for it is not easy to discover any traces of a proclamation, canon or statute published to enforce the use of it."*

Our critic certainly does not refer to any.

Moreover, neither Bunyan, Sunday (See Chapter 8) nor DeWitt Talmage (Chapter 10, Section 10.1), all of whom believed the AV1611 to be "*perfect*", were Anglican.

Neither Dr. Ruckman nor Dr. Vance, who also believe the AV1611 to be perfect, could be described as "*Anglican*" by ANY stretch of the imagination.

Here is Darrell Moore, of Hyles Anderson College, a Baptist work, cited by Dr. Ruckman (46) p 23: *"The only translation which has preserved the words of God without change down through the course of history is THE KING JAMES VERSION OF THE BIBLE. All other translations of the Bible come from the Westcott and Hort text, which IS KNOWN TO BE A PERVERTED TEXT. I often hear it said that the KING JAMES VERSION is too hard to understand because of the language that is used but the honest truth is that the Spirit of God is the One who gives light concerning the scriptures and He is quite capable of helping ANYONE understand WHAT THE BIBLE SAYS. If you have a KING JAMES VERSION of the Bible, you can feel comfortable knowing that this is the preserved, inspired, and infallible WORD OF GOD."*

Our critic regards the AV1611 translators as having "s***corned the more***

outspoken Puritans as "self conceited Brethren."" This term, for which he gives no reference, is from *The Epistle Dedicatory* of the AV1611 and the full quotation, which he did not give, is as follows:

'So that if, on the one side, we shall be traduced by Popish Persons at home or abroad, who therefore will malign us, because we are poor instruments to make God's holy Truth to be yet more and more known unto the people, whom they desire still to keep in ignorance and darkness; or if, on the other side, we shall be maligned by self conceited Brethren, who run their own ways, and give liking unto nothing, but what is framed by themselves, and hammered on their anvil; we may rest secure, supported within by the truth and innocency of a good conscience, having walked in the ways of simplicity and integrity, as before the Lord;"

It becomes apparent WHY the AV1611 translators used the term "s*elf conceited Brethren*" when:

1. We compare "*we are poor instruments to make God's holy Truth to be yet more and more known*" with "**May I suggest that you . . . become acquainted with the standard scholarly works on the subject,**" found in our critic's introductory letter.
2. We compare "*give liking unto nothing, but what is framed by themselves*" with "**This version (the NIV) like every other must be subject to the original languages which I constantly consult**" and "**I would be very willing to help you in the study of Greek so that you could make a first hand judgment on these matters.**"

Our critic then claims that "**Though the translators claimed to steer a middle course the rules were in fact weighted against the Puritans.**" Nowhere does he substantiate this statement.

Both Paine (53) p 70–71 and Dr. Vance list the 15 rules for the translators. The only one which ostensibly could be construed as "*against the Puritans*" is Rule 3, which lays down that "*the old ecclesiastical words (were) to be kept.*"

Although the translators were to follow the "*Bishops' Bible*", according to Rule 1, Rule 14 allowed them to use the other English Protestant Translations "*when they agree better with the text.*" Our critic continues "**The translators not only used phrases from the Geneva Bible but also the Rheims translation and they constantly used Jerome's Latin Vulgate.**"

Use of phrases from the Geneva Bible by the translators would have been quite in order with Rule 14 above. Our critic gives no proof of "**constant use**" of the Latin Vulgate by the translators. Paine (53) p 77 states "*they had the Latin Vulgate, though that was suspect because it was popish.*"

The readings found in Erasmus' editions which are also found in the Vulgate have been discussed, Chapter 9, Section 9.6. The AV1611 translators had access to the Old Latin Text in order to verify these readings. No doubt many readings in the AV1611 which stem from the Old Latin and/or the Receptus Greek also survive in the Vulgate. This does not mean that the translators used the Vulgate "*constantly*". Our critic furnishes no proof of his assertion whatsoever.

The fact that the AV1611 translators obviously REJECTED readings found subsequently in Vaticanus and Sinaiticus shows that they did NOT rely heavily on the Vulgate, because the Vulgate is drawn largely from the text of those two codices. See Section 9.6.

Dr. Ruckman (1) p125 states: "*The AV translators knew ahead of time what Vaticanus and Sinaiticus said about scores of omissions, where the Alexandrian Jehudis hacked out 1 Corinthians 10:28, Romans 8:1, 1 Corinthians 11:24, Matthew 20:22, 1 Peter 4:14, Matthew 16:3, Mark 6:11, Colossians 1:14, Matthew 6:13, Acts 7:30, Romans 13:9, Acts 24:7, Mark 13:14, Acts 9:5–6, and a dozen other places.*

"*Having more spiritual understanding in 1611 than the Lockman Foundation that printed the Amplified Bible and the NASV in 1960, the AV translators discarded all of the Greek manuscripts THAT CONTAINED THE APOCRYPHA AS PART OF THE OLD TESTAMENT WITHOUT HAVING TO READ EITHER VATICANUS OR SINAITICUS. The Lockman Foundation and Hort (along with the committees of the RV, RSV, and NRSV of the National Councils of Churches), on the other hand, adopted manuscripts that contained the Apocrypha AS PART OF THE OLD TESTAMENT, although they were too YELLOW TO INCLUDE THEM IN THEIR PUBLICATIONS.*

"*Nice folks! I've met better folks at a bar in an Officer's Club on New Year's Eve.*"

As for the Rheims translation, the 1899 edition, revised by Bishop Challoner during 1749–1752, retains intact only 4 of the above 15 verses cited by Dr. Ruckman. These are Acts 9:6, 24:7, Romans 13:9 and Colossians 1:14. It changes "**broken**" to "delivered" in 1 Corinthians 11:24 and omits parts of the other 9 verses.

However, one should bear in mind the remarks of Wilkinson (2) p 240–241:

"*The Rheims-Douay has been repeatedly changed to approximate the King James. The result is that the Douay of 1600 and that of 1900 are not the same in many ways . . . Cardinal Wiseman wrote, 'To call it any longer the Douay or Rhemish is an abuse of terms. It has been altered and modified until scarcely any verse remains as it was originally published. In nearly every case, Challoner's changes took the form approximating to the Authorized Version.'"*

In the Preface to the 1989 reprint of the 1899 edition, the publishers say: *"The present Bible is the Challoner revision (1749–1752) of the Douay-Rheims Bible. Catholics owe the saintly Bishop Richard Challoner (1691–1781) a great debt of gratitude for undertaking this work . . . Some Catholics in England were even reading the King James version-a situation which Bishop Challoner knew had to be rectified."* Bishop Challoner and our critic would certainly agree on that.

Dr. Ruckman (1) p120 states with respect to Douay readings in the AV1611: *"The lame alibi that the King James' English words often match the Rheims' English wording is just one more of those peculiar Alexandrian twists that we find infesting the minds of the Professional Liars Club through the centuries. This time, the ENGLISH words have nothing to do with it; that is why the matter was brought up. THIS TIME, IT IS THE TEXTUAL BASIS. The textual basis of the Douay-Rheims is Jerome's Latin Vulgate, including seven Apocryphal books from the "Septuagint manuscripts" (written 250 years after the death of Jesus Christ)."*

The textual basis of the Douay Rheims is stated explicitly by the publishers to be *"The Latin Vulgate"*. Like the Vulgate, the Old Testament of the Douay Rheims includes the Apocrypha as part of the Scriptures.

Dr. Ruckman continues (1) p 96–97: *"Jerome's New Testament is basically Vaticanus and Sinaiticus, although . . . he occasionally retains the correct Old Latin Receptus AGAINST the Alexandrian corruptions from Egypt . . . Against his wishes, the Pope (Damasus) had the APOCRYPHA stuck into the Old Testament as part of the inspired canon. THIS IS HOW IT HAD APPEARED IN VATICANUS AND SINAITICUS."*

One should recall that Vaticanus and Sinaiticus are designated by the NIV as *"The most reliable early manuscripts"*, Chapter 1, Section 1.6. It should also be borne in mind that the Textual Basis of the AV1611 is the Greek Received Text in the New Testament and the Masoretic Hebrew Text in the Old Testament, both of which depart significantly from Vaticanus and Sinaiticus.

I turn now to our critic's remarks on the Apocrypha.

He states ***"The Apocrypha was included (in the "KJV"). Indeed Archbishop Abbot in 1615 insisted on its inclusion on pain of one year's*** *imprisonment. (The Westminster Confession of Faith has a much more "Protestant" attitude to the Apocrypha.) It was not until the last century that the omission of the Apocrypha became general . . . The 1629 edition was the first to omit the Apocrypha – but that led to episcopal disapproval."*

Our critic has ignored the information given in Chapter 4, Section 4.4, Chapter 5, Section 5.7. This information shows that the Apocrypha is NOT part of the scriptures in the AV1611. My copy of the 1611 Edition of the AV1611 contains the Apocrypha BETWEEN THE TESTAMENTS. This is the essential issue.

Dr. Gipp states (9) p 99–100 states *"In the days when our Bible was translated the Apocrypha was accepted reading based on its historical value, though not accepted as Scripture by anyone outside of the Catholic church. The King James translators therefore placed it BETWEEN the Old and New Testaments for its historical benefit to its readers. They did not integrate it into the Old Testament text as do the corrupt Alexandrian manuscripts . . . If having the Apocrypha BETWEEN the Testaments disqualifies it as authoritative, then the corrupt Vaticanus and Sinaiticus manuscripts from Alexandria, Egypt must be totally worthless since their authors obviously didn't have the conviction of the King James translators and incorporated its books into the text of the Old Testament thus giving it authority with Scripture."*

Remember that the NIV, which regards the two Egyptian mss. above in such high esteem, is regarded by our critic as *the most accurate translation available at present."*

The penalty imposed by Archbishop Abbot in 1615 is described in the TBS article (37) *The English Bible and the Apocrypha*, a copy of which has been in my possession for over 10 years. In a letter to me dated 5th April 1986, the then Editorial Secretary of the TBS, Mr. A.J. Brown, stated that *"Abbot's directive applied not only to the Authorised Version but to ALL printed Bibles, i.e. including the Geneva Bible."* The TBS library contains a copy of the Geneva Bible with the Apocrypha, printed 1578 and Mr. Brown's letter states that *"throughout the 16th century it was standard practice for the Apocrypha to be included in all English Bibles."* Inclusion of the Apocrypha, therefore, between the Testaments of the AV1611 can hardly be reckoned as a shortcoming of that particular Bible.

According to the TBS article, the Westminster Confession of Faith, to which our critic alludes, states: *"The books called Apocrypha, not being of Divine confirmation, are no part of the Canon of Scripture; and therefore are of no authority in the Church of God; not to be any otherwise approved, or made use of, than other human writings."*

This statement accords very much with the reasons given by the King James Translators for not incorporating the Apocrypha into the text. There were seven. Dr. Gipp gives 3 and 4 as follows (9) p 99:

"These books were never acknowledged as sacred Scriptures by the Jewish Church, and therefore were never sanctioned by our Lord.

"They were not allowed a place among the sacred books, during the first four centuries of the Christian Church."

I do not see that the difference between the attitude of the AV1611 translators and the Westminster Confession towards the Apocrypha is as great as our critic would have me believe.

It is ironic that the Westminster Confession of Faith (12) p 352 *"cites 1 Timothy 3:16 as THE verse attesting most strongly to the deity of Christ (Section 8, par. 2)."* Yet our critic regards this attestation to Christ's Deity – namely **"God was manifest in the flesh"** AV1611 – as a *"late, highly doubtful reading"*. See Chapter 14 of this work.

The TBS document gives 1629 as the year in which an AV1611 was published without the Apocrypha and indicates that *"it became much more common for the AV to appear without the Apocrypha"* after the 1820's. However, Dr. Ruckman (34) p 3 explicitly refers to *"An edition in 1613 without the Apocrypha between the Testaments."* He also lists the six main copies after 1611, p 18–19 as being those of 1613, 1644, 1664, 1701, 1769 and 1852, although he adds to this list elsewhere (1) p 34–35. The Editions of 1644 and 1664 were largely the work of John Canne and the 1664 Edition did not include the Apocrypha. Neither did Editions of 1662 and 1682 (37). Mr. Brown states in his letter to me that *"several editions of the AV did appear without the Apocrypha between 1611 and 1660."* Since the 1769 Edition is regarded as *"the standard copy"* and is also a revision of the 1701 Edition, I made the statement in Chapter 5, Section 5.7 that *"The Apocrypha was removed from the 1613 edition and most subsequent editions"* in the first draft of Volume 1. Obviously, that statement needs some clarification, which has been supplied both here and in the redraft of Volume 1.

However, none of this affects the essential issue, that the Apocrypha was NEVER included in the SCRIPTURES of the AV1611, although it WAS in the Greek mss. underlying the NIV. That was the issue which our critic was not – and is not – prepared to face.

11.2 "INTENTIONAL CHANGES" AND "UNAUTHORISED REVISIONS"

Moving on he then refers to "*intentional changes*" and "*unauthorised revisions*" in various Editions of the AV1611 "*which have altered the meaning.*" These were evidently so serious that "*as far back as 1831, public attention was drawn to the extent to which all modern reprints had departed from the original editions of 1611.*"

He also mentions two verses where "*changes in punctuation affects meaning*". These are **Psalm 42:9** and **Luke 22:40**

In Psalm 42:9, the 1611 AV1611, Oxford University Press, reads: "**I will say unto God, My rocke, why hast thou forgotten me? why go I mourning, because of the oppression of the enemy?**"

A contemporary AV1611, Cambridge University Press, reads: "**I will say unto God my rock, Why hast thou forgotten me? why go I mourning because of the oppression of the enemy?**"

The differences in punctuation are commas after "**God**" and "**mourning**" in the 1611 AV1611. They make NO difference to "*meaning*" WHATSOEVER. In EACH Edition, God is plainly the "**Rock**", Deuteronomy 32:31, Psalm 18:2 and David is addressing Him as such. In EACH Edition, David is complaining to God about the suffering inflicted on him by his foes.

In Luke 22:40, the 1611 AV1611 reads:

"**And when he was at the place, he said unto them, Pray, that ye enter not into temptation.**"

The contemporary AV1611 reads:

"**And when he was at the place, he said unto them, Pray that ye enter not into temptation.**"

The only difference is a comma after "**Pray**" in the 1611 AV1611. Once again, there is NO change in "*meaning.*" In EACH Edition, the Lord is exhorting His disciples to pray in order to avoid or resist temptation to sin.

Why would anyone think otherwise in the light of Matthew 6:13?

Why would anyone think otherwise reading THE NEXT FOUR VERSES, Luke 22:41–44? Resisting temptation is ALWAYS "**not MY will but THINE, be done!**"?

Why would anyone think otherwise when the Lord says in VERSE 46 "**pray, lest ye enter into temptation**" where BOTH Editions have the comma after "**pray**"?

While gnat-straining against the AV1611, our critic fails to explain the misleading footnote in the NIV which disputes the authenticity of verses 43 and 44. According to Burgon (13) p 79–81 and Hills (5) p 130–131, only A, B, R, T, N, W and P75 omit the verses, together with a few "*Caesarean*" mss. and a few copies of the versions. All the remaining mss. and copies of versions, being in the vast majority, contain the verses. Other citations date from the 2nd and 3rd centuries.

Our critic then turns his attack on "*the He and She editions of 1611*" which "*differ in hundreds of minute particulars and each has errors of its own.*" He mentions that "*413 changes were made*" in the 1613 Edition and that the 1638 Edition "s*howed evidence of extensive careful revision and it remained the standard text for well over a century.*" This sentence appears almost word-for-word in Beale's *A Pictorial History of the English Bible* (47).

Then he continues "*Even so William Kilburne in 1659 claimed to find 20,000 errors in six different editions printed in the 1650's.*"

Paine, above refers to the revisions made in 1638 as "*minor*" and over 72% of all textual variations were resolved by 1638. See Chapter 10, Section 10.13.

Dr. Ruckman's book on the variations in the Editions of the AV1611 (34) gives a far more detailed analysis than our critic's comments. I reproduce the RESULTS of that analysis, first where Dr. Ruckman is citing the conclusions of the Committee on Versions to the Board of Managers of the American Bible Society in 1852.

"*The results of the God-honoured, God-blessed revisions of the original 1611 text are as follows:*

"*That the edition of 1611, although prepared with very great care, was not free from typographical errors; and that, while most of these were corrected in the edition of 1613, others in much greater numbers were then introduced, which have since been removed.*

"*That the revision of Dr. Blaney made by collating the then current editions of Oxford and Cambridge with those of 1611 and 1701 had for its main object to restore the text of the English Bible to its original purity: and that this was successfully accomplished.*""

Dr. Ruckman continues (1) p 30 "*What surprises do you suppose these greenhorns and tenderfeet are going to pull on a man who has had an exact copy of the original 1611 edition (not a "fairly reasonable" facsimile published by Thomas Nelson and Sons) for more than twenty years and an original copy of a 1613 right off the press? Do you suppose someone is going to try to bamboozle him with "variants in the different editions of the King James Bible"?"* Evidently it is this 1613 copy which does not contain the Apocrypha, even between the Testaments (34) p 3.

I am surprised that our critic thinks it is *"impossible . . . to go back to the unrevised edition (of the AV1611)."* I have a copy of *The Holy Bible, An Exact Reprint in Roman Type, Page for Page of the Authorised Version Published in the Year 1611* on my desk as I write. It is published by the Oxford University Press and contains the Apocrypha BETWEEN the Testaments.

Dr. Ruckman continues *"I have Scrivener's complete list of all the variants in all of the editions of the AV* (The Authorised Edition of the English Bible: Its Subsequent Reprints and Modern Representatives, Cambridge Press, 1884). *You are going to impress us with the differences between the editions of the AV, are you? You are going to impress us by telling us that there were five or seven major editions, when we have a list which gives fourteen (1612, 1613, 1616, 1617, 1629, 1630 with the King's printers; then 1640, 1660, 1701, 1762, 1769, 1833, 1847–51 and 1858)? You have more "authoritative sources" than WE do on the KING JAMES BIBLE, do you? Well, I have the complete list of all the changes in all of the books of both Testaments, including FIVE APPENDICES which detail the readings of the Greek text used by the AV translators. Why did I not lose my faith in THE BOOK after reading every word in this work? As they say "down home": "It DO present a problem, don't it?""*

Our critic was careful to say that William Kilburne only *"CLAIMED"* to find *"20,000 errors in six different editions (of the AV1611)"*, not that he actually found them. However, he then follows this *"claim"* by asking *"The question inevitably arises – which of all these various revisions is the real KJV?"*

William Grady (45) p 168–170 replies as follows:

"When all else fails, detractors of the King James Bible will invariably ask their despised opponents, "WHICH Authorised Version do you believe, the 1611, 1613, 1767 or perhaps the 1850?" And while their bewildered victims are pondering this troublesome innuendo (analogous to such nonsense as "Have you quit beating your wife lately?"), they are subjected to an array of staggering statistics. Citing the Evangelical scholar Jack Lewis, Keylock quotes him as stating:

"Few people realise, for example, that thousands of textual errors have been found in the KJV. As early as 1659 William Kilburne found 20,000 errors in six KJV editions."

"Reckless statements such as Lewis' are incredibly misleading as the

extent of these so-called "errors" are never explained to be primarily lithographical (printing) and orthographical (spelling) in nature. In 1611, the art of printing was an occupation of the utmost drudgery. With every character being set by hand, a multitude of typographical errors was to be expected . . .

"In addition to printing flaws, there was a continual change in spelling for which to care. Lewis did not inform his readers that there was no such thing as proper spelling in the seventeenth century . . .

"A significant portion of these twenty thousand "textual errors" were in reality nothing more than changing "darke" to "dark" or "rann" to "ran." Who but a Nicolataine priest would categorize as serious revisions the normal follow-up corrections of mistakes at the press?

"It is impossible to overstate the duplicity of such critics who would weaken the faith of some with their preposterous reports of tens of thousands of errors in the Authorised Version . . . In his Appendix A (List of wrong readings of the Bible of 1611 amended in later editions) of his informative work, The Authorised Edition of the English Bible (1611), Its Subsequent Reprints and Modern Representatives, *Scrivener catalogued but a fraction of the inflated figures of modern scholarship.*

"Excluding marginal alterations and Apocrypha citings, this author has personally reviewed pages 147–194 and counted LESS THAN 800 CORRECTIONS. And even this figure is misleading when you consider that many of the instances were repetitious in nature. (Six such changes involved the corrected spelling of "**Nathanael**" *from the 1611's* "**Nathaneel**" *in John 1:45–49 and 21:2).*

"Whereas Geisler and Nix cited Goodspeed's denouncing of Dr. Blayney's 1769 Oxford edition for deviating from the Authorised Version in "at least 75,000 details," Scrivener alludes to less than two hundred as noteworthy of mention."

Our critic also asks *"**If revision has been tolerated and even encouraged in the past why should it be terminated now?**"*

That he should even ask such a question shows that, in true Nicolataine fashion, he tends to dismiss ANYTHING which is put forward as documented evidence by a mere layman. Nevertheless, I will respond to his question with the help of another layman, Norman Ward (11) p 43:

"The modern versions utilize as their manuscript base the corrupt texts of the Alexandrian tradition." Modern revision seeks to overthrow the PROTESTANT Text of the English Reformation with the ROMAN CATHOLIC text of the Dark Ages. This was extensively documented in Chapters 1 ,6, 7 especially with respect to mss. Aleph and B, Section 1.6,

the duplicity of Westcott and Hort, Section 6.2 and the Roman Catholic readings in the modern versions, Sections 7.2, 7.3.

Further documentation of the corrupt nature of the Alexandrian text will be found in Chapter 9. Mr. Ward continues:

"The modern versions change the word of God anywhere from 30,000 to 70,000 times. Confronted with this truth, the critic . . . countercharges that the AV has also been subject to some 20,000 changes. When using this line to destroy the faith of his reader in the AV1611, the critic conveniently "forgets" to mention the NATURE of the changes he is referring to. The changes in the modern versions involve elimination of words, phrases, verses, and whole passages of Scripture. They involve substitution of words, changes in verb tense and additions or elimination of articles, etc. These changes result in the denial of the virgin birth, the blood atonement, the miracles and the deity of Christ."

I documented 70 passages of Scripture in Chapters 5 and 7 where changes in the NIV attacked important doctrines and produced readings matching the Jerusalem Bible of the Roman Catholic church and the New World Translation of the Jehovah's Witnesses. See also Chapter 10, Section 10.15. Although our critic has made spurious attempts to justify some of these changes and has offered to present his *"position orally"* on others, the facts remain. His insistence in his introductory letter that *"critics . . . leave so much in the text which stands in complete contradiction to their alleged purposes"* is merely evasion.

NO further *"revision"* of the Holy Bible is warranted and the *"revisions"* from 1881 onwards were NEVER warranted. God has His Book, regardless of the *"position"* of ANY modern critic, including our critic.

Our critic also seeks to acquaint me with *"the facts"* about the findings of the American Bible Society, which I mentioned very briefly in Chapter 5, Section 5.7, stating *"It examined six editions of the KJV then circulating and found 24,000 variants in the text and punctuation."* These editions have been listed above. The nature of the variations has been discussed in some detail.

Our critic continues *"It claimed that "of the great number" there was not one which affected any doctrine or precept in the Bible. When the Society attempted a revision in 1860 it had to be abandoned because of protests from its supporters."*

The ESSENTIAL facts, some of which our critic has omitted, are summarised by McClure (57) p 223–224, Dr. Ruckman (34) p 3, 18–19

and William Grady (45) p 171. To these our critic's material adds
NOTHING which is essential.

Dr. Ruckman states *"the variations were just under 24,000 (this
includes chapter heading changes and marginal notes) and not one of
them was a rejection of the Received Greek Text of the New Testament or
the Received Hebrew Text of the Old Testament. Not one of them was an
intentional departure from the original words as written by the AV
translators."*

McClure states *"the number of variations in the text and punctuation
of these six copies was found to fall but little short of twenty-four
thousand. A vast amount! Quite enough to frighten us, till we read the
Committee's assurance, that "of all this great number, THERE IS NOT
ONE WHICH MARS THE INTEGRITY OF THE TEXT, or affects any
doctrine or precept of the Bible.""*

One should observe carefully the words which our critic omitted:
"THERE IS NOT ONE WHICH MARS THE INTEGRITY OF THE TEXT."
The omission is rather like that which one finds repeatedly in the NIV and
other modern *"revisions"*.

Dr. Ruckman and Dr. Grady cite the conclusions of the Society: *"The
English Bible as left by the translators has come down to us unaltered in
respect of its text . . . With the exception of typographical errors and
changes required by the progress of orthography in the English language,
the text of our present Bibles remains unchanged, and without variation
from the original copy as left by the translators . . . The present copies of
the Bible accord throughout with the edition of 1611."*

McClure, p 224, refers to the standard copy prepared by the American
Bible Society for future distribution. Dr. Ruckman describes it as *"the
Standard Edition, Octavo Reference Bible of 1852."* If this edition
appeared in 1852 as a Standard, it is understandable that there may have
been protests when a revision was attempted only eight years later.

I turn now to the *"plainly intentional changes"* in the AV1611, where
our critic insists that *"meaning is involved"* such that *"the present KJV
is quite different from that produced in 1611."*

2 Samuel 16:8

1611 AV1611	2001 AV1611
"thou art taken to thy mischief"'	**thou art taken in thy mischief'**

The present tense ensures that both readings have much the same sense
– "You are brought TO evil (i.e. TO mischief – Exodus 32:12, 14)" or

"You are caught IN evil" (i.e. IN mischief"). The situation described in the second reading would be the logical outcome of that described in the first. No real alteration of meaning is involved. Our critic is straining at a gnat.

Jeremiah 19:11

1611 AV1611	2001 AV1611
"as one breaketh a potters vessel that cannot bee made whole againe, and they shall bury them in Tophet, till there be no place else to bury."	"as one breaketh a potter's vessel, that cannot be made whole again: and they shall bury them in Tophet, till there be no place to bury."

Besides the obvious changes in punctuation and spelling, "**one**", "**them**" and "**there**" are in Italics in the 2001 reading.

The comma after "**vessel**" in the 2001 reading does not introduce any change in meaning because the spoiling of the potter's vessel is explained in Jeremiah 18:4. The second part of each reading indicates that Tophet, in the valley of Hinnom, 2 Kings 23:10, would be full of burial places until there were no additional places (1611 reading) or no places left (2001 reading).

Ezekiel 24:7

1611 AV1611	2001 AV1611
'she powred it upon the ground to couer it with dust"	'she poured it not upon the ground, to cover it with dust"

"Not" is in the Masoretic Hebrew text, which would suggest that the omission in the 1611 reading is a typographical error. This is apparent not only in the first part of verse 7, "**she set it upon the top of a rock**" but also in verse 8, which reads "**I have set her blood upon the top of a rock, that it should not be covered.**"

Ezekiel 46:23

1611 AV1611	2001 AV1611
"there was a new building round about"	"there was a row of building round about"

The context in BOTH Editions indicates that each corner of the court was surrounded by buildings. Of course they were NEW (1611 reading), the whole temple was NEW – it hasn't even been built yet. If the buildings were "**round about**" a corner, they would have to be in a ROW. Both readings are correct.

Leviticus 26:40

1611 AV1611	2001 AV1611
"**If they shall confess the iniquity of their fathers**"	"**If they shall confess their iniquity, and the iniquity of their fathers**"

"Their iniquity" is in the Masoretic text and therefore this would appear to be another typographical omission in the 1611 Bible, subsequently corrected. Note that the 1611 reading is not in error as it stands, only incomplete.

Psalm 18:47

Apart from changes in spelling and the use of italics for "**It is**" in the 2001 reading, the readings for BOTH Editions are IDENTICAL. I wonder if our critic checked this reading?

Matthew 12:23

1611 AV1611	2001 AV1611
"**Is this the sonne of David?**"	"**Is not this the son of David?**"

"Meti", which is "**not**" in an exclamatory sense as "What(?)", is found in Berry's TR but is untranslated, yielding almost the same reading as the 1611 Bible. The people's amazement in the context shows that BOTH readings have the same sense, although the 2001 reading is stronger because it includes the exclamatory term.

If the change is "*plainly intentional*", then like ALL the others, it was for the BETTER and the Lord has HONOURED it. The same CANNOT be said for ANY change made in ANY modern translation.

Matthew 13:45

Apart from changes in spelling, e.g. "**marchant**" to "**merchant**", the readings are IDENTICAL. I wonder if our critic checked THIS reading?

Matthew 16:16

1611 AV1611	2001 AV1611
"Christ the sonne"	**"the Christ the Son"**

Gail Riplinger's findings Chapter 10, Section 10.11 apply but here Peter is addressing "**the LORD'S Christ**", Luke 2:26 in BOTH readings. The readings in Mark 8:29 "**the Christ**" and Luke 9:20 "**the Christ of God**" are IDENTICAL in BOTH Editions.

Matthew 26:36

Apart from changes in spelling and the capital D in "**Disciples**" in the 1611 reading, the readings are IDENTICAL. Did our critic check this verse?

Matthew 26:75

"**Words**" in 1611 has been altered to "**word**" in 2001. Since the "**words**" or "**word**" are actually GIVEN IN THE VERSE, it surely doesn't seriously affect the meaning. Our critic continues to gnat-strain.

Mark 2:4

"**Preasse**" ("press") in 1611 has been altered to "**the press**" in 2001 (Times, Independent, News of the World, Telegraph etc.). Both readings indicate that a crowd had gathered which was causing a lot of "Press"ure (!) and the meaning is unaltered.

Mark 5:6

1611 AV1611	2001 AV1611
"he came and worshipped him"	**"he ran and worshipped him"**

Beale on p 47 of his *Pictorial History* (47) indicates that this was one of the changes made in 1638. The sense of the reading is not changed, except insofar as the 2001 rendition indicates that the man came QUICKLY.

Our critic fails to mention that the NIV entirely omitted "**worshipped**" from this verse. So did the DR, Douay Rheims, JB and NWT. The same omission by the NIV, DR, JB, NWT occurs in Matthew 8:2, 9:18, 15:25, 20:20, with "kneeling down", "adored", "bowed low" and "did obeisance" respectively being their alternatives. ALL these verses express worship of the Lord during His earthly ministry, before His resurrection. The NIV reinserts "**worshipped**" in Matthew 28:9, 10. In the AV1611, the Lord is worthy to be worshipped BEFORE His resurrection.

Moreover, the NIV retains "worship" in Mark 15:19, where it is a mockery, in Acts 19:27 with the DR, NWT, Romans 1:25 with the DR, JB, Colossians 2:18 with the JB, NWT, Revelation 13:4 with the NWT, 14:11, 16:2, 19:10, 19:20, 20:4, 22:8 all with the JB, NWT. Even though "worship" is the correct term, the context in the last ten verses is IDOLATRY.

Mark 10:18

1611 AV1611	2001 AV1611
"there is no man good, but one, that is God"	**"there is none good but one, that is, God"**

Both Editions have the same reading **"there is none good but one, that is, God"** in Matthew 19:17 and **"none is good, save one, that is, God"** in Luke 18:19 with differences only in italics or punctuation. In that respect the Edition of 1611 endorses the 2001 reading in Mark. While the 2001 reading has a broader sense and is therefore the better reading, the 1611 reading is nevertheless correct, for two reasons:

1. The context is Jesus Christ challenging the young man to believe He is "**God manifest in the flesh**", which He IS, 1 Timothy 3:16.
2. The term "**but one**" could be taken to mean "but ONE is good", in contrast to any MAN. See how the Lord uses that very sense less than 10 verses further on, in verse 27.

Once again, there is no significant effect on meaning.

Luke 1:3

1611 AV1611	2001 AV1611
"understanding of things"	**"understanding of all things"**

Luke is plainly referring to "**those things which are most surely believed among us**", verse 1 in BOTH Editions and "**those things wherein thou hast been instructed**" verse 4 in BOTH Editions. No change of meaning is involved.

Luke 19:9

1611 AV1611	2001 AV1611
"the sonne of Abraham"	**"a son of Abraham**

Both readings are correct, although again the 2001 reading has the broader sense. No Bible believer would ever be confused into thinking that Zacchaeus was "THE" son of Abraham, to the exclusion of all others, including Isaac.

In the very next verse the term "**the Son of man**" appears. Yet it is apparent from reading the Old Testament, especially Ezekiel, that The Lord Jesus Christ is not the ONLY "**son of man**" in the Bible. This is apparent even in the NIV.

John 5:18

The 1611 Edition has "**father**", the 2001 Edition has "**Father.**" Aside from that and minor differences in punctuation and spelling, the readings are identical and no change of meaning is involved.

John 15:20

1611 AV1611	2001 AV1611
"**The servant is not greater than the Lord**"	"**The servant is not greater than his lord**"

Obviously both readings are correct, although the 2001 reading matches that in John 13:16, which is identical in BOTH Editions. In John 15:20, the Lord is exhorting the disciples to REMEMBER what He told them in John 13:16. In both Editions it is quite plain WHO "**The Lord**" is and WHO "**his lord**" is, in the immediate context.

Acts 4:27

The readings are identical. BOTH Editions have the term "**holy child.**" See Section 10.8.

Acts 6:3

"**holy Ghost**" in 1611 is changed to "**Holy Ghost**" in 2001, the readings being otherwise identical – apart from the usual minor differences in punctuation and spelling which DO NOT affect meaning.

Romans 11:23

"**bide**" in 1611 is changed to "**abide**" in 2001. NO change of meaning is involved.

1 Corinthians 4:9

There are the usual minor changes in punctuation and spelling. Otherwise, the readings are identical, with NO change of meaning.

Our critic fails to mention the NIV's additions to the word of God in this verse. See Chapter 10, Section 10.10.

1 Corinthians 12:28
1611 AV1611	2001 AV1611
"helpes in gouernmets"	"helps, governments"

A literal rendering of Berry's TR appears to support the 2001 reading, so the change could be typographical.

However, BOTH Editions show that "**governments**" was a separate gift, Romans 12:8 and that "**helpers**" did help those with responsibility for church "**government**", such as Paul. See Romans 16:2, 3, 6, 2 Corinthians 11:28, 1 Timothy 3:5. Therefore, both readings would be correct.

The 2001 reading simply indicates that "**helps**" had a wider ministry than helping only in church government and reinforces Romans 12:8. Most significantly, the variation does NOT involve error, in EITHER Edition.

2 Corinthians 12:2
There are minor changes in spelling and punctuation and use of parentheses in the 2001 reading. Otherwise, the readings are identical.

1 Timothy 1:4
1611 AV1611	2001 AV1611
"edifying"	"godly edifying"

"Theou" or "**godly**" is found in Berry's TR. This would indicate that the change is typographical. The sense of the verse is NOT changed.

1 Timothy 4:16
The 1611 Edition has "**thy selfe**", the 2001 Edition has "**thyself.**" Apart from minor differences in spelling and punctuation, the readings otherwise are identical.

1 Peter 1:22
'**see that ye**" is in italics in the 2001 Edition. Apart from the usual minor differences in spelling and punctuation, which do NOT alter meaning, the readings are identical.

The last verse cited by our critic in this section is **John 5:12.** Originally it had been **1 John 5:12** but he has tippexed out the "**1**" in his document.

This shows that he did not check the verse in various Editions of the AV1611 because 1 John 5:12 IS the correct citation. John 5:12 is identical in BOTH Editions, even with respect to punctuation. I seriously doubt whether our critic checked ANY of the verses in this section.

The 2001 Edition adds "**of God**" to the second reading of "**the Son.**" Obviously, this does NOT alter the meaning of the verse in ANY way. "Theou" or "of God" is found in Berry's TR and so the addition is clearly typographical. This was another change made in 1638, (47) p 46. Our critic concludes this section as follows:

"***In general these changes were plainly intentional,***" which does NOT mean that they were incorrect, unwarranted or not prompted by the AUTHOR, the SPIRIT OF GOD, who like ANY human author, has the right to edit HIS OWN WORK.

He adds "s***o the present KJV is quite different from that produced in 1611.***"

As this work has shown repeatedly, the TRUTH OF THE MATTER is "***quite different***" from our critic's opinion.

11.3 'SOME EARLY PROTESTANT REACTIONS TO THE KJV"

Dr. Ruckman (1) p 8 refers to "*the standard attacks on the AV, which have been current for one hundred years (1880–1980):*

1. *The AV "HAS BEEN" (past tense) the most popular version.*
2. *It was a compromise translation.*
3. *Some people objected to it . . .*
4. *Inspiration applies only to the original manuscripts . . . THERE ISN'T ANY VERSE TO BACK (THIS) UP IN EITHER TESTAMENT.*
5. *(The) 1611 copy (doesn't) match word-for-word (the) AV of 1980. (This is why Thomas Nelson and Sons printed a reasonable facsimile of the 1611 – in hopes that it would destroy some more Christians' faith in the Book. Nice people. THEY ALSO PUBLISHED THE RSV OF THE NCCC.)*"

Dr. Ruckman has summarised our critic's objections to the Book quite well and added some that our critic didn't mention. See Reference 1.

Our critic states "***The KJV was not universally welcomed when it appeared and opposition to it, especially from the strongest Protestants, continued for many years.***"

The opposition did NOT come from either Bunyan or Cromwell, two of the most outstanding Protestants of the 17ᵗʰ Century. See Section 11.1.

He reiterates the falsehood which he put forward earlier, that *"(The KJV's) final triumph . . . was due to the dominant influence of the Church of England"*, adding *"and the absence of the kind of doctrinal comment which had characterised the Geneva Bible."*

"Doctrinal comment", of course, is NOT the issue. Availability of the word of God IS. See Section 11.1 for our critic's spurious reference to the *"dominant influence of the Church of England"*. Beale states *"(The AV1611) was the superlative English translation of the Word of Life. As a matter of fact, the very authorization of this "Authorized Version" came from the popular acclamation of the English-speaking world gradually "authorizing" it on the basis of its own merits and integrity. Although some vigorously opposed it for years, the venerable King James Version eventually replaced even the popular Geneva Bible. The King James translation of the Gospels and Epistles replaced the Geneva translation in the* Book of Common Prayer *in 1661."*

Of *"the strongest Protestants"* who opposed the AV1611, our critic has seen fit to divest only one, Hugh Broughton, of the cloak of anonymity. The reason is not hard to find. Wilkinson (2) p 300, states *"Only one name of prominence can be cited as an opponent of the King James Version at its birth . . . Hugh Broughton, the Hebraist, who wrote – "Tell His Majesty I had rather be rent in pieces by wild horses, than any such translation, by my consent, should be urged on our churches.""*

Paine (53) p 106–107 writes *"Broughton himself had urged a revised version and had hoped to be among those chosen for the work, but was left out because he was so acrid in his humours."* Paine indicates that Broughton's criticism above was part of a pamphlet in which *"he went on with the attack on (Bishop) Bancroft, who had no love for him."* Our critic refers to one such attack of Broughton's, without explaining whether it was justified or not. Richard Bancroft, Bishop of London and later Archbishop of Canterbury, was not one of the translators but had overall responsibility for the work.

Ironically, he had opposed it at first (53) p 1, rebuking the Puritan Rainolds for his petition and giving rise to James' remark which *"started the greatest writing project the world has ever known, and the greatest achievement of the reign of James 1 – the making of the English Bible which has ever since borne his name."*

"I could never yet see a Bible well translated in English, but I think that of the Geneva is the worst."

Paine indicates that James made this remark because he "*was quick to put both factions down.*" Given the characters of Bancroft and Rainolds, James was something of a lion-tamer. Modern Christianity knows little of such men.

Since Broughton was not selected for the work on the new Bible, he possibly had an axe to grind. This may explain his chagrin over the "*score of idle words to account for in the day of judgement,*" which he supposedly identified in Luke 3. Our critic alludes to these words without discussing them or even listing them.

However, Paine continues "*As the work went on even Hugh Broughton was softening somewhat his thoughts about the new version. In 1609 he wrote, "None should bear sway in translating but the able." But he added, "The king's care to have the law and gospel learnedly translated hath stirred much study and expectation of good, and all true hearted subjects will be ready for forbearance.""*

Broughton's change of heart should be remembered when our critic's attempts to denigrate James 1 are addressed.

Our critic continues with the accusations against Bancroft, Thomas Bilson, Bishop of Winchester and one of the reviewers of the translators' work and against the Holy Bible itself. With the exception of Broughton's invective above, the charges as our critic relays them are all anonymous and largely unsubstantiated.

The terms used to describe the AV1611 and its translators which he passes on for my benefit, on behalf of their unidentified sources, include "*blasphemy*", "*damnable corruptors of God's Word*", "*Intolerable deceit*", "*vile imposture*" and "*Atheism and Popery.*"

I suppose that these terms are examples of the "*moderate language*" which our critic commends on the first page of his opening section "***The Text of the New Testament***", Chapter 9.

"**As the bird by wandering, as the swallow by flying, so the curse causeless shall not come**" Proverbs 26:2.

Our critic further objects to "*Catholic*" words like "**charity**" and "**church**". The use of the word "**charity**" has been discussed, Chapter 10, Section 10.4. Dr. Ruckman states in his series on *The Alexandrian Cult*, Part 5 p 18

"*Is "charity" really passé? Is love GIVING? Can you love without GIVING (John 3:16)? If salvation isn't a "handout," what is it (2 Cor. 8:9)? If you left it "love" every time, wouldn't that give a "modern man" a false lead on "love"? Hollywood love is often GETTING, not giving; and it is often LUST, not love. If the AV translators were intelligent* enough to use both words (love and charity), why would one be so "archaic" that you had to alter the Bible in 31,000 places in order to "update" the word. There are more than 31,000 changes between ANY Bible that updates "charity" and the AV that retains it.

"When in doubt, smile at "good, godly, sound, sincere, evangelical translators" and put their work in the trash where it belongs. A reputation for goodness, godliness and orthodoxy is no alibi for lying and perverting the words of the living God."

Dr. Miles Smith has an enlightening comment on the word "**church**" from the Preface to the AV1611 p 26: "*We have on the one side avoided the scrupulosity of the Puritans, who leave the old Ecclesiastical words, and betake them to other, as when they put washing for Baptism, and Congregation instead of Church: as also on the other side we have shunned the obscurity of the Papists, in their Azimes, Tunic, Rational, Holocausts, Praepuce, Pasche, and a number of such like, whereof their late Translation is full, and that of purpose to darken the sense, that since they must needs translate the Bible, yet by the language thereof, it may be kept from being understood. But we desire that the Scripture may speak like itself, in the language of Canaan, that it may be understood even of the very vulgar.*"

The AV1611 translators knew what the real "*Catholic*" words were and avoided them. It is interesting that the group who would substitute "*congregation*" for "**church**" would also change "**baptism**" into "*washing*", which would make for some rather peculiar names for local churches. Moreover, inspection of the use of the word "**church**" in the New Testament indicates that there are many instances where "*congregation*" would NOT be appropriate.

These include Matthew 16:18, Ephesians 1:22, 3:10, 5:23, 24, 25, 27, 29, 32, Philippians 3:6, Colossians 1:18, 24, Revelation 1:20, among others. The simple, generic term "**church**" covers all the possibilities.

If our critic objects so strongly to the word "**church**", why did he choose to become a pastor of one without insisting that it first change its name to "*congregation*"? He gives no other alternative to the word "**church**".

One should compare the statement in his introductory letter to me "*I would be very willing to help you in the study of Greek so that you could make a first hand judgment on these matters*" with that of Dr. Smith: "*We desire that the Scripture may speak like itself . . . that it may be understood even of the very vulgar.*"

Our critic then repeats his complaint about the Apocrypha, ignoring once again the fact that it was placed BETWEEN the Testaments. He does not like the *"popish prints, plates and pictures"* of the 1611 Edition and the prefix *"Saint"* being given to some of the writers of Scripture, Matthew, Mark etc.

The plates in the 1611 Edition number two, at the beginning of the each of the Testaments, the Apocrypha apparently not meriting one. There are simple, inoffensive, decorative designs for section and Book headings and capital letters at the start of chapters. Although more intricate, these designs have no more significance for the WORDS of the Bible than the emblem on the front of the Hodder and Stoughton NIV, to which our critic apparently does not object.

The small circled © indicating COPYRIGHT in ANY modern translation is of FAR MORE significance than ANY of the pictures in the 1611 AV1611. See Chapter 5, Section 5.1.

Continuing to clutch at straws, our critic also objects to the Book headings such as "**The Gospel according to St. Matthew**" as having "*no basis in the Greek*", "*the Greek*" once again being undefined. In reply it may be said that neither do the chapter and verse divisions have any "*basis*" in the Greek manuscripts. It is common knowledge that they were added later (22) p 3, 13.

The objection to "*St. Matthew etc.*", which again does NOT affect the TEXT of the AV1611 stemmed from "*many Puritans*", according to our critic.

Aside from the fact that ALL Christians are entitled to be called "saints", Romans 1:7, it is quite apparent that the AV1611 has long outlasted the Puritans who disliked it. Sir Charles Firth has this penetrating comment on those whom Our critic apparently includes among "*the men of unquestioned orthodoxy*" in his informative biography on Oliver Cromwell p 477–478

"*Puritanism was spending its strength in the vain endeavour to make England Puritan by force. The enthusiasm which had undertaken to transform the world was being conformed to it. A change was coming over the party which supported the Protector; it had lost many of the 'men of conscience'; it had attracted many of the time-servers and camp-followers of politics; it was ceasing to be a party held together by religious interests, and becoming a coalition held together by material interests and political necessities.*"

Our critic alludes once more to the Westminster Assembly, "*which drew up the greatest of all Protestant confessions of faith*", according to him. It apparently included some members, unnamed and unnumbered, who wanted the AV1611 revised. The AV1611 WAS revised, of course, see the previous section and it remains for our critic to demonstrate that these revisions were insufficient and WHY. The course of church history certainly indicates that the AUTHOR and EDITOR-IN-CHIEF of the AV1611 WAS satisfied!

This *"greatest of all Protestant confessions"* certainly did not want the AV1611 reading in 1 Timothy 3:16 to be revised, although our critic apparently DOES. See Section 11.1.

He continues *"Actually a proposal to revise (the AV1611) came to nothing when the Long Parliament was dissolved in 1653."* The proposal must have been a "predestinated failure" Daniel 2:21 **"he removeth kings, and setteth up kings."**

Yet he goes on *"Agitation for revision from men of "unquestioned orthodoxy" continued well into the next century."* The AV1611 WAS revised in the 18th century, which fact I alluded to in Chapter 5, Section 5.7. Again our critic does not identify who these men were, who declared them to be *"orthodox"* and on what basis or of what their *"orthodoxy"* consisted.

11.4 "THE CONSIDERABLE INFLUENCE OF THE RHEIMS NT"

Our critic then turns his attention to the alleged influence of the Douay-Rheims version on the AV1611, which Alfred Pollard mentions in his very informative *Biographical Introduction to the 1611 AV1611*, p 27–28, of the Oxford Reprint. I will now compare the readings of the 1611 AV1611 with those of the Geneva Bible, 1599, Tyndale's New Testament, 1526 and the DR for the verses cited by our critic, where the influence of the DR *"is reflected in many of the KJV's phrases and terms"*.

The present day edition of the DR, first published in 1899, contains Challoner's revisions which have made it conform more closely with the AV1611 than the original 1582 edition. I have compared the three versions as follows.

The number of differences with respect to the 1611 AV1611 is equal to:

number of words changed + number of words added + number of words removed + number of changes of word order.

The number of differences appears after each verse quoted and the total at the end of the comparison.

Matthew 21:16

1611 AV1611	Geneva	Tyndale	DR
"And said unto him, Hearest thou what these say? And Jesus saith unto them, Yea, have ye never read, Out of the mouth of babes and sucklings thou hast perfected praise?"	"And said unto him, Hearest thou what these say? And Jesus said unto them, Yea: read ye never, By the mouth of babes and sucklings thou hast made perfect the praise?" 8	"And said unto him, Hearest thou what these say? Jesus said unto them, Have ye never read, Of the mouth of babes and sucklings thou hast ordained praise?" 5	"And said to him: Hearest thou what these say? And Jesus said to them, Yea, have you never read, Out of the mouth of infants and sucklings thou hast perfected praise?" 5

Matthew 24:40

1611 AV1611	Geneva	Tyndale	DR
"Then shall two be in the field, the one shall be taken, and the other left."	"Then two shall be in the fields, the one shall be received, and the other shall be refused." 6	"Then two shall be in the fields; the one shall be received, and the other shall be refused." 6	"Then two shall be in the field: one shall be taken, and one shall be left." 6

Matthew 26:30

1611 AV1611	Geneva	Tyndale	DR
"And when they had sung an hymn, they went out into the mount of Olives."	"And when they had sung a Psalm, they went out into the mount of Olives." 1	"And when they had said grace (sung an hymn), they went out into mount Olivet." 6	"And a hymn being said, they went out unto mount Olivet." 9

Luke 9:31

1611 AV1611	Geneva	Tyndale	DR
"Who appeared in glory, and spake of his decease, which he should accomplish at Jerusalem."	"Which appeared in glory, and told of his departing, which he should accomplish at Jerusalem."	"which appeared gloriously, and spake of his departing, which he should end at Jerusalem.'"	"Appearing in majesty. And they spoke of his decease that he should accomplish in Jerusalem."
	3	5	7

Acts 15:24

1611 AV1611	Geneva	Tyndale	DR
"Forasmuch as we have heard, that certain which went out from us, have troubled you with words, subverting your souls, saying, Ye must be circumcised, and keep the Law, to whom we gave no such commandment:"	"Forasmuch as we have heard, that certain which went out from us, have troubled you with words, and cumbered your minds, saying, Ye must be circumcised and keep the Law, to whom we gave no such commandment."	"Forasmuch as we have heard that certain which departed from us, have troubled you with words, and cumbered your minds saying, Ye must be circumcised, and keep the law, to whom we gave no such commandment."	"Forasmuch as we have heard, that some going out from us have troubled you with words, subverting your souls; to whom we gave no commandment:"
	3	5	13

The DR has omitted "**saying, Ye must be circumcised and keep the Law**" along with the NIV, JB, NWT, Ne, L, T, Tr, A

Acts 15:34

1611 AV1611	Geneva	Tyndale	DR
"**Notwithstanding it pleased Silas to abide there still.**"	"Notwithstanding Silas thought good to abide there still."	"Notwithstanding it pleased Silas to abide there still."	"But it seemed good unto Silas to remain there; and Judas alone departed to Jerusalem."
	4	0	12

Romans 1:1

1611 AV1611	Geneva	Tyndale	DR
"**Paul a servant of Jesus Christ, called to be an Apostle, separated unto the Gospel of God,**"	"Paul, a servant of Jesus Christ called to be an Apostle, put apart to preach the Gospel of God,"	"Paul, the servant of Jesus Christ, called unto the office of an apostle, put apart to preach the gospel of God,"	"Paul, a servant of Jesus Christ, called to be an apostle, separated unto the gospel of God,"
	4	10	0

Romans 2.5

1611 AV1611	Geneva	Tyndale	DR
"**But after thy hardness, and impenitent heart, treasurest up unto thyself wrath, against the day of wrath, and revelation of the righteous judgement of God:**"	"But thou, after thine hardness, and heart that cannot repent, heapest up as a treasure unto thy self wrath against the day of wrath, and of the declaration of the just judgement of God,"	"But thou after thine hard heart that cannot repent, heapest thee together the treasure of wrath against the day of vengeance; when shall be opened the righteous judgment of God;"	"But according to thy hardness and impenitent heart, thou treasurest up to thyself wrath, against the day of wrath, and revelation of the just judgment of God."
	12	18	5

Romans 5.8

1611 AV1611	Geneva	Tyndale	DR
"**But God commendeth his love towards us, in that while we were yet sinners, Christ died for us.**"	"But God setteth out his love toward us, seeing that while we were yet sinners, Christ died for us."	"But God setteth out his love that he hath to us; seeing that while we were yet sinners, Christ died for us."	"But God commendeth his charity towards us; because when as yet we were sinners, according to the time, (verse 9) Christ died for us;"
	4	7	9

1 Corinthians 15:33

1611 AV1611	Geneva	Tyndale	DR
"**Be not deceived: evil communications corrupt good manners.**"	"Be not deceived: evil speakings corrupt good manners."	"Be not deceived: malicious speakings corrupt good manners."	"Be not seduced: Evil communications corrupt good manners."
	1	2	1

2 Corinthians 10:10

1611 AV1611	Geneva	Tyndale	DR
"**For his letters (say they) are weighty and powerful, but his bodily presence is weak, and his speech contemptible.**"	"For the letters, sayeth he, are sore and strong, but his bodily presence is weak, and his speech is of no value."	"For the epistles (saith he,) are sore and strong; but his bodily presence is weak, and his speech homely."	"(For his epistles indeed, say they, are weighty and strong; but his bodily presence is weak, and his speech contemptible,)"
	8	7	3

Philippians 1:21

1611 AV1611	Geneva	Tyndale	DR
"For me to live is Christ, and to die is gain."	"For Christ is to me both in life and in death advantage."	"For Christ is to me life, and death is to me advantage."	"For to me, to live is Christ: and to die is gain."
	9	8	1

1 Timothy 1:15

1611 AV1611	Geneva	Tyndale	DR
"This is a faithful saying, and worthy of all acceptation, that Christ Jesus came into the world to save sinners, of whom I am chief."	"This is a true saying, and by all means worthy to be received, that Christ Jesus came into the world to save sinners, of whom I am chief."	"This is a true saying, and by all means worthy to be received, that Christ Jesus came into the world to save sinners; of whom I am chief."	"A faithful saying, and worthy of all acceptation, that Christ Jesus came into the world to save sinners, of whom I am the chief."
	7	7	3

2 Timothy 1:3

1611 AV1611	Geneva	Tyndale	DR
"I thank God, whom I serve from my forefathers with pure conscience, that without ceasing I have remembrance of thee in my prayers night and day,"	"I thank God, whom I serve from mine elders with pure conscience, that without ceasing I have remembrance of thee in my prayers night and day."	"I thank God, whom I serve from mine elders with pure conscience, that without ceasing I make mention of thee in my prayers night and day;"	"I give thanks to God, whom I serve from my forefathers with a pure conscience, that without ceasing, I have a remembrance of thee in my prayers, night and day."
	2	4	5

Hebrews 10:25

1611 AV1611	Geneva	Tyndale	DR
"Not forsaking the assembling of ourselves together, as the manner of some is: but exhorting one another, and so much the more, as ye see the day approaching."	"Not forsaking the fellowship that we have among ourselves, as the manner of some is: but let us exhort one another, and that so much the more, because ye see that the day draweth near."	"and let us not forsake the fellowship that we have among ourselves, as the manner of some is; but let us exhort one another: and that so much the more, because ye see that the day draweth nigh."	"Not forsaking our assembly, as some are accustomed; but comforting one another, and so much the more as you see the day approaching."
	14	18	12

Hebrews 12:23

1611 AV1611	Geneva	Tyndale	DR
"To the general assembly, and Church of the first borne, which are written in heaven, and to God the Judge of all, and to the spirits of just men made perfect:"	"And to the assembly and congregation of the first born, which are written in heaven, and to God the judge of all, and to the spirits of just and perfect men."	"And unto the congregation of the firstborn sons, which are written in heaven, and to God the judge of all, and to the spirits of just and perfect men,"	"And to the church of the firstborn, who are written in the heavens, and to God the judge of all, and to the spirits of the just made perfect,"
	6	9	7

James 1:5

1611 AV1611	Geneva	Tyndale	DR
"**If any of you lack wisdom, let him ask of God, that giveth to all men liberally, and upbraideth not: and it shall be given him.**"	"If any of you lack wisdom, let him ask of God, which giveth to all men liberally and reproacheth no man, and it shall be given him."	"If any that is among you lack wisdom, let him ask of God (which giveth to all men without endoubleness (liberally), and casteth no man in the teeth) and it shall be given him."	"But if any of you want wisdom, let him ask of God, who giveth to all men abundantly, and upbraideth not; and it shall be given him."
	4	13	4

1 John 1:9

1611 AV1611	Geneva	Tyndale	DR
"**If we confess our sins, he is faithful and just to forgive us our sins, and to cleanse us from all unrighteousness.**"	"If we acknowledge our sins, he is faithful and just to forgive us our sins, and to cleanse us from all unrighteousness."	"If we acknowledge our sins, he is faithful and just, to forgive us our sins, and to cleanse us from all unrighteousness."	"If we confess our sins, he is faithful and just, to forgive us our sins, and to cleanse us from all iniquity."
1		1	1

1 John 2:2

1611 AV1611	Geneva	Tyndale	DR
"And he is the propitiation for our sins: and not for ours only, but also for the sins of the whole world."	"And he is the reconciliation for our sins: and not for ours only but also for the sins of the whole world."	"And he it is that obtaineth grace for our sins: not for our sins only, but also for the sins of all the world."	"And he is the propitiation for our sins: and not for ours only, but also for those of the whole world."
	1	8	2

1 John 2:20

1611 AV1611	Geneva	Tyndale	DR
"But ye have an unction from the holy One and ye know all things."	"But ye have an ointment from that Holy One, and know all things."	"And ye have an ointment (unction) of the Holy Ghost, and ye know all things."	"But you have the unction from the Holy One, and know all things."
	3	3	3

1 John 3:21

1611 AV1611	Geneva	Tyndale	DR
"Beloved, if our heart condemn us not, then have we confidence towards God."	"Beloved, if our heart condemn us not, then have we boldness toward God."	"Tenderly beloved, if our hearts condemn us not, then have we trust to God-ward."	"Dearly beloved, if our heart do not reprehend us, we have confidence towards God:"
	2	4	6

Total differences in Geneva	99
Total differences in Geneva if Acts 15:34 is included in the comparison	103
Total differences in Tyndale, with or without Acts 15:34	146
Total differences in DR	102
Total differences in DR if Acts 15:34 is included in the comparison	114

Apart from changes in spelling, punctuation and italics, NONE OF WHICH affect meaning, the total number of differences in the above verses, including Acts 15:34, between the 1611 AV1611 and the 2001 AV1611 is zero.

The above 21 verses, including Acts 15:34 contain 426 words.

When one selects a passage of scripture of comparable length but from one Book only, such as Revelation 22, the following results are obtained, with the same definition of differences as above.

Total number of words	574
Total differences in Geneva	46
Total differences in Tyndale	77
Total differences in DR	110
Total differences in wording in 2001 AV1611	0

If word changes only are considered, the number of differences between Geneva, Tyndale and the AV1611 are only 25 and 38 respectively (26) Preface p 3. My figures are 22 and 37 respectively. See table that follows for the verse listings in Revelation 22.

When one combines the two sets of figures for the maximum number of differences from the AV1611, a figure of 149 is found for the Geneva, i.e. 103 + 46, 223 for Tyndale and 224 for the Douay-Rheims. When one allows for the alterations made in the Douay-Rheims to conform it to the AV1611, there is no compelling reason to suppose that the AV1611 translators were especially influenced by the Douay-Rheims.

The above figures agree with McClure's statement that the Geneva Bible agrees more closely with the AV1611 than any other Protestant Bible (57) p 67. The Jesuits had access to it for over twenty years before they began work on the Douay-Rheims. Why could not any apparent similarity between the DR and the AV1611 be attributable to the influence of the Geneva Bible? The latter was listed as one of the recommended translations under Rule 14 of the Rules for the AV1611 translators (53) p 71.

However, Paine states (53) p 128 *"The Douay Bible . . . differs remarkably from the King James Bible. In Psalm 23 it reads,* "Thou hast anointed my head with oil, and my chalice which inebriateth me, how goodly it is!" *Psalm 91 begins,* "He that dwelleth in the aid of the most High shall abide under the protection of the God of Jacob." *Verse 13 says* "Thou shalt walk upon the asp and the basilisk." *Isaiah (60):1 starts,* "Arise, be enlightened, O Jerusalem." *At places it seems almost as if the*

Roman and the King James Bibles had determined to make their words differ as much as they could, to show that their standpoints were poles apart."

Psalms 23 and 91 are actually Psalms 22 and 90 in the DR.

Revelation 22, Word Changes only for Geneva and Tyndale in Brackets

1611 AV1611	Geneva	Tyndale	DR
"1 **And he showed me a pure river of water of life, clear as crystal, proceeding out of the throne of God, and of the Lamb.**	"And he showed me a pure river of water of life, clear as crystal, proceeding out of the throne of God, and of the Lamb. 0	"And he showed me a pure river of water of life, pure as crystal, proceeding out of the seat of God and of the Lamb. 2, (2)	"And he showed me a river of water of life, clear as crystal, proceeding from the throne of God and of the Lamb. 3
2 **In the midst of the street of it, and of either side of the river, was there the tree of life, which bare twelve manner of fruits, and yielded her fruit every month: and the leaves of the tree were for the healing of the nations.**	In the midst of the street of it, and of either side of the river was the tree of life, which bare twelve manner of fruits, and gave fruit every month: and the leaves of the tree served to heal the nations with. 9 (4)	In the midst of the street of it, and of either side of the river was there wood (tree) of life: which bare twelve manner of fruits: and gave fruit every month: and the leaves of the wood served to heal the people withal. 12 (6)	In the midst of the street thereof, and on both sides of the river, was the tree of life, bearing twelve fruits, yielding its fruits every month and the leaves of the tree were for the healing of the nations. 7
3 **And there shall be no more curse, but the throne of God, and of the Lamb shall be in it, and his servants shall serve him.**	And there shall be no more curse, but the throne of God and of the Lamb shall be in it, and his servants shall serve him. 0	And there shall be no more curse, but the seat of God and the Lamb shall be in it; and his servants shall serve him: 1 (1)	And there shall be no curse any more; but the throne of God and of the Lamb shall be in it, and his servants shall serve him. 2

1611 AV1611	Geneva	Tyndale	DR
4 And they shall see his face, and his name shall be in their foreheads.	And they shall see his face, and his Name shall be in their foreheads. 0	and shall see his face, and his name shall be in their foreheads. 1	And they shall see his face: and his name shall be on their foreheads. 1
5 And there shall be no night there, and they need no candle, neither light of the sun, for the Lord God giveth them light, and they shall reign for ever and ever.	And there shall be no night there, and they need no candle, neither light of the Sun: for the Lord God giveth them light, and they shall reign for evermore. 3 (1)	And there shall be no more night there and they need no candle, neither light of the sun; for the Lord God giveth them light, and they shall reign forevermore. 5 (1)	And night shall be no more: and they shall not need the light of the lamp, nor the light of the sun, because the Lord God shall enlighten them, and they shall reign for ever and ever. 14
6 And he said unto me, These sayings are faithful and true. And the Lord God of the holy Prophets sent his Angel to show unto his servants the things which must shortly be done.	And he said unto me, These words are faithful and true: and the Lord God of the holy Prophets sent his Angel to show unto his servants the things which must shortly be fulfilled. 2 (2)	And he said unto me, These sayings are faithful, and true. And the Lord God of saints and prophets sent his angel to show unto his servants, the things which must shortly be fulfilled. 4 (2)	And he said to me: These words are most faithful and true. And the Lord God of the spirits of the prophets sent his angel to show his servants the things which must be done shortly. 8
7 Behold, I come quickly: Blessed is he that keepeth the sayings of the prophecy of this book.	Behold, I come shortly. Blessed is he that keepeth the words of the prophecy of this book. 2 (2)	Behold, I come shortly. Happy is he that keepeth the sayings of the prophecy of this book. 2 (2)	And, Behold I come quickly. Blessed is he that keepeth the words of the prophecy of this book. 2

1611 AV1611	Geneva	Tyndale	DR
8. **And I John saw these things, and heard them. And when I had heard and seen, I fell down to worship before the feet of the Angel, which showed me these things.**	And I am John, which saw and heard these things: and when I had heard and seen, I fell down to worship before the feet of the Angel which showed me these things. 4	I am John, which saw these things and heard them. And when I had heard and seen, I fell down to worship before the feet of the angel which showed me these things. 3	And I, John, who have heard and seen these things. And after I had heard and seen, I fell down to adore before the feet of the angel, who showed me these things. 8
9. **Then saith he unto me, See thou do it not: for I am thy fellow servant, and of thy brethren the Prophets, and of them which keep the sayings of this book: worship God.**	But he said unto me, See thou do it not: for I am thy fellow servant, and of thy brethren the Prophets, and of them which keep the words of this book: worship God. 4 (2)	And he said unto me, See thou do it not, for I am thy fellow-servant and the fellow-servant of thy brethren the prophets, and of them which keep the saying of this book: but worship God. 8 (1)	And he said to me: See thou do it not: for I am thy fellow servant, and of thy brethren the prophets, and of them that keep the words of the prophecy of this book. Adore God. 10
10. **And he saith unto me, Seal not the sayings of the prophecy of this book: for the time is at hand.**	And he said unto me, Seal not the words of the prophecy of this book: for the time is at hand. 2 (1)	And he said unto me, Seal not the sayings of prophecy of this book, for the time is at hand. 2	And he saith to me: Seal not the words of the prophecy of this book: for the time is at hand. 2

1611 AV1611	Geneva	Tyndale	DR
11. **He that is unjust, let him be unjust still: and he which is filthy, let him be filthy still: and he that is righteous, let him be righteous still: and he that is holy, let him be holy still.**	He that is unjust, let him be unjust still: And he which is filthy, let him be filthy still: and he that is righteous, let him be righteous still: and he that is holy, let him be holy still. 0	He that doeth evil, let him do evil still: and he which is filthy, let him be filthy still: and he that is righteous, let him be more righteous: and he that is holy, let him be more holy. 8 (6)	He that hurteth, let him hurt still: and he that is filthy, let him be filthy still: and he that is just, let him be justified still: and he that is holy, let him be sanctified still. 8
12. **And behold I come quickly, and my reward is with me, to give every man according as his work shall be.**	And behold, I come shortly, and my reward is with me, to give to every man according as his work shall be. 1 (1)	And behold, I come shortly, and my reward is with me, to give every man according as his deeds shall be. 2 (2)	Behold, I come quickly; and my reward is with me, to render to every man according to his works. 6
13. **I am Alpha and Omega, the beginning and the end, the first and the last.**	I am Alpha and Omega, the beginning and the end, the first and the last. 0	I am Alpha and Omega, the beginning and the end, the first and the last. 0	I am Alpha and Omega, the first and the last, the beginning and the end. 0
14. **Blessed are they that do his commandments, that they may have right to the tree of life, and may enter in through the gates into the city.**	Blessed are they, that do his Commandments, that their right may be in the tree of Life, and may enter in through the gates into the City. 4 (2)	Blessed are they that do his commandments, that their power may be in the tree of life, and may enter in through the gates into the city. 5 (3)	Blessed are they that wash their robes in the blood of the Lamb: that they may have a right to the tree of life, and may enter in by the gates into the city. 10

1611 AV1611	Geneva	Tyndale	DR
15. **For without are dogs, and sorcerers, and whoremongers, and murderers, and idolaters, and whosoever loveth and maketh a lie.**	For without shall be dogs and enchanters, and whoremongers, and murderers, and idolaters, and whosoever loveth or maketh lies. 6 (2)	For without shall be dogs and enchanters, and whoremongers, and murderers, and idolaters, and whosoever loveth or maketh leasings (a lie). 5 (3)	Without are dogs, and sorcerers, and unchaste, and murderers, and servers of idols, and everyone that loveth and maketh a lie. 6
16. **I Jesus have sent mine Angel, to testify unto you these things in the Churches. I am the root and the offspring of David, and the bright and morning star.**	I Jesus have sent mine Angel, to testify unto you these things in the Churches: I am the root and the generation of David, and the bright morning star. 2 (1)	I Jesus sent mine angel to testify unto you these things in the congregations. I am the root and the generation of David, and the bright morning star. 4 (2)	I Jesus have sent my angel, to testify to you these things in the churches. I am the root and stock of David, the bright and morning star. 5
17. **And the Spirit and the Bride say, Come. And let him that heareth, say, Come. And let him that is athirst, come. And whosoever will, let him take the water of life freely.**	And the Spirit and the bride say, Come. And let him that heareth say, Come: and let him that is athirst, come: and let whosoever will, take of the water of life freely. 2 (1)	And the Spirit and the bride said, Come. And let him that heareth, say also Come. And let him that is athirst come. And let whosoever will, take of the water of life free. 5 (2)	And the spirit and the bride: Come. And he that heareth, let him say: Come. And he that thirsteth, let him: come. and he that will, let him take the water of life, freely 7

1611 AV1611	Geneva	Tyndale	DR
18. **For I testify unto every man that heareth the words of the prophecy of this book, If any man shall add unto these things, God shall add unto him the plagues, that are written in this book.**	For I protest unto every man that heareth the words of the prophecy of this book, If any man shall add unto these things, God shall add unto him the plagues that are written in this book.	I testify unto every man that heareth the words of prophecy of this book If any man shall add unto these things, God shall add unto him the plagues that are written in this book.	For I testify to every one that heareth the words of the prophecy of this book: If any man shall add to these things. God shall add unto him the plagues written in this book.
	1 (1)	2	4
19. **And if any man shall take away from the words of the book of this prophecy, God shall take away his part out of the book of life, and out of the holy city, and from the things which are written in this book.**	And if any man shall diminish of the words of the book of this prophecy, God shall take away his part out of the book of life, and out of the holy City, and from those things which are written in this book.	And if any man shall minish (take away) of the words of the book of this prophecy, God shall take away his part out of the book of life, and out of the holy city, and from those things which are written in this book.	And if any man shall take away from the words of the book of this prophecy, God shall take away his part out of the book of life, and out of the holy city, and from these things that are written in this book.
	4 (2)	4 (2)	1
20. **He which testifieth these things, saith, Surely, I come quickly. Amen. Even so, Come, Lord Jesus.**	He which testifieth these things, saith, Surely I come quickly, Amen. Even so, come Lord Jesus.	He which testifieth these things saith, Be it, I come quickly. Amen. Even so, come, Lord Jesus.	He that giveth testimony of these things, saith, Surely I come quickly: Amen. Come, Lord Jesus.
	0	2 (2)	6

1611 AV1611	Geneva	Tyndale	DR
21. **The grace of our Lord Jesus Christ be with you all. Amen.**'	The grace of our Lord Jesus Christ be with you all, Amen."	The grace of our Lord Jesus Christ be with you all. Amen."	The grace of our Lord Jesus Christ be with you all. Amen."
	0	0	0

Further to Paine's comments above,Dr. Ruckman (4) p 160ff and J.J. Ray (7) p 33ff have listed many important AV1611 readings omitted or altered by the Douay Rheims, showing that it is actually much closer to the modern versions than it is to the AV1611. Some of these readings are as follows:

Verse	Omission or Alteration	Against the AV1611
Matthew 5:22	"without a cause"	DR, RV, NIV, JB, NWT, Ne, L, T, (Tr, A)
Matthew 6:13	"For thine is the kingdom, the power and the glory, forever"	DR, RV, NIV, JB, NWT, G, L, T, Tr, A, W
Matthew 9:13	"to repentance"	DR, RV, NIV, JB, NWT, Ne, G, L, T, Tr, A, W
Matthew 16:3	"O ye hypocrites"	DR, RV, NIV, JB, NWT, Ne, L, T, Tr, A
Matthew 20:22	"and to be baptized with the baptism that I am baptized with"	DR, RV, NIV, JB, NWT, Ne, G, L, T, Tr, A
Matthew 25:13	"wherein the Son of man cometh"	DR, RV, NIV, JB, NWT, Ne, G, L, T, Tr, A
Matthew 26:60	"yet found they none"	DR, RV, NIV, JB, NWT, Ne, G, (L), T, Tr, A
Mark 1:2	"the prophets" changed to "Isaiah the prophet"	DR, RV, NIV, JB, NWT, Ne, G, L, T, Tr, A, W
Mark 2:17	"to repentance"	DR, RV, NIV, JB, NWT, Ne, G, L, T, Tr, A, W
Mark 6:11	"Verily I say unto you, It shall be more tolerable for Sodom and Gomorrha in the day of judgment, than for that city"	DR, RV, NIV, JB, NWT, Ne, G,(L),T, Tr, A

Verse	Omission or Alteration	Against the AV1611
Mark 10:21	"take up the cross"	DR, RV, NIV, JB, NWT, Ne, (L), T, Tr
Mark 11:10	"that cometh in the name of the Lord"	DR, RV, NIV, NWT, Ne, G, L, T, Tr, A, W
Mark 13:14	'spoken of by Daniel the prophet"	DR, RV, NIV, JB, NWT, Ne, G, (L), T, Tr, A
Luke 2:33	"Joseph" changed to "his father"	DR, RV, NIV, JB, NWT, Ne, G, T, Tr, A
Luke 2:43	"Joseph" changed to "his parents"	DR, RV, NIV, JB, NWT, Ne, L, T, Tr, A
Luke 4:8	"Get thee behind me, Satan"	DR, RV, NIV, JB, NWT, Ne, G, (L), T, Tr, A
Luke 10:21	"Holy" added	DR, RV, NIV, JB, NWT, Ne, L, T, Tr, A. See Section 10.3.
Luke 11:2, 4	"Our", "which art in heaven", "as in heaven so in earth", "but deliver us from evil"	DR, RV, NIV, JB, NWT, Ne, G, T, Tr, A. L regards the third phrase as "doubtful."
John 7:39	"Holy"	DR, RV, NIV, JB, NWT, Ne, L, T, (Tr, A).
John 17:12	"in the world"	DR, RV, NIV, JB, NWT, Ne, L, T, Tr, A
Acts 2:30	"according to the flesh, he would raise up Christ"	DR, RV, NIV, JB, NWT, Ne, G, L, T, Tr, A
Acts 4:25	"by the Holy Spirit" and "our father" or similar added	DR, RV, NIV, JB, NWT, Ne, L, T, Tr, A. See Section 10.3
Acts 7:30	"of the Lord"	DR, RV, NIV, JB, NWT, Ne, L, T, Tr, A
Acts 15:24	'saying, Ye must be circumcised and keep the Law"	DR, RV, NIV, JB, NWT, Ne, L, T, Tr, A
Acts 16:7	"of Jesus" added	DR, RV, NIV, JB, NWT, Ne, G, L, T, Tr, A. See Section 10.3.
Acts 16:31	"Christ"	DR, RV, NIV, JB, NWT, Ne, L, T, Tr, A
Acts 17:26	"blood"	DR, RV, NIV, JB, NWT, Ne, L, T, Tr, (A).

Verse	Omission or Alteration	Against the AV1611
Acts 23:9	"Let us not fight against God"	DR, RV, NIV, JB, NWT, Ne, G, L, T, Tr, A,
Romans 1:16	"of Christ"	DR, RV, NIV, JB, NWT, Ne, G, L, T, Tr, A, W
Romans 8:1	"but after the spirit"	DR, RV, NIV, JB, NWT, Ne, G, L, T, Tr, A, W
Romans 11:6	"But if it be of works, then is it no longer grace: otherwise work is no more work"	DR, RV, NIV, JB, NWT, Ne, G, L, T, Tr, (A).
Romans 14:6	"and he that regardeth not the day, to the Lord he doth not regard it"	DR, RV, NIV, JB, NWT, Ne, L, T, Tr, (A).
1 Corinthians 2:13	"Holy"	Dr, RV, NIV, JB, NWT, Ne, G, L, T, Tr, A, W
1 Corinthians 6:20	"and in your spirit, which are God's"	DR, RV, NIV, JB, NWT, Ne, G, L, T, Tr, A, W
1 Corinthians 10:28	"for the earth is the Lord's and the fulness thereof"	DR, RV, NIV, JB, NWT, Ne, G, L, T, Tr, A, W
1 Corinthians 15:47	"the Lord"	DR, RV, NIV, JB, NWT, Ne, L, T, Tr, A
2 Corinthians 4:10	"the Lord"	DR, RV, NIV, JB, NWT, Ne, G, L, T, Tr, A, W
Galatians 3:17	"in Christ"	DR, RV, NIV, JB, NWT, Ne, L, T, Tr, A
Ephesians 3:9	"by Jesus Christ"	DR, RV, NIV, JB, NWT, Ne, G, L, T, Tr, A, W
1 Thessalonians 1:1	"from God our Father, and the Lord Jesus Christ"	DR, RV, NIV, JB, NWT, Ne, (L), T, Tr, A
1 Timothy 3:16	"God" altered to "which" or "who" or "He" or "He who"	DR, RV, NIV, JB, NWT, Ne, G, L, T, Tr, A, W
1 Timothy 6:5	"from such withdraw thyself"	DR, RV, NIV, JB, NWT, Ne, L, T, Tr, A, W
Hebrews 1:3	"by himself"	DR, RV, NIV, JB, NWT, Ne, L, T, Tr, A
Hebrews 7:21	"after the order of Melchisedec"	DR, RV, NIV, JB, NWT, Ne, T, Tr, A

Verse	Omission or Alteration	Against the AV1611
Hebrews 10:30	'saith the Lord"	DR, RV, NIV, JB, NWT, Ne, T, Tr
Hebrews 10:34	"in heaven"	DR, RV, NIV, JB, NWT, Ne, L, T, Tr, A, W
Hebrews 11:11	"was delivered of a child"	DR, RV, NIV, JB, NWT, Ne, G, L, T, Tr, A
James 5:16	"faults" changed to "sins"	DR, RV, NIV, JB, NWT, Ne, L, T, Tr
1 Peter 1:22	"through the Spirit"	DR, RV, NIV, JB, NWT, Ne, L, T, Tr, A, W
1 Peter 3:15	"the Lord God" is altered to "Christ as Lord" or "the Lord Christ"	DR, RV, NIV, JB, NWT, Ne, L, T, Tr, A, W
1 Peter 4:14	"on their part he is evil spoken of, but on your part he is glorified"	DR, RV, NIV, JB, NWT, Ne, L, T, Tr, A
1 John 3:1	"and we are" or similar added	DR (has "and should be"), RV, NIV, JB, NWT, Ne, L, T, Tr, A
1 John 4:3	"Christ is come in the flesh"	DR, RV, NIV, JB, NWT, Ne, L, T, Tr, A
Revelation 1:11	"I am Alpha and Omega, the first and the last"	DR, RV, NIV, JB, NWT, Ne, G, L, T, Tr, A, W
Revelation 12:12	"the inhabiters of"	DR, RV, NIV, JB, NWT, Ne, G, L, T, Tr, A, W
Revelation 16:17	"of heaven"	DR, RV, NIV, JB, NWT, Ne, L, T, Tr, A, W
Revelation 20:12	"God" is changed to "the throne" or "his throne"	DR, RV, NIV, JB, NWT, Ne, G, L, T, Tr, A, W
Revelation 21:24	"of them which are saved"	DR, RV, NIV, JB, NWT, Ne, G, L, T, Tr, A, W
Revelation 22:14	"do his commandments" has been changed to "wash their robes"	DR, RV, NIV, JB, NWT, Ne, L, T, Tr, A

This list totals 60 verses, three times the number cited by our critic as 'evidence' of "*the considerable influence*" of the Douay Rheims bible on the AV1611.

None of the verses listed by our critic were proved by him to have introduced error into the AV1611 from the DR. Neither did he prove that the readings in the DR could not have been influenced by the Geneva Bible. When the list of comparisons between the AV1611, Tyndale and the DR was extended to include Revelation 22, it was found that the differences between the AV1611 and the DR were approximately the same as the differences between the AV1611 and the 1526 Edition of Tyndale.

I believe that it is easy to see WHICH versions reflect "*the considerable influence*" of the Douay-Rheims. They do NOT include ANY Edition of the AV1611.

12

"Some Biographical Notes on Men Connected With the KJV"

12.1 DESIDERIUS ERASMUS

Our critic continues his attack on the Holy Bible by inveighing against some of the principal men associated with its publication. He has refuted none of the information on Erasmus, Section 2.1 and indeed has hardly addressed them. Instead, he reiterates his disdain for the sources used by Erasmus for his Greek New Testament, in particular those for Revelation and Acts 9:6. See Section 9.6.

He then states "*1 John 5:7, 8 taken from the Vulgate was in Erasmus' 3rd edition owing to pressure from the church of Rome.*" See Chapter 14.

His invective against Erasmus continues: "*Erasmus never left the RC church yet in 1881 translators are accused of being "Romanists" because some of their readings are akin to the Vulgate.*"

The principle 1881 translators, Westcott and Hort, are accused of being "*Romanists*" because they WERE Romanists, even if clandestinely. Wilkinson (2) p 277ff describes their Mariolatry, anti-Protestantism, Ritualism and Papal Atonement Doctrine. See Section 6.2 and Ray (7) p 24ff.

As for their translation, Wilkinson states (2) p 293: "*(Their) radical Greek New Testament . . . in the main, follows the Vatican and Sinaiticus Manuscripts.*" Aleph (Sinaiticus) and B (Vaticanus) are the basis for Jerome's Vulgate, Section 10.1.

The definitive work on the Greek text used by Westcott and Hort, demonstrating beyond any shadow of doubt that it is the corrupt Alexandrian text of the Roman Catholic church, is of course that of

Burgon (13) *The Revision Revised*. Our critic refutes NONE of Burgon's evidence. He does not discuss it or even address it.

Section 7.3 gives many examples of the correspondence between the RV of 1881 and Aleph and B. They amount to considerably more than just "*some readings*". 60 examples may be found above, showing the repeated matching of the RV with the DR "*translated from the Latin Vulgate*" ACCORDING TO ITS PUBLISHERS.

Dr. Gipp (14) Chapter 8, not only verifies Wilkinson's statements but adds that Westcott and Hort believed in purgatory and Romish 'Baptismal Regeneration' and were strongly influenced by Cardinal Newman. Dr. Gipp reached these conclusions by a thorough study of the biographies and letters of these two translators.

William Grady (45) p 214 reached the same conclusion from a similar, exhaustive study. "*Having carefully read both the* Life and Letters of Brooke Foss Westcott *by his son Arthur Westcott (1903) and the* Life and Letters of Fenton John Anthony Hort *by his son Arthur Fenton Hort (1896), this author is firmly convinced . . . that Drs. Westcott and Hort were A PAIR OF UNSAVED LIBERALS WHOSE OPEN VATICAN SYMPATHIES CAST THEM AS THE CONSUMMATE JESUIT PLANTS!*"

Dr. Grady then substantiates his conclusion with the following 28 pages of his book.

Our critic gives NO evidence of having carried any study of Westcott and Hort ANYWHERE NEAR as exhaustive as those by Dr. Gipp and Dr. Grady.

He concludes his notes on Erasmus with the statement "***Erasmus might have protested about the abuses of the RC church but he still remained a member of that church. He had no understanding of salvation in the way that Luther did and firmly resisted the Gospel which Luther preached.***"

Nothing in our critic's closing remarks about Erasmus relates in any way to the GREEK TEXT which Erasmus produced. In this respect, Dr. Ruckman (1) p 162 states " "*The Index*" *is the Council of Trent's list of forbidden books; no translation from the Textus Receptus has ever gotten off the list. The Fourth Rule of the Index by this Council said that the Bible could only be read with the permission of a Catholic Bishop, and then only if it was a Bible put out by Catholic AUTHORS. When the RV came out – using the Catholic Greek text for the ASV, NIV, and NASV – it was immediately recommended by Roman Catholic officials. NO translation from Erasmus into any language was ever recommended by any Catholic official ONE time in 400 years (1530–1930).*"

There was no *"might have"* about Erasmus" protests against Rome. Dr. Gipp (9) p 149ff cites him as follows *"This monarchy of the Roman pontiff is the pest of Christendom."* Dr. Gipp adds *"He berated the papacy, the priesthood and the over indulgences of the monks . . . He was offered a bishopric in hopes that it would silence his criticism. He rejected the bribe flat."*

Concerning Luther and the Gospel of salvation by grace through faith, Dr. Gipp shows that our critic has totally misrepresented Erasmus. I quote from Dr. Gipp as follows:

"Of Luther he said, "I favor Luther as much as I can, even if my cause is everywhere linked with his." He wrote several letters on Luther's behalf, and wholeheartedly agreed with him that salvation was entirely by grace, not works . . . And what was "the gospel" to which Erasmus referred? We will let him speak for himself.

" "Our hope is in the mercy of God and the merits of Christ." Of Jesus Christ he stated, "He . . . nailed our sins to the cross, sealed our redemption with his blood." He boldly stated that no rites of the Church were necessary for an individual's salvation. "The way to enter Paradise," he said, "is the way of the penitent thief, say simply, Thy will be done. The world to me is crucified and I to the world."

As for Erasmus never having left the RC church, Dr. Hills (5) p 194–195 states: *"In 1535, he again returned to Basel and died there the following year in the midst of his Protestant friends, without relations of any sort, so far as known, with the Roman Catholic Church."*

Our critic continues with William Tyndale.

12.2 WILLIAM TYNDALE

He draws attention to Tyndale's use of words "congregation" and "love" instead of "**church**" and "**charity**" as in the AV1611. These terms, adds our critic, would have pleased *"the RC apologist Sir Thomas More."* Even if they had, they certainly gave no displeasure to Bunyan, Cromwell, Talmage, Sunday, Ruckman, Gipp, Donovan, Vance and Grady, none of whom could be described as *"RC apologists."* See Sections 10.4, 18.3.

The word "**congregation**" is used repeatedly in the Old Testament. Its sole use in the New Testament, Acts 13:43 is with respect to the assembly of a Jewish synagogue. The word "**church**", therefore, although used once with respect to Israel, Acts 7:38, has therefore both a New Testament emphasis and an emphasis on SAVED GENTILES.

Our critic then resorts to Tyndale's use of "flock" in **John 10:16**, together with Luther and Coverdale – he could have added Matthew's Bible of 1537 – to "*correct*" the AV1611's use of "**fold**". Apparently, the AV1611 was "*under the influence of the Vulgate*" in this place. (The DR reads "fold" in this place.)

He also states "***Bishop Westcott (no less!) in his commentary on John points out that the erroneous Vulgate rendering has "served in no small degree to confirm and extend the false claim of the Roman see.""***

Bishop Westcott's commentary on John will be discussed later. As for "*the false claim of the Roman see*" it nevertheless managed to stake a claim on Westcott. Dr. Gipp (14) p 133 states "*Dr. Westcott was also deeply devoted to John Newman, the Roman Catholic defector who took 150 Church of England clergymen with him when he made the change. Those of his disciples who did not make the physical change, made the spiritual change to Romanism, though many, like Westcott, never admitted it.*"

It would have compromised their ministry to do so. See Grady's conclusion above.

Our critic concludes his remarks on John 10:16 as follows "***Happily modern versions have gone back to Tyndale. Who is right – the Protestant Reformer Tyndale and modern versions or the KJV with its pro-Roman emphasis?***"

One of the "*modern versions*" which has "*gone back to Tyndale*" is the Jerusalem Bible, which reads "flock" in the second part of John 10:16. Would our critic regard THIS "bible" as being "*Pro-Roman?*"

Another modern version which has "*gone back to Tyndale*" is the New World Translation of the Jehovah's Witnesses, which also reads "flock" in this place.

So I could well ask, who is right, the AV1611, which has NEVER been removed from the Index of the Council of Trent, or the JB, which has NEVER been ON the Index and the NWT, which is from the same Augean stable as the JB – and for that matter, the NIV?

In John 10:16 the AV1611 (in 1611 AND 1998) reads "**And other sheep I have, which are not of this fold: them also I must bring, and they shall hear my voice; and there shall be one fold, and one shepherd.**"

The "s**hepherd**" had already identified Himself TWICE BEFORE in the chapter, in verses 11 and 14. He is not any POPE.

The "**fold**" had been identified in verse 1, as an enclosure with a door. The Lord, verse 7, identifies HIMSELF as "**the door**", so that He is both "the Shepherd of the sheep" and "the door of the sheep", the twin metaphors signifying both his care and protection for his followers.

Although there are two different Greek words for "**fold**" in verse 16, the latter rendered elsewhere as "**flock**", Matthew 26:31, Luke 2:8, 1 Corinthians 9:7, the Lord is clearly speaking of "**this fold**" on both occasions in the verse.

Therefore, use of the word "flock" in verse 16 obscures this sense because "flocks" plural are not mentioned anywhere in the preceding 15 verses of the chapter, not even in the NIV.

Of "**this fold**" the Lord says, verse 9, "**I am the door; by me if any man enter in, he shall be saved.**"

The Lord says, verse 16, that He has "**other sheep**", NOT "other FLOCKS." They are HIS sheep but they are STRAYS and He is going to seek them out and bring them to HIMSELF, ONE BY ONE IF NECESSARY.

WHY ELSE WOULD HE HAVE TOLD THE PARABLE OF THE LOST SHEEP IN LUKE 15:4–7?

Thus far I have been making spiritual application. Dr. Ruckman gives the doctrinal application in his taped study on John. Essentially it is as follows:

The Lord has "other sheep", which are already "**my flock**", Ezekiel 34:8 but they are SCATTERED, Ezekiel 34:5. He says "**I will seek out my sheep**", verse 12 "**and will bring them to their own land**" verse 13. THIS is the "**one fold**" of verse 16.

Either way, no sound commentator could infer support for "*the false claim of the Roman see*" from the AV1611 reading in John 10:16 by ANY stretch of the imagination.

Moreover, where the word "**flock**" is used metaphorically in the New Testament, Luke 12:32, Acts 20:28, 29, 1 Corinthians 9:7 (both literal and metaphorical), 1 Peter 5:2, 3 it always denotes a local congregation or assembly. In this respect therefore, the "**one fold**" would consist of MANY flocks. The AV translators used the word "**fold**" and thereby avoided the error of implying that there was only ONE flock – a reading which in itself actually SUPPORTS "*the false claim of the Roman see.*"

Other "*Pro-Roman*" readings in the NIV etc. are listed in Chapter 5, Section 5.7. They are Matthew 1:25, 23:14, Acts 8:37, Colossians 1:14, James 5:16, 2 Peter 1:20. Our critic discussed only ONE of them, Acts 8:37, in any detail and referred specifically to only one other, Colossians 1:14.

McClure (57) p71 states with respect to the supposedly "*Pro-Roman*" nature of the AV1611, *"The printing of the English Bible has proved to be by far the mightiest barrier ever reared to repel the advance of Popery, and to damage the resources of Popery."* On the rare occasions when Tyndale, Luther, Coverdale etc. depart from the AV1611, UNKNOWINGLY, unlike ALL modern critics of the AV1611, the AV1611 will always correct THEM.

Our critic continues *"Tyndale has, also like many modern versions, correctly,* "Only Son" *in John 3:16, 18."* He does not care to mention that, among the *"correct"* modern versions which have "only Son" in John 3:16, 18 is the Jerusalem bible of the Roman Catholic church, although the NWT correctly retains "only begotten." See Section 7.3.

He also neglects to mention that Tyndale retains "only begotten" in John 1:14, 18 and 1 John 4:9, where the same Greek word "monogenes" is used as in John 3:16, 18. **"Only begotten"** is yet another portion of the word of God which our critic wishes to alter. See Chapter 14.

His last comment on Tyndale is with respect to **Acts 7:45** and **Hebrews 4:8**. Tyndale here agrees with the NIV etc. in inserting "Joshua" instead of **"Jesus."** His explanation is as follows *"The reason why the KJV puts* "Jesus" *has nothing to do with your theological but highly implausible explanation. It lies simply in the rules drawn up by King James that there should be no attempt to maintain uniformity between the OT and the NT. Hence the OT gives the Hebrew form of the name and the NT gives the Greek form of the name."*

What our critic calls *"Your theological but highly implausible explanation"* is not mine but Dr. Ruckman's and was referenced as such, Section 5.7.

Further, the explanation was not *"theological"* but BIBLICAL. THREE passages of Scripture were cited, including one entire Chapter of the Book of Revelation, Chapter 18. (Another relevant passage would be **1 Kings 16:34**.) In his denunciation of what the Lord has graciously shown Dr. Ruckman, our critic discussed NONE of these references in relation to Acts 7:45 and Hebrews 4:8.

The rules were not drawn up by King James but *"Bishop Bancroft, with advice from others, had prepared or at least approved"* these rules (53) p 70.

Our critic ought at least to have quoted the rule to which he refers. It is Rule 2 and states:

"The names of the prophets and holy writers with the other names of the text to be retained as nigh as may be, according as they were vulgarly used." This rule obviously aims at authenticity with respect to common

contemporary usage of proper names, not deliberate non-uniformity between the Old Testament and New Testament.

It is also interesting that in Acts 7, the names of Abraham, Isaac, Jacob, Joseph, Moses, Aaron, David and Solomon appear exactly as they do in the Old Testament. Why not Joshua, if "Joshua" is the correct rendering? If "**Jesus**" is merely "Joshua", am I supposed to believe that not ONE of the other EIGHT names had a "*Greek form*", especially when Our critic is so quick to point out "**Esaias**", "**Jeremy**", "**Elias**" etc.?

Moreover, why is "**Saul**" referred to as such in verse 58, when he was also called "**Paul**", Acts 13:9? Doesn't "**Saul**" have a "*Greek form*"? It is, after all, a HEBREW name, 1 Samuel 9:2.

Elsewhere our critic criticises the AV1611 for "***Failure to render the same Hebrew and Greek word by the same English equivalent.***" See Section 10.8. This is very ironic.

After all, "Iesou" is "**Jesus**" everywhere else in the New Testament.

He provides NO statement from ANY of the AV1611 translators that they were applying their Rule 2 in using the name "**Jesus**" in Acts 7:45.

I continue with Dr. Ruckman's study of Acts 7:45 and Hebrews 4:8, from his Commentary on Acts, p 225. See also *Problem Texts* (17) p 337–338 and Section 5.7.

"*The Greek text (any Greek text anywhere) says* Iesou (*Greek for* '**Jesus**'), *and if your 'Bible' says* "Joshua", *you have an inferior translation produced by inconsistent critics who cared nothing about ANY Greek text in a showdown. God the Holy Spirit wrote* '**Jesus**' . . . *to remind you that when Jesus returns He enters the land of Canaan by the same route Joshua entered, attacking a cursed city (Revelation 17,18) after a seven year period (Joshua 6:15). His rule will be a military dictatorship (Psalm 110, Revelation 20), as Joshua's was, and the celestial phenomena of Joshua 10:12 will accompany His Advent (Matthew 24:29, Luke 21:25). Furthermore, the Jews will divide the land (Ezekiel 40–48) and repossess it at this time.*

"*Moral: where scholars find 'mistakes' in the King James Bible, the HOLY SPIRIT has often given an ADVANCED REVELATION expressly for the purpose of confounding the 'leading authorities who agree.'*"

Moreover, Joshua 5:13–15 and Exodus 23:21 reveal that "**the captain of the Lord's host**" is "**the captain of their salvation**" Hebrews 2:10, JESUS, to Whom Joshua was subordinate for the entire campaign, Joshua 4:14, 6:27, 7:6–13, 10:25, 42.

Our critic's next biographical note is with respect to King James 1.

12.3 KING JAMES 1

In Section 4.1 I cited Dr. Ruckman's evaluation of James 1 as *"The most hated character in English history for Greek and Hebrew scholars in the Protestant church, especially the modern fundamentalist branch."*

Our critic's note on James bears this out. His profound hatred for King James 1 is rivalled only by his evident hatred for the Holy Bible with which James' name is associated for all time.

He begins his denigration of James with the statement *"I am afraid your attempt to present James 1 in glowing colours hardly does justice to the facts of history. Actually he was a scoundrel. Serious historians speak of his "ingrained habit of intrigue" and point out that the immorality of his court was hardly more despicable than the imbecility of his government."*

He also refers to James' *"insufferable vanity"* and his *"malice and cruelty"* of which the Presbyterian ministers in Scotland evidently bore the brunt before James ascended the English throne.

No doubt this is more of the *"moderate language"* which our critic found so commendable with respect to the Holy Bible associated with James. See Section 11.3.

Hence our critic's diatribe prompts certain questions. For example:

Does he identify any of the *"serious historians"*, including one whom he describes as *"a great enthusiast for the KJV"*? No.

Despite specific charges which he later brings against James, does he supply proof of an *"INGRAINED habit of intrigue"*? No.

Does he supply any proof of James" *"insufferable vanity"* and the *"immorality of his court"*, which accusation is no doubt intended to include James himself? No.

Does he supply any proof against James of *"the imbecility of his government"*? No.

Most of the material on James in Chapter 4 was stated specifically to consist of extracts from a Christian Newsletter, *Battle Cry* Sept./Oct. 1985. A copy of the item could have been forwarded to our critic upon request. Although the author, Baptist Pastor David Ralston, does not explicitly reference every quotation about James which he uses in his article, he does list his sources. They include the well-known works by Caroline Bingham, William McElwee and Lady Antonia Fraser.

Any objective examination of these extracts would reveal that their main purpose was not to present James himself in any hue whatsoever. The purpose was to highlight the outstanding achievements of James' reign, culminating in the publication of the Authorised Version. Whatever his shortcomings, James was a saved man whom God had endowed with great wisdom, great courage and Royal authority, essential qualifications for being "*the principal Mover and Author of the work*" of making "*God's holy Truth to be yet more and more known unto the people.*"

The extracts given in Chapter 4 were obviously meant to illustrate this. God's work through James was described with respect to the study which I cited by Dr. Ruckman on Ecclesiastes 8:4, Acts 1:8 and Romans 13:1–4, more scriptures which our critic did not see fit to discuss.

It is instructive that he cannot actually refute any of James' achievements, in spite of his calumny against James himself. He even grudgingly concedes that James founded the Province of Ulster, although he disparages this achievement with the statement "*I do not think any altruistic motives should be ascribed to his settlement of Ulster nor is there much evidence that its later evangelical character was particularly indebted to James.*"

One may take comfort that whatever happens to be the truth of James' motives about Ulster, it does not depend on what our critic thinks or doesn't think. I did not ascribe ANY motive to James' settlement of Ulster in Chapter 4. I simply listed it as one of his achievements, which God has honoured. It is misleading for our critic to imply otherwise.

As for "*its later evangelical character*", there is probably NO evidence to attribute it directly to James. By the time Ulster had sufficiently divested itself of political and religious turmoil in order to assume this "*character*", James was DEAD.

However, our critic overlooks the fact that Ulster Protestantism IS indebted to THE BOOK which is associated with James. Among the strongest evangelical Protestants in Ulster today are the Free Presbyterians, whose outstanding leader is Dr. Ian Paisley. Both he and the pastors associated with him, including the Rev. Ivan Foster of Kilskeery Free Presbyterian Church, are firm in their adherence to the Authorised Version. The Lord has sustained them and vindicated their stand for His Book for over two decades "**in troublous times**" and continues to do so. See reference in Volume 1 to Dr. Paisley's web page.

Our critic also attacks James" motives for encouraging the work on the AV1611. He states "*One historian who was a great enthusiast for the KJV conceded that the real reason for his patronage of the KJV was not any great love for the Word of God but the king's shrewdness in seeing that a new translation would add to the glory of his reign and enhance his fancied reputation as a theologian . . . (the KJV was) the only glorious thing connected with his shifty and unworthy rule and his ambiguous career. He was thoroughly despicable and in no way entitled to his name bound up all through the ages with an enterprise so holy."*

Here is some more "*moderate language,*" I suppose. As for the above verdict, it would appear that "**the God of heaven**" who "**removeth kings, and setteth up kings**", Daniel 2:19–21, thought differently – much to the chagrin of "s*erious historians."*

Our critic's condemnation of James' motives reflects a certain inconsistency with respect to his introductory letter in which he takes me to task for "***repeatedly attributing the lowest possible motives to textual critics and translators . . . (which) is hardly likely to lead to a fair and balanced approach.***"

It would seem, however, that "***attributing the lowest possible motives***" to "*the principal Mover and Author*", in human terms, of the AV1611 and to ANY of his other achievements, DOES "*lead to a fair and balanced approach."*

Double standard. 'Heads I win, tails you lose.'

Ralston makes it clear that much of the criticism of James stems from two main sources. One was "*M. Fontenay, an agent for Mary Stuart who plotted for James' throne" and who "fostered much of the slanderous assault against the king."* The other was Anthony Weldon, "*who successfully blackened King James through the pen portrait he first published in 1650 . . . Antonia Fraser writes, "In fairness to James, (Weldon) should never be quoted without the important rider that he had been excluded from Court circles and had in consequence, a pathological hatred of the Stuarts. Weldon has had his revenge for the slight injuries done to him."* "

Our critic draws attention to James' provocative statement about the Geneva Bible, Section 11.3, "***as the worst of all versions – when actually it was a very good version.***"

McClure (57) p 67, states "*The new version (AV1611) agreed much more with the Geneva than any other; though the huffing king, at Hampton Court Conference, reproached it as "the worst of all.""*. See Section 11.4. McClure was clearly no admirer of James. However, if his assessments of the Geneva Bible and the AV1611 are taken together with our critic's, a curious result emerges.

A Bible which is closer to the AV1611 "*than any other*" (McClure) is "***a very good version***" (our critic). The Texts of the Geneva and the AV1611 may agree to within 5% in the New Testament. Yet according to our critic, the AV1611 is at best "***a manifestly fallible translation***" with "*incorrect renderings of the Hebrew and Greek*" *which are* "*INNUMERABLE*" (my emphasis). Indeed, according to our critic and "*the strongest Protestants*", who prefer to remain anonymous, the AV1611 is actually an "*intolerable deceit*" and a "*vile imposture.*"

It seems strange that the differences between the AV1611 and the Geneva are such that they give rise to such a glaring overall discrepancy. I am surprised that our critic did not list some examples.

Note that the correspondence between Biblical Texts being discussed here is with respect to their actual wording, Section 11.4, not variant readings, Section 9.2.

Paine, however, gives the context of James' remark and shows how it led to the publication of the AV1611, which supplanted all other Bibles "*on the basis of its own merits and integrity,*" Section 11.3.

'**Surely the wrath of man shall praise thee**" Psalm 76:10.

Paine also indicates that James' objection to the Geneva Bible was not, in fact, aimed primarily at its TEXT. "*Some of the marginal notes in the Geneva version . . . disturbed him: they seemed to scoff at kings. If the Bible threatened him, it must be changed. Away with all marginal notes! And indeed . . . many (were) based on dogma now outworn. James may have had some right on his side; he was far from witless.*"

Our critic further denigrates James for his treatment of the Puritans, Presbyterians and other non-conformists.

"*Despite his presbyterian upbringing in Scotland he favoured the High Church in England . . . When Puritans asked for the removal of superstitious practices in the Church of England which offended their Protestant consciences his well known reply was that he would make them conform or "harry them out of the land." As a result many godly men suffered at his hands.*"

However, our critic refers to only one, Thomas Helwys, a Baptist.

"*When in 1612 one of the early Baptists Thomas Helwys, made a plea (as he faced persecution) for liberty of conscience for all, James promptly imprisoned him. He died in prison some time before 1616.*"

Paine (53) p 10, also gives the context of James' "*harrying*" *of the Puritans following their request for the removal of* "*superstitious practices.*" He states "*so clever was his handling of the meeting that, although he gave the Puritan pleaders no satisfaction and actually threatened to harry them out of the land, he appeared to some observers to lean towards them. Indeed, the dean of the chapel said that on that day the king played the Puritan.*"

Paine continues "*after all the talk ended, it seemed (the Puritans) had won nothing. Indeed there was only one gain: the new Bible.*"

Of that "*one gain*", Paine, p 11, has a much more generous assessment than our critic: "*Tyndale's prayer was now answered in full: James 1 had ordered what Tyndale died to do.*"

Grady (45) p 153, makes the following observation "*With the "attitude adjustment" of Henry VIII occurring in answer to the martyr's prayer, "Open the King's eyes," we stand in awe at God's moving of the apostrophe, three-quarters of a century later to, "Open the KINGS' eyes!"*"

Of James' attitude to the Puritans, Dr. Ruckman (16) p 412, states: "*James was supposed to have said that Presbyterianism "agreeth as well with monarchy as God and the Devil." Subjective bigots (ready to catch at any straw in the wind) would take such a statement to mean that James rejected the idea of a New Testament local church; however, the Presbyterianism James spoke of was the Reformed brand of Calvin's theocracy at Geneva: it was a MONARCHY within itself and just as deadly to a nation as the popacracy at Rome.*"

Of Thomas Helwys, Ralston states: "*The Puritans and Baptists, both sincere and holy people, resisted the attempt to be brought under the authority of the Bishop. The ageing James had given religious freedom but now, without his approval, the Puritans suffered persecution by the official church. In 1612, James imprisoned Thomas Helwys, a Baptist preacher. Helwys had preached that the King and the Church of England had no right to dictate religious beliefs for English subjects.*"

In no way does Ralston condone James' treatment of Helwys. However, his description of Helwys' preaching appears closer to the truth than our critic's evaluation of it as "***a plea for liberty of conscience for all.***"

William Estep, in *The Anabaptist Story* p 223–224 refers to Helwys' "*vigorous plea for complete religious liberty*" and cites some of its salient passages:

"*Heare, o king, and dispise not ye counsell of ye poore, and let their complaints come before thee. The king is a mortall man, and not God therefore hath no power over ye immortall soules of his subjects, to make lawes and ordinances for them, and to set spirituall Lords over them . . .*

"*That Christ alone is King of Israell, & sitts upon Davids Throne, & that the King ought to be a subject of his Kingdome.*"

Estep states that Helwys identified the Church of England with the second beast of Revelation 13. Given the 'ministry' of this second beast,

Revelation 13:13–15 and his ultimate end, Revelation 19:20, I cannot believe that Helwys' interpretation was correct. However, it no doubt antagonised the Anglican hierarchy and probably James himself, who was the official head of the Church of England. Moreover, the contents of Helwys' statement, quoted above, read more like a demand than a plea and Estep also describes it as an admonition, p 223.

Thomas Helwys was a brave and godly man who championed a cause with scriptural foundation. James' reaction to him was despotic. However, in the light of the above and of Solomon's warnings, "**The wrath of a king is as messengers of death: but a wise man will pacify it**" Proverbs 16:14 and "**Where the word of a king is, there is power: and who may say unto him, What doest thou?**" Ecclesiastes 8:4, brave, godly Thomas Helwys may have overreached himself.

Ralston is frank about James' failures in his later years but again, gives the context. James died in 1625, aged 66.

"Due to disease and stroke, he had gradually ceased to rule long before he had ceased to reign . . . James had developed symptoms of early senility and whose symptoms were growing worse. It may have been this undiagnosed disease which accounts for his peculiar and unorthodox behaviour in later years. Again, it could have been the results of a backslidden and carnal life of a Christian who lapsed into sin."

If, however, James is reckoned to be *"a scoundrel"* for his various misdemeanours, of which the imprisonment of Helwys is the ONLY one that our critic actually specifies, what should one make of John Calvin? John Calvin burnt Michael Servetus at the stake for disagreeing with him on a point of doctrine. Under Calvin's theocracy in Geneva, a child was whipped publicly for calling his mother a thief and *"a girl who struck her parents was beheaded to vindicate the dignity of the Fifth Commandment"* (16) p 366.

Yet John Calvin is almost universally admired by fundamentalists, including our critic.

I cannot help being drawn to Ralston's conclusion. *"Do the critics of the Holy Word of God believe they can discredit the preserved authoritative scriptures by destroying the reputation of the man who helped bring it to the people? I am of the conviction that this indeed is the real cause of the slander against James."*

Moreover, I cannot help wondering, especially in the light of our critic's invitation to teach me Greek, if Ralston has not highlighted the real reason for our critic's antagonism against James. *"King James was regarded by those of his own time as "The British Solomon." He wanted*

*the Holy Word of God to be in the hands of people, not chained to pulpits
or hoarded in the cellars to be read only by Greek scholars."*

Although "*King James was the first earthly monarch to encourage the
propagation of Bibles (whereas) not one Catholic ruler of Italy, Spain,
Germany, Austria, France or Poland ever encouraged anyone*" (1) p 164,
our critic implies that James had papist leanings.

He states "***Most interesting of all was James' attitude to the RC
Church. While he dealt with priests severely since they posed a political
threat to the country, he nevertheless said to the English Parliament*** "*I
acknowledge the RC Church to be our mother church although defiled
with some infirmities and corruptions.*"

Our critic then adds, as if I was supposed to be aghast at this horrific
disclosure, "***Can you imagine any of the Protestant Reformers talking
like that?***"

I don't have to imagine some of the inane comments made by "*strong*"
and mostly anonymous "*protestants*" about the BOOK which James
sanctioned, which has done more to damage the cause of popery than any
other, Section 12.2. Our critic has very helpfully supplied them, although
he does not mention their sources. Neither does he mention any EFFECT
that James' remark had on subsequent events. The remark may simply
have been provocative, like his criticism of the Geneva Bible.

I certainly don"t have to imagine the "*interesting*" attitude which the
RC church had towards JAMES. It tried to BLOW HIM OFF THE FACE
OF THE EARTH. I find Our critic's careful omission of this fact VERY
"*interesting*". See Section 11.1.

I also find it "*interesting*" that our critic neglects to mention that
"*James DID allow the Puritans to assemble and put out an anti-Catholic
Version of the Bible with a note in the Preface that the pope was the "MAN
OF SIN"*" (16) p 412–413. No note to that effect will be found in the
Preface of ANY modern version.

Dr. Ruckman (1) p 164–166 also states "*King James promoted the
word of God after seeing Roman Catholics brutally murdering people in
violent brawls while he was growing up, and he promoted the word of
God although he had been baptized as a Roman Catholic . . . Alongside
the translating committees of 1901 (ASV) and 1970 (NIV), he was a
Biblical genius; he approved of a text that CORRECTED more than 50
FALSE READINGS FOUND IN THEIR WORKS.*"

Is THIS the attitude of a "*pro-Roman*" ruler?

Moreover, our critic apparently fails to appreciate the fact that James'
remark was evidently made publicly, where it could obviously have been

seized upon by his enemies and used against him. It was hardly an auspicious start to a supposed Jesuit plot implicating James. What is even more "*interesting*" is the freedom which the Puritans enjoyed at Hampton Court in denouncing the Roman church to the king's face. Paine (53) p 4 states "*Rainolds won his laugh later when, in the argument against Romish customs, he said, "The Bishop of Rome hath no authority in this land."* "

As for James' actual remark itself, I am reminded of the exchange between an RC priest and John Wesley, described by Grady (45) p 191:

"*When a priest asked John Wesley where HIS religion was before the Reformation, the no-nonsense Methodist replied, "In the same place your face was before you washed it – BEHIND THE DIRT!"* " For a detailed study of the life of James 1, see *King James . . . Unjustly Accused?* by Stephen A. Coston, Sr., KönigsWort, 1996, available from the Bible Baptist Bookstore.

I conclude these comments on James 1 with another extract from Ralston's article:

"*In great melancholy by his wife's death, he wrote about his faith in the resurrection:*

"*She's changed, not dead, for sure no good prince dies, But as the sun sets, only for to rise.*"

Can our critic imagine a "*scoundrel*" talking like THAT?

12.4 LANCELOT ANDREWES

Our critic's next biographical note deals with Lancelot Andrewes, Dean of Westminster and chairman of the AV1611 translating committee. Paine (53) p 16, states that "*Andrewes was a man for all to like, and one whose fame has lasted. There are over a million words by and about him in print.*"

Our critic refers to "*the linguistic skills of Lancelot Andrewes*" but adds "*interestingly you do not say anything about his theology. "This is a relevant matter*" insists our critic, "*in view of your belief that the KJV was the Protestant Reformers' Bible.*"

Apart from Hugh Broughton, Section 11.3, our critic does not mention one prominent English reformer after 1611 who did not eventually give his allegiance to the AV1611 as the standard Bible.

There is nothing particularly interesting about my omission of Andrewes' theology in Section 4.2 because the translators did not use their theology to influence the TEXT of the AV1611. Our critic has failed to prove otherwise, with respect to ANY of the translators, including Lancelot Andrewes. See Sections 11.1, 11.3 and 12.1. Our critic continues:

"Andrewes . . . had a long way to go in really embracing Protestant doctrine. He practised sacramental confession, believed in prayers for the dead, orderly ceremonial with Lights, incense and "all the externals of historic Catholic usage." Significantly a Jesuit priest, William Weston, who met him decided "he was not altogether opposed to the Catholic faith.""

I find it very *"significant"* to compare our critic's statements in his introductory letter:

"It seems to me a most serious spiritual matter when a manifestly fallible translation (the AV1611) made by men who taken as a body were not wholly orthodox, is preferred to the God breathed originals" (which our critic does not have) and *"This version (the NIV) LIKE EVERY OTHER must be subject to the original languages which I constantly consult"* (my emphasis) with the following comments from Robert Militello, who was trained by Jesuits before he was led to Christ. Mr. Militello's testimony was published in the July/August 1986 issue of *The Churchman's Magazine*:

"Jesuits . . . promote the idea of looking to a man rather than to Scripture. They do this rather subtly by declaring that (no) Bible is inerrant, that only the original manuscripts were inspired, and that since they are lost, believers must look to teachers and scholars as the final authority."

What did our critic say? *"I would be very willing to help you in the study of Greek so that you could make a first hand judgment on these matters."* Mr. Militello continues:

"In the New Testament class we used the Douay Rheims version, although others were accepted. Only the Authorised King James was not to be used, for this was a product of the hated Reformation . . . Jesuits have dedicated their lives to undoing the Reformation and the Bible it produced for the English-speaking world – the Authorised Version. Christian colleges now teach that only the original manuscripts were inspired and that all Bibles have errors."

It would appear that where the TEXT OF THE HOLY BIBLE IS CONCERNED, our critic is himself *"not altogether opposed to the Catholic faith."*

Paine writes p 20 *"While Andrewes valued a high ritual, he never forced it on others. He had the highest scruples in giving preferments to the clergy, abhorred simony and strove always to find the fittest man for any place he had to fill."*

McClure (57) p 79–80, adds *"Henry, Earl of Huntingdon, took him into the North of England; where he was the means of converting many papists by his preaching and disputations . . . (King James) had published a "Defence of the Rights of Kings," in opposition to the arrogant claims of the Popes. He was answered most bitterly by the celebrated Cardinal Bellarmine. The King set Dr. Andrewes to refute the Cardinal; which he did in a learned and spirited quarto, highly commended by Casaubon (classical scholar, Professor at Geneva and Montpellier, sub-librarian to Henry IV in Paris). To that quarto, the Cardinal made no reply."*

Reviewing Andrewes' life and ministry, Dr. Gipp states (14) p 185 *"He was not a man of 'head knowledge' only. He was a man of great practical preaching ability and an ardent opponent of Rome."*

Despite his love of ritual, Andrewes could never have been part of a religious system whose titular head insisted *"It is necessary to salvation that every man should submit to the Pope." (Boniface VIII* Unum Sanctum, *1303.)*

I am surprised that our critic did not mention Andrewes' insistence that Bartholomew Legate be burned at the stake (53) p 142, in his efforts to denigrate this translator, Jeremiah 17:9. The Holy Bible's verdict on this undoubted blemish on Andrewes' testimony is given in Ecclesiastes 7:20.

"For there is not a just man upon earth, that doeth good, and sinneth not."

12.5 WESLEY AND SPURGEON

Our critic then turns his attention to Wesley and Spurgeon. He says *"You mention the names of several famous preachers who used the KJV."* See Chapter 1, Section 1.7 Our critic continues *"Living at the time when they did, can you tell me what alternative they had?"*

I am amazed at this question. In the previous two pages of his own document he mentions two complete English Bibles, apart from the Douay-Rheims, which were in existence before the birth of Bunyan, who was the earliest preacher which I listed. These were Coverdale's and the Geneva. I also mentioned Matthew's Bible of 1537 in Section 3.3. If these were superior to the AV1611, the Geneva being *"a very good version"* according to our critic, Section 12.3, why didn't Wesley and Spurgeon preach from them?

Moreover, our critic makes much of Wesley's *"careful and independent study of the Greek original"* by which he *"produced a revised edition of the KJV in 1755."* Wesley's revision went through five editions (22) p 39. Why didn't Spurgeon use it? It was certainly available to him. Dr. Vance (22) p 44–46, lists three complete English bible translations published before 1850, which was about when Spurgeon was converted. Dr. Vance also shows that numerous English translations of the New Testament were available to both Wesley and Spurgeon.

Our critic admonishes me for not mentioning *"that Wesley and Spurgeon did not have an uncritical attitude to the KJV."* Neither did I mention that Wesley thought that *"some scriptures seemed to teach that it was possible for a MAN to fall away from salvation"* (16) p 411. Neither did I mention that Spurgeon led less than a tenth of the number of souls to Christ that Charles Finney did, who was a contemporary of Spurgeon's. Dr. Ruckman estimates Finney's converts as 500,000 in *The History of the New Testament Church* Volume 2 p 67.

Dr. Ruckman explains in his taped study on 1 Thessalonians that *"Spurgeon was a Calvinist."* Although only a moderate Calvinist, Spurgeon's theology nevertheless stifled his ministry. Dr. Vance states in his exhaustive study *The Other Side of Calvinism* p 351: *"There is no question as to what a Calvinist believes: God plays both sides of a chess game, and the members of the human race are the pieces, some pawns, some kings, but all puppets to be arbitrarily moved to heaven or hell as God sees fit."* Dr. Vance p 352 cites Wesley's cry of alarm and indignation: *"But if this be so, then is all preaching vain."*

Dr. Ruckman gives the number of Spurgeon's converts as 12,000.

The reason that I mentioned Wesley and Spurgeon in relation to the AV1611 was that they were faithful to it for most of their ministries and God honoured their faithfulness.

Our critic states that Wesley's revision *"contained 12,000 alterations"* of which *"three quarters . . . were accepted by the revisers in the next century."* Ray (7) p 34ff lists 38 portions of Scripture omitted or altered by Wesley. Our critic further insists, without proof, that *"If Wesley had the knowledge we now have the text he would undoubtedly have suggested many more alterations than he did."*

On the contrary, if Wesley had *"had the knowledge we now have"*, especially that furnished by Burgon, Scrivener, Pickering, Colwell, Riplinger, Ruckman and others, I think it highly likely that he would have confessed his sin of altering God's words and made appropriate restitution.

It seems that either Wesley or one of his editors at least started to make amends. Our critic states that Wesley *"omitted* "**through his blood**" *in Cols. 1:14 . . . exactly the position of modern versions on this textual matter. Yet you use his name for supporting your position on the KJV."*

Our critic by-passed the information given in Chapter 7, Section 7.3, which showed that the modern versions omitting "**through his blood**" include the JB and NWT and that the AV1611 reading is found in citations from the 2nd century. See Section 10.3.

However, Ray (7) p 50, 69 shows that Wesley's New Testament did NOT omit "**through his blood**" in Colossians 1:14! It would appear then, that either Wesley or one of his editors eventually decided to leave *"the position of modern versions on this textual matter"* and return to my *"position on the KJV."*

Nevertheless, Wesley's translation, like all revisions of the AV1611, paled into insignificance less than 100 years after it was first published, the last edition appearing in 1839 (22) p 39. Likewise, the 1881 RV, whose translators made 36,000 changes to the scriptures, Section 6.1, has long since faded into obscurity. The NIV and all the others will doubtless follow suit.

Our critic states in the section of his document entitled *"The effect of modern versions"* *"There was certainly no diminution in the blessing of God on the ministries of Wesley and Spurgeon because they challenged the KJV at various points."*

In answer to this assertion, which is unaccompanied by ANY discussion of relevant facts, Dr. Ruckman concludes in *The History of the New Testament Church* Volume 2, p 26 that *"Wesley's life and preaching were ruled by one Book, even though he translated some on his own. That one Book was his final authority in all matters of faith, preaching, doctrine and practice."* I would add that Dr. Ruckman's conclusion is based upon his own research of the available historical material, which he references and which includes Wesley's own Journal.

Nowhere does our critic give any indication that Wesley actually replaced the AV1611 with his own New Testament to any appreciable extent during his ministry. If he did not do so then as long as Wesley was ruled by the BOOK, obviously God would continue to uphold his ministry.

Spurgeon's case is rather different.

Our critic states that Spurgeon recognised *"the superiority of (the RV's) underlying Greek text."* He also quotes Spurgeon as rejecting *"the latter part of Roms. 8:1 in the KJV as* "*a gloss inserted in later copies*

*by some penman who was wise enough in his own conceit to think he
could mend the Bible.*""

The "*superiority*" of the Alexandrian text which underlies the RV and
subsequent apostate corruptions including the NIV, has been discussed
in Chapter 9. References 1–7, 12, 13, 16, 45 in particular will greatly
amplify the discussion.

The second half of Romans 8:1 is yet another omission stemming from
G, L, T, Tr, A, W which occurs in the NIV, JB, NWT and partially in the
DR. See Sections 7.3, 11.4. Dr. Ruckman (35) states in his book *Satan's
Masterpiece, The New ASV* p 67–68. "*Romans 8:1 has lost half of its text,
although verse 13 in the context would tell any fool why it should have
remained in the scripture.*"

Neither Spurgeon nor Our critic apparently looked at the context.
Romans 8:13 says "**For if ye live after the flesh, ye shall die: but if ye
through the Spirit do mortify the deeds of the body, ye shall live.**"

Dr. Ruckman continues "*Naturally, the Holy Spirit has preserved the
"original Greek text" in all four families of manuscripts and the majority
of uncials and cursives in any century. You will find this reading preserved
in its infallible purity in the King James Version of 1611.*"

Our critic then commends Spurgeon for adding the words "And we
are" to 1 John 3:1, from the RV and "*the Vulgate and the Alexandrian
family of MSS.*" See Section 10.3. Spurgeon evidently believed that these
words "*are clearly the words of inspiration.*" "*This fragment*" said
Spurgeon "*has been dropped by our older translators and it is too
precious to be lost.*"

The Jesuits who translated the Douay Rheims thought so too. Their
version reads "that we should be called, and should be the sons of God."
See Section 11.4. Tyndale, whom they burnt at the stake, did NOT. His
New Testament reads as the AV1611 "that we should be called the sons
of God."

Spurgeon then evidently preached "*a marvellous sermon on the
assured position of the child of God from the Revised Version.*" Our
critic concludes this section with the statement "*In the light of these facts
I wonder why you used his name in your own support.*"

Any "*support*" accruing from Spurgeon's name was aimed at
vindicating the AV1611 as the pure word of God. It was not advanced for
my particular benefit.

The reason that I used Spurgeon's name in support of the AV1611 was
simply to show that God honours the ministry of a man who is faithful to
it, which Spurgeon was, for most of his ministry.

William Grady (45) p 235 describes God's blessing on Spurgeon's early ministry. *"After being saved for only two years, a seventeen-year-old Spurgeon was called to pastor the Waterbeach Church of London in 1852. Using a King James Bible, the teenage pastor converted nearly his entire community."* There follows a detailed description from Spurgeon's own autobiography.

However, Spurgeon, like any other Christian, had a carnal nature, which was manifest towards the end of his ministry. Dr. Ruckman states (48) p 28–29: *"God is no respector of persons. Whenever, and wherever, Spurgeon messed with that Book (the AV), God messed with his mind . . . Spurgeon began to correct the Protestant reformation text, in the universal language, with the DEAD language of the Alexandrian text (RV) used for the Jesuit Rheims Bible of 1582. God trapped him and stumbled him (Ezek. 14:1–6). God is no respector of persons.*

" "The first Sabbath after his return from the sunny South – February 8, 1891 – the pastor (Spurgeon) preached at the Tabernacle from Isaiah 62:6, 7, using both the Authorised and Revised Versions . . . He had been especially struck with the revisers rendering of the text." The Lord took Charles H. Spurgeon home the year after he preached that message (C.H. Spurgeon Autobiography, Vol. 2, Banner of Truth Trust, p. 497)."

Spurgeon was only 58 years old when he died. In spite of our critic's opinion, see above, the Lord had cut short the ministry of *"the Prince of preachers."* Dr. Ruckman concludes:

"Today, his "tabernacle" is a ghostly monument."

12.6 WESTCOTT, HORT AND BURGON

Our critic continues his biographical notes with Westcott, Hort and Burgon.

Although not in agreement with all of Westcott's writings, our critic insists that *"there is much of value in his works especially his commentaries."* He declares *"That on John is superb and in it his commitment to Christ's deity and the miraculous is unwavering."* According to him, Westcott *"also provides the classic five point proof for the apostolic authorship of the fourth Gospel which is still in use by conservative scholars."*

What about Bible believers? How many of THEM need Westcott's *"five point proof"*?

I have never thought that anyone who read the last six verses of John's Gospel would need ANY FURTHER PROOF for *"the apostolic*

authorship of the fourth Gospel *'* if he was prepared to believe the BOOK as it STOOD.

Of Westcott's *"**superb**"* commentary on John, Dr. Ruckman has some informative observations (44) p 44ff.

""God is spoken of as THE FATHER and as 'my Father.' Generally it may be said that the former title expresses the original relation of God to being and specially to HUMANITY . . ." (Westcott on John, *p. 79–80). Comment by Donald Waite of Dallas Theological Seminary, "This is HERESY of the first dimension"* (Heresies of Westcott and Hort, *Waite, p. 9).*

""The thought . . . is here traced back to its most absolute form as resting on the essential power of God in his relation of UNIVERSAL FATHERHOOD" (Westcott on John, *p. 159). This is Westcott's* Commentary on John *that Custer has been citing . . . How on earth did Custer miss these references unless he himself believes in the* "universal fatherhood of God"?"

""Viewed from another point of sight it is the revelation of the DIVINE IN MEN, realized in and through Christ" (Westcott on John, *p.246). That is* "brilliant scholarship" *is it? "But the last error (the priesthood of all believers, 1 Peter 2:9) can hardly be expelled until Protestants unlearn the crazy horror of THE PRIESTHOOD (of Rome)"* (Life and Letters of Hort, *Vol. 2, p. 50) . . . The Alexandrian Cult is a priesthood in itself claiming special knowledge and special privileges that no Christian* "layman" *has! After all, all we have is the HOLY BIBLE (AV1611), they have the* "plenary, infallible, verbally inspired original autographs"!

""From the very beginning we see A POWER in action hostile to God" (Westcott on John, *p. 106). Did you mean "DEVIL," doctor? Could it have been Satan? "But the visible supremacy of THE POWER of evil inspiring to evil" (Hort on* Revelation, *p. 27). The references are to SATAN. Hort and Westcott have reduced him to a "power." Typical modernistic doctrine of Liberals in the NCCC.*

""And by his Baptism Christ fulfilled for the humanity which He took to Himself though not for Himself, the CONDITION OF REGENERATION" (Westcott on water baptism using 1 John 5:6, Commentary on John, *p. 181).*

""The bosom of the Father (LIKE HEAVEN) is a STATE and NOT a PLACE" (Westcott on John, *p. 15). Then Christ was a liar (John 14:1–3). But in case He wasn't, what will happen to Westcott and Custer? Custer was citing the* Commentary on John *(Custer, p. 26,27) and couldn't find this remarkable heresy in the FIRST CHAPTER.*

" *"Eternal life is the never ending EFFORT after this knowledge of God"* (Westcott on **John**, *p. 196). What is Custer doing . . . writing two pages to justify a HERETIC who thinks that eternal life is by SELF-EFFORT?"*

Dr. Ruckman continues (44) p 46: *"In Westcott's* Commentary on John *there are eleven references to the Universal Fatherhood of God and the Universal Salvation of mankind as a mass (Commentary, pp. 20, 52, 219, 155, 4, 27, 43, 59, 70 and 140) . . . The reader can get Westcott's Commentary and CHECK the pages listed above."*

This is Westcott's "*superb*" Commentary, according to our critic.

He then refers to what I *"allege Westcott and Hort have said about various matters."* See Section 6.1.

I did not *"ALLEGE"* anything. Our critic is lying. I cited three sources for the statements of Westcott and Hort, Dr. Fuller (2) p 277–282, Dr. Gipp (14) p 116–118 and Gail Riplinger (12) p 400–435. The statements were referenced from the *Life and Letters* of both Westcott and Hort with volume and page numbers quoted. See also Section 12.1.

However, our critic tries to dismiss these statements of Westcott and Hort as "*old hat*" – which does NOT prove that they are untrue – and as "*quite irrelevant to the textual debate.*"

The statements show that Westcott and Hort were NOT Bible believers and that they were determined to rid the church of "*the vile Textus Receptus*" and replace it with the corrupt text of the ROMAN CATHOLIC CHURCH. They believed that they could approach the New Testament like any other "*ancient text*" and that it was filled with errors (14) p 112. Their obsession with spiritism shows that they were guided by DEMONS.

Dr. Gipp (14) p 167 concludes after his extensive study on the lives and letters of Westcott and Hort: *"It can be safely said that if Westcott and Hort were not two Jesuit priests acting on secret orders from the Vatican, that two Jesuit priests acting under such orders COULD NOT HAVE DONE A BETTER JOB OF OVERTHROWING THE AUTHORITY OF GOD's TRUE BIBLE AND ESTABLISHING THE PRO-ROMAN CATHOLIC TEXT OF ALEXANDRIA, EGYPT!"*

Gail Riplinger (12) p 429 states *"This 'new' (W-H) text had a sinister start. In 1851, THE YEAR Westcott, Hort and Lightfoot began the Ghostly Guild, they set in motion their notion of a 'New' Greek Text. Appendix A chronicles their 30 year involvement in secret esoteric activities WHILE they were creating this 'New' text. In the VERY letter in which Hort hatched the 'New' Ghostly Guild, he christened 'villainous' the Greek*

Text which had, at his admission, been "the Traditional Text of 1530 years standing.""

And this is *"quite IRRELEVANT to the textual debate"*??

Yet our critic insists *"Their (W-H) arguments have been tested and retested by a host of scholars from various viewpoints. As a result the value and significance of their work have been widely acknowledged."*

Westcott and Hort's *"arguments"* were tested exhaustively by Dean Burgon at the time these arguments were put forward. See *The Revision Revised* (13).

Burgon summarised his findings as follows p 397: *"My contention is, – NOT that the Theory of Drs. Westcott and Hort rests on an INSECURE foundation, but, that it rests on NO FOUNDATION AT ALL."*

Our critic supplies NO *"foundation"* WHATSOEVER for the theories of Westcott and Hort. The evidence overwhelmingly supports Burgon. See Chapter 9.

I listed several outstanding scholars in Section 9.2 whose research has vindicated Burgon, NOT Westcott and Hort. They include Hodges, Hoskier, Hills, Pickering and Wilkinson who all published work in this century. They are joined by Aland, Colwell and Klijn Sections 9.4, 9.5 who carried out a thorough investigation of Patristic quotations and the papyri. It is the papyri which our critic prizes so highly as *"much more and earlier evidence which was not available to Westcott and Burgon"*.

Yet the conclusions of the scholars who actually studied this evidence are that the papyri are POOR manuscripts but which nevertheless support the TR MORE than the Alexandrian text of Westcott and Hort. See Section 9.5.

Of *"the host of scholars"* who *"tested and retested"* the *"arguments"* of Westcott and Hort and *"widely acknowledged"* their *"value and significance"*, our critic mentions only one, Benjamin Warfield. He describes Warfield as *"a conservative of the conservatives who was one of the greatest defenders of Reformed orthodoxy in this Century."* Of the *"tests"* and *"retests"* which Warfield supposedly applied to Westcott and Hort's *"arguments"* our critic simply says that Burgon failed to convince him and that he wrote *"books on infallibility and inerrancy"* which *"are still in print and continue to be greatly valued by conservatives."*

Dr. Ruckman (4) p 211 mentions Warfield in a list of *"A-millenial baby-sprinklers."* Did Warfield include *"baby-sprinkling"* in his *"greatest defence"* of *"Reformed Orthodoxy"*? Was he right to do so, according to the SCRIPTURE?

Concerning Warfield's books on "*inerrancy and infallibility*", I am tempted to ask "*inerrancy and infallibility*" of WHAT? Was it 'the Bible"? If so, WHICH Bible? Our critic does not say.

Given that Warfield rejected Burgon's evidence, did he write anything that REFUTED Burgon's evidence? If so, what and why doesn't our critic say so?

The truth is that Burgon's work has NEVER been refuted, neither by Westcott, Hort, Ellicott, Bruce, Kenyon, Warfield, Machen, Robertson, Vine nor E.H. Palmer. See Grady (45) Glossary. Burgon's work has never even been addressed, let alone answered.

The situation up to 1990 has been summarised by Radmacher and Hodges in the Appendix to their book (23). "*Burgon's strictures on Westcott and Hort have never been responded to in any detailed and coherent way by any specialist in this field. The handbooks on textual criticism, from which seminary students study, tend to dismiss Burgon peremptorily.*"

Warfield's rejection of Burgon's evidence stemmed from his belief that Westcott and Hort theories were "*parts of God's singular care and providence in preserving His inspired Word pure*" (5) p 110. Dr. Hills continues:

"*Dr. Warfield's thinking was not entirely unified. Through his mind ran two separate trains of thought which not even he could join together. The one train of thought was dogmatic, going back to the Protestant Reformation. When following this train of thought Dr. Warfield regarded Christianity as true. The other train of thought was apologetic, going back to the rationalistic viewpoint of the 18th century. When following this train of thought Dr. Warfield regarded Christianity as merely probable. And this same divided outlook was shared by Dr. Warfield's colleagues at Princeton Seminary and by conservative theologians and scholars generally throughout the 19th and early 20th century. Even today this split-level thinking is still a factor to be reckoned with in conservative circles, although in far too many instances it has passed over into modernism.*

"*Dr. Warfield's treatment of the New Testament text illustrates this cleavage in his thinking. In the realm of dogmatics he agreed with the Westminster Confession that the New Testament text had been "kept pure in all ages" by God's "singular care and providence," but in the realm of New Testament textual criticism he agreed with Westcott and Hort in ignoring God's providence and even went so far as to assert that the same methods were to be applied to the text of the New Testament that would be applied to the text of a morning newspaper. It was to bridge the gap between his dogmatics and his New Testament textual criticism that he suggested that God had worked providentially through Tischendorf, Tregelles, and Westcott and Hort to preserve the New Testament text. But this suggestion leads to conclusions which are extremely bizarre and inconsistent. It would have us believe that during the manuscript period orthodox Christians corrupted the New Testament text, that the text used by the Protestant Reformers was the worst of all, and that the True Text was not restored until the 19th century, when Tregelles brought it forth out of the Pope's library, when Tischendorf rescued it from a waste basket on Mt. Sinai, and when Westcott and Hort were providentially guided to construct a theory of it which ignores God's special providence and treats the text of the New Testament like the text of any other ancient book. But if the True New Testament Text was lost for 1500 years, how can we be sure that it has ever been found again?"*

Our critic says of John Burgon that he *"was a strong controversialist"*, which has nothing to do with the EVIDENCE that Burgon advanced and which our critic does not even attempt to address.

Instead, he evades Burgon's evidence by chiding me with *"it is interesting to note that you do not mention that he (as a high churchman) argued his case on the grounds of "Catholic antiquity"." "This same argument,"* says our critic, *"has often been used to support infant baptism and the historic episcopate."*

I wonder if Warfield used it for that purpose, believing in infant baptism as he did.

Since our critic does not DEFINE Burgon's use of the term *"Catholic antiquity"*, I will do so from The Preface of *The Revision Revised* p xxvii.

"The method I persistently advocate in every case of a supposed doubtful Reading, (I say it for the last time, and request that I may be no more misrepresented,) is, that AN APPEAL SHALL BE UNRESERVEDLY MADE TO CATHOLIC ANTIQUITY; and THAT THE COMBINED VERDICT OF MANUSCRIPTS, VERSIONS, FATHERS, shall be regarded as decisive."

In other words, when Burgon used the term *"Catholic antiquity"*, he was referring to the *"combined verdict of Manuscripts, Versions, Fathers."* His use of the term had nothing to do with *"infant baptism and the historic episcopate."*

Our critic also overlooked the summary which I gave of Burgon's methods. See Section 6.3.

Even though Burgon championed the TR and the AV1611 by the above method, he was not, of course, infallible. See Section 9.6. Nevertheless, he was genuinely scientific, which is more than can be said of Westcott and Hort.

Our critic continues *"You do not seem to realise that in the last 100 years many important changes have taken place in the study of the NT text."* Apart from a rehash of his earlier remarks on *"eclecticism"*, Section 9.8, our critic does not seem to think that any of them are important enough to list, let alone discuss.

He then repeats the party line *"The result of further work on the text and of MSS discoveries since 1881 have generally vindicated Westcott, though some modifications to his position have taken place."*

"Further work" has done nothing of the kind. See Sections 9.4, 9.5, 9.8. Instead of being *"widely acknowledged"*, Westcott and Hort's theories have been *"widely abandoned"*.

Genuine Bible believers never took them seriously to start with. Nevertheless, our critic continues *"evidence for an earlier date for the Byzantine text has not been found, and its secondary character continues to be affirmed."*

This statement consists of two blatant lies in a row. See Chapter 9.

Yet he continues, still with the party line *"Contrary to what is still believed in the KJV-only lobby modern editions of the NT are not dominated by Vaticanus and Sinaiticus. Modern scholars show that they were overestimated by Westcott."*

"Modern scholars" have shown nothing of the kind. Burgon, Miller and Scrivener showed that BEFORE 1900. See Sections 1.6, 9.3, 9.5.

Section 9.2 discusses our critic's repeated assertion about *"modern editions . . . not dominated by Vaticanus and Sinaiticus"*, where the NIV notes were cited indicating that Aleph and B were *"the most reliable early manuscripts."* It was further discussed in Section 9.3, where the MAIN sources for modern New Testaments were LISTED. It was noted there that of this list *"B and Aleph . . . usually head it."*

Our critic did NOT list ANY sources for modern Greek New Testaments in this portion of his document, apart from Aleph and B!

The only other sources which our critic mentions anywhere in his document which have supposedly *"vindicated Westcott"* are the papyri. The discussions in Sections 9.2 and 9.5 show that the truth is the REVERSE of our critic's claims. See also Burgon's comments earlier about Westcott and Hort's *"foundation"*.

Concluding this section, he states *"No modern editor follows one Greek text type to the exclusion of all others"* and chides me again with the statement *"It is a pity that in condemning modern versions of the NT you have not troubled to find out about the work of modern textual critics and the principles on which they arrive at their conclusions.*"

Our critic does NOT state WHICH Greek texts modern editors use and in what proportions. Nor does he state WHY they choose those particular proportions except by means of the bald assertion earlier in his document that the Alexandrian text has "*better credentials*" simply because it is older. See Section 9.3.

Nor does he seem to appreciate that the AV1611 is from an "*eclectic*" text and that he is being rather inconsistent in criticising Erasmus for employing essentially the same principle of "*eclecticism*" which he endorses. See Section 9.8. (It is, of course, difficult to see how modern editors would use anything but texts which conflict with the TR, if, like our critic, they believed it to be "*demonstrably secondary*" and "*a late development*" characterised by "*harmonisation and conflation*" – in spite of all the evidence to the contrary. See Section 9.4.)

Moreover, our critic does NOT state WHO these "*modern textual critics*" are, nor does he include BIBLE BELIEF as a "*principle*" upon which "*they arrive at their conclusions.*"

This omission I find most significant, given the words of the Lord in Psalm 138:2:

"For thou hast magnified thy word above all thy name."

If the Lord's WORD is ABOVE the Name which is above EVERY NAME, Philippians 2:9–11, how can mere scholars exalt their "*scholarship*" above that WORD? See Section 10.15.

The MAIN principles of "*modern textual critics*" WERE, in fact, described in Chapter 6. The salient features of these "principles" were given as follows:

1. Rejection of the Received Text on the basis of the OPINIONS of "higher critics" Sections 6.1. See also Section 9.2.
2. A subjective exaltation of codices Aleph and B, on the basis of AGE alone, Sections 1.3, 6.2. See also Section 9.8.
3. An assumption of a "recension" of the Traditional Text at Antioch in the 4th century, Sections 6.2. See also Section 9.4.
4. A belief that the Text of the New Testament is to be approached like ANY OTHER ANCIENT TEXT, Section 6.2. See also Hills' comments on Warfield.

Brake's comments (18) p 209–210 on the "*Method of Textual Criticism*" are worth repeating:

"*The basic method of textual criticism for those who view the original text as lying under the old manuscripts (A, B, Aleph, C, D) is essentially subjective . . . (citing Hodges) this is a poor substitute for evidence, and the history of human thought proves it to be most uncertain. Today's consensus is too frequently tomorrow's curiosity."*

"But, in the final analysis, subjectivism is a retreat from the hard and demanding task of original thought and research. Conservatives who give way to eclecticism and subjectivism, instead of rising to the challenge of fresh, original work, deserve to be left behind by the moving stream of events."" For example, more detailed collation of the extant cursive mss. is needed. See J.A. Moorman's comments on the so called *"Majority text"* of the NKJV (41).

Gail Riplinger, (12) p 492–511 shows how editors of modern Greek texts and new versions appear to have little or no *"consistency"* in use of their sources. They will sometimes ignore the oldest source in order to select a reading from available Greek mss. which detracts from an important doctrinal reading as found in the AV1611. Compare 1 Corinthians 10:9 and 11:24. Theirs is essentially the position of J.J. Griesbach, 1745–1812, who stated that *"When there are many variant readings in one place, that reading which more than the others manifestly favours the dogmas of the orthodox is deservedly regarded with suspicion"*. See Hills (5) p 65 and Section 10.3. Some of Mrs. Riplinger's examples are as follows. P46 is one of the 2nd–3rd century papyri and predates Aleph and B by at least 100 years.

Verse Altered by the NIV	Manuscripts	Doctrine Affected
1 Corinthians 7:15	Ignores Aleph Follows P46, B, Majority	
1 Corinthians 10:9	Ignores P46 and Majority Follows Aleph and B	AV1611: **'Neither let us tempt Christ'** NIV: 'We should not test the Lord' The NIV reading denies the Deity of Christ by failing to identify Him as **'God'** who sent **fiery serpents'**, Numbers 21:6.
1 Corinthians 11:24	Ignores Majority Follows P46, Aleph, B	AV1611: **'this is my body which is broken for you'**

		NIV: "This is my body, which is for you". The NIV reading denies that Christ's body was "**broken**" or "**pierced**" on the cross, John 19:37.
1 Corinthians 13:3	Ignores P46, Aleph, B Follows Majority	
1 Corinthians 14:38	Ignores P46, B, Majority Follows Aleph	

The favoured manuscripts are diametrically opposite in 1 Corinthians 11:24 and 13:3. Mrs Riplinger states p 500, *"The "accepted principles of the science of textual criticism" used to justify this 'shell game' . . . are illustrations of Timothy's "science falsely so called" and can be summarised in one sentence – "I believe the writer is probably more likely to have said this"."*

Dr. Ruckman has some further examples of inconsistency amongst editors of Greek New Testaments, namely Westcott, Hort and Nestle (4) Chapter 7. I have inserted Ricker Berry's notes on the *"authorities"* for the alterations which predate Nestle's 21st edition. This edition contains all of the alterations cited.

"A. John 14:7. At the close of the verse "αυτον" ("him") has been omitted. However, "αυτον" is not only in the Receptus of the A.V.1611, it is found also in P66 (2nd century), representing the papyrus, Aleph, and A (4th and 5th century . . .), D (5th century . . .), Theta (9th century . . .), the Vulgate and the majority of the remaining witnesses. This preponderant evidence is nullified by two manuscripts (which contain the Apocrypha!) – "B" (4th century), and "C" from the 5th century. L, Tr, A contain the alteration.

"B. John 8:38. Near the end of the verse the reader will see that "εωρακατε" ("ye have seen") has been deleted and "ηκουσατε" ("ye heard") inserted. The reading (A.V. 1611) is upheld by P66 (2nd century), Aleph (4th century), D (5th century), the Receptus manuscripts, and the Syriac palimpset of the 4th century. Nestle gives no documentation for the reading of his text and leaves us to assume that "B" and "A" have the reading "ηκουσατε". Since Aleph can cancel "B" in antiquity, and D can cancel "A" in antiquity, we are left with the Receptus manuscripts (which make up the bulk of any set of manuscripts), and a 2nd century papyrus reading, which reads as the A.V. 1611." L, T, Tr, A contain the alteration.

At example E, sub-example 3, Dr. Ruckman makes an amazing disclosure:

"*E 3.* "Ο δε Πετρος αναστας εδραμεν επι το μνημειον και παρακνψας βλεπει τα οθοσια κειμενα, και απηλθεν προς αντον θανμαζων το γεγονος" *(Luke 24:12).*

On this last reading (Luke 24:12) the whole scholastic farce is suddenly manifested where the Freshman student can see it. The reading given above is the reading of the A.V. 1611." (It is omitted in the 1971 edition of the RSV but inserted in the NIV of 1973.) Dr. Ruckman continues:

"*But what have we here?!*

"*The reading is supported by Vaticanus! Not only does "B" (Vaticanus) support the A.V. 1611 reading, but this time P75, Aleph, A, C, Theta, and the Old Latin, and Old Syriac all contain the reading!*" (L),T, (Tr) omit the verse or regard it as "*doubtful*".

"*What have we here?!*

"*How did this A.V. 1611 reading get omitted in a "New" Bible based on "older Manuscripts?" What is this "older manuscript" that is more authoritative than A, B, C, Aleph, Theta, and P75? Why bless my soul, it is "D" (Bezae Cantabrigiensis) from the 5th century.*

"*What could have possessed Nestle . . . to suddenly reverse field and accept one Western manuscript as a higher authority than 4 Alexandrian Manuscripts which included Vaticanus?! . . . The truth of the matter is the verse had to be deleted to sustain and maintain the theory of W&H that the Syrian type text (A.V. 1611) was a "conflation" of Western and Alexandrian readings. The lengths to which these "scholars" will go to bolster this incompetent and ridiculous theory is now demonstrated, in Luke 24:12.*"

Dr. Ruckman gives several more examples, together with another 34 in his books *The Bible Babel* and *Problem Texts*, Appendix 6, demonstrating that, although the modern Greek editors "prefer" the Vaticanus ms., B, they will use ANY ms. to contradict the AV1611 and may well DISCARD B if it AGREES with the AV1611.

Section 7.3 shows the subjective nature of "*eclecticism*". A summary follows, with respect to the departures of the RV, NIV from the AV1611, listing mss. sources followed by Greek editors listed after ;. Unless otherwise stated, Ne, JB, NWT match the RV, NIV and the RV matches the Westcott-Hort Greek text. I have listed major Greek sources. J.A. Moorman, (39), (41), has a much more detailed listing.

Verse	Omission or Alteration	Against the AV1611
Matthew 1:25	"firstborn"	RV, NIV using Aleph, B, Z, 2 cursives; L, T, Tr, A.
Matthew 5:22	"without a cause"	RV, NIV using Aleph, B; L, T, (Tr, A)
Matthew 5:44	"bless them that curse you, do good to them that hate you, despitefully use you"	RV, NIV using Aleph, B, 7 cursives; L, T, Tr, A
Matthew 6:13	"for thine is the kingdom, and the power, and the glory, forever. Amen"	RV, NIV using Aleph, B, D, Z, 6 cursives; G, L, T, Tr, A, W
Matthew 18:11	"For the Son of man is come to save that which was lost"	RV, NIV using Aleph, B, L, 3 cursives; L, T, Tr, (A)
Matthew 23:14	Woe unto you, scribes and Pharisees, hypocrites! for ye devour widows houses, and for a pretence make long prayer: therefore ye shall receive the greater damnation"	RV, NIV using, Aleph, B, D; L, T, Tr, A
Matthew 27:35	"that it might be fulfilled which was spoken by the prophet, They parted my garments among them, and upon my vesture did they cast lots"	RV, NIV, using Majority mss.; G, L, T, Tr, A. See Section 9.6.
Mark 9:44, 46	"Where their worm dieth not, and the fire is not quenched"	RV, NIV using Aleph, B; T, (Tr).
Mark 16:9–20	See notes under "Against the AV1611".	Verses disputed in NIV using Aleph, B. RV contains them, although Westcott and Hort's Greek text omits them. Verses omitted by T, (A).
Luke 2:33	"Joseph" has been altered to "the child's father"	Alteration in RV, NIV using Aleph, B; G, T, Tr, A
Luke 4:18	"to heal the brokenhearted"	RV, NIV, using Aleph, B; G, (L), T, Tr, A

Verse	Omission or Alteration	Against the AV1611
Luke 9:54–56	"even as Elias did", "and said, Ye know not what manner of spirit ye are of", "For the Son of man is not come to destroy men's lives, but to save them"	RV, NIV, using Aleph, B, "a few disreputable allies" (13) p 316; T, (Tr), A (first clause), L, T, Tr, A (remaining clauses)
Luke 11:2, 4	"Our," "which art in heaven," "as in heaven, so in earth," "but deliver us from evil"	RV, NIV, using Marcion, Aleph and B, (last clause); G, T, Tr, A (first two clauses), G, (L),T, Tr, A (third clause), G, T, Tr, A (final clause)
Luke 17:36	"Two men shall be in the field; the one shall be taken, and the other left"	RV, NIV, using Majority mss.; all Greek editions except Stephanus' 4th, Beza and Elzevir
Luke 23:38	"in letters of Greek, and Latin, and Hebrew"	RV, NIV, using B, C, L; (L), T, Tr, (A)
Luke 23:42	"he said unto Jesus, Lord" has been changed to "He said "Jesus""	Alteration in RV, NIV using P75, Aleph, B, C, L; T, Tr. A
John 3:13	"which is in heaven"	NIV using P66, P75, Aleph, B, L; T (7) p 42
John 3:15	'should not perish"	omitted by RV, NIV using (L), T, Tr, A.
John 3:15	"whosoever believeth in him should not perish, but have eternal life" altered to "everyone who believes may have eternal life in him"	RV, NIV, JB. Ne, NWT read as the AV1611.
John 5:3b-4	"waiting for the moving of the water. For an angel went down at a certain season into the pool, and troubled the water: whosoever then first after the troubling of the water stepped in was made whole of whatsoever disease he had"	RV, NIV, NWT, Ne using P66, P75, Aleph, A, B, C, L, 0125 (verse 3b), P66, P75, Aleph, B, C*, D, W supp, 0125, cursive 33; (G), T, Tr, A. JB converts "angel" to "angel of the Lord" using DR and Lachmann but otherwise retains the words.

Verse	Omission or Alteration	Against the AV1611
John 7:53–8:11	See notes under "Against the AV1611".	Verses disputed in NIV using Aleph, B, T as the only unequivocal mss. omitting them. (G), L, T, Tr, A omit the verses. RV retains them but W-H Greek text omits them.
John 9:35	"**son of God**" has been altered to "Son of man"	Alteration in NIV using P66, P75, Aleph, B, D; T. RV reads as AV1611 but W-H Greek text has the alteration.
Acts 8:37	"**And Philip said, If thou believest with all thine heart, thou mayest. And he answered and said, I believe that Jesus Christ is the Son of God**"	Verse omitted by RV, NIV using Majority mss.; G, L, T, Tr, A. See Section 9.6.
Acts 9:5, 6	"**the Lord**", "**it is hard for thee to kick against the pricks. And he trembling and astonished said, Lord, what wilt thou have me to do?**"	RV, NIV using Majority mss.; L, T, Tr, A, W. G omits the second reading but not the first. See Section 9.6.
Romans 13:9	"**thou shalt not bear false witness**"	RV, NIV using G, L, T, Tr, A, W. Aleph HAS the reading, (35). J.A. Moorman (39) cites P46, A, B, D.
Romans 14:10	"**judgment seat of Christ**" has been altered to "judgment seat of God"	RV, NIV using Aleph, B, D2 and other Alexandrian and Western mss.; L, T, Tr, A, W
1 Corinthians 10:28	"**for the earth is the Lord's and the fulness thereof**"	RV, NIV, using G, L, T, Tr, A, W
1 Corinthians 11:24	"**broken**"	RV, NIV using Aleph, B, A, C, 2 cursives; L, T, Tr, A
Ephesians 3:9	"**by Jesus Christ**"	RV, NIV using G, L, T, Tr, A, W. J.A. Moorman (39) cites P46, Aleph, A, B, C, D
Colossians 1:14	"**through his blood**"	RV, NIV using Aleph, B, A, C, D (BBB Feb., 1992); G, L, T, Tr, A, W

Verse	Omission or Alteration	Against the AV1611
1 Timothy 3:16	"**God**" has been altered to "He" or "Who"	RV, NIV using Aleph, D, cursive "Paul 17" as the only unequivocal Greek mss.; G, L, T, Tr, A, W
James 5:16	"**faults**" has been altered to "sins"	RV, NIV using Aleph, B, A, P; L, T, Tr
1 John 4:3	"**Christ is come in the flesh**"	RV, NIV using B, A, Psi, L, T, Tr, A
1 John 5:7–8	"**in heaven, the Father, the Word, and the Holy Ghost: and these three are one. And there are three that bear witness in earth**"	RV NIV, using Majority mss.; G, L, T, Tr, A, W

33 passages of scripture have here been listed, totalling 62 verses. 5 of the modern readings, or 7 verses, are based on the Majority mss. and the rest are from the Alexandrian and/or Western mss.. Agreement between the AV1611 and the Majority mss. for the above verses is over 85%, which is typical. See Sections 1.3, 7.3.

Where verses were not attested by the Majority mss., the TR editors and AV1611 translators consulted other ancient sources to vindicate the authenticity of readings. There are variations between editions of the TR but they are few compared to the variations between the "*oldest and best mss.*" See Sections 9.3, 9.6.

The list of examples, which is not exhaustive reveals that:

1. Aleph and B are repeatedly among the sources of variation from the AV1611 and therefore highly influential to this day, even if not "dominant".
2. "New discoveries" and "much more and earlier evidence", such as P66 and P75, are used to cut out MORE of the Scriptures.
3. There is appreciable inconsistency in the "eclecticism" or use of mss. sources by modern editors for no apparent reason except to change the Text of the AV1611.
4. There is appreciable inconsistency among modern editors, from Griesbach onwards with respect to what should or should NOT be "scripture".
5. Approximately 85% of AV1611 readings are supported by the Majority of mss..

Gail Riplinger (12) p 499ff, 630ff lists many further examples of the inconsistency of the "*eclecticism and subjectivism*" of "*modern textual critics*". Her penetrating summary of "*the work of modern textual critics and the principles on which they arrive at their conclusions*", so beloved by our critic, bears repeating.

"*The "accepted principles of the science of textual criticism" used to justify this 'shell game' . . . are illustrations of Timothy's "science falsely so called" and can be summarised in one sentence – "I believe the writer is probably more likely to have said this".*"

The final volume in this series addresses some of the discrepancies between the Holy Bible, AV1611 and the NIV in more detail and discusses certain passages of scripture that our critic describes as "***Disputed Texts***".

13

"The NIV – Apostate?" (Yes)

13.1 "THE "TOTALLY EVANGELICAL" NIV"

Our critic begins with the statement "*I notice that one of your illustrations describes the NIV as apostate. This is, I am afraid, simply ludicrous.*" The illustration is Figure 5.

He evidently failed to "*notice*" that in the nine pages immediately preceding Figure 5, in the version of Chapters 1–7 which he received, 110 verses were listed where the NIV agreed with the JB or NWT or BOTH AGAINST the AV1611. The latter category numbered 101 of the 110 examples given. The equivalent result for the extended list now found in Volume 1 is 171 of 192 verses, or almost 90%.

Also, he cited ANOTHER 66 VERSES, which do not appear in Sections 7.3 or 12.6, where the NIV agrees with BOTH the JB and NWT in 51 or 77%! Those repeated are Daniel 3:25, Mark 6:20, Acts 2:47, 4:27, 30, 9:6. In addition, this study has revealed a further 60+ verses where the NIV reading has been found to be either incorrect or inferior to the AV1611. See Sections 10.15, 12.6. Overall, the agreement between the NIV, JB, NWT against the AV1611 for the entire New Testament appears to be approximately 80%. See Section 10.15.

Moreover, 61 verses have been listed in the previous chapter to show the influence on the text of the NIV of Greek editors who were mostly unsaved heretics and who were NOT in perfect agreement.

60 verses have been listed which show that omissions in the NIV obviously stem from the Douay-Rheims version of the Roman Catholic church. See Section 11.4.

I am then supposed to believe that the NIV is NOT "*apostate*"? I find that proposition somewhat "*ludicrous*".

Moreover, Figure 5 is obviously the frontispiece of a BOOK. If he is so convinced that the NIV is NOT apostate, why did he not ask to see a copy of that book, so that he could refute its contents, no doubt with the help of "*the standard scholarly works on the subject*"?

Our critic then states that "***The hundred scholars responsible for (the NIV) came from all the main Protestant denominations and all had to subscribe to the high view of Scripture as set out in the Westminster Confession, the Belgic Confession and the New Hampshire Confession.***"

If the "*hundred scholars*" had such a "*high view of Scripture*" – which is not necessarily the same as actually BELIEVING ANY BIBLE to be the pure word of God AND the FINAL AUTHORITY – WHY did they VIOLATE The Westminster Confession of Faith in Section 8, Para. 2, of that Confession, (3) p 25?

""*Two whole perfect and distinct natures, the Godhead and the manhood, were inseparably joined together in one Person . . . Which Person is very God and very man, yet one Christ . . .*" The Scripture proofs annexed to section 8, para. 2, include 1 Timothy 3:16, "**God was manifest in the flesh.**" *The Westminster Divines evidently regarded this verse as one of the essential proofs of the Trinitarian doctrine of the Bible, that the Father is God, the Son is God and the Holy Spirit is God.*"

Our critic and the NIV translators "*evidently regarded*" the Westminster Divines as having been deceived by a "*late highly doubtful reading*" – according to our critic. See Sections 11.1 and Chapter 14 of this work.

Yet our critic insists that the NIV translators "*were totally evangelical*" in the "*historic doctrinal sense*" whereas "***The KJV consisted of many high churchmen and so could hardly be claimed to be translated by a completely orthodox evangelical body.***"

Dr. Laurence Chaderton was one of the AV1611 translators. His sermons won 40 of the clergy to Christ, Section 4.2. Does our critic mention ANY NIV translator whose sermons have won even half that number to Christ? No.

Dr. Lancelot Andrewes was one of the AV1611 translators – AND a high churchman. "*He was the means of converting many papists by his preaching and disputations*" Section 12.4.

Does our critic mention even one NIV translator whose "*preaching and disputations*" have been "*the means of converting many papists*"? No.

Regardless of who translated the AV1611, Finney and Sunday between them led 1,500,000 souls to Christ because they believed the AV1611 to be the pure word of God from cover to cover. See Chapter 8 and Section 12.5.

Does our critic name any two preachers who have led even one-tenth of that number to Christ with a "*totally evangelical*" NIV? No.

Dr. Peter Trumper (58) p 10, has some penetrating observations about "*all the main Protestant denominations*" among the NIV translators:

"*Reading the Preface of the NIV . . . We are told that "Anglican, Assemblies of God, Baptist, Brethren, Christian Reformed, Church of Christ, Evangelical Free, Lutheran, Mennonite, Methodist, Nazarene, Presbyterian, Wesleyan and other churches – helped to safeguard the translation from sectarian bias. That is quite a cross section! . . . Are we to be palmed off so easily? There are some queer fish swimming about in these denominations, all blithely calling themselves "evangelical." By the way, what about that ominous-sounding phrase, "and other churches"? What other churches? The reader should demand to know.*"

The TBS (56) have answered Dr. Trumper's questions in their *Quarterly Record*, Oct.-Dec. 1987 No. 501, p 8. "*Advice was also sought from Jewish, Roman Catholic, and atheistic scholars, according to a news release by the publishers.*"

The TBS article continues, p 11 "*Attention must also be drawn to the fact that, although the NIV professes to be an evangelical translation, the Greek text on which it is mainly based was not prepared by evangelical scholars but by the editors of the United Bible Societies' Greek New Testament. The UBS editors included several who deny the inerrancy of the Holy Scriptures, working in co-operation with a Roman Catholic Cardinal, Carlo Martini. The soundness of a translation which relies upon such a source must be questioned by every one of the NIV's evangelical readers.*"

Not by our critic, who on this occasion appears quite ready to ignore "***evidence which is inconvenient to one's case***" although he has "***collected, for a number of years, literature taking a similar approach.***"

Would he consider Cardinal Martini to be "*totally evangelical*" in the "*historic doctrinal sense*" of the word?

Anyone wishing to confirm the similarity between the NIV and UBS texts should consult the marginal notes in the Samuel Bagster 1982 British usage edition of the NKJV.

Dr. Trumper is obviously quite justified in his assessment of the NIV translating committee as having "*an ecumenical flavour*" rather than an evangelical one.

E.L. Bynum (58) p 8, (59) p 5–6, comments about these "*totally evangelical*" scholars:

" *"New Evangelical" schools are heavily represented on the translation committee. Among others, we find that this committee contains six men from Trinity Evangelical Divinity School, and several from Fuller, Wheaton, Dallas and even Oral Roberts University. Why does Oral Roberts University need to be represented? How sad to see Clyde T. Francisco of Southern Baptist Theological Seminary represented. In the early 60's Dr. Ralph Elliott stirred a furor in his book, "The Message of Genesis". Dr. Elliott's book denied the historical accuracy of the first 12 chapters of Genesis.*"

'Evolutionary progress!' Westcott only denied the first three. See Sections 6.1, 12.6.

Pastor Bynum continues:

"*Adam meant mankind and Moses did not write the Pentateuch, the tower of Babel is a parable, Enoch was not translated, and the age of the men before the flood is doubtful, these as well as other heresies are contained in Elliott's book. And where did Elliott get his ideas? In his introduction he said, "Though the material in this book is mine, and I do not wish anyone else to be charged with its deficiencies, I do wish to express my appreciation to DR. CLYDE T. FRANCISCO, my teacher and later a colleague on the faculty of Southern Baptist Theological Seminary, Louisville, Kentucky. It was in an eclective course in the Pentateuch under his guidance that I first gained inspiration and purpose to attempt a serious study on the Book of Genesis. THUS, I AM SURE THAT MANY OF THE INSIGHTS WHICH CULMINATED IN MY OWN MIND WERE PLACED THERE IN SEED-BED FASHION BY HIM.*" "

Pastor Bynum concludes "*To this date we have never heard of Dr. Francisco denying this.*"

Yet I am assured that Dr. Francisco is "*totally evangelical*" in the "*historic doctrinal sense*" of the word.

What of Edwin Palmer, the "*coordinator of all the work on the NIV*" (12) p 230–233? Gail Riplinger states "*He . . . "selected all of the personnel of the initial translation committee.*" He also edited the NIV Study Bible which Zondervan says includes the "*liberal position.*" His scandalous and sacrilegious statement will stun and shock the reader. In one of his books he quotes a verse from his NIV, then says:

"This (his NIV) shows the great error that is so prevalent today in some orthodox Protestant circles, namely that regeneration depends on faith . . . and that in order to be born again man must first accept Jesus as his Saviour."" The verse in question is John 1:13.

The AV1611 reads "**Which were born, not of blood, nor of the will of the flesh, nor of the will of man, but of God.**"

The NIV reads "children born not of natural descent, nor of human decision or a husband's will, but born of God."

Palmer's error and that of the NIV is seen in the words "nor of human decision". "Human decision" is EXACTLY how ANY individual is "born of God."

Although no-one can "will" himself to be "born of God", the Bible extends an open invitation to anyone to AVAIL himself of the new birth:

"**Whosoever WILL, let him take of the water of life FREELY**" Revelation 21:17.

It is a "human decision" whether to receive the Lord Jesus Christ, John 1:12, 3:36 or to reject Him, John 3:36, 12:48. God cannot make that decision for ANYONE. It is an individual matter for "**whosoever believeth in him,**" John 3:16.

Having made the right "human decision", that individual is then empowered to become a son of God by the new birth, John 3:3. Gail Riplinger continues:

"If he denies "faith" and each individual's responsibility to "accept Jesus as his Saviour," what does he offer in its place?

"Luke 21:19

"NIV "By standing firm you will save yourself."

"AV1611 "**In your patience possess ye your souls.**"

"He is not alone in his views. Another "liberal" new version editor comments regarding this switch in Luke 21:19:

""Of all the changes in the RV, that in Luke 21:19 is the one to which I look with most hope. We think of our souls as something to complete . . .""

The RV reads "In your patience ye shall win your souls." This is also the sense of the NIV, namely that salvation depends on an individual striving for it, to gain his soul as a prize at the end. In the AV1611, the believer in the context by his patience keeps what he HAS – his soul. Doctrinally, the passage applies to the tribulation, Matthew 24:13, where patience in trial is an element of salvation. Gail Riplinger continues:

"Palmer devoted an entire chapter in his book, The Five Points of Calvinism, to disprove the idea that "man still has the ability to ask God's *help for salvation." His "Five Points" form a Satanic pentagram. His book is so irrational that he is periodically forced to interrupt himself with comments like, " . . . as contradictory as that may seem?" In defense of the obviously unscriptural character of his chapters, he quips, "The lack of a (scripture) text does not destroy their character." He whittles away at John 3:16 and concludes that the view "that Christ loved the whole world equally and gave himself up for the world" is wrong . . .*

"(Palmer) says, "God intends that salvation shall be for only a few . . ." Sounding like one of the Jehovah Witness 144,000 he says, "God chose only a certain number to be saved." "For God so loved the world" becomes "only those whom he loved . . . would be saved . . . If God loves us, we are called" . . .

"Palmer's chapter on the 'Elect' elite is reflected in his translation of 1 Thessalonians 1:4, "he has chosen you." *He admits his change "suggests the opposite of" the KJV's* **"your election of God."** *In his system, God elects a few 'winners'. In Christianity, God calls ALL sinners, but few elect to respond. Palmer denies that man should respond . . . Palmer believes, "Man is entirely passive." He points to his alteration of John 1:13 asserting that it "proves" man has no free will."*

1 Thessalonians 1:9 bears out Mrs. Riplinger's analysis. She continues:

"His 'elite' were serenaded by the heavenly host in Luke 2:14 in the NIV . . . However, in the KJV the good will of God was extended to all men, not his favorite 'God-pleasing' elect.

"NIV reads "Glory to God in the highest, and on earth peace to men on whom his favor rests."

"KJV reads **"Glory to God in the highest and on earth peace, good will toward men."**

"Here, the new versions follow manuscripts Aleph, B, C and D. Their Greek differs from the overwhelming majority of manuscripts by one letter, 's'. The former has the genitive "eudokios", *while the latter has the nominative* "eudokia" *. . . the KJV and the Majority text reading of* "eudokia" *is attested by not only MOST MSS but also by the oldest witnesses.*

2nd Century:	Syriac Version and Irenaeus
3rd Century:	Coptic Version and the Apostolic Constitution
4th Century:	Eusebius, Aphraates, Titus, Didymus, Gregory, Cyril, Epiphanus, Ephraem, Philo, Chrysostom.

"In their passion to give space to Satan's sermon, (the NIV committee) follow four corrupt fourth and fifth century MSS while ignoring a total of

53 ancient witnesses including 16 belonging to the second, third and fourth centuries and 37 from the fifth, sixth, seventh and eighth centuries.

"*Although the advertisements for the NIV boast that it was translated by a committee of 100 scholars, Palmer's hand picked CBT (Committee on Bible Translation)* "*would choose a translation other than that of the initial or intermediate or general editorial committees.*" *Therefore Palmer and his cronies could ignore all three intermediate committees and make their own translation. This is evident in verses such as Romans 1:28 where a concept from Palmer's chapter entitled* "*Total Depravity*" *finds its way. He admits his purposeful switch saying,* "*Paul was not speaking of the reprobate but the depraved*" . . . "

"*His power and influence can also be seen in the Commonwealth edition of the NIV in which* "*Edwin Palmer* . . . *agreed with many of the changes himself to save time.*" *(The Greek Textus Receptus is often ignored by critics who insist Erasmus hurried it along to save time.) Palmer's Calvinism did not rest with his influence in the NIV. The New King James Committee boasts seven members who subscribe to Palmer's elite 'Elect' and damned 'depraved' classes.*"

Yet Palmer is supposed to be "*totally evangelical*" in the "*historic doctrinal sense*" of the word.

13.2 "THE "HIGH CHRISTOLOGY" OF THE NIV"

Our critic then insists that "***In a number of instances the NIV is much clearer for the deity of Christ, and the deity and personality of the Holy Spirit than the KJV.***"

He seeks to illustrate this assertion by reference to "***five key texts affirming the deity of Christ about which there is no textual controversy John 1:1; Romans 9:5; Titus 2:13; Hebs 1:8; 2 Peter 1:1 In terms of presenting a high Christology the NIV scores 5 out of 5 while the KJV scores 3 out of 5.***"

I assume that by "*a high Christology*" our critic means that the verses indicate that Jesus is God. He then extends this list to eight, "***where the Greek text can be understood (either in the light of the best Greek MSS. or correct grammatical interpretation) to call Christ God.***"

Observe that our critic does NOT specify WHICH mss. are "*the best Greek mss.*", nor does he allow for the fact that INTERPRETATIONS belong to GOD, Genesis 40:8, not Greek grammarians.

His eight verses are John 1:1, 1:18, Acts 20:28, Romans 9:5, 2 Thess. 1:12, Titus 2:13, Hebs. 1:8, 2 Peter 1:1. He concludes "***The KJV accepts*** *only 4 out of 8 as referring to Christ's deity, while the NIV accepts 7 out of 8. Yet the NIV is supposed to be apostate!"*

Dr. Ruckman (1) p ii-iii, 346 states *"Between 1970 and 1984, several writers tried to bluster, blow, stick out their chicken breasts, and prove that such corruptions as the ASV, RV, NIV, NASV, RSV, and others did not attack the Deity of Christ. In order to do this, they deliberately side-stepped ALL of the salient verses that dealt with it (see Acts 4:27; 1 Tim. 3:16; Acts 20:28; Luke 2:33; Luke 23:42; John 3:13; et al.) and chose other verses that were NOT salient . . . John 1:1, which is not salient; John 1:18 (where (Custer (44)) had accepted the Arian teaching of the Jehovah's Witnesses); Romans 9:5, which is not salient; Titus 2:13, which is not salient; and Hebrews 1:8, which is not salient."*

Although our critic's list of eight verses includes Acts 20:28, this is only possible because the NIV WENT BACK to the AV1611 reading from the RSV reading "of the Lord", which the NIV nevertheless RETAINED in the margin.

Otherwise, our critic's list bears an uncanny resemblance to the verses cited by Dr. Ruckman as *"not salient"* by comparison with the verses he lists which DO emphasise Christ's Deity.

Once again, Gail Riplinger reveals the subterfuge to which our critic has resorted (12) p 369–371. She refers to a book by *"D.A. Carson, a most forward new version advocate"* entitled The King James Version Debate.

"(Carson) proceeds to give, as 'advanced work,' a small chart from the promotional brochures used to 'advance' the sale of new versions. It quickly becomes apparent that he must mean – 'advanced con artistry' not 'advanced' scholarship. The chart is composed of only eight verses, which he calls, "all the verses of the New Testament that can be translated in such a way that they directly call Jesus, 'God'." (He must be using a new version.) In fact, only three of the eight deal with the deity of Christ at all. (Books such as Nave's Topical Bible *or* Lockyer's *classic* All the Doctrines of the Bible *do not even mention these five other verses under the heading 'Deity of Christ.' However, these books do cite many of the verses covered in this book which are omitted by the new versions.)*

"The following is an abridgement of the trumped-up chart used by new version publishers and Carson.

"VERSES THAT IDENTIFY JESUS AS GOD

Verse	KJV	NIV
John 1:1	Yes	Yes
John 1:18	No	Yes

John 20:28	Yes	Yes
Rom. 9:5	Yes	Yes
2 Thess. 1:12	No	No
Titus 2:13	No	Yes
Heb. 1:8	Yes	Yes
2 Pet. 1:1	No	Yes

For brevity, I have omitted the NASV, which is also included in the chart.

Our critic's list has Acts 20:28 instead of John 20:28. The discrepancy is minor because the NIV reads as the AV1611 in Acts 20:28, while both versions are awarded a *"Yes"* by Carson for John 20:28. However, there is a slight advantage for Our critic in using Acts 20:28 because in John 20:28 the NIV reads "Thomas answered, 'My Lord and my God!'"

The AV1611 reads **And Thomas answered AND SAID UNTO HIM, My Lord and my God**" (my emphasis). The AV1611 puts much greater emphasis on the fact that Thomas is addressing Jesus. The NIV agrees with the JB. The RV, NWT, Ne and other Greek texts read with the AV1611.

Gail Riplinger continues *"The KJV's four out of eight verses marked 'No', to which Carson points to support his claim that "the KJV missed half" of the verses on Christ's deity, prove to be straw men which fall with a touch of scholarly inspection.*

1. *John 1:18 (p 339, 342) The term* "the only begotten Son" *is seen in the vast majority of MSS and is witnessed to the earliest extant record of John 1:18, Tertullian in A.D. 150 . . . The word* "only begotten" *emphasises too strongly the distinction between Jesus Christ, the begotten Son, and believers who are adopted sons.* "Only begotten" *also flattens any New Age assertion that Jesus is one in a long line of avatars. The 'censored' versions stand ready to support those unscriptural schemers who subscribe to a Son who was not 'begotten'.*

    ""*He, Jesus, is the unique Son of God . . . but there have been lots of others like him . . . he was a guide and I can be just like him" New Ager.*

    " "*The only Son, Jesus is mankind's Saviour. The second advent of Jesus is in Korea" Reverend Moon.*

    " "*The Spirit of Eternity is One . . . God the Mother is omniscient*

. . . The only Son is Christ, and Christ is Love" The Aquarian Gospel of Jesus Christ . . .

"*The jarring tone of 'Christians' harmonising with cultists is confounding. (Recall that Palmer hand picked the members of the NIV committee and had the final say on all translations.)*

" *"The Holy Spirit did not beget the Son" Edwin Palmer NIV Committee Executive Secretary."*

I will discuss John 1:18 further in relation to Scriptures which our critic wishes to delete from the Bible. Mrs Riplinger continues , p 370:

2. *2 Thessalonians 1:12: ALL versions read* "our God and the Lord Jesus Christ." *The originator of the chart thinks a comma should be added (after* "God"*).* (Author's note: I believe that Mrs. Riplinger means that the "and" in the clause should be replaced by a comma.)
3. *Titus 2:13: ALL Greek texts have the wording of the KJV,* "God and our Saviour Jesus Christ." *None render it as the new versions do.*
4. *2 Peter 1:1 Lewis Foster, NIV and NKJV committee member, reveals WHY new version editors insert Christ's deity in Peter and Titus, yet removed it (in) nearly 100 other places. "Some would point out that in passages Titus and 2 Peter, the expression of the deity of Christ has been strengthened by renderings even in liberal translations. What many do not realize is that even here the strong affirmation of deity is used to serve a purpose. The liberal translator ordinarily denies that Paul wrote Titus or that Peter wrote 2 Peter. He points to the very language deifying Jesus as an indication of the later date of these epistles when Paul and Peter could not have written them."*
5. *2 Thessalonians 1:12, Titus 2:13, and 2 Peter 1:1 are called "hendiades," from the Greek "hen, dia dyoin," 'one by two'. Grammatically it is the "expression of an idea by two nouns connected by "and", instead of by a noun and an adjunct. It would be like introducing one's spouse as "my wife and best friend.""*

Dr. Ruckman adds (1) p iii "*Any fool could have seen the same construction in Isaiah 45:21.*"

The AV1611 reading in Titus 2:13 and 2 Peter 1:1 is actually a superior testimony to the Deity of the Lord Jesus Christ than the NIV variation. "Our God", NIV, simply designates the Lord as God of the Christians. The expression "**God and our Saviour**", AV1611, shows that the Lord is GOD universally but effectually the Saviour of the Christian. Doctrinally, the Lord is, of course, "**Saviour of the world**" John 4:42.

Our critic also maintains that "*1 Peter 3:15 is another example of the KJV missing the deity of Christ. This verse is based on Isaiah 8:13 and is typical of many instances in the NT where what is spoken of God in the OT is ascribed to Christ in the NT – writers are thereby affirming his deity. The KJV using an inferior text misses this clear affirmation that Christ is God.*"

The accusation that the AV1611 has "*an inferior text*" has been answered in Chapter 9.

The relevant portion of 1 Peter 3:15 in the AV1611 reads "**But sanctify the Lord God in your hearts:**"

The relevant portion of Isaiah 8:13 in the AV1611 reads "**Sanctify the Lord of hosts himself;**"

The corresponding readings in the NIV are "But in your hearts set apart Christ as Lord." 1 Peter 3:15 and "The Lord Almighty is the one you are to regard as holy," Isaiah 8:13. In his reference to Isaiah 8:13, our critic by-passed the attacks by the NIV on Christ's deity in the very next chapter, verse 6. See Section 5.6.

Agreeing with the NIV in 1 Peter 3:15 are the DR, RV, JB, NWT, Ne, L, T, Tr, A, W, Section 11.4.

The association between 1 Peter 3:15 and Isaiah 8:13 is much clearer in the AV1611 than in the NIV because the AV1611 uses the word "**sanctify**" in each verse.

In fact, the NIV has subtly erased ALL DIRECT REFERENCE TO DEITY in the verse. Thanks to the modern editors – see above – it has omitted the word "**God**". Moreover, the term "Christ AS Lord" NIV, is NOT identical to "**Christ IS THE Lord**" 1 Corinthians 12:3. The RV, NIV, JB, NWT all omit "**the**".

The term "Christ AS Lord" appears nowhere in the Bible for this simple reason. Christ IS the Lord. He should not be only likened to the Lord by the word "as" which in the NIV construction appears as a relative pronoun denoting comparison of high quality, which is not necessarily identical quality.

Elsewhere in his letter Peter uses the word "**as**" in this proverbial sense:
"**as of a lamb**" 1:19, "**the lamb of God**" John 1:29 but not a literal lamb.
"**as grass**" 1:24, obviously not literal grass.
"**As newborn babes**" 2:2, spiritual babes but not literal babies.
"**as lively stones**" 2:5, not literal stones.
"**as sheep**" 2:25, not literal sheep.
"**as a roaring lion**" 5:8, not a literal lion.

The same sense is found in 2 Samuel 19:27 and Galatians 4:14.

The NIV uses "like" instead of "as" in all of these verses except in 1:19, where no pronoun is used and in Galatians 4:14 where "as if" is used. No doubt it uses "as" in 1 Peter 3:15 because "like" would not fit easily into the wording of the sentence but "as" here retains the same sense.

13.3 "THE DIFFERENT TREATMENT BY THE NIV OF THE HOLY SPIRIT"

Our critic continues: "*The different treatment by the KJV and the NIV of the deity and personality of the Holy Spirit in the following verses is revealing also.*"

Among the verses listed here by our critic are several which have been discussed in Sections 10.3, 11.4 which see; Luke 10:21, Acts 4:25 and Acts 16:7.

Evidently **Matthew 22:43** "**in spirit**" AV1611, should be "by the Spirit" RV ("in" instead of "by"), NIV, JB. NWT has "by inspiration". Both Ne and Berry's TR translate as the AV1611. Presumably the modern translators desire to force Matthew 22:43 to match Mark 12:36, where the AV1611 has "**by the Holy Ghost,**" with the same in the NIV except that "Ghost" is given as "Spirit."

The modern revisers thereby lose the cross references to Psalm 51:10–12, which show from the statements in Matthew and Mark that David's prayer was answered and that his pledge in verse 13 was fulfilled.

Moral: "*When the Bible says one thing and scholarship says another, scholarship can go plumb to the devil!*" Billy Sunday, Chapter 8.

Our critic's next reference is **Acts 11:28**, where "**by the spirit**" AV1611 should be "through the Spirit" DR ("by" instead of "**through**"), RV (as DR), NIV, JB. NWT has "through the spirit" and the Greek texts have "the Spirit".

The AV1611 is supposedly in error because "s**pirit**" has not been capitalised as in the NIV etc.. This objection overlooks the fact that "spirit" is not capitalised by the NIV in John 4:24, although the reference is to the Person of God Himself. The DR, JB have "spirit" together with the Greek texts, although the RV and NWT read with the AV1611, which has "**spirit.**"

The NIV gives another evasive reading in 1 Kings 22:22–24 and 2 Chronicles 20:20–23, showing that the translators were unable to distinguish between a LYING spirit and "**the Spirit of the Lord**" AV1611.

This is what happens when a verse on SPIRITUAL DISCERNMENT is altered, 1 John 4:3. See Section 11.4.

I find that Walker's Concordance, Kregel Publications Inc., 1976 distinguishes between "S" and "s" in reference to "Spirit" and "spirit." Young's does not preserve this distinction. Although I have not checked all the references – they are very numerous – it appears that in the New Testament, "**Spirit**" is the designation for the Third Person of the Godhead. In the Old Testament, "**spirit**" is sometimes used when the work or ministry of the Holy Spirit is the subject of the passage. See Isaiah 11:2 and Ezekiel 1:12, 2:2, 3:12. Agabus appears to have been a prophet with a roving commission, Acts 11:28, 21:10 and could have had a prophetic ministry similar to that of John the Baptist, Luke 1:17, who was likened to an Old Testament prophet, namely Elijah, Matthew 11:14.

Given that Agabus had some association, therefore, with Old Testament prophetic ministry, it would be entirely appropriate for him to be speaking "**by the spirit,**" small "s". He did, after all, speak words of "**spirit and life,**" John 6:63.

I have thus far been speaking of the word "**spirit**" as found in the Cambridge Cameo Edition of the AV1611. (The Oxford 1611 AV1611 also has "**spirit**" in Acts 11:28.) However, Walker's Concordance and the Cambridge Concord Edition of the AV1611 have "**spirit**" in Acts 11:28 – which would also be entirely appropriate because Agabus was part of the New Testament Church and ministering to that Body. Both readings can therefore be justified and our critic is merely gnat-straining.

He then objects to "**the Spirit itself**" AV1611, in **Romans 8:16, 26**, claiming the reading should be "himself," DR, RV, NIV, JB. The NWT and Berry's TR have "itself," Ne has both readings.

There are some manifestations of the Spirit of God, Ezekiel 1:20, 21, Revelation 4:5, where application of gender to "**spirit**" would not be appropriate. The modern alteration obscures this revelation.

Dr. Gipp (9) p 97–98, replies to our critic's charge as follows: "*The word translated "**itself**" in Romans 8:26 is "pneuma" which means "spirit" . . . "pneuma" is a NEUTER, a fact which is known to even first year Greek language students. Thus, the King James Bible CORRECTLY translates pneuma "itself" because it would be grammatically incorrect to translate it "himself" as many of today's inferior translations do. Since critics of the King James Bible like to deride it for pretended "mistranslations" of the Greek, it seems hypocritical indeed to criticise it* *here for properly translating the Greek. Then to add insult to ignorance they laud other versions such as . . . the NIV which INCORRECTLY render pneuma as* "himself."

'*Secondly, in adding to their hypocrisy and exposing their disdain for God's Bible, these same critics . . . will promote translations such as the NIV which call God a* "What" *in Acts 17:23. The Authorised Version correctly renders it* "**Whom.**"

"*Thirdly . . . is a statement that Jesus Christ makes in John chapter 4 while dealing with the woman at the well . . .*

"**Ye worship ye know not what: we know WHAT we worship . . .**"

"*To whom is Jesus referring by the word* "**what**"*? The next verse defines His statement perfectly.*

'"**But the hour cometh, and now is, when the true worshippers shall worship THE FATHER in spirit and in truth: for the Father seeketh such to worship him.**"

"*Thus we see that Jesus finds referring to His own Father as* "**what**" *in verse 22 a NON-ISSUE.*"

Our critic's next objection is in **Ephesians 1:17** where "**the spirit of wisdom**" AV1611 should be "the Spirit of wisdom" (not "Wisdom" as in our critic's document), NIV. The modern alteration obscures the cross reference to Isaiah 11:2 and the spiritual wisdom now available to the Christian. The alteration also creates confusion because Ephesians 1:17 is a prayer on behalf of SAINTS, verse 1, who already HAVE "**the Spirit,**" Romans 8:9.

Our critic's last objection is **Philippians 3:3**. The AV1611 reading is "**we . . . worship God in the spirit.**" The NIV reading is "we who worship by the Spirit of God.", similarly with the RV, JB, NWT ("God's spirit"), Ne, L, T, Tr, A, W.

The comparison speaks for itself. The Bible believer follows the example of the Lord Jesus Christ and WORSHIPS GOD IN SPIRIT, John 4:22–24. The modern revisers "**worship YE KNOW NOT WHAT.**"

Gail Riplinger (12) p 383–384 lists several verses where reference to the Holy Ghost has been weakened or removed in the modern versions "*from 'ecumenical' pressures not from Greek manuscript evidence.*"

Matthew 12:31

"**the Holy Ghost**" AV1611, "the Spirit" DR, RV, NIV, JB, NWT ("spirit"), Ne and the other Greek texts. "**Holy**" is italicised in the AV1611.

John 7:39
"**the Holy Ghost**" AV1611, "the Spirit" DR, RV, NIV, JB, NWT ("spirit"), Ne, L, T, (Tr, A). "The original writing on the oldest papyri (P66) says "the Holy Ghost" (12) p 383. See Section 11.4.

Acts 6:3
"**the Holy Ghost**" AV1611, "the Spirit" RV, NIV, JB, NWT ("spirit"), Ne, G, L, T, Tr, A

Acts 8:18
"**the Holy Ghost**" AV1611, "the Spirit" NIV, JB, NWT ("spirit"), Ne, T, (Tr), A. "The earliest papyri (P45 and 74) say "Holy Ghost" " (12) p 383.

Romans 8:1
See Section 11.4.

Romans 15:19
"**the Spirit of God**" AV1611, "the Spirit" NIV, Ne. DR and other modern versions have "Holy Ghost" or "Holy Spirit" as do G, L, Tr, (A), W. "The earliest papyri (2nd century P46), Aleph, Nestle's 26th edition, and the Majority Greek Text agree on the reading, "**the Spirit of God.**" (NIV) follows ONE 4th century manuscript, B" (12) p 383.

1 Corinthians 2:13
"**the Holy Ghost**" AV1611, "the Spirit" DR, RV, NIV, JB, NWT ("spirit"), Ne, G, L, T, Tr, A, W. See Section 11.4

1 Peter 1:22. See Section 11.4.

Our critic listed 9 verses on the Spirit, or spirit, in which his criticisms of the AV1611 have been shown to be unjustified and in which deficiencies in the modern translations have been revealed. In addition, a further 8 verses have been cited with respect to the Spirit of God, where criticisms of the NIV etc. are FULLY JUSTIFIED.

Taking this section as a whole, NONE of our critic's criticisms of the AV1611 withstand close scrutiny. NEITHER DO HIS ATTEMPTS TO UPHOLD THE NIV AS A 'BIBLE.'

Yet he concludes "*It is ludicrous to say that the NIV is apostate compared with the KJV. Rather the boot is on the other foot.*"

This last statement displays our critic's hatred for the Authorised Holy

Bible like no other in his entire document. The AV1611, which has had the breath of God upon it for nearly four centuries, Chapter 10, Section 10.3, is declared by him to be "***apostate.***" Our critic would do well to ponder Romans 14:12, where Paul is speaking to CHRISTIANS;

"So then every one of us shall give account of himself to God"

and marshall his arguments carefully, far more carefully than he has for this document.

A final note on the NIV comes from an article in the *Bible Believers' Bulletin*, October 1993, entitled *The New International Perversion*. I quote from the article: "*One of the literary consultants for the NIV translating committee is a LESBIAN . . . Her name is Dr. Mollenkott. In the* Episcopal Witness *(June 1991, pp. 20–23), another woman, Sue Pierce, asked her, "Why was it important to both of you to come out as lesbians?" The sex pervert's reply was, "My lesbianism has always been a part of me . . . what I did ultimately realise was that GOD CREATED ME AS I WAS, and that this is where life was meaningful.*"

And I am supposed to believe that this individual is "*totally evangelical*" in the "*historic doctrinal sense*" of the word?

13.4 "NIV AND RCs"

Our critic's comments here are in response to the statement in Chapter 5, Section 5.7 wherein I note that the Catholic Truth Society sell the NIV but not the AV1611.

This note was based on an observation made some years ago by J.E. North (58) p 20. It prompts our critic to inform me that "***a Gallup survey . . . indicated that in England and Wales 13% RCs used the KJV and only 2% used the NIV. 8% RC churches used the KJV and 0% used NIV.***"

Our critic has ignored an obvious implication of these figures. They show that 85–90 % RCs "*use*" – not "believe," Section 10.15 – something OTHER THAN the AV1611 or the NIV.

Although the DR is a possibility, it is most likely to be the Jerusalem Bible, JB, as I confirmed in a telephone call to the CTS on 11th November 1994. The lady who answered said that they "*usually recommend the JB.*" This work has shown repeatedly that the 'bible' which the NIV agrees with consistently and most frequently AGAINST the AV1611 is the JB. The results of the poll are therefore no indictment of the AV1611.

I asked the lady in the CTS about this Gallup survey cited by our critic. She had no knowledge of it whatsoever, so it could not have received very wide publicity amongst Catholics. This dear lady then confirmed that the CTS do sell the NIV – of which they had a few – but NOT the AV1611. It is not considered to be a 'Catholic' Bible. This would suggest that RCs are not persuaded of the AV1611's *"Pro-Roman emphasis"* even if our critic is.

However, the lady in the CTS suggested that I contact the Cathedral Bookshop next to St. Paul's, Westminster. Upon doing so, I spoke to another dear lady, whom I think had a Spanish accent, who informed me that they DID sell BOTH the AV1611 AND the NIV! However, she had not heard of the Gallup survey either, so perhaps our critic should send them the results. It may help their marketing strategy.

Again our critic criticises the AV1611 for its *"**Elizabethan English**"* which *"**means less and less to people in the twentieth century.**"*

Whatever the AV1611 or any Bible may or may not mean *"to people in the twentieth century"* the facts of the matter do not appear to mean much to our critic. He has obviously not researched the language of the AV1611 very thoroughly. See Section 10.14.

Our critic's only other statement in this section which requires any discussion is that *"**Theologically there is nothing objectionable in the KJV to the RC position which is not also in the NIV.**"*

The key to this statement is the word *"Theologically"*. It puts the discussion in the realm of what the Bible TEACHES – or is presumed to teach – and separates it from the actual WORDS of the Bible. The statement is akin to the time-honoured excuse for replacing the AV1611 with *"**some new thing**"* Acts 17:21: "Any version is all right as long as it contains the fundamentals of the faith", Section 5.7.

I gave a list of verses in Section 5.2 where WORDS had been changed to support, or at least not to offend RC teaching. To this list could be added John 1:42, compare the AV1611 with the NIV and its footnote. The only attention which our critic gave to those verses was to ATTACK the AV1611 readings and to SUPPORT the RC readings. See the discussion in Section 12.5 on Colossians 1:14 and the discussion on Acts 8:37 to follow.

13.5 "THE EFFECT OF MODERN VERSIONS"

Our critic's comments here would be in response to the statement by Dr. Gipp, Section 5.5, the material found in Section 6.3 and Figure 4 *A Flood of Revisions.*

Our critic does not refute, discuss or even address ANY of the information in any of these sources. Instead, he asserts "***Your claim that our present national moral decline is the result of reading modern versions is a complete non sequitur.***" (A "*non sequitur*" is "*that which does not follow*" for those who do not understand Latin any better than Elizabethan English.)

I didn"t attribute ANY decline to "*reading modern versions*". The root cause of the decline is the REJECTION of "Imperial Text" of the AV1611. Figure 4 makes this clear. Our critic simply evaded the issue.

Moreover, although he is apparently CONVINCED about what is NOT the cause of "*our present national moral decline*", he is quite unable to state what IS the cause of this decline. I am surprised at this silence on our critic's part, given the vehemence of his opening statement.

He continues "***modern versions do not present a different God, a different Christ, a different salvation, or a different morality. To suggest otherwise is absolutely untrue.***"

Gail Riplinger does not "*suggest*" anything of the sort. She proves it. It is the main thesis of her book, which our critic should have read before passing judgement. See Section 13.1 for a small sample.

For another example, consider Isaiah 14:12a in the AV1611: "**How art thou fallen from heaven, O Lucifer, son of the morning!**" and in the NIV: "How you have fallen from heaven, O morning star, son of the dawn!"

Mrs Riplinger explains (12) p 42–43: "*Twentieth century versions have removed the name Lucifer, thereby eliminating the ONLY reference to him in the entire bible . . . The Hebrew is* "helel, ben shachar," *which is accurately translated,* "**Lucifer, son of the morning.**" *The NIV . . . give(s) an English translation AS IF the Hebrew said,* "*shachar kobab, ben shachar*" *or* "morning star, son of the morning (or dawn)". *Yet the word for star (*kobab*) appears nowhere in the text. Also* "morning" *appears only once, as the KJV shows, not twice as new versions indicate . . .*

"*The ultimate blasphemy occurs when the* "morning star" *takes* "Lucifer's" *place in Isaiah 14. Jesus Christ is the* "**morning star**" *and is identified as such in Revelation 22:16, 2:28 and 2 Peter 1:19. With this slight of hand switch, Satan not only slyly slips out of the picture but lives up to his name* "**the accuser**" *(Revelation 12:10) by attempting to make Jesus Christ the subject of the diatribe in Isaiah 14.*"

And the new versions do not present "*a different Christ*"?

"**Prove all things; hold fast that which is good. Abstain from all appearance of evil**" 1 Thessalonians 5:21,22.

Our critic then insists that "***The logic of your position is that only those*** *churches using the KJV are enjoying the blessing of God and making a real impact on the outside world. This is far from the case and some of those very churches are in fact in severe decline."*

The stark TRUTH of our critic's *"position"* is that he must resort to misrepresentation in order to maintain that *"position."* Leaving aside the fact that his statement consists of generalities only, I attach no importance whatsoever to simply *"using"* the AV1611. I have even heard our critic *"use"* the AV1611. What is vital is whether or not an individual or church BELIEVES the AV1611 and OBEYS it. See Section 10.15.

Our critic continues *"In this country very many of the finest churches, with the strongest Bible teaching, the godliest members, the fullest prayer meetings, the most faithful and fruitful ministries and the greatest impact for good, use and commend the NIV etc and have done so for a long time . . . To deny this is simply closing one's eyes to inconvenient facts."*

What facts? Apart from stating that he does not mean the Charismatic movement, our critic has not given me any facts. Again, his statement consists entirely of generalities and subjective ones at that. I am reminded of the words of the Apostle Paul in 2 Corinthians 10:12:

"For we dare not make ourselves of the number, or compare ourselves with some that commend themselves: but they measuring themselves by themselves, and comparing themselves among themselves, are not wise."

One *"fact"* that is painfully evident is that this contingent of *"the finest churches"* is unable to reverse the national decline, in spite of their recommendation of the NIV etc *"for a long time."*

In other words, they have had 20 to 25 years to accomplish what Wesley and Whitefield achieved in less than 15 – with the AV1611. I seriously doubt whether these *"finest churches"* have even arrested the decline. Rev. M.J. Roberts, editor of *The Banner of Truth* Magazine and minister of Greyfriars Free Church in Inverness, would seem to agree. I quote from his address in the TBS *Quarterly Record*, No. 529, October to December 1994:

"The Bible is a lost book in Britain today. It has little influence on national life any more . . . We have to admit that we are not seeing souls converted in great numbers. It does not matter where you go. Go to Wales, to Scotland, or to England here. Few are being converted in these days. Where are the days when the Bible was being blessed to the conversion of thousands and ten thousands? . . . The problem is here. This book is not being read so as to bring light to bear upon men's lives. Therefore

the tragedy is that men are not being converted to Christ. Could any curse in this life be greater? Could any judgment be more awful than this?"
  No.

14

Some "Disputed Texts"

14.1 1 JOHN 5:7

I now address the final section of our critic's document, where he seeks to justify the excision of several verses or words of scripture from the Holy Bible.

The first is 1 John 5:7, 8 **"in heaven, the Father, the Word, and the Holy Ghost: and these three are one. And there are three that bear witness in earth."** See Sections 1.2, 7.3 for a summary of the mss. evidence in support of these verses.

Our critic states *"These words are not quoted by any of the Greek Fathers and are absent from all early versions. The oldest citation of this verse is in a 4th Century Latin treatise called Liber apologeticus . . . It probably began as allegorical exegesis in a marginal gloss."*

Our critic gives no evidence to prove that ONLY Greek writers are to be taken as authentic witnesses. Christian writers who cited the words in question BEFORE the 4th Century are Tatian (A.D. 180), Tertullian (A.D. 200) and Cyprian (A.D. 225) (12) p 381, (42) p 7–8. Athanasius cited the words in A.D. 350. J.A. Moorman (41) indicates that Priscillian, who cited the verse in 385 A.D., is the author of *Liber apolgeticus*.

The early versions which cite the verse are the Old Syriac (170 A.D.) and the Old Latin (A.D. 200) (12) p 381, (42) p 8, despite our critic's opinion that *"This verse did not become established in the Old Latin until the fifth century."* Wilkinson (2) p 213, citing Nolan, says of the Old Italic Bible, which existed in A.D. 157 (2) p 208, that *"it has supplied him with the unequivocal testimony of a truly apostolical branch of the primitive church, that the celebrated text of the heavenly witnesses (1 John*

5:7) was adopted in the version which prevailed in the Latin Church, previously to the introduction of the modern Vulgate."

He then states *"It was not in Jerome's Vulgate despite the opinion of John Gill . . . this text was not in the Vulgate till the beginning of the 9th Century."* Our critic did not read Section 7.3 very carefully. I quoted from MacLean (40) p 25, with respect to GREEK copies in the possession of Robert Stephanus. MacLean cites Gill as saying *"As to its (1 John 5:7–8) being wanting in some Greek manuscripts . . . it need only be said that it is found in many others . . . out of sixteen ancient copies of Robert Stephens', nine of them had it."*

I made no reference to Gill's opinion of the text of the Vulgate, although Jerome cites the words in 450 A.D. *"in his epistle to Eustochium and wants to know why it was excluded from some texts"*, (40) p 25, (42) p 7.

Our critic continues *"the words are not an integral part of the Byzantine textual tradition."* This is of no consequence because the AV1611 translators were not obliged to adhere rigidly to *"the Byzantine textual tradition"* where that *"tradition"* was defective. Their text was ECLECTIC. See Section 9.8, (42) p 8 and they had with them six Waldensian Bibles, whose Text contained 1 John 5:7–8 and which dated from the 2nd Century (2) p 208, 212–213.

Our critic then states *"The verse is found in only four very late Greek MSS . . . probably all post date Erasmus' second edition. It is generally agreed that Erasmus reluctantly included the verse in his third edition under pressure from Rome. The Greek manuscript which was "found" for him was translated at the time from the Vulgate."*

I originally stated in Section 7.3 that the words are found in only two of the 500–600 extant Greek mss. of 1 John and in the margins of two others (17) p 334. I gave the mss., respectively, as Codex 61, Codex Ravianus, 88 and 629. Dr. Hills (5) p 209 and Dr. Ruckman in a later work (42) indicate that the disputed words of 1 John 5:7, 8 are actually in the text of Codex 629.

Concerning Erasmus' inclusion of 1 John 5:7–8 in his 3rd Edition of the TR, Dr. Hills (5) p 209, explains that it was NOT *"pressure from Rome"* that influenced him but Erasmus' promise *"to restore (1 John 5:7–8) if but one Greek manuscript could be found which contained it . . . Many critics believe that (Codex 61) was written at Oxford for the special purpose of refuting Erasmus, and this is what Erasmus himself suggested in his notes."*

This is clearly our critic's belief. He also assumes that Ms. 61 came from the Vulgate. However, Dr. Ruckman (42) p 6–7, has a more searching analysis:

"*How about that Manuscript 61 at Dublin?*

"*Well, according to Professor Michaelis (cited in Prof. Armin Panning's "New Testament Criticism"), Manuscript 61 has four chapters in Mark that possess three coincidences with Old Syriac, two of which also agree with the Old Itala: ALL READINGS DIFFER FROM EVERY GREEK MANUSCRIPT EXTANT IN ANY FAMILY. The Old Itala was written long before 200 A.D., and the Old Syriac dates from before 170 (Tatian's Diatesseron).*

"*Manuscript 61 was supposed to have been written between 1519 and 1522; the question becomes us, "FROM WHAT?" Not from Ximenes's Polyglot – his wasn't out yet. Not from Erasmus, for it doesn't match his "Greek" in many places. The literal affinities of Manuscript 61 are with the SYRIAC (Acts 11:26), and that version WAS NOT KNOWN IN EUROPE UNTIL 1552 (Moses Mardin).*"

Our critic adds "***Luther did not include the verse in his translation of the Bible.***" This is a half truth. Beale (47) p 65 states "*The passage of the three witnesses (1 John 5:7b-8a) did not appear in Luther's Bible until 1574–1575, when a Frankfort publisher inserted it for the first time . . . The passage does not appear in a Wittenberg edition until 1596.*"

However, since then, 1 John 5:7–8 has remained in Luther's Bible (7) p 34. Moreover, Tyndale DID include 1 John 5:7–8 in his New Testament.

Our critic remarks that "***some defenders of the KJV are prepared to agree now that it did not form part of the original text,***" which shows that even Bible believers can give way to apostasy. Our critic observes that J.N. Darby omitted the verse from his New Testament, which I knew anyway (7) p 53. I would add that Darby's New Testament, like Wesley's, the RV, RSV etc. has long since joined the ranks of versions now obsolete or nearly obsolete. In any event, Darby's New Testament had little influence outside of the exclusive Brethren.

Our critic lied again in his concluding statements on 1 John 5:7–8:

"***To imply that the doctrine of the Trinity depends on this verse and that to question it is to deny that doctrine, is absolutely unacceptable.***"

Our critic is here springing to the defence of Origen, who "*would correct the word of God (in the originals or otherwise) as quickly as (he) would take a breath of air*" (16) p 82.

I did not imply ANYWHERE that the doctrine of the Trinity DEPENDS on this verse, to the extent that the doctrine cannot be proved without it, although I would never seek to do so.

However, 1 John 5:7–8 is undoubtedly the strongest verse in the Bible on the Trinity. There is no doubt that Origen rejected the doctrine of the Trinity and his infidelity to this doctrine very likely prompted him to attack the verse. See Section 1.2.

The TBS *Quarterly Record*, Jan.-Mar. 1993, No. 522, p 9, cites R.L. Dabney as follows:

"There are strong probable grounds to conclude, that the text of Scriptures current in the East received a mischievous modification at the hands of the famous Origen. Those who are best acquainted with the history of Christian opinion know best, that Origen was the great corrupter, and the source, or at least earliest channel, of nearly all the speculative errors which plagued the church in after ages . . . He disbelieved the full inspiration and infallibility of the Scriptures, holding that the inspired men apprehended and stated many things obscurely . . . He expressly denied the con substantial unity of the Persons and the proper incarnation of the Godhead – the very propositions most clearly asserted in the doctrinal various readings we have under review.

"The weight of probability is greatly in favour of this theory, viz., THAT THE ANTI-TRINITARIANS, FINDING CERTAIN CODICES IN WHICH THESE DOCTRINAL READINGS HAD BEEN ALREADY LOST THROUGH THE LICENTIOUS CRITICISM OF ORIGEN AND HIS SCHOOL, INDUSTRIOUSLY DIFFUSED THEM, WHILE THEY ALSO DID WHAT THEY DARED TO ADD TO THE OMISSIONS OF SIMILAR READINGS."

Given our critic's offer to teach me Greek, it is instructive to quote from the TBS *Notes on the Vindication of 1 John 5:7*. See also Riplinger (12) p 382 and Ruckman (42) p 5–6.

"The internal evidence against the omission is as follows:

"The masculine article, numeral and participle HOI TREIS MARTUROUNTES, *are made to agree directly with three neuters, an insuperable and very bald grammatical difficulty. If the disputed words are allowed to remain, they agree with two masculines and one neuter noun* HO PATER, HO LOGOS, KAI TO HAGION PNEUMA *and, according to the rule of syntax, the masculines among the group control the gender over a neuter connected with them. Then the occurrence of the masculines* TREIS MARTUROUNTES *in verse 8 agreeing with the neuters* PNEUMA, HUDOR, *and* HAIMA *may be accounted for by the power of attraction, well known in Greek syntax."* This is probably sufficient. How did our critic miss it?

When one reviews ALL the evidence, it is noteworthy that 1 John

5:7–8 satisfies at least 5, if not 6 of Burgon's 7 tests of truth, Section 6.2, (3) p 264ff. Only *"number of witnesses"* and in consequence some *"respectability of witnesses"* is lacking, through omission.

Finally, in view of our critic's high regard for the Westminster Confession, Sections 11.1, 11.3, I quote from the TBS article, No. 522, again, citing:

"These supporters believe the passage rightly belongs in the Scriptures, as does the Society, as did the writers of the Westminster Confession of Faith (3) . . .

"Note 3. Westminster Confession of Faith, Chapter II. iii. In the Scripture proofs for the statement of the Trinity, "God the Father, God the Son, and God the Holy Ghost", 1 John 5:7 is quoted." More *"evidence inconvenient"*, which our critic ignored.

14.2 1 TIMOTHY 3:16

Our critic's next attack is on the verse used by the Westminster Divines in support of the Deity of Christ, 1 Timothy 3:16, which reads "**God was manifest in the flesh.**" See Section 13.1.

Our critic states *"**The manuscript evidence is decidedly in favour of "He". "God" has no support at all in the early manuscripts nor the versions. It does not appear in the quotations of any of the Fathers before the late 4th Century. No uncial (in the first hand) supports it before the 8th Century. By contrast 'He' is in the earliest extant codices (except Vaticanus which does not include the Pastorals) the quotations of the Ante Nicene Fathers, and various versions in other languages.**"*

Taking his first assertion, none of the manuscript evidence is in favour of "He". ALL the manuscript evidence is in favour of either "God" or "Who" or "Which". I described in Section 6.2 how "THEOS" or "*God*", which is found in the majority of manuscripts and is written "THS", can easily be changed into "OS", "Who", or "O", "Which".

Pickering (3) p 260 summarises Burgon's findings on 1 Timothy 3:16 as follows:

"Burgon found that 300 Greek MSS (uncial, minuscule, lectionary) read the word "God" in 1 Timothy 3:16 and only seven did not."

Our critic has ignored all of this evidence. The ONLY early witness which could be in favour of "Who" is Aleph (5) p 137. The bad character of this manuscript has been discussed in detail. See Chapter 1, Section 1.6 and Chapter 9.

The TBS Publication No. 10 *God Was Manifest in the Flesh* states that *"(Aleph) was characterised by numerous alterations and omissions."*

Dr. Hills states further that *"The Traditional Text reads* "God was manifest in the flesh", *with A (according to Scrivener), C (according to the* "almost supernaturally accurate" *Hoskier) . . . the Western text (represented by D2 and the Latin versions) reads* "which was manifest in the flesh.""*

Burgon (13) p 479 identifies D2 as *"the VIth-century codex Claromontanus D", the ONLY Greek manuscript containing* "which.""* Yet Gail Riplinger (12) p 352 states *"The uncials, Aleph and especially A and C, have been altered here so that EITHER* "God" *or* "who" *can be deduced."*

This is hardly evidence *"decidedly in favour of* "He"."* Moreover, Gail Riplinger states (12) p 353 *"Those few copies that have* "who" *in place of* "God" *do not have a complete sentence. There is no subject without* "God". *In addition, a neuter noun* "mystery" *cannot be followed by the masculine pronoun* "who." *To avoid having a clause with no subject, the NIV and JW bible arbitrarily drop the word* "who" *and invent a new word,* "He" *. . . By making these additions and subtractions, the new versions, in 1 Timothy 3:16, follow no Greek manuscripts at all, not even the five late uncials."* She states that these five mss. are of the 9th, 12th and 13th centuries.

Dr. Hills states (5) p 138 *"But if the Greek is* "who", *how can the English be* "He"? *This is not translation but the creation of an entirely new reading."*

Concerning the versions, Burgon (13) p 426, 448 shows that the Old Latin does NOT bear witness to "He" but rather to "O", "which" and that *"From a copy so depraved, the Latin Version was altered in the second century."* See Hills, above. The TBS Publication No. 10, p 8, states *"While the Syriac* "Peshitto" *version has been justly described as* "the oldest and one of the most excellent of the versions . . . It was evidently influenced by Greek manuscripts like Codex D and the Latin versions, which have* "which was manifested" *. . . It is probable that the earliest Syriac copies had* "God was manifested.""*

"One of the Syriac versions which was remarkable for its literal adherence to the Greek was attributed to Philoxenus Bishop of Hierapolis in Eastern Syria, A.D. 488–518. This version actually includes the name of God in 1 Timothy 3:16 and indicates that Philoxenus found "God" *in the Greek or Syriac copies in his hands."*

As for the quotations by the fathers, Burgon (13) p 479 found only

Gelasius (A.D. 476) and *"an unknown author of . . . uncertain date"* citing "which" and NOT ONE citing "who." By contrast, the fathers citing "God" are numerous. They include Gregory of Nyssa (d. A.D. 394, TBS No. 10), who *"in at least 22 places, knew of no other reading but "Theos""* (13) p 45. Patristic citations before 400 A.D. include (13) p 486ff:

Barnabus and Ignatius	A.D. 90
Hippolytus	A.D. 190
Dionysius of Alexandria	circa A.D. 264
Gregory Thaumaturgus and Apostolic Constitutions	also 3rd Century
Didymus	circa A.D. 330, "clearly witnesses to what was the reading of the first quarter of the IVth century."
Gregory of Nazianzus	A.D. 355
Diodorus	A.D. 370

Burgon allows that the testimonies before 300 A.D., apart from Dionysius, are *"open to cavil"* because *"the very early Fathers are ever observed to quote Scripture thus partially."* However, they do NOT bear witness to "he", "who" or "which".

Our critic states that *"the earliest uncials . . . call Christ "God" elsewhere in the New Testament"* but he does not SAY where! In any case, this is beside the point. The point is the WORDING of 1 Timothy 3:16, **"God was manifest in the flesh"** which our critic evaded.

Again, reviewing ALL the evidence, it is significant that 1 Timothy 3:16 certainly meets 6 if not all of Burgon's tests of truth. It may be that some *"respectability of witnesses"* is lacking in the aberrant readings of some ancient versions but other *"respectable"* witnesses are numerous.

Our critic's parting shot on this reading is that *"**the idea that questioning the authenticity of one late highly doubtful reading, means denying the truth that Christ is God manifest in the flesh, is quite indefensible. This truth is taught repeatedly in the N.T. especially in Johannine and Pauline theology.**"*

In reply, it can be said unequivocally that the reading is NOT *"late."* Nor is it *"highly doubtful"*, although our critic's *"evidence"* certainly IS. Once again, the point at issue is NOT what the Bible TEACHES but what the BIBLE SAYS.

Unless there is certainty about what the Bible SAYS, there can no certainty about what it TEACHES, although fundamentalists who worship their egos and their education may find this hard to accept. Reference to "*theology*" is merely more evasion. One wonders what the Westminster Divines would have made of our critic's evaluation of 1 Timothy 3:16.

"**All the words that I command thee . . . speak unto them; diminish not a word**" Jeremiah 26:2.

14.3 ACTS 8:37

Our critic's next attack on the Holy Bible is against Acts 8:37, Section 7.3. He states that "*Uncial E of the 8ᵗʰ Century is the earliest known Greek MS to include this passage. It is basically a Western addition and is omitted from P45 (early 3ʳᵈ Century) and the earliest uncials. The grammatical construction of the Ethiopian's confession is quite un-Lukan. There is no reason at all why scribes should have omitted this material if it had stood originally in the text. It possibly began as a marginal gloss.*"

Note that our critic gives no evidence for Acts 8:37 being "*a Western addition*" or originating "*as a marginal gloss*". Neither does he explain why, if the reading was false, the NIV etc. retain the verse numbering sequence of the AV1611. He continues: "*Prominent among those early Fathers who quote the verse are those whom you describe as the "Founding Fathers of the Roman Church" . . . The verse is not in the Alexandrian family or even the Byzantine! It found its way into the received text and hence into the KJV via Erasmus who . . . took the words from the margin of another manuscript.*"

In answer I shall quote first from Dr. Hills (5) p 201 "*As J.A. Alexander (1857) suggested, this verse, though genuine, was omitted by many scribes, "as unfriendly to the practice of delaying baptism, which had become common, if not prevalent, before the end of the 3ʳᵈ century."*"

Dr. Hills has advanced a good reason "*why scribes should have omitted this material*", if they were not Bible believers. Our critic has overlooked this. Dr. Hills continues:

"*Hence the verse is absent from the majority of the Greek manuscripts. But it is present in some of them, including E (6ᵗʰ or 7ᵗʰ century). It is cited by Irenaeus (c. 180) and Cyprian (c. 250) and is found in the Old Latin and the Vulgate. In his notes Erasmus says that he took this reading from the margin of 4ap and incorporated it into the Textus Receptus.*" Dr. Ruckman (1) p 316, places E in the 8th century but in the 6th to 7th century in an earlier work (17) p 331.

Our critic therefore adds little or nothing to the information which I summarised in Section 7.3. The difference is that Dr. Hills acknowledges the graciousness of *"divine providence"* in supplying ALL of the New Testament from several sources, Section 9.6. By contrast, our critic seems ready to reject such providence if it did not see fit to locate a reading in the text with, in his opinion, *"better credentials"*. See Section 9.3.

As for the lack of the verse in particular *"families"*, although this classification is often used for convenience (5) p 120, it is nevertheless a HOAX, Section 9.4.

In reference to the *"un-Lukan"* grammar of the Ethiopian's confession, why wouldn"t it be *"un-Lukan"*, if indeed it is? The man speaking was an AFRICAN. The man writing the Book of Acts was a JEW! See Romans 3:1–2. Even though our critic is referring specifically to grammar, I am reminded of Dr. Hill's statement (5) p 158, *"Arguments from literary style are notoriously weak"*. I continue with Dr. Ruckman (1) p 236–237:

"Those who first threw (Acts 8:37) out were P45 and P74, followed by the Cult (Sinaiticus, Vaticanus, "C", the Sahidic, and the Bohairic; and then the Harclean and Peshitta Syriac, after Origen messed with them). It is also missing from cursives 049, 056, 0142, 436, 326, 1241, 1505, 2127, 181, 81, 88 and several others.

"To offset this vast array of African scholarship produced by half-baked apostates, we have the verse, in whole or in part, in the works of Irenaeus (190 A.D.), Tertullian (200 A.D.), Cyprian (255 A.D.), Pacian (370 A.D.), Ambrose, uncial manuscript E, Old Latin manuscripts, Old Syriac manuscripts, plus the Armenian and Georgian translations. It is also found in cursive 629 . . . (from) the dates of the Church Fathers listed above, we find the verse being quoted 100 to 200 YEARS BEFORE SINAITICUS OR VATICANUS WERE WRITTEN.

"So, we quote it 100 years AFTER the REVISED VERSION of Hort fell to pieces with the British Empire. (Why give up a good thing just because a destructive critic doesn"t like it?)"

Why indeed? Dr. Ruckman (17) p 331 states that Acts 8:37 *"has an unbroken chain of testimony from the Old Latin (second century) . . . to the present time."* Reviewing the evidence therefore, one finds that Acts 8:37, like 1 John 5:7–8, fulfils at least 5 of Burgon's 7 tests.

Cursive 629 also has 1 John 5:7–8 in its margin, see above, no doubt also by God's gracious provision. Our critic again resorts to misrepresentation in attacking this verse. He states *"**Once again it has to be said that the idea that challenging the authenticity of this verse is to question the importance of personal salvation is utterly ludicrous.**"*

I put forth no such *"idea"* at all in Section 7.3 What I said was *"Note that Luke 23:42, John 9:35, Acts 8:37 and 9:5, 6 are all passages which deal with INDIVIDUAL SALVATION*". FIVE verses were cited, not ONE. (I could have added a sixth, Acts 16:31, where "**Christ**" is omitted by the DR, RV, NIV, JB, NWT, Ne thanks as usual to L, T, Tr, A, Section 11.4). If our critic had read my statement carefully and LOOKED AT THE VERSES, he would have seen that they deal with THE SALVATION OF INDIVIDUAL SOULS, two of whom were saved by the LORD JESUS CHRIST HIMSELF!

I was not referring to the "*subject*" of "*personal salvation*" in the abstract – of which our critic does not cite even ONE of the "*hundreds of statements*" in the New Testament that he insists deal with it, according to this section of his document. The critics obviously mutilated verses which gave specific examples of SOUL-WINNING. Whatever their "*motives*" in so doing – and these may have been as sincere as Eve's, Genesis 3:6! – their ACTIONS and the RESULTS of those actions are ABOMINABLE!

Our critic then states "*Incidentally some of the manuscripts which have Acts 8:37 also have in v. 39* "**the Spirit of the Lord fell upon the eunuch**" and poses the question "*Why is this not in the KJV?*"

There are at least three good reasons.

1. The AV1611 translators, being much more scholarly than the modern translators and endowed with much greater spiritual wisdom, Luke 21:15, were able to discern between the authentic reading and the false one. Lacking this discernment, the modern translators rejected BOTH readings.
2. The spurious reading in Acts 8:39 no doubt lacks number, respectability, continuity and variety of witnesses. It may also lack antiquity and the context, as defined by Burgon (3) p 264 ff, may be suspect.
3. There are two references in the Book of Acts to the Holy Ghost falling upon individuals, 10:44 and 11:15. They deal with incidents in Acts 2:3, 4 and 10:44. In each case there were Jews present and the gift of TONGUES was manifested, magnifying God as a SIGN to these Jews, 1 Corinthians 1:22, Acts 2:5–11, 10:45–46, 11:17–18. In Acts 8:39 NEITHER condition applies and therefore internal considerations mitigate against the reading.

The reading therefore fails 5 TO 7 of Burgon's tests and is therefore rightly rejected.

Our critic concludes this section by stating his disapproval at my having described Irenaeus, Cyprian and Augustine as "*the "founding fathers" of the RC church*" Section 1.2

"**Such a judgment,**" he says "**represents far too simplistic a view of church history and it also ignores the debt which all serious theologians of all schools acknowledge the early Fathers.**"

Our critic naturally ignored the reference that accompanied my allusion to these "*founding fathers*". I will therefore quote it in full.

Dr. Ruckman states (4) p 76 "*The Roman Group (Western Fathers) is going to be a group of Catholics who worship traditions and look to an authoritative Hierarchy instead of an authoritative Bible. Irenaeus (130–202) is there, with his baby sprinkling to ensure that members of the family won't leave the church. Cyprian (200–258) is present to make the Bishop into a god and Augustine (354–430) is there to teach that the sacraments are the "means of salvation."*

"*The Western group is going to approach the Bible exactly as the College of Cardinals approaches it today, and any man in the group (with the exception of Tertullian (160–220) could walk into St. Peter's and get a "blessing" from the service.*"

The references from which Dr. Ruckman gleaned this material (4) p 203, include *History of the Christian Church* Philip Schaff, Eerdmans, 1910, *A Source Book for Ancient Church History* Joseph Ayer, Charles Scribner and Sons, N.Y., 1952, *A History of the Christian Church* Williston Walker, Scribners N.Y., 1918 and the well-known work *Nicene and Post-Nicene Fathers* Volume 1, Eerdmans, Grand Rapids Michigan 1952 Reprint.

Elsewhere (16) p 62, 63 Dr. Ruckman states: "*It was Cyprian . . . (contemporary of Origen), who stated that the church was built on Peter, that Peter was in Rome, and that the Roman church was not Satan's seat but "THE CHAIR OF PETER." In the carnal mind of Cyprian's unregenerate nature, the Roman church was the "fountain of unity and the MOTHER of the Catholic Church.*"

"*The seeds of the papacy are found in the writings of Cyprian and . . . The germs of the papacy can also be found in the writings of Irenaeus . . . who calls Rome the "greatest" and oldest church "acknowledged by ALL" and founded by Paul and Peter. What is Irenaeus' SCRIPTURAL AUTHORITY for saying that Peter helped found the Roman church? Quite naturally it was none: Peter in Rome is the figment of someone's conceited imagination.*"

And on p 93 "*Philip Schaff says that Origen was responsible for the acceptance of infant baptism. G.H. Orchard (*A Concise History of the

Baptists *Lexington, Kent. 1956) says that the first indication of infant baptism as a "Catholic" belief (to prove Catholic faith in line with "Holy Mother Church") was stated by Aurelius Augustine . . . an African, who thought, as Origen (an African), that the Septuagint with the Apocrypha was inspired."*

And on p 95, 104–105 *"It is apparent that the body of oral traditions, which eventually leavened and corrupted the Christian church and transformed it into the Papal church, came from the "church fathers," of whom Augustine was one . . . He also caused the murder of several hundred Christians during his lifetime and was directly responsible for the death of several hundred thousand after his own death. He also shut up the kingdom against men and prevented them from finding Christ by teaching them that the new birth was water sprinkling in the Roman catholic church. In short, he was a Bible-perverting liar."*

And our critic would have me believe that a *"debt"* is owed to a *"Bible-perverting liar"* and others like him?

Our critic speaks in this section of the *"**pressures**"* that the early fathers were under, in order to excuse their *"**unbalanced statements**"* and *"**incorrect theological judgments**"* – which Dr. Ruckman has shown to have been Bible-perverting LIES. See above.

Then our critic poses the question *"**But in any case who has yet written the perfect theological text book?**"*

I can answer that question very simply. God the Holy Spirit. His "text book" is the Holy Bible, AV1611. I have a copy on my desk as I write.

Our critic maintains that I am *"**quite mistaken**"* to call Origen *"**a gnostic**"* because *"**it has been correctly said of him by a reliable church historian** "He battled against the gnostics . . . **His principal work De Principiis is the first example of a positive and well rounded system of theology.**"*

R.L. Dabney, Section14.1, showed that Origen also battled against THE BIBLE and against BIBLE BELIEF. Moreover, however *"positive and well rounded"* Origen's theology may have been, it was steeped in HERESY. See Section 1.2.

Dr. Ruckman (16) p 81–82 continues: *""Gnosticism" . . . simply means "smart aleck." A Gnostic was a "knower" . . . these super elect were always characterised by advanced knowledge and higher light of a "higher nature than you poor common peons, etc.," . . . The all-star "team" for Alexandria, chronologically speaking, would look like this: Plato (427–347 B.C.), Philo (20 B.C.-50 A.D.), Pantaenus (145–200 A.D.), Clement (150–215 A.D.), and finally Origen (184–254 A.D.). These are the founding fathers of the Alexandrian Cult ... founded and sustained by Gnostic Greek philosophers, (it) comes to invade every branch of science, philosophy, religion and education in the western world for twenty centuries, and its members range from out-and-out Atheists and Communists ... through dead orthodox theologians (Barth, Brunner, Berkhof ... Machen, Warfield, Lightfoot, etc.) ... "*

Gail Riplinger (12) p 526 states " "The History of Heresy" *calls Origen a 'Christian Gnostic' who was pronounced a 'heretic' by a series of general synods.*

"The philosophical school, based in Alexandria, had seen as its head Pantaenus, a pagan gnostic, followed by Clement, who was succeeded by Origen ... Philip Lee, author of "Against the Protestant Gnostics" *and graduate of Princeton and Harvard Divinity Schools observes: " "The Alexandrian school was indeed one of the historical moments in the church's closest proximity to gnostic heresy ... (For) Clement and Origen ... gnosis (hidden wisdom), far from being a forbidden word, was a basic tenet of their system ... (T)he word gnosis is the key to Clement's work." "*

And also, it would seem, to Origen's false teaching and BIBLE PERVERSION.

Bernard Ramm, in *Protestant Biblical Interpretation* Baker Book House 1970, states p 32–33

"Origen is in the Aristobulus-Philo-Pantaenus-Clement tradition ... He wanted to escape the crudities of the lay people who were literalists to the point of taking everything symbolic or metaphorical or poetic literally ... "The Bible is one vast allegory, a tremendous sacrament in which every detail is symbolic," writes Danielou of Origen's fundamental thesis. The Bible is a spiritual book, and its meaning is found only by spiritualizing it."

The *"meaning"* of the Bible is found by BELIEVING it and OBEYING it, Psalm 119:66, 99, 100. Ramm certainly does not believe that the AV1611 is the FINAL AUTHORITY. However, his evaluation of Origen as a *"Christian"* gnostic closely matches that of Riplinger and Ruckman, 2 Corinthians 13:1, even if expressed in milder language.

14.4 JOHN 1:18

Our critic's next attack on the Holy Bible is against John 1:18, where he objects to the expression "**only begotten Son**" on the grounds that:

"Both external evidence (Most reliable manuscripts and the earliest fathers) and internal evidence (A later scribe has clearly harmonised

*with other passages in John which read "only" or "only begotten" Son
. . .) plainly indicate that John originally wrote "God" not "Son."*

*"This is another example where the KJV (here using a defective
manuscript and not at this point being guilty of incorrect translation as
in 2 Peter and Titus) fails to affirm that Jesus is God."*

The supposed *"incorrect translations"* in 2 Peter and Titus have been
discussed in Section 13.2. I alluded briefly there to the evidence for John
1:18, which included the vast majority of mss.and the earliest extant
record. See also Section 7.3, which our critic ignored.

Our critic does not state what the *"most reliable manuscripts"* are nor
which *"defective manuscript"* the AV1611 translators used. I will now
make up for these deficiencies, first from Dr. Hills (5) p 133–134: *"The
Only Begotten Son Versus Only Begotten God"*

"John 1:18 . . . This verse exhibits the following four-fold variation:

(1) "the only begotten Son," Traditional Text, Latin versions, Curetonian
Syriac.
(2) "only begotten God," Pap 66, Aleph, B, C, L, W-H
(3) "the only begotten God" Pap 75
(4) "(the) only begotten," read by one Latin manuscript."

Dr. Ruckman (17) p 331 states that "The" has been added to the Aleph
reading by its FOURTH corrector.

It has been shown how the few places in the Traditional Text which
are defective have been rectified from other sources. See Sections 9.6,
14.1, 14.3.

However, Dr. Hills shows that the *"most reliable manuscripts"*,
according to our critic are, in fact, P66, P75, Aleph, B, C, L although he
has said, Section 12.6, that *"Modern editions of the NT are not
dominated by Vaticanus and Sinaiticus"* which were *"overestimated by
Westcott"* and that to imagine otherwise *"is quite fallacious."*
Nevertheless, our critic has revealed here that Aleph and B are still
AMONG the most dominant mss.. They are, of course, prominent
amongst the sources used to corrupt the New Testament Text. See
Sections 9.8, 12.6. Their depraved character, which our critic has NOT
refuted, in spite of his assertions about *"quality"* and *"reliability"* was
covered in Sections 1.6, 9.3, 9.5, 9.8.

The corrupt nature of P66 and P75 has also been discussed and it has been
shown that they agree with the TR as much as, if not more than with the
Alexandrian text, Section 9.5.

What of the other sources, which are with Aleph and B, the "*Most reliable manuscripts*"?

Of C, Codex Ephraemi, Dr. Ruckman (1) p 315, (17) p 408 describes it as a "*palimpsest*" "*which simply means a worked-over work that has been partly erased, with another text written over it . . . written in the fifth-century A.D . . .*

"*It is very incomplete, containing now only sixty-four Old Testament leaves and 145 New Testament leaves . . . All New Testament books are present except for 2 Thessalonians and 2 John . . . (but) it omits Genesis, Exodus, Leviticus, Numbers, Deuteronomy, Joshua, Judges, 1 and 2 Samuel, 1 and 2 Kings and all of the major and minor prophets.*"

Burgon says of this ms. (13) p 325 "*Codex C, after having had 'at least three correctors very busily at work upon it' (in the VIth and IXth centuries), finally (in the XIIth) was fairly obliterated, – literally scraped out, – to make room for the writings of a Syrian Father.*"

Hoskier further demonstrated the unreliability of C, together with P47, Aleph and A (3) p 290, in his "*complete collation of the book of Revelation*". Hoskier identified "*two large groups of MSS which exhibit a high degree of stability within themselves, but between which the cleavage is remarkably sharp . . . P47, Aleph, A, C – "vacillate surprisingly from side to side.*"" This result indicates that the Alexandrian mss. are themselves "*an eclectic text.*"

Burgon also noted the tendency of C to disagree with Aleph and B, Section 9.3. He discusses in detail (13) p 11–17 the variations, describing C as "*fragmentary*" and concludes "*It is discovered that in the 111 (out of 320) pages of an ordinary copy of the Greek Testament, in which alone these five manuscripts are collectively available for comparison in the Gospels . . . The readings peculiar to A . . . are 133: those peculiar to C are 170. But those of B amount to 197: while Aleph exhibits 443: and the readings peculiar to D . . . are no fewer than 1829 . . . We submit that these facts . . . are by no means calculated to inspire confidence in codices B, Aleph, C, D.*"

Of Codex L, Burgon (18) p 81–82 states "*Of the eighth or ninth century . . . It is chiefly remarkable for the correspondence of its readings with those of Codex B and with certain of the citations in Origen . . . a peculiarity which recommends Codex L . . . to the special favour of a school with which whatever is found in Codex B is necessarily right.*"

Burgon continues: "*(Codex L) is described as the work of an ignorant foreign copyist . . . who is found to have been wholly incompetent to determine which reading to adopt and which to reject . . . evidently incapable of distinguishing the grossest fabrication from the genuine text.*"

Certain it is that he interrupts himself, at the end of (Mark 16:8) to write as follows:

'*Something to this effect is also met with:* "All that was commanded them they immediately rehearsed unto Peter and the rest. And after things, from East even unto West, did Jesus Himself send forth by their means the holy and incorruptible message of eternal Salvation." "*But this also is met with after the words,* 'For they were afraid': "Now, when He was risen early, the first day of the week," *etc.*""

Burgon therefore describes L, with this interruption, as exhibiting "*an exceedingly vicious text.*"

Yet if L is one of the "*most reliable MSS*" and the field of textual criticism is "*not dominated by Vaticanus and Sinaiticus*" Section 12.6 of this work, why is not the above reading from L in the NIV?

Having identified our critic's "*most reliable MSS*", I return to the variant readings, listed by Dr. Hills. Gail Riplinger states (12) p 338–339:

"*Arius (260–336), a student of Origen's, crusaded for Jesus as* "the begotten God," *only to be met by campaigning Christians like Athanasius (296–373), Hilary (315–367), and Ambrose (339–397) armed with* "the only begotten Son" *in their canon's mouth.*" Dr. Ruckman (4) p 119 mentions Chrysostom (347–407) as also opposing Arius' teachings. Gail Riplinger continues:

"*The further swell of Arianism by A.D. 330 prompted Constantine to replace semi-Arian Eusebius of Caesarea with Arian Eusebius of Nicodemia . . . It is in this climate that Constantine requested the production of manuscripts B and Aleph. Their use of* "only begotten God" *in John 1:18 was no doubt a political expedient.*

"*The term* "the only begotten Son" *is seen in the vast majority of MSS and is witnessed to by the earliest extant record of John 1:18, Tertullian in A.D. 150. Even Allen Wikgren of the UBS Greek New Testament committee admits:*

"*"It is doubtful that the author would have written* "begotten God" *which may be a primitive, transcriptual error in the Alexandrian tradition.*""

Note that our critic neglected to list Tertullian amongst his "*earliest Fathers*", none of whom he actually identified. Gail Riplinger strips away the veil of anonymity.

"*The critical apparatus of the UBS Greek New Testament cites P66, P75, Aleph, B ,C, and L, as well as Valentinus (who changed* "begotten Son" *to* "begotten God"*), Theodotus, Clement, Origen and Arius, as support for their use of* "begotten God," *in spite of the doctrinal bias of* *these witnesses."*

She cites Westcott from his "*superb*", Section 12.6, commentary *The Gospel According to St. John* p 159 as follows:

"*"It is impossible to suppose that two beings distinct in essence could be equal in power. We find ourselves met by difficulty which belongs to the idea of begetting . . . If we keep both (Arianism and Sabellianism) before us we may hope to attain . . . to that knowledge of the truth.""* Dr. Hills (5) p 34 explains "*The teaching of Sabellius (220 A.D.) (was) that the Father, the Son, and the Holy Spirit are merely three ways in which God has revealed Himself . . . these false doctrines culminated in the greatest heresy of all, namely, the contention of Arius (318 A.D.) that before the foundation of the world God the Father had created the Son out of nothing."*

It now becomes apparent why our critic then states "***Much scholarly discussion has centred around whether monogenes means* "only begotten" *or* "only" . . . *I am inclined to believe that the better translation is* "only", *this indicating Christ's uniqueness.*"

Having insisted, along with Valentinus, Origen, Arius etc. that John 1:18 should read "God" instead of "**Son**," our critic CANNOT agree with "**begotten.**" The reason is clear. As Dr. Ruckman states (4) p 119 "*The teaching that Jesus Christ is a "god," begotten in Eternity (or sometime before Genesis 1:1) is the official theology of the Jehovah's Witnesses.*"

It is also Edwin Palmer's theology, "*From all eternity the Father begat the Son*" (12) p 339. The reason why Palmer's NIV (Hodder & Stoughton 1979) omits "begotten" from John 1:18 and reads "No-one has ever seen God, but God the only (Son)" is discussed in Section 13.2. However, there is some confusion in the ranks of NIV editors because the Gideon edition, 1983, REINSERTS "begotten" and reads "No-one has ever seen God, but the only begotten (Son)." The Gideon edition re-inserted "begotten" in John 1:14, 1:18, 3:16, 3:18; Acts 13:33; Hebrews 1:5, 5:5 and 1 John 4:19 exactly where the AV1611 has it and from where the H&S NIV removed it.

However, bracketing of the word "Son" in both editions of the NIV mean that the editors regard the word as UNCERTAIN, p viii Preface. Neither NIV, therefore, is absolutely clear that Jesus Christ is even referred to in John 1:18.

Earlier in his document, our critic asked "***which of all these various revisions is the real KJV?***", Section 11.2. One could now reasonably pose a similar question (58) p 18 *"Which version of the New International Version is the true version of the New International Version?"*

To return to "monogenes," the TBS Article No. 58 *The Only Begotten Son* cites *"Professor Cremer's great Lexicon of N.T. Greek . . . " as giving* "monogenes – "only-begotten."". Gail Riplinger (12) p 342 states *"The Greek word preceding "Son" . . . is always* "monogenes," *a two part word in which* "mono" *means* 'only' *or* 'one' *and* "genes" *means* 'begotten', 'born', 'come forth'. *Buschel, in his definitive treatise on the meaning of the word* 'monogenes' *said, "It means only-begotten." All inter-linear Greek-English New Testaments translate it as such."*

Nestle is no exception and even Vine – no friend of the AV1611 – gives "only begotten" as the meaning of "monogenes", adding that it *"has the meaning "only" of human offspring, in Luke 7:12; 8:42; 9:38."*

Vine has a more honest assessment of the three verses in Luke than our critic, who cites them to justify rendering "monogenes" as "only" IMMEDIATELY after referring to CHRIST's uniqueness – see above.

The *"uniqueness"* of the Lord Jesus Christ was that He did NOT have a human father! The three individuals in Luke DID! D.A. Carson also uses the verses in Luke to obscure the meaning of "monogenes" (48) p 36. Obviously it is not necessary to translate "genes" in these verses – nor would it be good style. (Isaac, Hebrews 11:17, is an exception because *"he was a type of Jesus Christ (see Gal. 3:16), the only son begotten by promise and command (Gen. 17:21, Gal. 4:28)"* (48) p 37.)

Our critic then claims that the distinction between "only" and "**only begotten**" was not drawn *"until Jerome's Vulgate"* which allegedly influenced *"the KJV."* See Section 11.1. The TBS Article No. 58 flatly refutes this: *"The Old Latin translation was made not later than the 2nd. century, and it is significant that the translators who were in a position to know how the word* MONOGENES *was understood by contemporary Greek Christians, rendered it* UNIGENTIUS – "only-begotten," *not* UNICUS – "only". *It is therefore clear that the rendering* "**only begotten Son**" *in the Authorised Version is well supported by ancient evidence."*

The Old Latin pre-dated Jerome by 200 years (2) p 344.

Our critic continues to defend "only" by means of theology. *"While . . . others in the Bible are called* "**sons of God**" *there is a radical and fundamental difference in Christ's sonship compared with theirs (Matt.11:25–27) . . . Others are sons in a derivative and much lesser sense since they are sinners dependent on God's grace. In Johannine theology Christ's Sonship is equivalent to equality with the Father (John 5:18). In this sense he is truly the Only Son. To attempt to suggest*

that Christ's Sonship is different only in degree but not in kind is to take
essentially a Unitarian position."

This is our critic's reaction to the simple statement in Section 7.3 *"the*
modern reading (of John 1:18) cannot be correct, according to Job 1:6,
Luke 3:38 and John 1:12, which show that Jesus Christ is NOT God's
"one and only son.""

Our critic did not check the verses. Job 1:6 was a reference to
ANGELS, who HAD kept "**their first estate**", Jude 6 and had NOT
sinned, 2 Peter 2:4 and were NOT therefore "*sinners dependent on God's*
grace". Luke 3:38 was a reference to ADAM, who was God's son
BEFORE he sinned.

John 1:12 refers, of course, to those who are God's sons by adoption
– not "*derivation*", having received Christ by faith, Ephesians 1:5.
Although "*they are sinners dependent on God's grace*", nowhere does
the Bible speak of them as sons in a "*much lesser sense*". Quite the reverse
is true:

"**For we are members of his body, of his flesh, and of his bones**"
Ephesians 5:30.

"**For both he that sanctifieth and they who are sanctified are all of**
one: for which cause he is not ashamed to call them brethren"
Hebrews 2:11.

"**Herein is our love made perfect, that we may have boldness in the**
day of judgment; because as he is, so are we in this world" 1 John 4:17.

Of course these verses refer to one's STANDING in Christ. One's state
may be different.

Our critic's reference to Unitarianism is ironic. It is the JW's, the
modern Unitarians who have adopted the reading from our critic's "*most*
reliable MSS." for their New World Translation, NWT. It was their
spiritual ancestors who made the change in the first place (12) p 338–339.

It is also ironic that our critic seeks to alter or eliminate the scriptures
that most strongly OPPOSE Unitarianism. See remarks on 1 John 5:7–8
and 1 Timothy 3:16.

Moreover, Christ's Sonship HAS to be "*different in kind*". NO OTHER
SON OF GOD WAS VIRGIN BORN! The expression "**only-begotten**"
makes this abundantly clear, as the fulfilment of Isaiah's prophecy, Isaiah
7:14.

Finally, no matter how much our critic resorts to theology, or what the
Bible is said to teach, Section 14.2, the Bible SAYS that God has other "**sons**".
The expression "one and only Son" is therefore misleading with respect to

Jesus Christ. The confusion is not resolved by *"theology"* but by **"comparing spiritual things with spiritual"** 1 Corinthians 2:13.

Our critic then gives his exposition of John 1:18 *"The meaning of John 1:18 is* "the only one *(or, if you prefer,* "the only begotten"*)* himself God, who is in the bosom of the Father" *or* "The only one, who is the same as God, is at the Father's side". *There is no clearer affirmation of Christ's deity."*

There isn't? I can think of two without trying.

"For there are three that bear record in heaven, the Father, the Word, and the Holy Ghost: and these three are one" 1 John 5:7.

"God was manifest in the flesh" 1 Timothy 3:16.

As for our critic's statement itself, I would make the following observations:

1. "The only one" is NOT the same as "the only begotten" – see above and Section 13.2.
2. IF the latter reading is chosen, one has "the only begotten God" after all, which is standard J.W. theology – see above.
3. However, the wording of scripture is NOT decided by what "you prefer". It is decided by what God WROTE, Exodus 31:18, or commanded to be WRITTEN, Jeremiah 30:2, 36:2, Revelation 1:11 and which He PRESERVED, Psalm 12:6, 7.
4. "In the bosom of the Father" is NOT the same as "at the Father's side", Exodus 4:6, Ruth 4:16.
5. "The same as God" is not necessarily identical with "himself God". The devil could be described as "the same as Christ" in that both were anointed, Ezekiel 28:14, Acts 10:38.

Our critic concludes this section with *"the Chalcedonian Definition 451 in which Christological orthodoxy was finally crystallized. In it Christ is confessed as the one and same Son and only begotten (or only) God."*

Dr. Hills (5) p 35 states *"Guided therefore by these teachings of the New Testament Scriptures, the Church was able to formulate at Nicea (324 A.D.) and at Chalcedon (451 A.D.) the true doctrine of the holy Trinity and of the incarnation of Christ."*

Nevertheless, Dr. Hills shows, p 34, that the teachings upon which the councils were dependent, went back to THE WORDS OF SCRIPTURE in John 1:1, 4, 14. That is the whole issue. What did God SAY and where are God's WORDS? Dr. Ruckman (16) p 171–172, however, furnishes a note of caution:

*"The fourth ecumenical Council of Chalcedon was held in 451 A.D .
. . .they decided among other things that the Apostle Peter was speaking
through (Pope) Leo and also that anyone who disagreed with Leo I was
CURSED. Not content with this state of things, they took three more shots
of cocaine (or heroin: the historians are divided!) and decided (as good
"Bible-believing Christians") that a man was a BLASPHEMER OF
CHRIST if he refused to call Mary "the Mother of God.""*

"Christological orthodoxy", therefore, did not prevent the Council of
Chalcedon from being most UN-orthodox, in the matter of FINAL
AUTHORITY!

14.5 LUKE 2:33

Our critic's last attack on the Holy Bible is against Luke 2:33, where he
maintains that "**Joseph and his mother**" AV1611 should be "the child's
father and mother" or similar, as in the DR, RV, NIV, JB, NWT, Ne, G,
T, Tr, A. The versions listed have also changed "**Joseph**" to "his parents"
in verse 43, except that Lachmann substitutes for Griesbach in this
alteration, Section 11.4.

Our critic states *"The reading "father" is definitely in the best
manuscripts but as these same manuscripts also teach the virgin birth,
that must determine the way "father" is construed."*

Of *"the best manuscripts"* Dr. Ruckman (4) p 65 states *"The readings
of Luke 2:33, Acts 8:37, and 1 Timothy 3:16 in the "new bibles" are NOT
"neutral readings." They are the "LXX" readings from Origen's
stenographers (preserved in Vaticanus) and they are no more "neutral"
than the writings of Voltaire (1694–1778) and Tom Paine (1737–1809)."*

Brenton's LXX IS Vaticanus, except in places where Alexandrinus
was used. See Section 1.2.

G.W. Anderson in the TBS publication *The Greek New Testament*
states *"The Sinai manuscript and the Vatican manuscript (c. 4th century)
. . .form the basis of the Greek New Testament, referred to as the Critical
Text, which has been in widespread use since the late 19th century. In
recent years there has been an attempt to improve this text by calling it
an "eclectic" text (meaning that many other manuscripts were consulted
in its editing and evolution) but it is still a text which has as its central
foundation these two manuscripts . . .*

*"The modern reconstructed Critical Text omits reference to the Virgin
Birth in Luke 2:33."*

It is appropriate to insert one more comment about *"eclecticism"* Section 12.6.

Pickering (3) p 293 states *"The most serious defect of the eclectic method is that it is ESSENTIALLY SUBJECTIVE. This defect is indeed serious because it renders the method hopeless – certainty as to the text of the New Testament is thereby impossible. Colwell has made an astute observation as to the true nature of the eclectic method . . . "We need to recognise that the editing of an eclectic text rests upon conjectures.""*

Concerning Luke 2:33, Wilkinson (2) p 220 states *"where the Received Text read:* **"And Joseph and his mother marvelled at those things which were spoken of him,"** . . . *Jerome's text read:* "His father and mother marvelled," *etc.."* Jerome's text, the Latin Vulgate IS the text of Vaticanus and Sinaiticus, Section 10.1.

Dr. Ruckman adds (29) p 43 *"The reading* **"Joseph"** *is found – not* "his father" *– in a greater number of older Latin witnesses, and nearly all Caesarean – type texts read,* **"Joseph and his mother,"** *not* "His father and mother.""* The Old Latin pre-dates Jerome AND Vaticanus and Sinaiticus by 200 years (2) p 344.

In sum, the reading which our critic advocates comes from a text which has Aleph and B as *"its central foundation"*. These are evidently STILL *"**the best manuscripts,**"* although our critic has carefully avoided designating them as such when he actually mentions them. He tries instead to deflect attention AWAY from them, probably because their CONTENTS can too easily be CHECKED. See Sections 1.6, 14.4. J.A. Moorman (39) cites Aleph, B, D, L, W as having the NIV reading.

Our critic explains neither how Aleph and B *"**teach the virgin birth**"* nor HOW, nor even WHY THEY *"**must determine the way** "father" is construed"*. His lame excuse for the depraved reading in B and Aleph (13) p 161, is entirely UNSUPPORTED by ANY Scripture from ANY Bible!

Actually, the HOLY BIBLE determines how ""father" *is to be construed"*. See Isaiah 45:10 and Matthew 1:16. Fathers BEGET children. Joseph DID NOT beget the Lord Jesus Christ, Matthew 1:20 and he is therefore NOT referred to in the AV1611 as the Lord's "father".

Our critic thinks that *"**it is extraordinary that (I) do not go on to challenge the KJV for similar statements later on in the same chapter. e.g.** **His parents went to Jerusalem** (Luke 2:41) and* "**Thy Father and I have sought thee sorrowing**" *(Luke 2:48)."*

It is *"extraordinary"* that our critic is unable to solve the simplest problems with respect to the words of scripture.

At least ONE Biblical reference to Joseph and Mary as the Lord's **"parents,"** Luke 2:41, would be quite in order to illustrate the fact that they were all of the same PARENTAGE. Joseph **"was of the house and lineage of David"** Luke 2:4, Matthew 1:1–17 as indeed was Mary, Luke 3:23–31 and the Lord Himself, Luke 3:23, Matthew 1:16. At least one such reference is necessary to substantiate the claim that the Lord has on **"the throne of his father David:"** Luke 1:32–33. See also Luke 2:27. The necessity for a VIRGIN birth, Isaiah 7:14, was, of course, prophesied by Jeremiah, Jeremiah 22:30.

Luke 3:23 uses the expression **"(as was supposed)"**, indicating that Jesus' true identity was not to be revealed until John the Baptist could **"go before the face of the Lord to prepare his ways;"** Luke 1:76–80. John was in the deserts until Jesus was thirty years old, Luke 3:23. This explains why Mary uses the term **"father"** – small "f" in the AV1611, including the 1611 AV1611, not capital "F" as in our critic's document. She is CONCEALING the Lord's identity. Dr. Ruckman states in *Satan's Masterpiece – the New ASV* (35) p 37, "*Mary is covering up for a birth record (John 8:41) which the Pharisees knew when she calls Joseph His* "father.""

Nevertheless, the Lord corrects her in the very next verse, 49, with **"I must be about my Father's business?"** Jesus is here calling God His **"Father"** – capital "F", because at the time He was **"in the temple"**, verse 46, NOT a carpenter's shop!

Moreover, a devout Jewish woman would hardly have called her husband by his first name in public. There are no instances of such open familiarity in the Bible. Being of **"chaste conversation"** 1 Peter 3:2, she is far more likely to have called him **"lord"** 1 Peter 3:6.

Finally, as Dr. Ruckman points out, p 37 above, "*Luke 2:33 (and verse 43) is the direct statement of a LICENSED PHYSICIAN speaking UNDER THE INSPIRATION OF THE HOLY GHOST.*"

Our critic's last gasp with this passage deals with manuscript variations. "***The readings on which the KJV was later based for 2:41 and 2:48 were themselves suspected by some scribes of denying the virgin birth. As a result other manuscripts have put in 2:41*** "Joseph and Mary" (*Greek MSS*) ***and*** "Joseph and his mother" (*Latin MSS*). ***In 2:48*** "We" ***has replaced*** "Thy Father and I". "*so by this same token that you condemn modern versions for denying the Virgin birth you will have to condemn the KJV also if you act consistently.*"

In "*consistent*" fashion, our critic does not say WHICH manuscripts, nor what proportion they represent of those manuscripts which testify to the AV1611 readings – which in these verses correspond to the modern readings anyway.

The BIBLICAL explanations for the AV1611 readings in Luke 2:41, 48 have been given above. They do not depend on scribal suspicions. If I am to "*act consistently*", I will be faithful to what the BIBLE, AV1611, SAYS and reject TOTALLY anything which CONTRADICTS what it says or CASTS DOUBT on what it says.

That includes modern versions, renegade Greek texts, mutilated manuscripts, scholarly conjectures and the opinions of our critic. It will be appreciated that his "*authorities*" for overthrowing the AV1611 range from the non-extant "*originals*", the corrupt Alexandrian "*best mss.*" and papyri fragments, through to the 'high mindedness' of dead orthodox theologians and Greek New Testament editors and the occasional lapses of 'good, godly men' such as Wesley, Darby, Luther, Spurgeon etc., where they saw fit to tamper with the word of God.

Associate Pastor Brian Donovan of Pensacola Bible Baptist Church has described how the new bibles stem from an unholy spirit because they remove the words "**Christ is come in the flesh**" from 1 John 4:3. Our critic has tried to cast doubt on 1 John 5:7, 8, 1 Timothy 3:16, Acts 8:37, John 1:18 and Luke 2:33, all verses which are in some way associated with the coming of the Lord Jesus Christ "**in the flesh**". He is led by an unholy spirit.

The Bible believer seeking to resist the confusion of the closing days of the Church Age can take comfort in Psalm 119:140:

"Thy word is very pure; therefore thy servant loveth it."

14.6 LUKE 17:21, ADDENDUM

Following the initial study in response to the criticisms discussed above, part of the wording found in Luke 17:21 has been drawn to the author's attention for consideration. The words in question are quoted as follows from the various versions.

"**within you**" AV1611 ("among you" marg.), Tyndale, Geneva, DR, RV, Ne, NIV ("among you" marg.), NKJV

"among you" JB

"in your midst" or similar, NWT, Berry, i.e. Stephanus' TR, RSV, NASV – New American Standard Version. The latter two sources have been listed in order to show that the reading cited had support among some of the earlier popular versions.

The Greek construction is identical in both Nestle's and Berry's texts;

"εντος υπων" or "entos humon" although translated differently in their respective interlinear English texts. (One notes in passing that where Luke uses the phrase "**in their midst**" Luke 24:36, the Greek construction in both Berry and Nestle is "εν μεσω αυτων" or "en mesos hautou", approximately. This seems to be Luke's rendering of the phrase throughout his Gospel.)

The basic issue therefore is one of translation, as in the cases of Acts 3:13, 26, 4:27, 30 – see Section 10.8 – rather than textual variation. The issue may be set out as follows.

The reading of the AV1611 is sometimes objected to on the grounds that "**the kingdom of God**" could not be "**within**" the tradition-bound Pharisees who were antagonistic to the Lord Jesus Christ, especially insofar as the Apostle Paul describes this kingdom as "**righteousness, and peace, and joy in the Holy Ghost**" Romans 14:17. Moreover, how could the Lord legitimately exhort His disciples in Matthew 6:33 to "**seek ye first the kingdom of God and his righteousness**" if such a kingdom was already "**within**" them?

It has on occasion been proposed therefore that the reading "in your midst", as found in the NWT etc., or even "among you" as in the JB, should be preferred as a means of resolving this apparent dilemma. Such a reading is said to draw attention to the Lord Himself, as Heir Apparent to the throne of this kingdom, because He was literally in the midst of His hearers at the moment of speaking. This alternative rendering would then point to a fulfilment of the prophecies of Luke 1:32, 33, which Gabriel had delivered to Mary and deflect any possibility that "**the kingdom**" could pertain to a Pharisaic religious system, which has its obvious modern counterpart in the form of Roman Catholicism.

The scripture readily acknowledges the Kingship of the Lord Jesus Christ, Zechariah 9:9, Matthew 21:5, John 18:36, 37 and the prophecies of Luke 1:32, 33 will have their literal fulfilment in Him. However, Luke 17:20 indicates that "**the kingdom of God cometh not with observation**" which in turn shows that the reference in verse 21 is not primarily to the Lord Himself as a contemporary visible ruler – although He will be such, Revelation 11:17, 18.

Any kingdom, by definition, must of course have a ruler, whose duty it is to "**reign**" Luke 19:12, 14 and a ruler who abides by scripture "**must be just, ruling in the fear of God**" 2 Samuel 23:3 but as Matthew 6:33 and Romans 14:17 indicate, "**the kingdom of God**" is associated with *inner* righteousness and therefore "**the fear of God**" must also be *inward*. Even in the Old Testament, before the advent of the new birth, it was recognised that God's rule should be internal and that the fear of Him was the means of resisting evil:

"So did not I, because of the fear of God" Nehemiah 5:15b.

"Behold, the fear of the Lord, that is wisdom; and to depart from evil is understanding" Job 28:28b.

"And by the fear of the Lord men depart from evil" Proverbs 16:6b.

David therefore prays **"search me, O God, and know my heart: try me, and know my thoughts: And see if there be any wicked way in me, and lead me in the way everlasting"** Psalm 139:23, 24. Proverbs 20:27 reveals that the spirit of man is the means by which the Lord carries out this search:

"The spirit of man is the candle of the Lord, searching all the inward parts of the belly". Thus the Lord **"lighteth every man that cometh into the world"** John 1:9b.

God's internal 'register' of His fear and of the legitimacy of His righteous rule within the individual, upon which His **"candle"** throws light, includes the conscience and an innate sense of right and wrong, whether or not this sense is heeded, as Paul explains, with reference to an Old Testament setting:

"For when the Gentiles, which have not the law, do by nature the things contained in the law, these having not the law, are a law unto themselves: which show the work of the law written in their hearts, their conscience also bearing witness, and their thoughts the meanwhile accusing or else excusing one another" Romans 2:14, 15.

Both Jew and Gentile possess this internal 'register' as shown in the incident of the woman caught in adultery:

"And they which heard it, being convicted by their own conscience, went out one by one, beginning at the eldest, even unto the last: and Jesus was left alone, and the woman standing in the midst" John 8:9. (The Greek construction of the phrase **"in the midst"** is similar to that of Luke 24:36.)

One may therefore associate the conscience with an innate sense of God's standard of right and wrong, that He illuminates by means of the spirit of man, even in an unsaved person, thus bearing witness to His intrinsic right of ruler-ship over that individual, a right established originally by the act of creation, Genesis 2:7.

In that sense, **"the kingdom of God is within you"** Luke 17:21 and this kingdom is totally foreign to any system of ritualistic religious observances, such as either Roman Catholicism or 1st century Pharisaism. Whether or not the individual submits to the rule of the kingdom or in effect is prepared to "**seek…first the kingdom of God and his righteousness**" Matthew 6:33 is a matter of the will.

"**For whosoever shall call upon the name shall be saved**" Romans 10:13.

"**Whosover will, let him take the water of life freely**" Revelation 22:17b

References

1. *The Christian's Handbook of Biblical Scholarship* Dr. Peter S. Ruckman, Bible Baptist Bookstore, P.O. Box 7135, Pensacola FL. 32504, 1988.
2. *Which Bible?* 5th Edit. David Otis Fuller, D.D., Grand Rapids International Publications, P.O. Box 2607, Grand Rapids, Michigan 49501, 1984.
3. *True or False?* 2nd Edition, Edit. Dr. David Otis Fuller, D.D., Grand Rapids International Publications, 1983.
4. *The Christian's Handbook of Manuscript Evidence* Dr. Peter S. Ruckman, Pensacola Bible Press, P.O. Box 86, Palatka, Florida 32077, 1976.
5. *The King James Version Defended* 3rd Edit. Edward F. Hills Th.D, Christian Research Press, P.O. Box 2013, Des Moines, Iowa 50310, 1979.
6. *Let's Weigh the Evidence* Barry Burton, Chick Publications, P.O. Box 662, Chino, CA 91710, 1983.
7. *God Only Wrote One Bible* Jasper James Ray, The Eye Opener Publishers, P.O. Box 7944, Eugene, Oregon USA 97401, 1980. See also *New Eye Opener* leaflet.
8. *Perfected or Perverted?* Norman Ward, Which Bible? Society Inc., 605 Deeming, S.E., P.O. Box 7096, Grand Rapids.
9. *The Answer Book* Dr. Samuel C. Gipp, Th.D., Samuel C. Gipp, 1989.
10. *Supplement to The Inheritance Paper No. 9* J. Coad, Totnes, Devon.
11. *Famine In The Land* Norman Ward, Which Bible? Society Inc.
12. *New Age Bible Versions* Gail Riplinger, Bible and Literary Missionary Foundation, 1993.
13. *The Revision Revised* Dean John William Burgon, Centennial Edition, 1883–1983, A.G. Hobbs Publications, P.O. Box 14218, Fort Worth TX76117, 1983.
14. *An Understandable History Of The Bible* Rev. Samuel C. Gipp Th.D., Samuel C. Gipp, 1987.
15. *The Inheritance Paper 9* J. Coad, Totnes, Devon.

16. *The History of the New Testament Church Vol. 1* Dr. Peter S. Ruckman, Bible Baptist Bookstore, 1982.

17. *Problem Texts* Dr. Peter S. Ruckman, Pensacola Bible Institute Press, P.O. Box 7135, Pensacola, Florida 32504, 1980.

18. *Counterfeit or Genuine? Mark 16? John 8?* 2nd Edition, Edit. Dr. David Otis Fuller, D.D., Grand Rapids International Publications, 1984.

19. *Interlinear Hebrew/English Old Testament*, 3 Vols. Jay P.Green, (edit.) The Eye Opener Publishers, 1983.

20. *The Monarch of the Books* Dr. Peter S. Ruckman, Bible Baptist Bookstore, 1980.

21. *The History of the Waldenses* Rev. J.A. Wylie, LL.D., reprinted by Church History Research and Archives, 1985.

22. *A Brief History of English Bible Translations* Dr. Laurence M. Vance, Vance Publications, 1993.

23. *The NIV Reconsidered* Earl Radmacher and Zane C. Hodges, Kerugma, Inc. 1990.

24. *John Wycliffe The Dawn of The Reformation* David Fountain, Mayflower Christian Books, 1984.

25. *William Tyndale, His Life and Times* S. M. Houghton, M.A., FOCUS Christian Ministries Trust, 6 Orchard Road, Lewes, East Sussex, BN7 2HB, 1985.

26. *The Newe Testament by William Tyndale (1526)* John Wesley Sawyer, The Martyrs Bible Series Volume 1, 1989.

27. *Pioneers of the Reformation in England* Marcus Loane, Church Book Room Press, Ltd., 1964.

28. *The Newe Testament of Matthew's Bible 1537 AD* John Wesley Sawyer, The Martyrs Bible Series Volume 2, 1989.

29. *The Bible Babel* Dr. Peter S. Ruckman, The Bible Baptist Bookstore, 1981.

30. *Why I Believe the King James Version is the Word of God* Dr. Peter S. Ruckman, Bible Baptist Bookstore, 1988.

31. *Desecrating God's Word* William A. De Jonge, Bible Truth Society.(tract), obtained from FOCUS.

32. *A Bible Word List and Daily Reading Scheme* The Trinitarian Bible Society, London.

33. *A Treasury of Evangelical Writings* Edit. Dr. David Otis Fuller, D.D., Kregel Publications, Grand Rapids, Michigan 49501, 1980.

34. *Differences in the King James Version Editions* Dr. Peter S. Ruckman, Bible Baptist Bookstore, 1983.

35. *The New ASV-Satan's Masterpiece* Dr. Peter S. Ruckman, Bible Baptist Bookstore, 1983.

36. *The Bible Believer's Commentary Series, Genesis, Exodus, Job, Proverbs, Minor Prophets (Hosea-Nahum), Matthew, Acts, Gal-Eph-Phil-Col.,*

Hebrews, Revelation Dr. Peter S.Ruckman, Bible Baptist Bookstore, 1970–87.

37. Articles and Reprints from *The Quarterly Record* The Trinitarian Bible Society, London:
    Topics: *The Bible-A Sure Foundation, Common Bible?, Divine Inspiration of the Holy Scriptures, English Bible and Apocrypha, Excellence of the AV, Good Will Toward Men, Holding Fast the Faithful Word, The Holy Bible, Holy Trinity, The Image of God, Important Omissions, Italic Type, Plain Reasons Why We Keep the AV, Of the Resurrection of Christ, Rome and Reunion, Standing on a Rock, The Only Begotten Son, Who is the Rock?, The Word Baptism in the KJV, What is Wrong with the Modern Versions? etc.*
    Verses: Gen. 37:3, 2 Sam. 15:7, Matt. 6:13, Mk. 6:20, 16:9–20, Jn. 1:1, 5:3, 4, 17:24, Acts 2:47, 13:48, Rom. 8:14–16, 9:5, 1 Cor. 11:23, 24, 1 Tim. 3:16, 2 Tim. 2:24–26, 3:16, 17, Heb. 1:6, 2 Pet. 1:20, 21, 1 John 5:7, Rev. 22:14.
    Versions: NIV, NKJV, RSV, GN, LB, AMP, NASV, NEB, NWT, JB, NJB, etc. See references 43–45 for particular articles.

38. *Believing Bible Study* Edward F. Hills, Th.D, Second Edition, the Christian Research Press, 1977.

39. *Early Manuscripts and the Authorized Version* J. A. Moorman, B.F.T. #1825, 900 Park Avenue, Collingswood, N.J. 08108. Also obtainable from A.V. Publications Corp. P.O. Box 280, Ararat, VA 24053.

40. *The Providential Preservation of the Greek Text of the New Testament* Rev. W. Maclean M.A., Westminster Standard, 1983.

41. *When the KJV Departs from the "Majority" Text* J. A. Moorman B.F.T. #1825, 900 Park Avenue, Collingswood, N.J. 08108.

42. *1 John 5:7* Dr. Peter S. Ruckman, Bible Baptist Bookstore, 1990.

43. *The NIV* Dr. Peter S. Ruckman, Bible Baptist Bookstore, 1990.

44. *Custer's Last Stand* Dr. Peter S. Ruckman, Bible Baptist Bookstore, 1981. This is a reply to a book by Dr. Stewart Custer, of Bob Jones University, entitled *The Truth About the King James Version Controversy*.

45. *Final Authority* William P. Grady, Grady Publications, P.O. Box 506, Schereville, Indiana, 1993.

46. *The Last Grenade* Dr. Peter S. Ruckman, Bible Baptist Bookstore, 1990.

47. *A Pictorial History of Our English Bible* David Beale, Bob Jones University Press, Greenville, South Carolina 29614, 1982.

48. *How To Teach The Original Greek* Dr. Peter S. Ruckman, Bible Baptist Bookstore, 1992.

49. *Interlinear Greek-English New Testament, (Stephens (Stephanus) 1550 Greek Text)* George. R. Berry, (edit.) The Eye Opener Publishers.

50. *New International Version Article No. 74* G.W. and D.E. Anderson, Trinitarian Bible Society, London.

51. *The Holy Bible New International Version Article No. 19* Trinitarian Bible Society.

52. *Expository Dictionary of Bible Words* W.E.Vine, Marshall, Morgan & Scott, Basingstoke, Hants.1981.
53. *The Men Behind the KJV* Gustavus S. Paine, Baker Book House, 1977.
54. *King James Onlyism In Action* Dr. Peter S. Ruckman, Bible Baptist Bookstore, 1992.
55. *Analytical Concordance to the Holy Bible* Robert Young, United Society For Christian Literature, Lutterworth Press, 8th Edition, London, 1973.
56. Items from the *TBS Quarterly Record*, No. 473, Oct.-Dec. 1980 and No. 501, Oct.-Dec. 1987.
57. *Translators Revived* Alexander McClure, from the 1858 Edition, Maranatha Bible Society, Post Office Box 466 Litchfield, Michigan.
58. *Should We Trust The New International Version?* FOCUS Christian Ministries Trust.
59. *Why Not The NIV?* G.R. Guile, Amainthakarai Gospel Hall, Post Office Box No. 2501, Madras-600 029, India.

Bibliography

Books considered to be of particular assistance are listed in **Bold** type.

Beale, David *A Pictorial History of Our English Bible* Bob Jones University Press, Greenville, South Carolina 29614, 1982.

Berry, George R. (edit.) *Interlinear Greek-English New Testament (Stephens (Stephanus) 1550 Greek Text)* The Eye Opener Publishers, P.O. Box 7944, Eugene, Oregon USA 97401.

Brown, Michael H. *The 1599 Geneva Bible* L.L. Brown Publishing, 561 Melton Road, Ozark, MO 65721, 1995.

Burgon, Dean J.W. *The Revision Revised* Centennial Edition, 1883–1983, A.G. Hobbs Publications, P.O. Box 14218, Fort Worth, TX76117.

Burton, B.D. *Let's Weigh the Evidence* Chick Publications, P.O. Box 662, Chino, CA 91710, 1983.

Coad, J. *The Inheritance Paper 9*, Totnes, Devon.

Coad, J. *Supplement to The Inheritance Paper 9*, Totnes, Devon.

De Jonge, W.A. *Desecrating God's Word* (tract), FOCUS Christian Ministries Trust, 6 Orchard Road, Lewes, East Sussex, BN7 2HB, 1985.

Fountain, David *John Wycliffe The Dawn of The Reformation* Mayflower Christian Books, 1984.

Fuller, Dr. David Otis, D.D. *Which Bible?* 5th Edition, Grand Rapids International Publications, P.O. Box 2607, Grand Rapids, Michigan 49501, 1984.

Fuller, Dr. David Otis, D.D. *True or False?* 2nd Edition, Grand Rapids International Publications, 1983.

Fuller, Dr. David Otis, D.D. *Counterfeit or Genuine? Mark 16? John 8?* 2nd Edition, Grand Rapids International Publications, 1984.

Fuller, Dr. David Otis, D.D. *A Comparison of the NWT and the NIV* (tract), Which Bible? Society, Inc., 605 Deeming, S.E., P.O. Box 7096, Grand Rapids.

Fuller, Dr. David Otis, D.D., Edit. *A Treasury of Evangelical Writings*, 1980.

Gilmore, A. (by courtesy) *The New International Version* Verse listing.

Gipp, Rev. Samuel C. Th.D. *An Understandable History Of The Bible* Samuel C. Gipp, 1987.

Gipp, Dr. Samuel C. Th.D. *The Answer Book* Samuel C. Gipp, 1989.

Grady, William P. *Final Authority* Grady Publications, P.O. Box 506, Schereville, Indiana, 1993.

Green, Jay P. (edit.) *Interlinear Hebrew/English Old Testament* 3 Vols., The Eye Opener Publishers, 1983.

Guile, G.R. *Why Not The NIV?* Amainthakarai Gospel Hall, Post Office Box No. 2501, Madras-600 029, India.

Hills, Dr. E.F. *The King James Version Defended* 3rd Edition, The Christian Research Press, P.O. Box 2013, Des Moines, Iowa 50310, 1979.

Hills, Dr. E.F. *Believing Bible Study* 2nd Edition, The Christian Research Press, 1977.

Houghton, S. M., M.A. *William Tyndale, His Life and Times* FOCUS.

Jones, F. *The New KJV versus The KJV 1611 AD* 8222 Glencliffe Lane, Houston, TX 77070.

Loane, Marcus *Pioneers of the Reformation in England* Church Book Room Press, Ltd., 1964.

Maclean, W. *The Providential Preservation of the Greek Text of the New Testament* Westminster Standard, obtained from FOCUS.

McClure, Alexander *Translators Revived* from the 1858 Edition, Maranatha Bible Society, Post Office Box 466, Litchfield, Michigan.

Moorman, J. A. *Early Manuscripts and the Authorized Version* B.F.T. #1825, 900 Park Avenue, Collingswood, N.J. 08108. Also obtainable from A.V. Publications Corp. P.O. Box 280, Ararat, VA 24053.

Moorman, J. A. *When the KJV Departs from the "Majority" Text* B.F.T. #1825, 900 Park Avenue, Collingswood, N.J. 08108.

North, J.E. *Should we Trust the NIV?* FOCUS.

Paine, Gustavus S. *The Men Behind the KJV* Baker Book House 1977.

Peoples Gospel Hour *Did God Write a Book? The Living Bible Review of the NIV and NASV Is the NKJV the Word of God? The RSV* FOCUS.

Radmacher, Earl and Hodges, Zane C. *The NIV Reconsidered* Kerugma, Inc. 1990.

Ray, Jasper J. *The New Eye Opener* (tract), The Eye Opener Publishers.

Ray, Jasper J. *God Only Wrote One Bible* The Eye Opener Publishers, 1980.

Riplinger, Gail *New Age Bible Versions* Bible and Literary Missionary Foundation, 1993.

Riplinger, Gail *Which Bible is God's Word?* Hearthstone Publishing, Ltd, 1994.

Ruckman, Dr. Peter S. *The Bible Babel* Bible Baptist Bookstore, P.O. Box 7135, Pensacola FL. 32504, 1981.

Ruckman, Dr. Peter S. *The Bible Believer's Commentary Series, Genesis, Exodus, Job, Proverbs, Minor Prophets (Hosea-Nahum), Matthew, Acts, Gal-Eph-Phil-Col., Hebrews, Revelation* Bible Baptist Bookstore, 1970–87.

Ruckman, Dr. Peter S. *The Christian's Handbook of Biblical Scholarship* Bible Baptist Bookstore, Pensacola FL. 32514, 1988.

Ruckman, Dr. Peter S. *The Christian's Handbook of Manuscript Evidence* Pensacola Bible Press, P.O. Box 86, Palatka, Florida 32077, 1976.

Ruckman, Dr. Peter S. *Custer's Last Stand* Bible Baptist Bookstore, 1981. This is a reply to a book by Dr. Stewart Custer, of Bob Jones University, entitled *The Truth About the King James Version Controversy.*

Ruckman, Dr. Peter S. *Differences in the King James Version Editions* Bible Baptist Bookstore, 1983.

Ruckman, Dr. Peter S. *The History of the New Testament Church Vol. 1* Bible Baptist Bookstore, 1982.

Ruckman, Dr. Peter S. *How To Teach The Original Greek* Bible Baptist Bookstore, 1992.

Ruckman, Dr. Peter S. *1 John 5:7* Bible Baptist Bookstore, 1990.

Ruckman, Dr. Peter S. *King James Onlyism In Action* Bible Baptist Bookstore, 1992.

Ruckman, Dr. Peter S. *The Last Grenad*e Bible Baptist Bookstore, 1990

Ruckman, Dr. Peter S. *The Monarch of the Books* Bible Baptist Bookstore, 1980.

Ruckman, Dr. Peter S. *The New ASV-Satan's Masterpiece* Bible Baptist Bookstore, 1983.

Ruckman, Dr. Peter S. *The NIV* Bible Baptist Bookstore, 1990.

Ruckman, Dr. Peter S. *About the 'New' King James Bible* Bible Baptist Bookstore, 1983.

Ruckman, Dr. Peter S. *About the New Scofield Reference Bible* Bible Baptist Bookstore, 1980.

Ruckman, Dr. Peter S. *Problem Texts* Pensacola Bible Institute Press, P.O. Box 7135, Pensacola, Florida 32504, 1980.

Ruckman, Dr. Peter S. *Why I Believe the King James Version is the Word of God* Bible Baptist Bookstore, 1988.

Salliby, Chick *If The Foundations Be Destroyed* Word and Prayer Ministries, P.O. Box 361, Fiskdale, MA 01518–0361, 1994.

Sawyer, John Wesley *The Newe Testament by William Tyndale (1526)* The Martyrs Bible Series Volume 1, 1989.

Sawyer, John Wesley *The Newe Testament of Matthew's Bible 1537 AD* The Martyrs Bible Series Volume 2, 1989.

The Trinitarian Bible Society, London *A Bible Word List and Daily Reading Scheme.*

The Trinitarian Bible Society, London, Articles and Reprints from *The Quarterly Record* on:

Topics: *The Bible-A Sure Foundation, Common Bible?, Divine Inspiration of the Holy Scriptures, English Bible and Apocrypha, Excellence of the AV, Good Will Toward Men, Holding Fast the Faithful Word, The Holy Bible, Holy Trinity, The Image of God, Important Omissions, Italic Type, Plain*

Reasons Why We Keep the AV, Of the Resurrection of Christ, Rome and Reunion, Standing on a Rock, The Only Begotten Son, Who is the Rock?, The Word Baptism in the KJV, What is Wrong with the Modern Versions? etc.
Verses: Gen. 37:3, 2 Sam. 15:7, Matt. 6:13, Mk. 6:20, 16:9–20, Jn. 1:1, 5:3, 4, 17:24, Acts 2:47, 13:48, Rom. 8:14–16, 9:5, 1 Cor. 11:23, 24, 1 Tim. 3:16, 2 Tim. 2:24–26, 3:16, 17, Heb. 1:6, 2 Pet. 1:20, 21, 1 John 5:7, Rev. 22:14.
Versions: NIV, NKJV, RSV, GN, LB, AMP, NASV, NEB, NWT, JB, NJB, etc.

Vance, Dr. Laurence M. *A Brief History of English Bible Translations* Vance Publications, 1993.

Vine, W.E. *Expository Dictionary of Bible Words* Marshall, Morgan & Scott, Basingstoke, Hants. 1981.

Ward, N. *Perfected or Perverted?* Which Bible? Society Inc..

Ward, N. *Famine in the Land* Which Bible? Society Inc..

Wylie, Rev. J.A., LL.D. *The History of the Waldenses* reprinted by Church History Research and Archives, 1985.

Young, Robert *Analytical Concordance to the Holy Bible* United Society For Christian Literature, Lutterworth Press, 8th Edition, London 1973.